THE
TATA
GROUP

ADVANCE PRAISE FOR THE BOOK

'What a terrific book! The Tata businesses articulated a stakeholder philosophy more than 100 years before it was "(re)discovered" by the West. This book is a great example of why we need more business history that is global. And it serves as an icon for how we can learn about businesses that can work all over the world'—R. Edward Freeman, professor, University of Virginia, USA

'A commendable, riveting account of impeccable integrity, grit, passion and perseverance that defines the Tata Group—an iconic brand synonymous with visionary leadership and ethical, inspirational business practices. That torch lit almost two centuries ago continues to blaze a trail worthy of accolade and emulation!'—Venu Srinivasan, chairman and managing director, TVS Motor Company and Sundaram-Clayton; director, Tata Sons board

'The story of the House of Tata inspires us by showing that service and success can go hand-in-hand, especially amidst turbulence and change. Shashank does this story much justice'—Tarun Khanna, professor, Harvard Business School; author, *Trust: Creating the Foundation for Entrepreneurship in Developing Countries*

'Tata is a microcosm of India—gyroscopically balanced, colloidally stable, complex, large, highly diverse, yet unified by a soft glue. This book suggests the secret formulation of that glue, which has helped Tata remain India's no. 1 corporate for over eighty years, ever since corporate rankings have been measured in India. I found it a great read!'—R. Gopalakrishnan, former director, Tata Sons; vice chairman, Hindustan Unilever; author, *A Biography of Innovations: From Birth to Maturity*

'This book highlights the Tata principles of business and their success strategies by analysing the potential and performance of business in India over the last 150 years. From colonial rule to Independence, from Licence Raj to the dawn of globalization, the Tata saga has been deeply interwoven with the destiny of a resurgent nation. Shashank narrates this great story with passion and a deep sense of purpose. If there was one book to be read on the Tata Group, this would be worth the time'—Dipak C. Jain, president (European), China Europe International Business School, Shanghai; former dean, INSEAD (France) and Kellogg School of Management (USA)

'Shashank Shah narrates the Tata story with great passion. You will find in this book a broad sweep of Tata history and a wealth of interesting anecdotes, which beautifully illustrate the character of the Tata Group. The author has revisited many crossroads and brings to vivid life many defining moments, which will inspire you and also make you reflect. You will thoroughly enjoy the interesting stories, the engaging narration and the invaluable lessons that this book holds for all of us'—Harish Bhat, brand custodian, Tata Sons; author, *Tata Log* and *The Curious Marketer*

'This book provides a fascinating overview of the story of India's most admired group as a torchbearer of industrial capitalism for 150 years. Through a simple narrative, exciting stories and insightful analysis, Shashank decodes the Tata way of business that has enabled them to emerge as a trailblazer on the global platform. A definitive book on the subject, and a must-read for all who wish to build successful businesses with a social conscience'—Debashis Chatterjee, professor and director, IIM Kozhikode; author, *Invincible Arjuna*

'As India's biggest business group since records began in 1939, the Tata Group has an incredibly rich history of growth and successes, of mysteries and failures spread over 150 years. Shashank's paring and peeling of the Tata Group into seven sections with a clear relationship between the parts is remarkable. I am sure his readers and students will appreciate the crispness of the omnibus that is *The Tata Group: From Torchbearers to Trailblazers*'—Gita Piramal, business historian; author, *Business Maharajas*

'Tata is not just India's largest conglomerate, but one of the world's most important businesses. In *The Tata Group: From Torchbearers to Trailblazers*, Shashank has written the definitive history of the enterprise that spearheaded India's new era of globalization, while also providing a colourful account of how it will play a critical role in the country's economic future'—James Crabtree, associate professor, National University of Singapore; former Mumbai bureau chief, *Financial Times*; author, *The Billionaire Raj*

THE TATA GROUP

From Torchbearers
to Trailblazers

SHASHANK SHAH

PORTFOLIO
PENGUIN

An imprint of Penguin Random House

PORTFOLIO

USA | Canada | UK | Ireland | Australia
New Zealand | India | South Africa | China

Portfolio is part of the Penguin Random House group of companies
whose addresses can be found at global.penguinrandomhouse.com

Published by Penguin Random House India Pvt. Ltd
7th Floor, Infinity Tower C, DLF Cyber City,
Gurgaon 122 002, Haryana, India

Penguin
Random House
India

First published in Portfolio by Penguin Random House India 2018

ISBN 9780670090679

Typeset in Minion Pro by Manipal Digital Systems, Manipal
Printed at Replika Press Pvt. Ltd, India

www.penguin.co.in

MIX
Paper from
responsible sources
FSC® C016779

To

crores of Indians
endeavouring to build a nation with nobility and ability

CONTENTS

INTRODUCING AN INSTITUTION THAT NEEDS NO INTRODUCTION

Tata. A name synonymous with Indian industry. A name known to Indians for generations. A name acknowledged for adventure and achievement, excellence and ethics, innovation and integrity, perseverance and performance, reformation and responsibility, struggle and success. A name known for salt, software, cars, communications, perfumes, pesticides, tea, trucks, housing, hospitality, steel and gold. A name that greets every other Indian every single day.

Some stunning statistics reveal the scale of the Tata Group. Established in 1868, it is India's largest conglomerate, with products and services in over 150 countries, and operations in 100 countries across six continents. The Tata Group has over 100 operating companies of which twenty-nine are publicly listed in India. With nearly 700,000 employees, it is India's third largest employer after the Indian railways and defence forces. Its total revenues exceed ₹6.7 lakh crore ($100 billion). By 2018, roughly 67 per cent of the group's revenues came from international operations, making it India's largest conglomerate with global exposure.[1] Tata Group's market capitalization[2] of nearly ₹9.45 lakh crore ($145 billion) equated to 6.6 per cent of the Bombay Stock Exchange (BSE). With the highest market capitalization among all business houses in India, the Tata Group enjoys the trust of over 40-lakh shareholders. The group has also been a significant contributor to India's growth story. In 2018, it contributed about 4 per cent to the country's GDP and paid 2.24 per cent of the total taxation in India, amounting to a whopping ₹47,195 crore—the highest by any corporate group. This is almost equal to the total taxes collected by the entire state of Andhra Pradesh in 2017.

The distinguishing factors are not limited to its size alone. In both Indian and multinational conglomerates/businesses, the one who steers the company forward is the one with the maximum personal wealth in the organization— Jeff Bezos, Bill Gates, Warren Buffett and Mukesh Ambani to name a few. Particularly in the case of large businesses, the founders and leaders are among the wealthiest in the world. A major reason being the equity stake they have in the companies they own and run. In case of the Tata Group, neither the Tata family nor chairman emeritus Ratan Tata appear in the list of India's wealthiest families. This is in stark contrast to promoters of Indian conglomerates that rank below the Tata Group in size like Reliance Industries, Aditya Birla Group, Bharti Group and others whose net worth tops that of Ratan Tata. For example, Forbes indicated Mukesh Ambani being worth $40 billion, Kumar Mangalam Birla $10 billion and Sunil Bharti Mittal $8 billion in 2018. Other top Indian businessmen who run large businesses within an industry such as Uday Kotak and Azim Premji were worth $12 billion and $15 billion respectively. This wasn't just the case with Ratan Tata. It was true in the case of former chairman J.R.D. Tata as well. In November 1985, an article in the *Bombay* magazine reported that J.R.D. Tata's personal wealth was nearly ₹28 crore. J.R.D. remonstrated the publication and placed on record that his wife's and his personal investments, including an apartment were valued at ₹60 lakh. All other shares in his name were only as a trustee of public charitable trusts in which he had no personal interest. This speaks volumes of the simplicity and transparency of J.R.D., the only businessman to have been conferred the Bharat Ratna, India's highest civilian award. It also intrigues us as to why the Tatas are not the richest businessmen in India, though the Tata Group is India's numero uno conglomerate.

The answer takes us back a hundred years, when Sir Ratan Tata, son of Tata Group founder Jamsetji Nusserwanji Tata, donated a sizeable portion of his estate to a trust in his name—Sir Ratan Tata Trust. Jamsetji's elder son, Sir Dorab Tata followed suit. In 1938, he donated his entire estate and belongings, including his pearl-studded tiepin and his late wife's jewellery, the Jubilee diamond (twice the size of the Koh-i-Noor) among others, to a public charitable trust—Sir Dorabji Tata Trust. The trustees of these Tata Trusts were empowered to sell all the property and jewellery for funding public welfare projects, but were not permitted to withdraw the shares the Tata siblings held with Tata Sons. Thus, through the trusts, they sought to ensure the integrity of the parent firm, and ensure corporate perpetuity as a means to wealth creation for nation building and social well-being. These two trusts own nearly 50 per cent of Tata Sons, the promoting company of the Tata Group and a significant shareholder of over a 100 operating Tata companies in seven major areas, including communications and information technology, manufacturing, services, realty and infrastructure, consumer and retail, defence and aerospace, and financial services. By FY 2017, Tata Sons' investments were valued at ₹5 lakh crore, consolidated revenues at ₹1.73 lakh crore, and profits of ₹18,431 crore.

Professor Gras of Harvard Business School, founder of the academic discipline of business history, noted many decades ago, 'The Tatas have done much to introduce industrial capitalism in India in place of the old mercantile and petty capitalism. As the companies progressed, they socialized the business by transferring much of the ownership to charitable trusts. And we in our time have thought that we [America] were original in some of this socialization from within!'[3]

The Tata companies are commonly referred to as the Tata Group. The elected chairman of the Tata Sons board is recognized as the Tata Group chairman. Tata Sons became a deemed public company with effect from 1 May 1975 because of a change in law. Since 2013, modified legislation permitted Tata Sons to become a private limited company again. It opted to do so and from 8 November 2017 it became a private limited company. Accordingly, its shares cannot be sold without board approval. In 2018, about 66 per cent of the equity capital of Tata Sons was held by fifteen philanthropic trusts endowed by various members of the Tata family over many generations. The Shapoorji Pallonji (SP) Group held around 18.4 per cent stake in Tata Sons,[4] about 13 per cent was held Tata Group companies and the remaining 3 per cent by Tata family members. Of this, Ratan Tata's holding is a mere 0.83 per cent. The Tata Trusts are mandated to annually spend 85 per cent of their dividend earnings on social welfare projects. From this, one can imagine the substantial amount of money ploughed back into the society by the Tata Group.

It is this one-of-its-kind holding structure of the Tata Group that distinguishes it in the firmament of India Inc. It resembles India's joint family system where the Tata Trusts are like the grandfather, Tata Sons like the father, and operating companies like dynamic children. The Tata Sons board consists of managing directors of several leading Tata companies, industry captains, academics and technocrats. The Tata Group is also very different from its peer conglomerates in the developed world such as Johnson & Johnson or GE, or its peers in India, Reliance, ITC or Larsen & Toubro, where the parent company is publicly listed but subsidiaries are not. In the Tata Group, the operating companies are publicly listed, but the holding company (Tata Sons) is not. Each of the operating companies have an independent board of directors, who collectively take decisions in the best interests of the company, its shareholders and a larger ecosystem of stakeholders. Tata Sons' presence on the board of operating companies is usually through the chairman, who facilitates decisions that would create long-term value for its shareholders.

This magnificent edifice of munificence is not one of recent origin. It has been built brick-by-brick over 150 years. Its roots are grounded in a heritage that goes back over thirteen centuries. To acquaint ourselves with it, let's go to the shores of Gujarat on one fine afternoon in the ninth century AD when the first group of native Zoroastrians persecuted for religious conversion during the Islamic invasion of Persia landed in India.

CHAPTER 1

ENERGY OF A PROPHET, COURAGE OF A PIONEER

The Gujarat harbour was on the maritime routes between ancient Persia (present-day Iran) and India, and there were extensive and mutual trade relations even before the Christian Era. Interestingly, the term 'Parasikas' has been used to refer to the people west of the Sindhu (Indus) river in the Puranas and the Mahabharata. This indicates that their arrival on Indian shores was not an act of coincidence but a matter of conviction that they would get refuge in this majestic country that spread from the Hindu Kush Mountains in the northwest to the borders of Thailand in the southeast.

The 'Qessa-ye-Sanjan' (the story of Sanjan) is a sixteenth-century poem that elaborates on the travails and persecution of the Zoroastrians after the fall of the Sassanid Empire (651 AD). An apocryphal legend mentioned in the 'Qessa' details an interaction between a group of Zoroastrian priests who landed in Sanjan (present-day Valsad district) and Jadi Rana, the Hindu Rajput king who ruled over Gujarat. When the Dastur (chief priest) sought permission to settle down in his kingdom, the Rana felt apprehensive about granting asylum to people who looked like warriors. He sent a cup full of milk indicating that his kingdom was already full. In response, the Dastur added a pinch of sugar in the brimming cup indicating that his tribe would add sweetness but not cause it to overflow. The Rana was impressed with the allusion and asked for an account of their religion. He even laid down some preconditions on language, customs and the usage of weapons before agreeing to grant them sanctuary. The Dastur readily agreed and emphasized several common features between Zoroastrianism and Hinduism, including reverence for nature and the highest levels of purity observed by women. The Rana was satisfied, and the migrants were accepted.

The place where those Zoroastrian refugees settled is believed to have been named by them after Sanjan in Greater Khorasan, northeast Persia, from where they originated. Contemporary genetic studies are consistent with the historically recorded migration of these populations to South Asia in

1

the seventh century and in agreement with their assimilation into the Indian subcontinent's population and cultural milieu 'like sugar in milk'.[1] Modern-day scholars also highlight several similarities between the Avesta (Zoroastrian holy book) and the Vedas and conclude that both texts are likely to have been derived from the same source. No wonder the Vedic scriptures emphasized 'Ekam Sat, Viprah Bahuda Vadanti' (truth is one, scholars interpret it in myriad ways).

At its zenith, the Persian Empire extended from Egypt near the Mediterranean Sea to Sind on the shores of the Arabian Sea. The prophet of the Zoroastrian faith—Zarathustra—is said to have been born around 1500 BC. He founded one of the world's first monotheistic religions that acknowledged the supreme divine principle as Ahura Mazda. Under his inspiration, the Persian Empire established Zoroastrianism as the state religion. Zarathustra's message was that life was a struggle between the forces of good and evil, with good emerging victorious by the power of righteousness. The adherents of the faith accept a commitment to fight evil that reveals itself as the ills of human society. If Christ asked his followers to love their neighbours, Zarathustra asked his followers to attain happiness by making others happy. 'Humata, Hukhta, Hvarshta' (good thoughts, good words, good deeds) were key maxims of the faith. Interestingly, the first declaration of human rights is said to have been prepared during the reign of Cyrus the Great (559–30 BC), who was influenced by the message of Zarathustra. In 1971, then United Nations Secretary General U. Thant promoted the relic as an 'ancient declaration of human rights', which is now housed in the UN building in New York.

As for the Parsis (meaning Persian in the native language), followers of the Zoroastrian faith in India, they truly lived up to the assurance given to Jadi Rana 1200 years ago. The development of Bombay in the eighteenth and nineteenth centuries, is indistinguishably linked with the prosperity of Parsis. They not only flourished but also contributed immensely to the well-being of the country they made their new home. While maintaining their own cultural identity they did not fail to recognize themselves as Indian. Dadabhai Naoroji, the first Asian to occupy a seat in the British Parliament, once said, 'Whether I am a Hindu, a Mohammedan, a Parsi, a Christian, or of any other creed, I am above all an Indian. Our country is India; our nationality is Indian.'

With just over 50,000 Parsis in India during the 2011 census, the quantum of contribution the community has made and continues to make to India is supremely impressive. A demographic minority, they rarely claim privileges. Instead, they give back to the nation as industrialists, scientists, lawyers or educators. Interestingly, the term 'Parsi' in Sanskrit means 'one who gives alms'.

In the last couple of centuries, one of their greatest contributions has been philanthropy. Mahatma Gandhi had acknowledged this fact when he said, 'I am proud of my country, India, for having produced the splendid Zoroastrian stock, in numbers beneath contempt, but in charity and philanthropy perhaps unequalled and certainly unsurpassed.' Among the several illustrious and generous Parsi households, the House of Tata leads the pack.

The founder of the Tata empire is born

An elaboration of religious philosophy, principles and practices may seem out of place in a book on India's leading business house. However, the Parsi heritage and value systems have played a central role in the Tata way of business. The intimate application of its fundamental tenets would be increasingly evident as we unravel the Tata tale. Contemporary records of young men who qualified as Zoroastrian priests going back to the thirteenth century indicate the name of the Tatas. The Tata family had a strong connection with traditional Parsi religion and each generation of the Tatas typically included a priest of the Zoroastrian faith. In such a lineage was born Nusserwanji in 1822 in the town of Navsari (Gujarat). He was the first in the fifteenth generation of the Tata family to move out of formal priestly duties for trade and commerce. He apprenticed with a Hindu banker and saved enough money to start his own business.

On 3 March 1839, at the age of seventeen, Nusserwanji and Jeevanbai had a son, Jamsetji. A decade later, Nusserwanji left Navsari for Bombay and after settling down called his son. In 1852, Jamsetji arrived in Bombay. Four years later, he joined the Elphinstone College and graduated in 1858. In the same year, he married Heerabai Daboo. A year later, their first son Dorabji, was born. While Jamsetji delighted in liberal English education, he also witnessed with dismay how the British brutally quelled the 1859 uprising. On the steps of Bombay's Town Hall, India was transformed into a British colony.

Young Jamsetji joined Nusserwanji's firm and was sent to Shanghai and Hong Kong to develop trade with China, export cotton and opium, and import silk, tea, cinnamon, copper, brass and Chinese gold.[2] He started and stabilized a branch of the company, where Nusserwanji, Kaliandas and Premchand Roychand were principal partners. The American Civil War (1861–65) brought a cotton boom to Bombay. The war had caused a blockade of ships that brought American cotton to England. The British mill owners soon realized that Indian cotton was the alternative to keep them alive, and were willing to pay twice the normal price for its cotton. Nusserwanji's firm and many others made bumper profits. On the partners' insistence, Jamsetji sailed from Bombay to England to set up a cotton agency in December 1864.[3] He carried bills of exchange and securities on the cotton market. However, even before his ship docked on the London harbour, the American Civil War ended. The Manchester mills once again had their stock of American cotton; the Indian cotton market collapsed. The scripts he was carrying had become worthless overnight; Jamsetji was penniless in the British capital.

Not the one to lose hope in adversity, he brilliantly negotiated with the shrewd bankers at the Bank of England and the Royal Exchange. This was perhaps his first independent display of business acumen. They were so impressed with the integrity of the twenty-five-year-old lad from India that they appointed him his own liquidator with an allowance of 20 pounds a month. Nusserwanji had to sell his seven-storied house in Bombay to discharge debts. But the creditors were paid in full. During his four-year-long stay in London, two fellow Parsis helped him—Dadabhai Naoroji and Pherozeshah Mehta. Both were eminent freedom fighters in India's struggle for independence. This association, which was to last a lifetime, probably sowed the seeds of nationalism in young Jamsetji.

The Tata story begins

Worldwide conquests had made the small island of Britain a mighty power. 'The empire on which the sun never sets', is how Christopher North described His Majesty's rule. The British Empire was at the acme of its supremacy, and when Jamsetji visited Manchester, the greatest of the Lancashire cotton cities, he marvelled at its mills. What struck him the most were its industrial slums, which were as dark and sulphurous as 'the medieval vision of hell'. He was appalled at the contrast between poverty and prosperity in the world's most efficacious country. This inspired in him the ambition of creating another Manchester in the East and equipping India with the power to make for herself, with Indian labour and capital, the cotton fabrics that she would use in large quantities, and thereby make a dent in the British dominance of India's textile industry. All this, while ensuring the highest standards of labour and human dignity. Historically, Indian cotton goods had been in great demand for over 2000 years. A Roman historian had complained that Indian textiles were draining Rome of its gold. It was the British Raj (henceforth referred to as 'the Raj') that had made concerted efforts from the eighteenth century to destroy the hand-crafted Indian products and impose the dominance of machine-made British products.[4]

Wiser for the experience garnered by nine years of working with his father, Jamsetji started his first independent venture in 1868—a trading firm with a capital of ₹21,000. This marked the formal beginning of the Tata Group. Like his father, Jamsetji was also ordained as a Zoroastrian priest. He brought those value systems into business, and made Humata, Hukhta, Hvarshta, the fundamental tenets of the Parsi faith as his motto and inscribed it on his family coat of arms. Acknowledged as the founder of the Tata Group, Jamsetji is often referred to as the 'father of Indian industry'. Business historian Dwijendra Tripathi observed, 'Jamsetji continues to occupy a unique, unrivalled position in the annals of Indian business. There never has been even a mild challenge to his supremacy. None is in sight, either.' His actions and enterprises reveal the truth of this assertion.

Among Jamsetji's first initiatives in 1869 was the acquisition of a derelict and bankrupt oil mill at Chinchpokli in the industrial hub of Bombay. He converted it into a cotton mill and named it Alexandra Mills, after the Princess of Wales. Within two years he turned it around and sold it for a significant profit to Kesowji Naik, a local cotton merchant. He once again headed to Britain for an intensive study of the Lancashire cotton industry. On his return, in September 1874, he registered the Central India Spinning, Weaving and Manufacturing Company, with a seed capital of ₹15 lakh Jamsetji was thirty-five; the Tata odyssey had just begun.

Tatas' textile tale

India was called the jewel in Queen Victoria's crown. In 1877, the British Parliament offered her a promotion. She became the Empress of India. The same year there was a drought in south India followed by famine and a cholera outbreak. Over 50-lakh people died in this natural catastrophe. This did not affect the Delhi Durbar where Victoria was proclaimed Empress in absentia on 1 January 1877.[5] On the same day, Jamsetji inaugurated his Empress Mills in Nagpur, considered the heartland of cotton. His decision to opt for Nagpur was much against the prevalent preference of setting up mills in Bombay, which was regarded as the 'Cottonopolis of India'.

Jamsetji acquired 10 acres of marshy land from the Raja of Nagpur and sought the help of a Marwari banker for funds to reclaim the land and make it a suitable site for a large factory. The banker refused to back a man who was 'wasting gold by sinking it into the ground'. Several years later, he apologetically admitted that he was wrong, and that Jamsetji had actually 'put in earth and taken out gold'.[6] Tata's rationale was vindicated as Nagpur was located close to the source of raw materials, land was cheap and the central location of Nagpur benefited distribution.[7] Even before the mill attained significant success, in 1880, he established a reserve and renewal fund and an insurance fund to allocate funds for repairs and replacements, depreciation and extensions. The consequent improvement in quality and quantity of work more than justified the large amounts spent for the purpose.[8] These far-sighted practices were much ahead of times, and were faithfully carried forward by his successors making them a part of the Tata way of business.

Jamsetji imported more than half a dozen men for his staff of departmental foremen from Lancashire who taught techniques of handling the textile machinery to the Indian workforce. He appointed Sir Bazonji Dadabhai Mehta, then goods superintendent of railways, as manager of Empress Mills, who remained a loyal lieutenant and successfully carried out Jamsetji's vision of making Empress India's foremost cotton mill. The use of the ring spindle revolutionized the manufacture of high-quality cotton yarn, which was extensively exported to Central and East Asia. Shareholders were handsomely rewarded with 90 per cent dividend during the boom period. The profits earned by them led to the development of the equity cult in India.

Jamsetji went beyond prevailing practices for labour welfare. He wanted his enterprise to be different from what he had witnessed in Manchester. At Empress Mills,[9] workers—men and women—were provided benefits denied elsewhere in the world, and much before such measures were made statutory for all Indian enterprises. These have been elaborated in later chapters. The outcome was that when absenteeism in the textile industry was as high as 20 per cent, at Empress Mills it dropped to nearly nil. Jamsetji also tried to introduce a more liberal system of management centred on a managing director (MD) and a board. This was at a time when almost every industrial firm in India was organized as a managing agency concern (roughly a cross between a holding company and an investment bank) under tight family control. The move proved too radical and forced him to fall back upon the prevailing Indian structure. Nearly a century later, when the managing agency system was abolished, an independent system based on a board of directors became mandatory in India. A century earlier, Jamsetji's focus on transparent corporate governance, empowering managers, engaging with labour, and promoting multi-stakeholder welfare had demonstrated his vision of a harmonious industrial future. No doubt, he was referred to as 'the man who saw tomorrow'.

In 1886, Jamsetji acquired the Dharamsi Mills at Kurla (Bombay) and named it Swadeshi Mills. The change in nomenclature was indicative of a changing mindset. From Alexandra and Empress, the use of the word 'Swadeshi' for the new mill represented his increasing nationalistic passion, much before it became a nationwide political cry. While benchmarking with best practices from Britain, he envisaged 'an India for Indians'. His dream was that the yarn from the Swadeshi Mills would be finer than any British yarn in the international market. For this, he even visited Japan and familiarized himself with latest technical innovations. When the mill initially made losses, he realized its deficiency and overhauled the equipment. For this, he even revoked his family trust and used the capital to pull the mill out of crisis. The outcome was impressive. Swadeshi Mills' cotton products gave direct competition to British imports. He even tied up with an enterprising Greek agent who soon started replacing Austrian and Italian cloth in the Levant with Swadeshi cloth. His vision had come true, and once again, Indian textiles became the toast of international markets. In 1903, he founded his last textile enterprise by acquiring the Advanced Mills in Ahmedabad and equipping it with state-of-the-art plant and machinery. All through, Jamsetji liberally shared his knowledge with fellow mill owners. His biographer Frank Harris recalls an occasion when a mill owner sought his advice. Jamsetji shared his view with such sincerity that the mill owner did not believe him and took a decision contrary to Tata's advice. Later, when his decision proved wrong, he realized Jamsetji's genuineness of intent.

Tata's reputation as a captain of the Indian industry can be attributed in substantial measure to the successful turnaround of his four textile mills. Yet, his mind was full of ideas. Some of these remained ideas, like his vision of developing a miniature Venice in Juhu (suburban Bombay) complete with canals. This was at a time when Worli was considered a godforsaken place and Forjet Hill and Santacruz were sites for fox hunting! One hundred and fifty years later, these are Mumbai's plush residential localities. Some others fructified but with limited success, like the Tata Line, a shipping company he started to challenge the dominance of British-controlled shipping lines whose exorbitant rates were affecting the profitability of Indian mills. He also initiated projects to resuscitate certain native industries, such as bringing Japanese experts to develop silk cultivation (sericulture) in Bangalore. The Tata Silk Farm developed in 1902 played a catalytic role in reviving silk cultivation in south India. Many of India's sericulture veterans were among Tata Silk Farm's first trainees. The Government of India replicated the Tata model in Sri Lanka and north India. Some Tata ventures reaped financial rewards; some others failed. Indubitably, Jamsetji made a lot of money through diverse business interests. But he never remained a mere moneymaker.

Tata Sons is founded

In 1887, Jamsetji converted his trading business into a company. He found
Tata and Sons with Dorabji and Heerabai's nephew Ratanji Dadabhoy (R.D.)
Tata.[10] Ratan, Jamsetji's second son, was only sixteen years then, and added as
a partner two years later. By virtue of controlling the largest trading business
and Empress Mills, the flagship company, Jamsetji became the chairman
of Tata and Sons. Tata and Sons was the managing agency through which
investments in various Tata enterprises were managed. Under the managing
agency system that began in India under the colonial rule, a managing agent
(either an individual or a company) would be appointed to manage one or
more joint stock companies. The managing agent also held shares in the
managed companies and controlled their boards of directors. This limited
liability system was introduced in early nineteenth century to facilitate trade
and investment by British businesses in India, and was eventually adopted by
Indian businesses.[11]

In Jamsetji's lifetime, the Tatas had transformed itself from a small trading
company, often considered as a backbencher in the Bombay industrial circuit,
and emerged as the largest indigenously financed and managed industrial
group in India. Unlike its British counterparts, the Tatas' style of business was
characterized by a desire to experiment with investments in new technology
and a non-aversion to risking private capital. For example, in 1881, Jamsetji
put up an electric light installation to run Empress Mills at night, and even
experimented a double-shift for two years. When it did not give results as
expected, the electric installation was scrapped.

The prevailing practice was calculating managing agents' remuneration
on sales. In contrast, Jamsetji established a system at Tata and Sons to claim
5 per cent commission on net profits. This ensured that a loss-making firm
wasn't burdened. He was probably the first mill owner to even allow for
depreciation while calculating net profits. These systems and processes were
eventually adopted across the managing agency system in India.[12] The British
managing agency houses preferred an individualistic small-firm approach to
business and refused to diversify into newer industrial sectors after World War
I, especially in steel, chemicals, construction and transport. These were exactly
the areas in which the Tatas invested substantially through new enterprises.
Their nationalist outlook played a significant role in large investments in new
industries despite conditions of uncertainty.

Sir Lawrence Jenkins, chief justice of Bombay, once told an audience
that when speaking of the hardships of the poor, Jamsetji's eyes were filled

with tears.[13] His philanthropic vision like his industrial forethought was distinct from prevailing wisdom, and developed in parallel to his industrial success. He once mentioned:

> There is one kind of charity common enough among us . . . It is that patchwork philanthropy which clothes the ragged, feeds the poor, and heals the sick. I am far from decrying the noble spirit which seeks to help a poor or suffering fellow being . . . However, what advances a nation or a community is not so much to prop up its weakest and most helpless members, but to lift up the best and the most gifted, so as to make them of the greatest service to the country.

To this end, Jamsetji established the J.N. Tata Endowment in 1892 to enable Indian students to pursue higher studies overseas. By 1924, two out of every five Indians coming into the elite Indian Civil Service were Tata scholars. By 2016, there were more than 5000 J.N. Tata scholars all over the world. Some of the illustrious names include K.R. Narayanan, former president of India, and scientists Jayant Narlikar, Raja Ramanna and Raghunath Mashelkar. I too was a beneficiary when invited as a visiting scholar to Harvard Business School.

The Taj Mahal Hotel shines on Bombay's firmament

Tata and Sons prospered as did the city of Bombay. For the sake of the city he loved the most, Jamsetji wanted to develop a grand hotel that was equivalent to any other in Europe. On 1 November 1889, he bought the lease of 2.5 acres of reclaimed land near the Bombay harbour. The construction began in 1900. So visionary were Jamsetji's plans that he even purchased two islands near Uran for guests at Taj to enjoy picnics![14] On 16 December 1903, an ailing Jamsetji presided over its inauguration. The construction was still in progress. However, the first wing with two complete floors and dozens of waiters welcomed seventeen guests that day. It was a culmination of his two-year-long efforts, when he went all over the world to shop for his dream hotel—electrical machinery from Dusseldorf, chandeliers from Berlin, fans from the USA, and the first-spun steel pillars from the Paris Exhibition, where the Eiffel Tower had been constructed only the previous decade. The architecture was a blend of Moorish domes, Florentine Renaissance and Oriental and Rajput styles. The hotel was the first building in Bombay to be illuminated by the new wonder—electric lamps. A 15-tonne carbon dioxide ice-making plant provided refrigeration and helped cool the suites. These were among the very first in India. So great was his passion that the money spent for the construction of Taj (over ₹20 lakh) was not from Tata and Sons, but from his personal funds. He had no desire to own the place. He wanted Taj to attract people to India. That is exactly what it did. A century later, the Taj Hotels continue to be the preferred choice of royalty and heads of states.[15]

For the future of India

In the 1880s, Field Marshal Lord Auchinleck had told the BBC that he and his friends were convinced that the British Raj in India would last a thousand years. For there was no way the British would let go the 'brightest jewel in the Crown'.[16] On the other side of the globe, Indian nationalists were striving hard for the nation's earliest redemption from the Raj. Though Jamsetji shared the patriotic sentiments of fellow nationalists, he firmly believed that India's industrial self-sufficiency was a prerequisite for its political independence. He once observed, 'Freedom without the strength to support it and, if need be, defend it, would be a cruel delusion. And the strength to defend freedom can itself only come from widespread industrialization and the infusion of modern science and technology into the country's economic life.' During his many travels, he compared his country with industrialized nations and came to three conclusions: first, no country that did not manufacture iron and steel could become industrially great; second, no sustained economic growth was possible without the aid of science and technical education; and third, the prosperity of his favourite city Bombay depended upon the provision of cheap electric power.[17] Incidentally, electric power and steel were the two pillars of the Soviets and of communism in Russia. He was convinced that these three schemes would be the harbingers of national growth. The last quarter-century of his life was dedicated to these three; and they in turn became the basis of the future Tata empire.

In his scrapbook, the very first page had a mention of a sentence by Thomas Carlyle (English author and philosopher) that he had heard in a speech made in 1867, 'The nation which has the steel will have the gold.' However, laws in British India discouraged private enterprises from mining. When demand for steel required for railways and defence production grew faster than supply, Lord Curzon, viceroy of British India, was forced by his superiors to liberalize the mining laws in 1899. Jamsetji had been waiting for this for twenty years. He set sail for England in the summer of 1900 to meet Lord Hamilton, Secretary of State for India, who was the only person with the power to issue orders to the viceroy and knew they would be obeyed. Hamilton was impressed with the

Tatas' three schemes and was most enthused with the idea of India producing its own steel. Jamsetji told Hamilton that if he built a steel plant at his age, it wouldn't be for personal gain but only because India needed it. He also shared the many obstacles put in his way by the Raj. Hamilton acknowledged his superordinate passion and assured him that he would write to Curzon to support him in all his schemes. In later years, Hamilton acknowledged Jamsetji as 'a political pioneer of the most reliable character'.

Enthused by Hamilton's commitment, Jamsetji set sail for America, where he was often called the J.P. Morgan of East Indies. Some newspapers even thought his name was John N. Tata! In Pittsburgh, he found the man he needed—Julian Kennedy, the foremost metallurgical engineer in the world. Kennedy advised larger survey of the iron ore deposits in India's hinterland before commencing operations. He sent him to Charles Page Perin in New York. When he finally reached Perin's office, he almost commanded, 'I want you to take charge as my consulting engineer. Mr Kennedy will build the steel plant wherever you advice and I will foot the bill. Will you come to India with me?' Jamsetji's enigmatic personality compelled Perin to listen. 'I was dumbfounded. But you do not know what character radiated from Tata's face, and kindliness too. I said I would go and I did,' recalled Perin several years later. Jamsetji believed in getting the best consultants to provide India with world-class enterprises. This was evident in all Tata ventures.

The Tatas' steel project was received with dismay in India and considered rather foolhardy. At the turn of the twentieth century, per capita consumption of steel in India was 0.5 kg compared to 318 kg in USA and 227 kg in Britain and Germany.[18] When Sir Frederick Upcott, chairman of the railway board, heard about the Tatas' steel venture, he remarked, 'Do you mean to say that the Tatas propose to make steel rails up to British specifications? Why, I will undertake to eat every pound of rail they succeed in making.' Yet, the Tatas were undeterred. After all, India was not new to steel making. It had a 2500-year-old history. Persian King Xerxes I had employed Indian archers using arrows tipped with Indian steel in the battle of Thermopylae in 480 BC. Eighty years later, Porus presented Alexander with 15 kg of Indian steel. Closer home, in 402 AD, the famous iron pillar weighing 6000 kg was erected by Chandragupta II near Delhi. Currently located near the Qutub Minar, it was the largest mass of iron to be cast in the ancient world. Its corrosion-resistant composition remains a testimony to the high level of skill achieved by ancient Indian ironsmiths in extraction and processing of iron.[19] What Jamsetji was attempting was in fact a revival of India's ancient capacity of indigenous steel-making, albeit with the most modern techniques.

Perin's partner Charles Weld arrived first in India in 1903. He and Dorabji prospected the jungles of central India for deposits of iron ore. They travelled by horse, bullock cart and foot, faced many a wild animal, and even made their tea in soda water. After months of unfruitful search, Weld wanted to leave but Jamsetji refused. In a letter to Dorabji, he visualized the steel city he wanted to build unlike the dismal steel towns he had seen in the USA. The catholicity of his vision is evident in his expression. He wrote, 'Be sure to lay wide streets planted with shady trees, every other of a quick-growing variety. Be sure that there is plenty of space for lawns and gardens. Reserve large areas for football, hockey and parks. Earmark areas for Hindu temples, Mohammedan mosques and Christian churches.' It was said of him that he united the daring courage of the American captain of industry with the German passion for details, and the contemporary Japanese spirit.

Given his age, and the extreme physical strain he had undergone over the previous five decades, Jamsetji was running a race against time. On his deathbed at Bad Nauheim (Germany), where he was undergoing treatment, he told R.D. Tata, 'Do not let things slide. Go on doing my work and increasing it, but if you cannot, do not lose what we have already done.' On 18 May, Dorabji and his wife, Meherbai, arrived in his presence and were feebly yet warmly welcomed by him. The next morning, 19 May, India's foremost industrial doyen slipped away in his sleep. Tributes poured in from all over the world. On his passing, Lord Curzon admitted, 'No Indian of the present generation had done more for the commerce and industry of India.'

CHAPTER 2

FOR THE LOVE OF INDIA

On 24 February 1904, former employee of the Geological Survey of India P.N. Bose, who was working with the Maharaja of Mayurbhanj, had written to Jamsetji about iron ore deposits in Mayurbhanj district and the maharaja's intent to support the Tatas' prospecting efforts in his kingdom. A year later, Perin, Weld and Bose discovered the 3000-feet-high Gorumahisani Hills (Odisha) with 60 per cent iron content in its soil. Their half-a-decade-long search had finally borne fruit. Yet, the plant site remained the holy grail. At long last, in 1907, Weld and Dorabji discovered a site at the confluence of Kharkai and Subarnarekha rivers near the village of Sakchi (Jharkhand), which was within easy reach from the Jharia coalfields, 90 km from Gorumahisani iron ore deposits and 300 km west of Calcutta.[1] It was the perfect place for the Tatas' steel plant.

Tata and Sons had already invested lakh during the prospecting process. The next objective before Dorabji, the new chairman of Tata and Sons, was raising finance. The popular opinion was that India did not have the money for supporting such an enterprise. Hence, the Tatas attempted to raise funds in Britain. However, the prevailing market situation, lack of faith in an Indian steel enterprise and the desire to have disproportionate control in its management deterred the British from investing in the Tatas' steel company. Disheartened, Dorabji returned to Bombay and decided to try his luck in India. By this time, the Swadeshi Movement had swept across the country. For over a century under the Raj, minerals from India were exported to America and Europe, and finished products were imported at high costs. At such a time, an Indian firm desirous of indigenous steel making was received with overwhelming optimism.

When the Tatas listed their company's shares for subscription on 26 August 1907, prospective investors besieged Tata and Sons' headquarters at the Navsari Building in Bombay. Within a span of twenty days, the entire capital (₹2.32 crore) was contributed by 8000 Indians. It was the largest amount ever subscribed for an industrial undertaking until then. The Tata Iron and Steel Company (TISCO) was born. Dorabji called it 'a purely Swadeshi enterprise

13

financed by Swadeshi money and managed by Swadeshi brains.' In 1912, TISCO (now Tata Steel) produced the first ingot of steel.

Two years later, World War I began. The Sakchi plant worked night and day; the furnaces flowed with rivers of molten iron that shone resplendently like gold. Between 1914 and 1918, Tata Steel supplied 2400 km of rail and 300,000 tonnes of steel to the Allied forces. 'If Upcott had carried out his undertaking, he would have had some slight indigestion,' remarked Dorabji in later years. On 2 January 1919, Viceroy Lord Chelmsford came to Sakchi and thanked the Tatas for their contribution to the war efforts. 'I can hardly imagine what we should have done during these four years if the Tata company had not been able to give us steel rails . . . This great enterprise has been due to the prescience, imagination and genius of late Mr Jamsetji Tata,' he said. In grateful acknowledgement he rechristened Sakchi to Jamshedpur, and the adjoining Kalimati railway station to Tatanagar.

Even before commercial production began, the Tata Main Hospital was set up in 1909, and town-building activities had begun in Sakchi. During the annual general meeting of 1923, R.D. Tata remarked:

> We are constantly accused of wasting money in the town of Jamshedpur. We are asked why it is necessary to spend so much on housing, sanitation, roads, hospitals and on welfare . . . People asking such question are sadly lacking in imagination. We are not putting a row of workmen's huts in Jamshedpur. We're building a city.

This focus on community well-being has remained the Tata way of business ever since. On the eve of Indian independence, Tata Steel had become self-sufficient and self-reliant in steel making. It was one of the lowest-cost producers in the world, the largest self-contained steel plant outside the USA and the USSR, and India's largest company. The director-in-charge was Sir Ardeshir Dalal, former ICS officer and a Tata scholar. Jamsetji's investments were finally falling into place.

An institute of higher learning by Indians for Indians

The convocation address by Chancellor Lord Reay at Bombay University in 1889 had spurred Jamsetji's vision for an institute of advanced research for the material and industrial welfare of India, the like of which even Britain did not have. He envisaged this institute providing postgraduate education and research training in sciences, technology and humanities at a time when there was no discourse around postgraduation and advanced scientific research in academic circles. These were areas Jamsetji believed as vital for a resurgent and independent India. He sent his son-in-law and trusted aide Burjorji Padshah to visit universities in Britain and the USA. After eighteen months of travel, Padshah returned to India and recommended Johns Hopkins University at Baltimore as a suitable model. In a letter dated 27 November 1896 to Lord Reay, governor of Bombay, Jamsetji wrote:

> Being blessed by the Mercy of Providence with more than a fair share of the world's goods, and persuaded that I owe much of my success in life to an unusual combination of favouring circumstances, I have felt incumbent on myself to help to provide a continuous sphere of such circumstances for my less fortunate countrymen.

In the letter he also elaborated the quantum of funds he proposed to commit to the institute and emphasized that he did not want it to be named after him. In the same year, he pledged almost half his fortune (consisting of fourteen buildings and four properties) worth ₹30 lakh (equivalent to ₹100 crore in 2018)[2] towards setting up the institute.[3] It was an unprecedented gesture, and a fabulous sum by any measure, especially in India. The press and the Congress party hailed Jamsetji's 'practical charity' and called him a true son of 'Mother Bharati'.

Support came from another legendary leader—Swami Vivekananda. The association between the monk and the merchant dated back to May 1893 when they were together on board the ship from Japan to Canada. When Jamsetji shared his vision for the institute, Vivekananda remarked, 'How wonderful it would be if we could combine the scientific and technological achievements of the West with the asceticism and humanism of India!' These words stayed with Jamsetji and five years later in November 1898, he personally wrote to him seeking his involvement and leadership for the proposed institute. Given his commitments with the Ramakrishna Mission, Swami Vivekananda could not spare time, but Sister Nivedita, his disciple, worked extensively to popularize the project with eminent educationists in the USA and Britain. She remained committed to the project till its fruition. In April 1899, *Prabuddha Bharat*, Ramakrishna Mission's mouthpiece, lauded the scheme.

> We are not aware if any project at once so opportune and so far reaching in its beneficent effects has ever been mooted in India . . . The scheme grasps the vital point of weakness in our national well-being with a clearness of vision and tightness of grip, the mastery of which is only equalled by the munificence of the gift that is being ushered to the public.

In December 1898, a distinguished committee of eminent citizens formed by Jamsetji Tata presented this plan before the Raj. Curzon wasn't convinced of the relevance and utility of such a grand scheme for India and the expenses it would entail. He dragged his feet and was non-committal on a government contribution. Several rounds of discussions and conferences followed. Curzon thought Jamsetji was fishing for a baronetcy (a hereditary title of honour). Jamsetji despised such ideas with indignation and declined the offer on two occasions. Despite Lord Hamilton's insistence, Curzon dodged the proposal for nearly half a decade. The British government thought that since the permission for the institute had not been given, at his advanced age, Jamsetji would divert the funds to his other industrial ventures. Instead, Jamsetji's solid resolve became visible from his explicit instruction to his sons in his will that the amount set aside for the institute should not be touched. He encouraged them to contribute part of their inheritance for this scheme and work towards its fruition.

A year after Jamsetji's death, and before completing his term as viceroy, Curzon finally gave permission for the institute.[4] The Maharaja of Mysore donated 370 acres of land for the project. In 1911, the Indian Institute of Science (IISc) at Bangalore finally opened its doors. Ever since, several notable scientists of India have been groomed in its classrooms. Its first Indian director was Sir C.V. Raman, the Nobel laureate. A century later, 2000 young scientists leave its portals every year to fulfil Jamsetji's dream of a technologically advanced and scientifically self-sufficient India.[5] His majestic statue at the entrance of IISc continues to remind them of his vision for our nation. IISc has consistently ranked as the best university in India and among the top fifty in Asia. What modern-day scholars refer to as 'strategic philanthropy' can be seen from Jamsetji's support for scientific and technical education a century ago, albeit its strategic focus was for India and not for the donor.

Clean energy for India's future commercial capital

Esplanade House, Jamsetji's palatial home in south Bombay, built at a cost of ₹6 lakh in 1885, was the first in the city to be electrified with its own generator. But he wasn't satisfied. His dream was to provide electricity for the entire city, that too clean energy. He was increasingly concerned about the smoking chimneys of Bombay causing air pollution. Jamsetji had envisaged hydroelectricity in 1875, seven years before the first commercial scale hydroelectric project was built in Wisconsin (USA). However, he was denied permission on two occasions. First, at the Marble Rocks on the Narmada river near Jabalpur; second, at the Dudhsagar Falls in Goa. During one of his visits to North America in the late 1890s, he even saw the generator installed by Westinghouse under the Niagara Falls. Thirty-five years later, in 1910, when the Tata Hydroelectric Company was established, Jamsetji's daring vision was implemented. He had envisaged impounding the monsoon rainfall by dams on the Western Ghats in the Sahyadri Mountain reservoirs (on the outskirts of Bombay) and then carrying the water down 1734 feet (ten times the height of the Niagara Falls) to drive the turbo generators in the valleys below. He proposed using the basic principles of physics and hydrodynamics to convert kinetic energy into potential energy for generating electricity. The electricity thus produced was to supply cheap and clean power to Bombay, particularly in the mills, and make it a smokeless city.

Contrary to popular belief, the Tatas' power project met with widespread opposition from existing licencees. They filed several petitions to the government and even to the Secretary of State for India in London seeking intervention to restrain the Bombay government from granting permission to the Tatas. After several consultations, the government decreed that it was impossible to prevent a scheme that provided cheap electricity to Bombay. However, it restricted the Tatas to bulk supply to factories and railways.[6] While inaugurating the project in February 1911, Dorabji, who deserves the highest praise for following his father's footsteps and fulfilling his vision, said, 'To my father, the hydroelectric project was not merely a dividend-earning scheme. It was a means to an end—the development of the manufacturing power of Bombay.' An army of 7000 workers installed pipelines from Germany, waterwheels from Switzerland, generators from America and cables from England on the steepest slopes and roughest terrains of Lonavala and Khandala. One of the three dams they constructed was more massive than the famous Aswan Dam on the Nile. The popular Lonavala Lake that tourists enjoy today was created by the Tatas for the power project. A truly audacious enterprise attempted only fourteen years after the Niagara Falls hydropower project, it was lauded even by the British government. Lord Sydenham, then governor of Bombay, observed, 'This project symbolizes the confidence of Indians in themselves.' Like Tata Steel, the Tatas' hydropower company was financed entirely with Indian money, predominantly by native princes.[7]

The task of generating hydropower was as daunting as that of popularizing its use with Bombay's smoke-spewing textile mills, eighty-three of whose owners were wedded to power generation through coal-based steam engines. The Tatas not only shared with each of them the advantage of 'clean and cheap' electricity, but also offered to buy back the steam engines in which the mills had substantially invested. It is noteworthy that a discourse around 'clean power' was initiated by the Tatas nearly a century before the world woke up to its imperative in the light of global warming. When inaugurated in February 1915, the Tatas' power station at Khopoli was the largest in India and its penstocks (pipes) the longest in the world! In 1916 and 1919, two corresponding firms— The Andhra Power Supply Company and The Tata Power Company—were established. In 2000, the three companies were merged into what is today known as Tata Power. One hundred years since inauguration, the Tatas' power companies continue to provide electricity to the city Jamsetji loved. They substantially contributed to Bombay's industrialization and suburban transport system by providing what the company calls 'invisible goodness'.

Experiments and experiences with new enterprises

Dorabji had inherited not only the leadership of the Tata companies but also the industrial genius and risk-taking abilities of his father. Under his headship, in the years preceding and succeeding World War I, Tata and Sons embarked on several enterprises in hitherto unexplored industries, including engineering, electrochemical, sugar and toiletries. The Indian Cement Company established by Tata and Sons at Porbandar (Gujarat) in 1912 was the first successful attempt at producing cement in India. The Tata Construction Company dented the British monopoly of massive infrastructure projects and built the Vaitarna Dam and several elongated railway bridges over the gargantuan rivers—Sindhu, Narmada, Godavari and Krishna. In 1917, the Tata Industrial Bank, first of its kind in India, was promoted. Its key objective was developing industrial resources of the country by Indian capital, and for starting manufacturing industries in India from raw materials obtained in the country. The New India Assurance Company providing services in general and life insurance was also established by Dorabji in 1919. It went on to become the largest composite Indian assurance company transacting all classes of insurance business with a robust pan-India distribution network and branches in the Middle East and Far East. While a dozen new Tata companies came into existence during this decade, there were changes in the parent company as well. In 1917, under the Indian Companies Act 1913, Tata and Sons was converted into a private limited firm and rechristened 'Tata Sons and Company Limited' with a capital of ₹1.7 crore. The expansion necessitated a larger headquarters befitting one of India's largest managing agency house. In 1921, the Tatas invited George Wittet, a Scottish architect, who was at that time designing the Gateway of India, to design the new Tata Group headquarters at Bombay.

Wittet agreed and 'Bombay House', the Tatas' majestic headquarters was inaugurated in 1924, around the same time when Viceroy Isaacs inaugurated the Gateway, 2 km away. Ever since, Bombay House, the epochal heritage building, has become synonymous with Tata Sons.

Unfortunately, the best of times soon ended. The group leadership realized that several new companies they had started were not aligned to the group's core competence. While they performed well and gave quick returns in the war years, they came crashing down in the post-war period when demand for several industrial products dried up. Despite best efforts to retain them, the Tatas had to divest most of them to remain afloat. The Tata Industrial Bank was merged with the Central Bank of India in 1923, and Tata Construction was acquired by eminent industrialist Walchand Hirachand Doshi in 1929. The difficult days even forced Tata Sons to sell half the managing agency firm running Tata Power to American and Foreign Power Company for a twenty-one-year period, a decision that was criticized by several nationalists.

Tata Steel would have met a similar fate but for the Himalayan efforts of Dorabji and R.D. Tata. During World War I, Tata Steel had stood by the imperial government in its hour of need. It expanded capacity to meet war requirements, and even let go of profits of ₹1 crore, by making products for defence purposes instead of those that gave handsome commercial returns. However, the post-war scenario was one of gloom. Spiralling costs combined with transport and labour difficulties created huge challenges. There was also a spurt in imports, and steel products were sold below prices they were sold in the country of origin. The Raj did little to protect the native steel industry, which needed protection against dumping, especially from Belgium and Japan.[8] To add misfortune to misery, the company's largest pig iron customer, Japan, was struck by an earthquake. As a result, Tata Steel's profits plummeted, and by 1922 it was staring at an existential crisis. There was no money to even pay wages. When one of the directors suggested that the Tatas should consider selling the company, R.D. Tata thundered, 'Over my dead body!'

This was the finest hour of Dorabji's leadership. To salvage his father's dream and the Tatas' flagship company, he pledged his personal wealth of ₹1 crore, including his wife's jewellery, and raised a loan from the Imperial Bank of India (now State Bank of India). R.D. Tata also reached out to the nationalist leaders in the Central Legislative Assembly of India for their help to protect India's steel industry. Leaders from both sides of the political spectrum—Motilal Nehru and Muhammad Ali Jinnah—wholeheartedly supported the Tatas, and tariffs were levied on imported steel. Complementing these efforts with a vigorous drive of cost cutting, Tata Steel was back on an even keel by the late 1920s. In the current scenario, when some errant businessmen have escaped to foreign countries and are fighting legal battles to save their personal fortunes, even without bothering about employees' salaries and jobs, the example of Dorabji mortgaging his wife's jewellery to pay wages to Tata Steel's workforce is remarkable.

Worthy sons of an iconic industrialist

The commercial challenges faced by the Tata companies never deterred the Tata siblings, though very different in temperament, from continuing the philanthropic legacy of their far-sighted father. Let's first look at the contribution of the younger son—Ratanji. Though included as a partner in Tata and Sons in 1896, his real interests lay in social and philanthropic causes. He passionately pursued his father's endeavours for the development of Bombay. One such scheme was the reclamation of the Mahim Creek. However, lack of support from the government and local citizenry hindered its execution. He contributed extensively to the efforts of freedom fighter Gopal Krishna Gokhale and his Servants of India Society in its formative years. Gokhale had acknowledged his munificence (₹1 lakh received over a decade) in a letter in 1909 stating, 'There is no parallel to your overwhelming generosity anywhere in the country.'

In 1911, he even financed the excavation of Pataliputra (present-day Patna) by the Archaeological Survey of India. It unearthed Ashoka's Palace built on the model of Persepolis (the ceremonial capital of the Achaemenid Empire in 550 BC). This further strengthened the hypothesis of the ancient link between Persia and India, of which the Tata family was emerging as a fine ambassador.

An avid art collector, Ratanji's collection of rare Western art and Chinese antiques formed the nucleus of the Prince of Wales Museum in Bombay. He also seeded the department of social sciences and funded a chair at the London School of Economics for the study of poverty and its alleviation. Its first beneficiary was Sir Clement Attlee who was the prime minister of England when India attained independence. For his noteworthy services to society, Ratanji was knighted by the Raj in 1916. He died at the age of forty-eight in 1918, yet endowed a corpus of ₹80 lakh, a sizeable portion of his estate as the Sir Ratan Tata Trust. His place as a director on Tata Sons' board was taken by his wife, Lady Navajbai Tata. She was the largest stockholder in Tata Sons and held the position until her demise in 1962. Since Ratanji died childless, the family council suggested that Navajbai adopt a male child as her heir. She adopted Naval Hormusji Tata, son of Ratanji's late cousin.

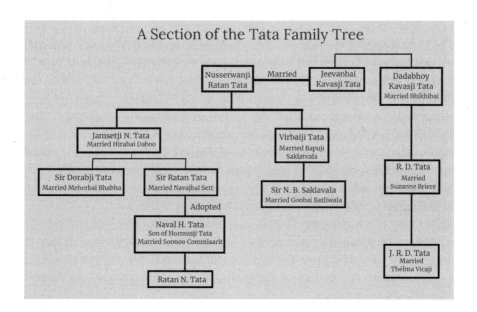

A Section of the Tata Family Tree

It was to the credit of Dorabji and with plentiful help from his partner, R.D. Tata, that Jamsetji's three schemes reached culmination. While Jamsetji was the man who gave the vision, Dorabji was the man with a passion for execution despite unprecedented infrastructural and resource challenges. For his outstanding contribution to India's industrial advancement, the Raj knighted him in 1910. As a student at Cambridge University, Dorabji had won honours for cricket and football. In later years, he wanted to support the passion for sports among his fellow citizens. From his own funds, he financed Indian participants for the 1920 and 1924 Olympics at Antwerp and Paris. He also supported the establishment of several institutions to promote sports, including the Willingdon Sports Club and the Parsi Gymkhana. Interestingly, Lady Meherbai Tata née Bhabha, a top tennis player herself, participated in the mixed doubles at the Paris Olympics. Dorabji also gave a handsome donation to his alma mater, and instituted a chair for Sanskrit studies at the Bhandarkar Oriental Research Institute, Pune. He had even offered to set up an Institute of Tropical Medicine at IISc with an endowment as large as that of Jamsetji. However, it was declined by the director as it was too much of a resource for the fledgling Institute to handle at that time.[9] It was eventually established in the year 1999.

Three months prior to his death in 1932, the childless Dorabji pledged a corpus of ₹1 crore that included all his belongings to Sir Dorabji Tata Trust (SDTT) with a mandate to support higher learning and alleviating poverty. His beloved wife had died of leukaemia in 1931. In her memory, he formed the

Lady Tata Memorial Trust for cancer research, and also intended to establish a radium wing for the study and cure of cancer in an existing hospital. Instead, his successors at Tata Sons initiated and completed the construction of India's first and one of the world's best-equipped cancer hospital, Tata Memorial Hospital, in 1941 at Bombay. The Sir Dorabji Tata Graduate School of Social Work was also funded by SDTT in 1936. It was later renamed the Tata Institute of Social Sciences (TISS), and is credited as Asia's oldest institute for professional social work. On his way to visit his wife's grave in England around her first death anniversary, Dorabji died at Bad Kissingen in Germany on 3 June 1932. His ashes were laid to rest beside hers. On their mausoleum were inscribed the words: Humata, Hukhta, Hvarshta.

CHAPTER 3

EVOLUTION OF INDIA'S NUMERO UNO

Seventy days after Jamsetji Tata shed his mortal coil, and 600 km west of Bad Nauheim, was born another Tata titan—Jehangir Ratanji Dadabhoy Tata—on 29 July 1904 in Paris. Jeh to his friends and family and J.R.D. to the world at large, he went on to guide the destiny of the Tata Group and catalyse the industrialization of independent India over the next nine decades. Believers in reincarnation could well hypothesize that it could very well have been Jamsetji Tata himself, who returned to fulfil his dreams for India in this new avatar!

In the years following the formation of Tata and Sons, a stark difference in the temperaments and leadership styles of Dorabji and R.D. Tata had emerged. Realizing that he may not be able to rise above the incompatibility, R.D. Tata relocated to France in 1900 to trade in pearls and precious stones. At the house of his French teacher in Paris, R.D. met his future wife—Suzanne Briere, the daughter of his teacher. Despite a huge difference in age and culture, R.D. decided to exchange the vows of matrimony and sought Jamsetji's blessings. Looking beyond orthodox reservations associated with an inter-religious marriage, the grandsire blessed the couple. In 1902, he celebrated their marriage with a special gathering at Kingston-on-Thames, which was, at that time, the largest gathering of Parsis to the West of the Suez Canal. Suzanne embraced Zoroastrianism and was given the name Sooni. To this couple was born J.R.D. and his four siblings.

Over the next two decades, J.R.D. attended schools in four cities—Bombay, Paris, London and Tokyo. Born a French citizen, he underwent a mandatory stint in the French army. Just when he was getting ready to enter Cambridge University for his undergraduate studies in engineering, R.D. Tata, advancing in age, called him to India to join the Tata business in December 1925. He requested his friend, John Peterson, former ICS officer and then director-in-charge of Tata Steel, to mentor J.R.D. His training consisted of seeing every letter before it went to Peterson, and once again after he had noted his comments on it. In later years, J.R.D. acknowledged his experience of working with Peterson as it taught him how an eminent ICS administrator worked. This was complemented by on-site training at Jamshedpur from early 1926.

Though he anticipated joining university at a later date, circumstances did not present J.R.D. the opportunity of undergoing university education. This remained his lifelong regret.

As J.R.D. was learning the nuances of the Tata way of business at Bombay and Jamshedpur, R.D. Tata passed away during a visit to France in 1926. Sooni had succumbed to tuberculosis three years earlier. In the two decades since Jamsetji's demise, R.D. had reconciled his differences with Dorabji and stood shoulder to shoulder with him in the accomplishment of the founder's vision. His passionate espousal of all causes related to India's industrialization were lauded by his peers. On his demise, Jamnalal Bajaj, founder of the Bajaj Group of companies, said, 'If all businessmen in India would acquire half his love for things Indian, there is no reason why all our enterprises should not flourish.'[1]

Tatas brace the Great Depression

R.D. Tata had bequeathed his shares to J.R.D. In all fairness, he divided them among the five siblings. However, he was nominated to step into his father's shoes. At the young age of twenty-two, he became a director on the board of Tata Sons. In his early years, he witnessed the turnaround of Tata Steel from the brink of closure, and even worked with Sir Homi Mody, director at Tata Steel, to reach out to small Indian manufacturers as customers for Tata Steel products. During the years leading to the Great Depression, the British government and executives were keen to protect their native steel industry. The alternative market developed by J.R.D. and Mody helped Tata Steel tide over the difficult years.[2] With the support of Peterson (who served the Tatas through 1931), J.R.D. even convinced Dorabji to invest in India's fledgling civil aviation sector. This led to the birth of Tata Airlines, a fascinating story we'll explore in a later chapter. By this time, J.R.D. had given up his French citizenship and embraced India as his country—legally and heartfully.

In 1932, after the demise of Dorabji, Sir Nowroji Saklatvala, Jamsetji's nephew (son of his sister Virbaiji and Bapuji) became the third chairman of Tata Sons. Nowroji had risen through the ranks at the Tatas' textile mills— he was nominated chairman of the Bombay Mill Owners' Association and even represented Indian employers at the International Labour Conference in Geneva. It wasn't surprising then that he introduced a novel profit-sharing programme for Tata employees and higher wages for the lowest-paid workers during his tenure.[3] He shared the Tata passion for sports, and was the first chairman of the Cricket Club of India (CCI) and developed the now historic

Brabourne Stadium. To date, his imposing photo frame welcomes visitors at the reception of CCI, alongside that of Jamsetji. J.R.D. was his right-hand man and assisted him in preparing speeches and in managing the affairs of Tata Steel and Tata Airlines. Both shared a great working relationship. Nowroji even set up J.R.D.'s office next to his at Bombay House, with a glass panel between the two rooms. Under his leadership, nothing new was started by Tata Sons except the Investment Corporation of India. It promoted companies and acquired holding in outside companies. This was also the period when the world was recovering from the Great Depression. Nowroji worked hard and ensured that the Tata goodwill was retained and enhanced.

In those years, the Tatas' cement companies faced severe headwinds. Like the steel industry, they became a victim of competition from imported British products. Due to exceptional efforts by Indian industrialists, the government agreed to impose tariff on imported cement but recommended greater consolidation and mutual agreements for pricing and sales among Indian companies. To avoid uneconomic competitiveness and improve production, marketing and consumption of cement within the country, Framroze Edulji Dinshaw, a leading legal luminary and businessman, and J.R.D. proposed a merger of the cement companies. Ten of the existing one dozen companies agreed. These included companies belonging to the Tatas, the Khataus, Killick Nixon and Dinshaw. However, Dinshaw passed away before the formation of the consolidated entity. The responsibility fell on the young shoulders of J.R.D., and he executed it with great conviction and commitment under Nowroji's guidance. In 1936, the Associated Cement Companies (ACC) came into being with an authorized capital of ₹8 crore.[4] Nowroji was its first chairman. Though it had doyens of Indian industry on its board, ACC remained a Tata-run and Tata-controlled company over the next six decades. The successful creation of ACC had demonstrated the capacities of young J.R.D. It was noticed by the leading lights on the board of Tata Sons. After all, they were looking for grooming the next chairman.

In 1938, during a visit to France, Nowroji suffered a fatal heart attack. He became the third consecutive Tata chairman to die in Europe. In a special board meeting of Tata Sons on 26 July 1938 at the Bombay House, the board of directors unanimously elected J.R.D. as the chairman of Tata Sons. Though just thirty-three, he had proved his credentials in the previous decade, and emerged a hero in his own right. He also had the blessings and approval of Lady Navajbai, the largest stockholder in Tata Sons at that time. To make light of his achievements at a young age, J.R.D. joked years later about his appointment as chairman as 'a moment of mental aberration'![5]

The J.R.D. era begins

When J.R.D. took over, the Tatas were the largest industrial house in India. The fourteen major companies under their control had combined annual sales of ₹280 crore. The young chairman was to preside over the 'first family' of India Inc. for the next half a century. Married to Thelma Vicaji, a half-English Parsi lady from Bombay, J.R.D. called himself an internationalist. He had a very different world view compared to his industry peers who were primarily born and bred in British India. This distinguished his thinking from the mainstream, but complemented the industrial discourse of that era. However, he modelled his style of leadership to that of Jamsetji, and always placed the nation before the company. He once said, 'To me, the Tatas and India are in many ways one and the same, and one of their purposes and the objective is to build India.' Like the founder, his priority was not moneymaking. 'None of my decisions were influenced by whether it would bring me money or wealth,' he once said.

With age on his side, and his characteristic enthusiasm, J.R.D. embarked on a mission to spread the Tatas' wings to newer industries and fly 'beyond the last blue mountain'. He had decided that he would not be like his predecessor—Nowroji, who spent most of his six years as chairman rushing from one board meeting to another, with hardly any time to do creative work. J.R.D. broke with the long-held tradition that the Tata Sons chairman would be the chairman of the operating Tata companies. He devolved powers to heavyweights within the group who had far greater experience than him. He gave the chairmanship of the power companies to Sir Homi Mody and shed the chairmanship of the textile companies. However, he was not interested in remaining a nominal chairman. He took an active interest in the affairs of Tata Sons and of two key companies where he had substantial experience—Tata Steel and Tata Airlines.

Exploring the establishment of new companies and grooming talent to lead them was another priority. As a result, the next decade saw the establishment of several new companies under the House of Tata. Tata Chemicals began in 1939; Tata Engineering and Locomotive Company (TELCO, now Tata Motors) in 1945; Air India International, India's first global airline, in 1948; and National Radio and Engineering Company (NELCO) in 1949. The Tatas' investment in basic industries through Tata Chemicals and TELCO was in continuation of Jamsetji's vision of contributing to India's industrialization through core-sector contributions. These initiatives were costly and intensive, and meant the holding of large funds from the public. In later years, they were even vulnerable to government interventions and nationalization. Some succeeded and some surrendered. Yet, the story of their inception, growth, challenges and revival to global heights makes for a fascinating read and has been captured in later chapters.

The beginning of World War II had stranded a brilliant young scientist from proceeding to Cambridge University for advanced research. The young man's exceptional ideas impressed Tata Trusts, which invested in his research by providing infrastructure and resources in Bangalore and Bombay. The man was Homi Jehangir Bhabha,[6] who became the founding father of India's atomic energy programme. The institutions he subsequently founded were also substantially funded by Tata Trusts—the Tata Institute for Fundamental Research (1945) and the Bhabha Atomic Research Centre (1954), which became the cradle of India's indigenous nuclear programme. It wasn't just the resources, but the time J.R.D. personally gave to the development of these institutions, which has played a significant role in their success and stature. For decades, he remained the president of the governing council of TIFR and the president of the court of IISc. In true Tata tradition, J.R.D. founded the J.R.D. Tata Trust in 1944 to help Indians through scholarships, grants and targeted programmes.[7] In the same year, the Tata way of business was acknowledged by US-based *Fortune* magazine. In its New Year special issue, it noted:

> . . . The House of Tata stands out like a power plant in a country of treadmills. To the Indian, the natively created House of Tata represents a source of national pride, a signpost on the rocky road toward an industrial future . . .
> It may go on to accomplish even more spectacular things than it has in the past. Without so expansive an immediate future, Tata will remain what it is today—one of India's greatest national assets, significant in itself, but still more significant as the promise of a far-off industrial future.

These observations proved prophetic. In the following years, the Tatas became pioneers in giving prominence to staff functions in a business organization. They were probably the first corporate organization in the world to have a department of economics and statistics, and a department of public relations in the early 1940s. In 1945, when management as a discipline was not fully developed even in Western countries, the Tatas set up Tata Industries—the first technocratic structure in Indian business. Eminent economists, lawyers and financial wizards were appointed to its board. None of them were shareholders, their expertise was used to benefit group companies.[8] Tata Industries was owned entirely by Tata Sons and became the managing agents of all Tata companies in place of Tata Sons. Besides the technocrats, directors of major Tata companies also sat on its board. This brought together the best

blend of experience and expertise to benefit and catalyse the growth of the
Tata Group in independent India. Between 1945 and 1970, Tata Industries
became the group's 'think tank' and spearheaded several new companies.

Tatas in independent India

The year of India's political independence marked the diamond jubilee of the
Tatas' existence. On 15 August 1947, J.R.D. sent a letter to all the employees of
the Tata Group. He wrote, ' . . . Let us together harness the Tatas' resources to
the task of national reconstruction and development, and thus play our part in
creating the better land . . . ' In 1757, when Robert Clive entered Murshidabad
(Bengal) after the winning the Battle of Plassey, he had commented that the
city was richer than London. Over the next two centuries of British rule in
India, Britain's share of world trade increased from 2 to 23 per cent. That of
India declined from 23 to 2 per cent. Britain's enrichment had been in direct
proportion to India's impoverishment.[9] At the dawn of political independence,
India had before herself a colossal task of economic and industrial revival.

The first decade of independent India has been described by historians as
the 'golden age of Indian industry'. Despite the government's licencing policy,
Tata companies, including TISCO, TELCO and NELCO, received generous
permissions of capacity expansion. The Tatas optimized the opportunities.
There were setbacks too. As part of the nationalization programme of the Nehru
government, Air India and New India Assurance Company were nationalized.
It was a bittersweet experience and the Tatas were witnessing the unfolding
of a new era of centralized planning that was dominated by intrusions in the
functioning and decision-making of private companies, including the likes of
the Tatas. J.R.D. was exasperated and used every opportunity to communicate to
the government about the need to balance private enterprise with public welfare.
In later chapters, we'll analyse the negative impact of these policies on the potential
of several Tata companies and of Indian industry for over three decades.

Amid this complex scenario, a unique request came from the Prime
Minister's Office (PMO) to the Tata Group—can't the Tatas make cosmetics
for Indian women? The Government of India had banned imports of all non-
essential items, including cosmetics and perfumes. In those years, there wasn't
a domestic cosmetic company, leaving elite women of Delhi superlatively
upset. They besieged the prime minister—both at home and at work. Indira
Gandhi, who was then the hostess of Teen Murti Bhavan, Prime Minister
Nehru's official residence, empathized with the women's representation and
assured them of her support. Another delegation of women blocked the prime

minister on his way to the external affairs ministry. Some were wailing at the insensitivity of the government at 'women's woes'. The PMO was flooded with telegrams and letters with the same request.

It was under such pressure that the Tatas and some other companies were requested to enter this new industry with the assurance of government support. This marked the beginning of Lakmé[10] (1952), a brand that became synonymous with Indian cosmetics. It was launched as a division of the Tata Oil Mills Company (TOMCO) in collaboration with a French enterprise. TOMCO was started at Tatapuram, in the backwaters of Cochin in 1917. The Tatas were one of the first to start an industry in Kerala. However, it took a quarter-century before the company turned profitable due to several factors, including global competition and local inadequacies. By the 1950s, TOMCO's Hamam bathing soap and 501 laundry soap had become household names. Intriguingly, the name 501 was an outcome of patriotic passion. In those years, there was a French soap called '500'. TOMCO felt that India could do better. They launched '501'!

The decade saw the establishment and acquisition of several companies and managing agency houses. Voltas (1954), which specialized in large-scale air conditioning, and Tata Finlay (1963) for tea plantations were notable additions. A decade later, when James Finlay wanted to divest their interests, the Tatas acquired their stake. Tata Finlay became Tata Tea, the number one tea-growing company in the world (by size). In 1960, Tata International and Tata Exports were formed to export Tata products and services to international markets. It was a revival of the old Tata expertise in trade that existed during the years of Jamsetji when Tata had offices in Osaka, Kobe, Shanghai, New York and Paris. Under its renewed international outreach, the Tatas ventured into precision equipment manufacturing in Singapore, palm oil refining in Malaysia and hotels and electricals in the Gulf countries. During a conversation, Syamal Gupta, former director at Tata Sons, recalled the success of TELCO trucks in Africa. In an environment where European products were popular, the Tatas' endeavours convinced local consumers of the quality of Indian products. This opened a new geography for several Indian companies, who benefited from the positive image created by the Tatas. In recognition, Gupta was appointed on the presidential advisory committees of five African countries. All through, the Tata way of business remained the undercurrent. Sumant Moolgaokar, then chairman of TELCO, had given clear instructions, 'Be part of the local economy. Don't focus on bringing money back to India.'

It was an opportune time for export-focused businesses as the government was conservative in sanctioning domestic industrial licences to discourage any kind of monopolistic situation. Between 1958 and 1967, the Tatas received approval for 198 of the 245 applications it submitted. In contrast, the Birla Group, the Tatas' closest competitor, received approval for 427 of its 855 applications.[11] While Birla was considered aggressive in its approach, the Tatas were perceived as risk-averse. In hindsight, it emerged that the Tatas focused on consolidation, which was more in alignment with the government policy than the expansionary strategy of the Birla Group that had sought permits for businesses across seventy-six industries.

The Tata Consultancy Services, the group's flagship company today, saw the light of day as an operating division in 1968. Its growth from a dozen software consultants to 400,000 software experts in fifty years has been mind-boggling, to say the least. The TCS story and its pioneering contribution in creating and globalizing India's IT industry has been reserved for another chapter. By mid-1960s, the number of companies under Tata Sons had increased to 150 and the total assets to over ₹500 crore. The most challenging decade for the group and India Inc. was about to begin.

Tata empire becomes a commonwealth of Tata companies

In 1966, after Indira Gandhi came to power, there were increasing efforts to limit the scope and scale of private sector companies. To this end, a series of legislations was introduced. One of these, which had an unprecedented effect on the House of Tata, was the abolition of the managing agency system on 2 April 1970. Under the new system, each Tata company became an independent entity with its own board of directors. The writ of Tata Sons was no longer implementable on them; its role was limited to advice and persuasion. With 74 per cent of the group run by managing agencies, the Tatas had to identify and bring on board hundreds of independent directors for its fifty manufacturing companies and 100 associate companies, almost instantaneously. The massive exercise was led by India's pre-eminent jurist—Nani Palkhivala, who joined Tata Sons as a director in 1961 and remained J.R.D.'s adviser on most legal matters for the next four decades.[12]

The abolition of the managing agency system severely impacted India Inc. Several companies were even liquidated. There were labour problems that emerged from division of employees and senior leaders across companies within a group. The Tata Group was particularly impacted because the stake of Tata Sons in most Tata companies was negligible. Interestingly, the stake of the Birla Group (through Pilani Investments) in Tata Steel was double (6 per cent) that of Tata Sons (3 per cent). Every year, before the AGM, G.D. Birla, head of the Birla empire, would sign and send his proxy form to J.R.D. for his decision and discretion. The cohesion of the group was maintained purely by the power of J.R.D.'s charismatic personality. He had nurtured and empowered every single leader within the Tata companies during their formative years. They admired him and were grateful for the trust he reposed in them. This was the soft power through which Tata Sons led the group companies for the next two decades. It also worked to the group's advantage as it was spared the sway of the draconian MRTP (Monopolies and Restrictive Trade Practices) Commission set up under the MRTP Act, 1970, the Tata Group emerged as a professionally run group of independent companies under the leadership of a nominal chairman.

During the 1970s, most Tata companies were chaired by the 'awesome foursome'. J.R.D. was the chairman of Tata Sons, Tata Industries and Tata Steel. Moolgaokar was the chairman of Tata Motors and ACC. Darbari Seth was the chairman of Tata Chemicals, Rallis India and Tata Tea. Naval Tata was the chairman of the textile and power companies.[13] A word on the role of Naval Tata is topical. Exactly thirty-two days younger to J.R.D., he joined Tata Sons as a director in 1941 and was the deputy chairman of Tata Sons from 1962 up to his death in 1989. However, his lifelong mission focused on reconciling differences between the labour and the management in India. He played a pivotal role at the International Labour Organization to whose governing council he was elected a record thirty-eight times. Under his presidency of the Indian Hockey Association, India won gold in three successive Olympics. He remained the face of the Tatas while manoeuvring through the arduous processes within the government's bureaucratic labyrinth.

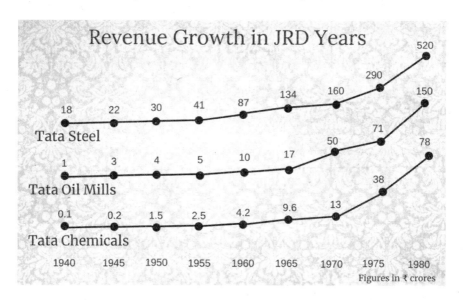

Revenue Growth in JRD Years

Figures in ₹ crores

The penultimate decade before liberalization

The 1980s began with a bang. There was a change in government at Delhi. Prime Minister Indira Gandhi wrested power from the Janata Party. The Tatas had also regained their numero uno position in India Inc. despite a difficult decade. Their combined assets had tripled over the previous decade and crossed ₹1540 crore. The octogenarian J.R.D. realized that it was time to bring a young leader at the helm of affairs. In October 1981, he appointed Ratan Tata, son of Naval Tata, as the chairman of Tata Industries.

Born in 1937 as the eldest son of Naval and Sonoo Tata, Ratan had completed his bachelor's in architecture and structural engineering at Cornell University in 1962. After a brief stint in Los Angeles, he returned to India at the insistence of his grandmother Lady Navajbai. She remained a dominant influence in his life since the divorce of his parents when he was ten. 'She taught me the values which I consider very important in myself,' he once said about her. After joining the Tata Group, he was sent to gain hands-on experience at Jamshedpur and worked on the shop floor at the Tata Motors and Tata Steel plants. He also assisted S.K. Nanavati, then director-in-charge at Tata Steel, to gain administrative experience. After six years in the Tata township, he was sent on an assignment to Australia. On his return, he was given two challenging assignments—turning around the Empress Mills at Nagpur and NELCO. Both had a troubled history and were bleeding when he took charge. He achieved profitability in both enterprises within a short period. In 1974, he was inducted as a director on the board of Tata Sons. He completed the advanced management programme at the Harvard Business School in 1975. Of Ratan Tata, J.R.D. had once said, 'Ratan is a much better manager than I am. He understands all the modern techniques of management. If I succeeded, it was only because of ideals. Ratan has both ideals and also the training of a manager.'[14]

Three months after his appointment at the helm of the Tata Industries, his mother was diagnosed with cancer. He prioritized her health over his professional commitment and spent four months by her side at the Sloan-Kettering Hospital in New York. However, during those four months, he formulated what came to be known as the 'Tata Strategic Plan 1983'. It consisted of six key focus areas: take back control of the operating companies; rebuild the group shareholding; invest and modernize; internationalize; dispose of underperforming 'sunset' businesses; and succession planning.[15] The plan proposed Tata Industries as the group's growth vehicle for investment in high-tech industries.

Despite J.R.D.'s support, the response from the Tata Sons board to the plan was lukewarm. The hardened attitudes developed in a laissez-faire environment while independently managing the Tata companies had created high levels of complacency among Tata stalwarts. Not one to succumb, Ratan Tata resized the plan to fit his pocket. He revived the relatively inactive Tata Industries that had an equity of just ₹60 lakh, by getting group companies to invest in it and then used those funds to set up next-gen companies such as Tata Telecommunications, Tata Honeywell, Tata Elxsi and Tata IBM.[16] Between 1982 and 1989, Tata Industries witnessed a tenfold rise in their capital and profits. The changing policy regime under Prime Minister Rajiv Gandhi had also created an encouraging macro environment. The warm working relationship between Rajiv and Ratan created the right synergies at the highest levels.

In the 1980s, the Tatas launched fourteen new companies. The most noteworthy was Titan Industries, which went on to become India's number one watch company. The Tatas' oldest surviving company achieved commendable scale during this period—the Taj Group of Hotels. Under the leadership of managing director Ajit Kerkar, five new Taj properties were constructed every two years between 1973 and 1987. Some of these were greenfield projects such as the Taj Mahal in Delhi, the Taj Bengal in Calcutta, and the Taj Coromandel in Madras. Many others were acquired, including the grandiose palaces of the erstwhile maharajas of Jaipur, Jodhpur and Udaipur. A select few were curated to showcase the place as an attractive destination on India's tourist map, such as the Taj Aguada Hermitage in Goa, which was selected in 1983, to host all Commonwealth heads of states, including Prime Minister Indira Gandhi and British Prime Minister Margaret Thatcher. Taj Malabar in Cochin was built to project Kerala as an attractive tourist destination in collaboration with the Kerala Tourism Development Corporation.

By 1988, Ratan Tata was nominated chairman of Tata Motors at the insistence of the ailing Moolgaokar. His first major challenge was the Rajan Nair-led labour strike at Tata Motors' Pune plant. He successfully thwarted it through multi-stakeholder negotiations, including with then chief minister of Maharashtra, Sharad Pawar. This became the talking point across political and corporate circles leading to an increasing conviction about his ability to lead the Tata Group. However, J.R.D. had not made up his mind about his successor at Tata Sons. As India was at the threshold of economic liberalization, the foremost question in everyone's mind was—who would lead India's largest conglomerate into the new millennium? Or would India's most iconic group of companies disintegrate?

CHAPTER 4

A NEW TATA FOR A NEW CENTURY

On 1 March 1991, J.R.D. Tata was to fly to Jamshedpur to participate in the annual Founder's Day celebrations held in Jamsetji's memory on 3 March. That morning he suffered from anginal pains. Yet, with help of painkillers he travelled to Jamshedpur and joined the annual festivities conducted with great fanfare. On his return, doctors recommended a week-long stay at Breach Candy Hospital in Mumbai. Ratan Tata, who had just returned from Stuttgart after a meeting with Mercedes, called on him at the hospital. The subsequent Monday, 18 March, J.R.D. was back in office. When Ratan met him, in his characteristic style, J.R.D. asked, 'Well, what's new?' 'Jeh, I saw you at the hospital on Friday! There's nothing new since I saw you last,' replied Ratan. 'Well, I have something new for you. I have decided to step down and name you my successor as chairman of Tata Sons,' said J.R.D.[1] Though appointed deputy chairman of Tata Sons in 1989, Ratan Tata was quite surprised at the sudden decision. What followed was amusing. 'Don't say about this to anyone now. I have to pick an auspicious day to do it,' said J.R.D.

At the Tata Sons board meeting on 25 March 1991, J.R.D. announced his decision to nominate Ratan Tata. Pallonji Shapoorji Mistry, the largest individual shareholder of Tata Sons, seconded the nomination and the new chairman was unanimously elected. J.R.D. was nominated chairman emeritus. As J.R.D. addressed the board one last time as the chairman of India's largest business house, he remembered several milestones achieved in the past fifty years while he was at the helm of the Tatas. Ratan Tata recalled that speech as an archival account of his experiences, but having not a word of praise about himself. Under J.R.D.'s leadership, Tata Group's assets had increased from ₹62 crore in 1939 to ₹10,000 crore in 1990. The group did it in an era that was marked by major government intrusions in private enterprises that scuttled substantial growth and delayed industrial expansion projects by decades. One could wonder how the Tatas and the Indian industry would have performed under J.R.D. if his ingenuous leadership would have been available when the Indian economy liberalized.

As J.R.D. rose from his chair that morning, and offered it to Ratan Tata, history was created. After fifty-three years, a new chairman occupied the august chair of Tata Sons. Except some differences of opinion expressed below the surface in previous years, the smooth transition in leadership was a vindication of a corporate culture J.R.D. had conscientiously built over five decades. Through personal example he had established that companies could be both value-driven and market-driven; that profits did not preclude ethical behaviour; that growth was possible without using political patronage to bend rules and cut corners; and that pursuit of wealth could be graceful.[2] Emotions were high in the boardroom that day as it was the end of an era. Posterity will never get an opportunity to relive those moments as the proceedings were not recorded. When asked how he would like to be remembered, J.R.D. said, 'As an honest man who tried to do what he thought was right.' Of J.R.D., Ratan Tata said several years later, 'His simplicity, his value systems and his sense of justice have stayed with me. He was like a second father to me. I could share with him much more than what I could with my father.' He never occupied J.R.D.'s corner office in Bombay House but continued to work out of the office given to him as chairman of Tata Industries. On 29 November 1993, J.R.D. passed away in Geneva at the age of eighty-nine, the fourth Tata chairman to die in Europe. To preserve his memory, his office was meticulously recreated with the same furniture, tapestry and photo frames at the Tata Archives in Pune for public viewing. I had an opportunity to see it during a visit.

The Ratan Tata era begins

The month of March 1991 was doubly significant. In a unique coincidence, as the Tatas embarked on a new journey with a new leader, India also embarked on a new journey of a liberalized market-based economy after dismantling the structural scaffoldings of a socialist approach under a centrally controlled economy. The balance of payments crisis requiring an International Monetary Fund bailout mandated several structural changes. Industrial licensing was abolished, and capital markets came alive. The Tata Sons that Ratan Tata inherited was India's largest business house with eighty-four companies (of which thirty-nine were listed), a turnover of ₹24,000 crore and profits of ₹2120 crore. Recalling those days, he highlighted two key legacies. One was a group high in ideals, values and ethics. The other was a group that had a board with several of its directors in their eighties. Many of whom were even unable to walk unassisted into the boardroom. 'Some very hard of hearing, some not

staying awake through meetings, but all rising to the occasion to not allow a
change to take place, whatever you may have wanted it to be.'[3] The former was
a strength that needed to be upheld and nurtured. The latter an area of concern
that had to be rectified to bring greater dynamism and youthful energy in the
company leadership.

In April 1992, two key initiatives that focused on leadership and
consolidation were announced. One was the revival of a much-ignored policy
that mandated retirement of executive and managing directors at sixty-five
years and chairmen at seventy-five years. A complementing initiative was
to revive the Tata tradition of the group chairman holding chairmanship in
major Tata companies. This was to ensure greater alignment in operating
companies' vision with the group vision, an area that had witnessed severe
lacunae in the 1980s after J.R.D. had handed over chairmanship of major Tata
companies to independent chairmen. There were hardened attitudes and
zealously guarded turfs that made change implementation difficult. Though
met with initial reservations by established leaders of group companies, often
referred to as 'satraps', both policy changes were implemented over the next
five years.

The second initiative was to increase the group's ownership in several
Tata companies through a rights issue. In the changed scenario that was open
to MNC takeovers, Ratan Tata believed that Tata Sons' holding in its major
operating companies should be more than symbolic. Though met with some
scepticism in the media, it was successfully completed in December 1995. Of
course, the Tata goodwill with financial institutions that held major stakes in
most Tata-promoted companies, sufficiently ring-fenced them from hostile
takeovers. N. Vaghul, then chairman of ICICI, had observed that any raider on
a Tata company would have to negotiate the barrier of goodwill that the group
enjoyed in abundance.[4]

Besides increasing Tata Sons' equity stake in major Tata companies,
consolidation also required shedding the flab and divesting non-core
companies from the group. Ratan Tata believed that in the era of free markets,
the Tatas were in many more areas than they should have been and needed
to refocus. One such company identified for divestment was TOMCO. The
market share of the ₹400-crore seventy-five-year-old soap major had tumbled
from 20 to 2 per cent, and was heavily in losses.

In 1993, a 2:15 share swap deal was worked out with Hindustan Unilever
(HUL) for Tata Sons' 20 per cent stake in TOMCO. HUL was keen to acquire
the company as it would enhance its market share to a third of the ₹3000-
crore soap and detergent industry, much to the chagrin of local competitors

like Nirma. The boards of both companies, the high court and also the financial institutions that held 43 per cent stake in TOMCO agreed to the merger.[5] According to a stand-alone agreement insisted by the Tatas, for three years, none of the 5500 employees, distributors and suppliers would be severed. Over the next decade, Tata Group divested several major companies in areas it considered non-core to its future growth strategy and where substantial investments would be required to be sustainable and competitive.[6] Some of the notable ones included Lakmé (cosmetics) to HUL, ACC (cement) to Gujarat Ambuja Cement, Merind (pharma) to Wockhardt, and Goodlass Nerolac (paints) to Kansai Paint Company.

The evolving free-market economy in India also necessitated major Tata companies to transition their focus from being product-centric and cost-focused to customer-centric and profits-focused. This wasn't a commercial strategy but an existential imperative to beat global competition tiptoeing into Indian markets. Ratan Tata identified the two flagship companies—Tata Steel and Tata Motors—for implementing this change. The two were among India's largest private sector companies and accounted for half of Tata Group's revenue and a third of its profits. He believed that if these two managed to achieve global benchmarks, other group companies would be inspired to follow their example. The transformational journey of these and other Tata companies becoming global leaders over the next two decades has been elaborated in subsequent chapters of this book. It encapsulates the persistence of an Indian business house in achieving global success.

By mid-1990s, the Tatas were exuding a newfound confidence and dynamism. Except for power and infrastructure sectors, they had entered or planned entry into most industries. A proposed collaboration between Bell Canada and Tata Telecom, a ₹100-crore open-ended mutual fund by Tata Finance and Kleinwort Benson, an agreement with the American Insurance Group for the soon-to-be-opened insurance sector, a ₹1300-crore domestic airline proposal with Singapore Airlines, a consortium to build the Bangalore International Airport, and a joint venture with Mercedes Benz for Indian-assembled Mercedes cars from Tata Motors' Pune plant were on the cards. Dinesh Vyas, former chief tax counsel to the group, noted that the Tatas were most sought after in the international business community as a collaborator, which enabled the group to enter new areas rather quickly. Ratan Tata reflected on the reasons for the Tatas not foraying into the infrastructure sector in substantial measure. 'There is a tendency amongst some bidders to take things on ridiculous terms and then trying to negotiate after the contract has been awarded. We don't do that and, therefore, lose out on that score.'[7]

The problem has persisted two decades later with L1 (lowest bidder) tender proposals preferred for most government projects.

In the year 2002, Ratan Tata completed sixty-five years and technically stepped aside from executive responsibilities across group companies. However, in that single decade as group chairman, the two key focus areas of increasing stake across major group companies and improving market performance of Tata companies across core sectors had been achieved. Most notably, between 1992 and 2002, Tata Sons' stake in Tata Steel had increased from 8 to 26 per cent and in Tata Motors from 17 to 32 per cent. Of the forty listed, fourteen companies had emerged as the fulcrum of the group. The major seven were Tata Steel, Tata Motors, Tata Tea, Tata Power, Indian Hotels, TCS and Tata Chemicals. The budding seven were Rallis, Voltas, Tata International, Tata Finance, Forbes Gokak, Tata Infotech and Titan.[8] These fourteen collectively contributed 85 per cent of group revenues and 90 per cent of profits. In a decade when several leading Indian business houses had disintegrated, Tata Group enhanced its consolidation and established its identity as India's largest and most-successful conglomerate. R. Gopalakrishnan, director at Tata Sons, described the transformation of the Tatas as 'the fantastic restoration without tinkering with the façade of a heritage monument'. This allegory could be appreciated from the key structural changes that were implemented within the group that eventually became its pillars of strength.

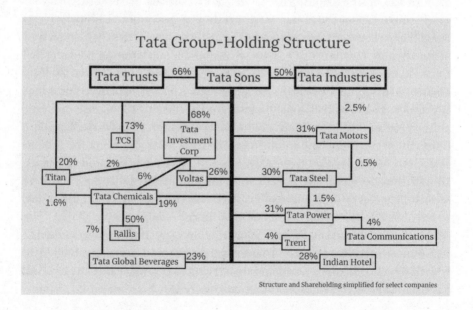

Tata Group-Holding Structure

Structure and Shareholding simplified for select companies

A new structure for the next century

In the 1980s and early 1990s, the Tata Group was described as a loose confederation of companies, where each company went its own way. Companies chose to call themselves part of the group only when they needed to, especially while raising funds from the market. The persona of J.R.D. and the personal loyalty he commanded had held the group and its operating companies together. Such was the passion for developing their company's identity that they often behaved as competitors rather than constituents of one conglomerate. Here is an interesting anecdote. At one time, Tata Steel was producing a certain kind of steel, which Tata Motors didn't want to use. It was the Licence Raj era, and Tata Motors sent out a notice to all steel plants saying that they should be allowed to import that type of steel. Tata Steel refused stating that they could make the steel for them. The matter was escalated to Tata Sons but wasn't resolved at Bombay House. Finally, both approached the Central government department, as in those days, government permissions for special imports were mandatory. Jamshed J. Irani represented Tata Steel and C.V. Tikekar represented Tata Motors. Both presented their viewpoints, but the government ruled in favour of Tata Steel, and refused import of steel for Tata Motors.

Ratan Tata was convinced that a persona-driven structure would not survive in a competitive economy. 'That was a time when many of our companies had their heads in the sand. The dominant impression was that we were less nimble than others, more resistant to change and extremely set in our ways,' Irani, former MD of Tata Steel, recalled. To beat this perception and effectively address the challenges, there was an urgent need for a structure where the group functioned as a cohesive entity that was proactive and nimble-footed to meet market requirements and beat competition. He believed in an institutionalized approach towards governance that would be long-lasting beyond any charisma that any individual leader may possess.

Consequently, several structural initiatives were undertaken at the corporate level. Notable among them was the establishment of the Group Corporate Centre (GCC) as the policy-framing board taking into cognizance the government's prevailing economic and industrial policies. It reported to Tata Sons board and provided several corporate services[9] to group companies on discretionary basis. The Group Executive Office (GEO) was the implementation arm for restructuring the group and forging its future direction. It interacted with group companies as the voice of the promoters and advised them to remain in businesses where they could establish themselves as globally competitive. The group chairman headed both the bodies.[10]

Tata Group's binding glue

Ratan Tata proposed that the best tribute to J.R.D.'s memory would be an award to honour and celebrate what J.R.D. had embodied all his life, and in turn, inspire a quest for excellence among the group companies. Accordingly, the J.R.D. QV Award was instituted in July 1994 as an annual commemoration. After studying several performance excellence frameworks in Singapore, Japan, Europe and the US, an apex committee at Tata Sons selected the Baldridge National Quality Programme as the methodology to be adopted across group companies for working towards winning the J.R.D. QV Award.

Tata Business Excellence Model

The Baldridge programme was found to be most appropriate for the Tata Group for two reasons. Firstly, it wasn't industry-centric but process-centric. In a group with over 100 companies representing diverse industries, an industry-agnostic model was most suitable. Secondly, two of the group companies—Tata Steel and Tata Honeywell—had already embarked on the implementation of the Baldridge programme. The Tata Group leadership decided and licensed its model from the Baldridge programme.

When the first results were announced post-assessment in August 1995, the average score across twelve companies was a depressing 215 out of 1000 points. It was an eye-opener for individual companies as well as the senior leadership. Till then, the primary focus of group companies had been on achieving production targets, expanding manufacturing facilities and improving profits compared to the previous year. However, the new framework required a transition to a customer-centric approach with superlative emphasis on process quality while benchmarking with the best-in-class practices from across global companies. This was a must in the post-liberalization era.

In the first meeting of eighty quality champions from across group companies in November 1995 at the Taj President in Mumbai, there was a common complaint—they were not receiving full support from their company leadership. At a first-of-its-kind gathering of 100 senior leaders of Tata Group companies

TBEM: Evaluation Process

JRDQV Award

If assessment score exceeds 600 out of the total 1,000 points, the company wins.

4

STAGE 3
Verify the detailed process descriptions implemented at grass root levels. Presentation of key findings.
3
Site Visit

STAGE 2
A team of 8-10 assessors from the group companies led by a mentor. Followed by meetings to arrive at consensus.

2 Evaluation by trained and certified assessors

STAGE 1
Proposal prepared by the applicant company on identified criteria
1
Self-analysis

at the same venue in January 1996, there was a common request—they needed a centralized resource group for guiding and pursuing the quality movement across group companies. Ratan Tata responded positively to this request, and in the same year, Tata Quality Management Services (TQMS) was set up with a mandate to assist Tata companies in achieving their business excellence and performance enhancement goals. More importantly, these meetings across group companies marked the change in the Tata Group culture from independent identities to a unified Tata family. Irani recollected that there hadn't been a single group-wide convention of this kind before. The intra-group quality movement had played a significant role in developing a common Tata identity.

Initially, there were consistent efforts to boost quality consciousness across group companies. Eventually, the quality movement transitioned to a movement of business excellence and the process of working towards the J.R.D.

QV Award was christened the Tata Business Excellence Model (TBEM) in 1998. To strengthen the ecosystem, TQMS was made a division of Tata Sons. Yet, the transition wasn't easy. Typically, process changes within a division take several months. And here we were talking about changing the way business processes were implemented across more than 100 companies. Moreover, how do you sustain a common Tata identity across group companies when by law they are governed independently by their own boards? One is through common values, in which case an institutional arrangement helps. TBEM created a structured scaffolding that provided a pathway for everybody.

In the first few years, the senior leadership across many group companies conjectured that an application using flowery language would help them win the J.R.D. QV award. They could not perceive TBEM as a tool to formulate their company strategy in a holistic manner. When no company could win the J.R.D. QV Award in the first six years, some of the CEOs suggested to Ratan Tata, 'Why not give this award to the highest scorer rather than wait for a threshold of 600 points?' The world benchmark for winning the MBNQA was 600 points. Anything below 600 was not recognized. Ratan Tata stood his ground and insisted that the Tatas would not recognize the highest scorer just because none of its companies were able to win the award. The group should adhere to world-class benchmarks. He invested enormous resources to provide an enabling ecosystem such that companies and their leadership could imbibe and implement TBEM within their companies.

Yet, as they say, the most difficult part of change is letting go. A former senior leader at TQMS shared an incident that brought forth the tough side of the chairman, who had all along played the role of the facilitator. This was at the group strategy forum meeting in the early years of the millennium that was chaired by Ratan Tata, where topmost CEOs of Tata companies interacted with directors of Tata Sons. Many companies were not yet convinced of the model and its benefits. A presentation was made at the meeting on the group's progress in business excellence as compared to other world-class companies. The Tatas' performance hadn't been good enough. At the end of the presentation, Ratan Tata asked the reason for this insufficiency. There was pin-drop silence. On being prodded further, a senior leader from TQMS confessed that CEOs of many companies were not providing the necessary support. The responsibility of anchoring the implementation of business excellence within the company was with the CEO, and they weren't taking enough interest. The stony silence in the room persisted. The chairman appeared truly upset. 'If that is the case, let us address it in the annual general management meeting,' he said. He took two slides from the presentation for the annual general management meeting, where 600 senior leaders across Tata companies met. During that meeting, he presented those slides and shared how the group companies were not doing well enough. In a rare display of displeasure, he gave an ultimatum to CEOs of some of the largest Tata companies, 'If somebody here is not willing to follow the guidelines and drive business excellence using TBEM, then I don't want to see you here next year.' This was not very usual of him. But it pained him that senior leaders across group companies were not able to see his grand vision. Seeing his commitment to TBEM as means to achieve that vision, a silent yet palpable change began across group companies. Slowly but surely, driven both by internal persuasion, and by the pressures of the marketplace, companies grew to understand the importance of business excellence as well as the role played by TBEM in helping them with a structure.

The Baldridge framework upgrades itself with newer elements every two years. This helped TBEM with valuable insights from the parent institution. TQMS introduced new elements in the evaluation process based on changing requirements—market factors, group performance in certain areas and geopolitical issues. For example, in 2003, corporate governance and knowledge management became part of TBEM. Between 2005 and 2007, sustainability and climate change became key elements of the TBEM process. Around 2008, Tata Group realized that it wasn't doing well enough on the parameter of safety. Thereafter, TQMS introduced a specific set of questions on safety in the TBEM evaluation process. From 2011–12, there was a big thrust on technology and digitization. To enable the group to achieve its customer-centricity objectives, customer promise was embedded in the TBEM criteria in 2015.

By 2017, over 760 TBEM assessments had been performed across group companies since inception. However, the high aspiration levels for the award could be seen from the fact that there had been only fifteen J.R.D. QV Award winners since 1995. Interestingly, six of these were from the Tata Steel Group. The others included: Tata Motors (2005), Titan (2006), Tata Chemicals (2007), Tata Power (2009), Rallis (2011), Tanishq (2012), Indian Hotels (2013) and Tata Power Delhi Distribution (2014). Moreover, TBEM had created a niche for itself in the Malcolm Baldridge ecosystem. During the TBEM convention in 2016 at Vivanta By Taj in New Delhi, Al Faber, President and CEO of the Baldrige Foundation, praised the Tata Group as a global benchmark in institutionalizing business excellence in a scalable and repeatable manner.

United we stand

In 1998, another vital initiative was implemented. This was with respect to the 'Tata' brand, which was loosely defined though widely used across hundreds of companies and thousands of products and services. 'We identified our brand

in 15–20 different ways, each company doing its own thing,' recalled Ratan
Tata. The group's top leadership realized the urgent need to clearly define
the brand, its ownership and usage. For those disinclined to such a mandate,
Ratan Tata argued:

> If you are to fight a Mitsubishi or an X or Y in the free India of tomorrow,
> you better have one rather than forty brands. You better have the ability to
> promote the brand in a meaningful manner . . . There may be a Mr Tata as a
> chairman, or there may not be a Mr Tata as chairman of the group . . . You
> have to institutionalise certain things.[11]

To achieve this end, the Brand Equity and Business Promotion (BEBP)
agreement was effected from 1998. The first step was the introduction of a
uniform brand mark to be used across Tata companies. After eighteen months
of intense engagement with a British design agency, Wolf Ollins, a stylized 'T'
inside a blue oval was selected as the new logo. A single font used for the 'Tata'
name gave it a contemporary identity. Both were launched in February 1999.
All Tata-promoted companies desirous of calling themselves a Tata company
and using this brand identity had to sign the BEBP agreement. An annual
contribution had to be paid by every subscribing Tata company to Tata Sons
as part of BEBP based on the degree of its association with the brand. This
payment was connected to their net income, and would be used by Tata Sons
for the development, promotion and protection of the unified Tata brand.
Signatories included Tata companies and subsidiaries in which the group held
at least 15 per cent equity and in which the Tatas (including Tata Sons and
cross-holdings through various Tata companies) were the largest shareholder
outside the major institutional shareholders.[12] During our conversation, Ratan
Tata recalled how BEBP was initially resented within the group that it was
beneficial only for the big companies. 'Eventually it was seen that the smaller
companies gained the most from being a part of the bigger group.'

The BEBP was an unprecedented initiative in corporate India, perhaps even
globally. Unni Krishnan, managing director of Brand Finance, acknowledged
the Tatas' brand value governance practices as among the best in the world. He
averred that hardly any global company had institutionalized brand-related
practices such as the Tatas.[13] Its importance could be realized from the fact that
the contribution of brand-driven businesses in the Tata Group increased from
19.1 per cent to the turnover in 1991 to 41.4 per cent in 2000, and was expected
to rise to over 60 per cent in the future.

CHAPTER 5

TATA CULTURE, A WAY OF LIFE

'We cautiously stayed away from businesses like cigarettes and alcohol. Certain businesses which are more prone to corruption we do not get into because we will not succeed in those businesses. You will always have the handicap, and to say that a particular peer got it because he gave a bribe is no consolation to you.'

Farokh N. Subedar

The BEBP agreement mandated two other initiatives, which formed the pillars of the 'new' Tata Group. One of the pillars was adherence to the TBEM, another was signing the Tata Code of Conduct (TCOC). The former told Tata companies how to enhance their performance using a certain business maturity model, the latter on how to conduct business. One would wonder the necessity of a code of conduct for a group that had the goodwill for being ethical, even during the most intimidating periods of the Indian regulatory system. There was a strong reason for this.

For a long time, the Tata culture and tradition varied from company to company. There wasn't a defined culture except that embodied in the leadership style of J.R.D. and other Tata stalwarts. After taking over as chairman of Tata Industries, Ratan Tata had expressed his concern about the heuristic nature of the group culture, its understanding and implementation. 'There is no booklet or orientation or induction programme, and yet if we seem to carry through, it is what we carry by interaction in terms of what our predecessors and leaders have given to us.'[1]

Codifying a century-long culture

TCOC was an attempt to codify the value systems on which the Tata Group had been built, and is often referred to as Ratan Tata's seminal contribution for perpetuating the long-held Tata ethos. It reinforced the five core values that the group espoused—integrity, understanding, excellence, unity and responsibility. Every employee and director of a Tata company subscribing to the BEBP had to sign the TCOC and abide by it in letter and spirit. This meant that lakhs of Tata employees became TCOC signatories, making it one of the most followed corporate code in the world. The CEO of every Tata company also had to submit an annual compliance on its adherence to BEBP and its two pillars—TCOC and TBEM.

A new TCOC containing twenty-five clauses was introduced in October 2008. In addition to defining the company's value system, it demarcated ethical behaviour for all stakeholders. TCOC clauses were regularly revised and refined to remain relevant for a diverse and globally expanding conglomerate. Tata Sons also issued a detailed reference manual for explaining 'Management of Business Ethics' in 1999. It was revised in 2008 for making it globally applicable. Gopalakrishnan called TCOC the Tatas' bible that contained 'all the dilemmas and questions of conduct that have come up. We (top leadership) are clergy that go around and say, "What troubles you in your heart?"'[2]

The chief executive of each Tata company also acted as the chief ethics officer. Regional meets of ethics counsellors, web-based modules for greater awareness of TCOC, exhaustive assessments, and a group-wide ethics network formed part of the energetic ethics ecosystem. [3] It wasn't surprising that Tata Steel was recognized by Ethisphere Institute as the world's most ethical company six times. That too in the metals and infrastructure sector where ethics and fair play were often called 'the last ball in the game'. 'This happens only if ethics are part of your DNA in terms of systems, processes[4] and the people that run the business,' emphasized Kulvin Suri, head of corporate communications at Tata Steel. The BEBP achieved threefold outcomes—a unified brand identity, a synergistic journey to business excellence and a renewed commitment to highest standards of ethics. All three strengthened the structure of a unified Tata Group.

Arun Maira, former chairman of Boston Consulting Group, highlighted the special problem all conglomerates face—the role of the centre.

> The diversity of the parts has to be respected. Each has its own specialties, and needs adequate freedom to manage its own affairs. But the parts cannot be left entirely to their own devices; otherwise there will be little cohesion in the group. The issues are what decision-making powers and functions should the divisions forego to the centre and what capabilities the centre should add to the divisions.[5]

Gopalakrishnan gave an insightful metaphor to explain what he called the parent-adult-child relationship that exists between Tata Sons and its operating companies.

Accordingly, each Tata company is an adult son, an individual citizen with his own board of directors who direct the company and its strategies. 'We treat them like adults, and with adults there will be occasional differences of opinion, but if the board of directors blesses it, that adult is free to do what he wants to do.' The only way the parent (Tata Sons) exercises its role is if the son (individual Tata companies) does something that is violently different from what the parent wants to do. 'In that situation, we would behave like an investor and cash out.'

Truth alone triumphs?

The Tata Group's mission is: 'To improve the quality of life of the communities we serve globally through long-term stakeholder value creation based on leadership with trust.' The whole recycling of wealth and prosperity between the firm earning the profit and the people who gave it the profit in the first place are the core of its business approach. The purpose was articulated in the 1890s by Jamsetji, repeated in the 1960s by J.R.D., and in the noughties by Ratan Tata, in different words. Yet, the consistency of the message was the same. Gopalakrishnan, who had worked with Unilever for thirty-five years before joining the Tata Group, underscored:

> The degree of commitment I have seen in the Tatas to playing out its purpose is quite exceptional. I always use that very Indian word 'sanskaar'— commitment to truth and certain value systems. Sanskaar is not something you forget easily. It provides checks and balances whereby we continue to stick to the path.

The visible synergy between the group's stated purpose (mission) and the actual practised purpose (culture) was evident during testing times. This invisible yet very palpable Tata culture can be understood from three instances. First, when it is challenged through a provocation to wrongdoing. We'll see this through individual and institutional examples. Second, when there is proof of transgression. We'll see this through a real example of a Tata company that failed on several legal and ethical parameters. Third, when something unprecedented is attempted in a corporate context. We'll see this through the example of the largest and most successful IPO of the Tata Group, when Tata Sons fulfilled its obligations to its shareholders and holding institutions—Tata Trusts.

Gopalakrishnan shared with me the example of a young accountant working in one of the Tata companies that imported goods. Very impressed with TCOC and convinced of Tata values, one of his job responsibilities was dealing with excise, customs and local tax department officials. During one of his interactions, a tax officer insisted that the Tata company should pay ₹10,000 a month (split between the officer, his boss and the accountant) to ensure hindrance-free processing of papers. The accountant protested but the officer was unyielding. What happened thereafter was startling. The accountant acted as the whistle-blower and wrote a complaint to the director general of the Anti-Corruption Bureau. The authorities promptly responded, and a trap was set. Both the tax officers got caught and were sent to jail. The accountant hadn't even informed his superiors about this entire chain of events because he was convinced that he had abided by TCOC. Gopalakrishnan received a call that evening informing him about the developments and that the same would be reported in the media the next day. He experienced mixed feelings. The manager in him felt that the accountant had been naïve in approaching the highest authorities for an act of corruption, without even consulting his seniors. The leader in him was pleased with the promptness of a young accountant convinced of the Tatas' culture and his resolve to book the culprits. This incident validated what T.R. Doongaji, then MD of Tata Services, shared with me:

> People are not necessarily evil or manipulative. If you can cultivate that goodness and communicate the value systems to the extent that employees feel that this is what we are really here for, and this is what the company recognizes most as compared to temporary materialistic successes, then I think that kind of culture can be retained.

Another example of abiding by TCOC at the institutional level was equally illustrative. Tata Motors had set up a bus manufacturing facility along with Marcopolo from Brazil at Lucknow. One of the major assignments was to manufacture buses for the Delhi Transport Corporation (DTC), which had the mandate of completely changing all its buses to contemporary CNG ones under Sheila Dikshit, then chief minister of Delhi. However, the bus plant wasn't getting pollution-control clearance from the Uttar Pradesh government. The company had promptly fulfilled the concerns highlighted by the government, and yet there was an inordinate delay. A senior Tata Motors leader personally met the chief secretary at Lucknow. The bureaucrat was concerned about the delay but expressed his inability as the decision was not in his hands. 'While I understand your problem, I can only represent your problems, nothing more,' he confessed.

The Tata Motors leadership recognized the indirect approach by political powers to extract some 'benefits' from the company, which was under tremendous pressure from the Delhi government and even had to pay a penalty for delay in delivery of buses. 'I met the officials twice and told him that the Tatas can do nothing other than what was stipulated by law,' he shared. Appointments with the chief minister sought on two occasions were denied. The waiting game continued for 4–5 months. The people in the bureaucracy were embarrassed. Whenever Tata representatives went for a follow-up, they would say, 'All your documents are in order. We don't understand why they aren't being processed.' This was around the time the Tatas had decided to relocate from Singur to Sanand. 'I tried telling them that this is what can happen if you don't allow us to manufacture in Uttar Pradesh; we will have to relocate the plant, and if we leave, Uttar Pradesh will be the loser,' the Tata Motors leader shared. After six months, bureaucracy blinked, and clearances were received. To cover up loss of production, Tata Motors had to put in tremendous amount of extra work, and employed more manpower for fulfilling DTC orders. Yet again, TCOC triumphed.

Resolving financial fiascos—the Tata way

Tata Finance was a lending company closely attached to Tata Motors (auto finance). A promising company desirous of being a one-stop shop in the highly lucrative financial services business, Tata Finance and its MD—Dilip Pendse—had grand plans. Unfortunately, the star financier got into speculative trading and property transactions. Pendse allegedly routed money raised from Tata Finance's deposit holders through two subsidiaries, Niskalp Investments and Inshallah Investments, to various new economy stocks, which tumbled during the dot-com crash of 2000–01.[6] There was a cover-up for several quarters in which he would settle transactions on a reporting day and then re-enter them. The alleged fraud came to light while Tata Finance's application for a ₹90-crore rights issue in 2001 was under scrutiny by SEBI. Through an anonymous whistle-blower and internal mumbling, the matter came to the notice of Tata Finance chairman and Tata Sons chairman. Subedar shared:

> At the first stage you don't even realize the intensity of the problem. Companies are normally run by the MD and a group of people he has recruited. In a group of our size, we do hear murmurs, but sometimes you don't have proof. This continued till a stage when we realized that there is some problem.

Tata Finance appointed A.F. Fergusson and Co. as an independent auditing firm to scrutinize the company's books. The investigation revealed that the

investments had caused Tata Finance a loss of nearly ₹500 crore, besides issues
of insider trading and dubious bookkeeping. Tata Sons decided to blow the
whistle themselves rather than sweep the matter under the carpet. Senior
directors of Tata Sons met the RBI governor and deputy governor and shared
the problem. Their reaction was encouraging and they were willing to extend
appropriate legal help. The matter was widely reported in the papers, and
received strong reactions from both ends of the spectrum. The Tatas filed a
case against Pendse and certain employees. Pendse claimed complicity of Tata
Sons leadership, a charge later invalidated. The Tatas continued to support the
case right up to the Supreme Court, and even encouraged a CBI enquiry into
the matter.[7]

As a non-banking financial company (NBFC), Tata Finance borrowed
six to seven times its net worth. Some amount was bank borrowing and a
large portion was public deposits. It had borrowings of ₹2700 crore, of which
₹875 crore belonged to 400,000 small depositors. Public deposits are largely
lent on the strength of the name of the promoter, in this case—the Tatas. The
group leadership was keen to protect the goodwill and trust the Tata name
enjoyed. It decided to protect the depositors. Did it have a legal obligation
to them? Probably not. Tata Finance was a separate company. Tata Sons as
a holding company could have ring-fenced the corporate liability and taken
legal recourse for liquidation. However, what the Tatas did subsequently can
be considered a benchmark in corporate governance practices following a
financial debacle. Especially when compared to global financial companies
that filed for bankruptcy and evaded responsibilities for similar dubious
investments during the 2008 financial crisis, where federal institutions were
forced to use taxpayers' money to save some of these 'too big to fail' investment
banking companies. It was also the Tata legacy that promoters went beyond
their legal mandate to save an enterprise during a downfall. Jamsetji had done
so for Swadeshi Mills in the 1880s and Dorabji for Tata Steel in the 1920s.

At a shareholders' meeting called for clarifying the issue in July 2001,
Ratan Tata admitted to the fraud committed on the company accounts and
assured depositors and shareholders that Tata Sons would stand by them.
Despite a contract that entitled Tata Finance to keep the deposits for 2–3 years,
Tata Sons decided to pay all those depositors who wanted to prematurely
withdraw their money. This was at a time when even Tata Sons did not know
the quantum of losses. Subedar recalled the subsequent days. 'I was sitting in
Tata Sons when the board took a decision. Every morning, the Tata Finance
CFO would call me and convey the amount of deposit money that was due
for repayment, and request a cheque. This continued for nearly twenty days.'

Even a helicopter was to be kept on standby in case of urgent need for funds by depositors. A small proportion of retail depositors did withdraw their money. But this was insignificant compared to the usual run on the bank that one witnesses in such scenarios. In total, Tata Sons and Tata Industries provided Tata Finance ₹615 crore in cash and corporate guarantees to tide over the crisis.[8]

In parallel, Tata Sons installed a new chairman and a new operating team at Tata Finance. It shrunk the business, securitized debts, sold fixed assets, and repaid banks and financial institutions. The remaining entity was merged into Tata Motors, with Tata Finance shareholders receiving Tata Motors shares. To strengthen corporate governance processes, Tata Sons also introduced a dual reporting structure across group companies. It mandated all Tata company CFOs to report to the group finance director at Tata Sons along with their respective managing directors. It also included 'prevention of insider trading' and 'protection to whistle-blowers' as elements of the TCOC. But for the debacle, Tata Finance would have contended with market leaders like HDFC and ICICI for consumers' purse strings given the Tata Group's financial muscle and an early-mover advantage in the 1990s.

Five years later, Tata Sons promoted a new finance company—Tata Capital. Praveen Kadle, former finance director at Tata Motors, who had overseen the merger of Tata Finance with Tata Motors, was nominated CEO. During our conversation, he reflected on the transition from Tata Finance to Tata Capital.

> The group supported Tata Finance both in financial terms and in restructuring the operations. We ensured that our customers were never at a loss irrespective of who made the mistake. At Tata Capital, we have extra responsibility to ensure that we don't allow that kind of a situation to recur. We have worked collectively and taken joint decisions to ensure that.

Within a decade, Tata Capital had 120 branches in seventy cities with a book size of ₹25,000 crore. The group had made significant progress in the financial services despite a five-year setback.

Besides the catalytic role played by Tata Sons in resolving the Tata Finance debacle, its actions were indicative of the stance the group leadership would take against errant employees, irrespective of their seniority in corporate hierarchy. This was Tata Group's approach to publicly reinforce its commitment to its culture and ethos—sternly dealing with legal and ethical aberrations. While addressing the annual conference of EXIM Bank USA in 2016, Ratan Tata underscored this approach:

You cannot vouchsafe the DNA of every single person you hire. However, you can show your commitment to value systems and ethics by how you deal with an errant employee when he veers away. In my time, we have been absolutely hard on such employees, no matter who it was. You broke the code, you left the company.

Nearly fifteen years after the Tata Finance debacle, Tata Sons once again entered the scene to rescue another operating company—Tata Teleservices. Founded in 1996, Tata Teleservices was the Tatas' venture (37 per cent stake) in the booming telecom market. In 2009, NTT DoCoMo, the Japanese telecom major, had picked up a 26 per cent equity stake[9] in the company for ₹13,176 crore. With a subscriber base of 2.5 crore across twenty circles, Tata DoCoMo aimed at reaching the top three spots in the world's second largest and fastest-growing mobile phone services market. However, due to several operational, competitive and regulatory reasons, the venture wasn't successful. Allegations of wrongdoing by vested interests and peers during the 2G scam were disproved by CBI investigations.[10] By 2014, the company's losses had wiped out its net worth. The same year, DoCoMo decided to divest its stake in the venture, which was acquired by the Tatas at $1.2 billion after a prolonged arbitration process.

By 2017, Tata Teleservices' debt had increased to nearly ₹30,000 crore. The interest could not be serviced by the earnings of the company. Tata Sons decided to pare down the debt by 50 per cent. Being a 55 per cent shareholder, it decided to put in the money, though other shareholders were not willing to do so. Tata Teleservices was to use those funds purely for debt repayment. Tata Sons also negotiated with lenders on behalf of the company. By October 2017, the consumer mobile business was merged in a cashless deal with Airtel. Along with access to additional spectrum and 4.2-crore new customers, Airtel had to absorb 5000 employees of Tata Teleservices. In January 2018, the Tata Group paid ₹17,000 crore to a consortium of banks for the debts of teleservices, with an assurance of paying the remaining ₹6000 crore in a second instalment. Tata Sons had issued corporate bonds to raise the funds.[11]

Tata Sons stood by its operating companies in difficult times. It had taken over financial responsibilities of its operating companies due to losses caused by financial demeanour (Tata Finance) and non-performance (Tata Teleservices). It was a rare example of a holding company going beyond legal essentials to ensure its goodwill is maintained and value systems retained. This synergy between the Tatas' holding and operating companies under adverse circumstances was noteworthy. Gopalakrishnan often described the Tata Group with the analogy of a tree. The parent—Tata Sons and Trusts formed the roots. The larger companies formed the tree's trunk and bigger branches, while the smaller companies were its smaller branches and leaves. The roots provided the nourishment in the form of values, ethics and strategic guidance to the entire tree. The topmost branches and leaves, though small, were important as they received the maximum exposure to sunlight and oxygen.[12]

'Why wasn't TCS floated during the IT boom?'

This has been a common question asked by analysts, investors and market-watchers for nearly two decades. The reasons exemplify the Tata way of business. In May 2004, the Atal Bihari Vajpayee-led NDA government lost the general elections. The BSE Sensex nosedived from an all-time high of 6250, to 4300. In an unfavourable milieu, TCS decided to go public in June 2004. In 2003, TCS had already become India's first billion-dollar software company. Though a much-awaited IPO, its timing raised apprehensions among investors and analysts. Half a decade earlier, in the penultimate year of the twentieth century, when valuation of IT stocks was skyrocketing, it was the best time to float TCS as an independent company that was operating until then as a division of Tata Sons. The promise of the opportunity on hand could be understood from the fact that a single e-commerce company like Amazon with a few thousand employees on its payroll commanded a greater market capitalization than the entire US steel industry that had a million employees. There was a lot of pressure from corporate watchers and market analysts on Tata Sons to consider listing TCS in those years. They even provided the kind of valuation TCS enjoyed. For example, Credit Suisse First Boston had valued TCS at $20.7 billion (₹97,000 crore). In the mid-1990s, the capitalization of the five or six biggest Tata companies was about ₹20,000 crore. If Tata Sons considered this option and monetized a relatively small percentage of the TCS stock after it went public, it could take every single listed Tata stock in India, including Tata Steel, Tata Motors, Tata Chemicals and Tata Power. Most Tata companies could also become debt-free. This was also one of the priority areas identified by Ratan Tata. Then why didn't the Tatas exploit the opportunity?

Mukund Rajan, then chief sustainability and group ethics officer, recalled that N.A. Soonawala, then vice chairman at Tata Sons, had shared some of these observations with chairman Ratan Tata and the benefits it would generate for Tata Sons. However, Ratan Tata turned it down:

> We all recognize that there is an IT bubble that is being built up. We can certainly list TCS and get a ridiculous valuation; but three–four years down

the line, after the bubble has burst and shareholders are still holding our stock, what they receive as dividends is in no way going to compensate them for the investment they would have made. They will remember that and hold it against us. As promoters, we cannot exploit the market because of a short-term situation.

His stance was a classic example of what the famous US footballer Curtis Martin once said: 'Never let a short-term desire get in the way of a long-term goal.' The listing could have created billions for the group but would have eventually erased the hard-earned money of millions of shareholders who had faith in the Tatas. The decision underscored the Tatas' priority to serve shareholder interests over group interests.

In 2004, when the decision for listing TCS was made, Tata Sons being the promoters of the issue agreed to retain 82.69 per cent stake in the newly formed Tata Consultancy Services Ltd., In June–July 2004, the ₹5000-crore TCS IPO emerged as the biggest IPO in India and the second-largest tech IPO in Asia. At the time of opening for trading on the bourses, it created a record by commanding a premium of 41 per cent and was oversubscribed 7.7 times. It had received a total application amount of ₹34,000 crore against the issue size of ₹5000 crore. However, behind this fascinatingly successful financial outcome, there was a superordinate story that reflected the standards of corporate governance at the highest levels of the Tata leadership.

Conscientious corporate governance

'If *niyat* [intention] is not correct, you cannot have good corporate governance. I should sit on the board like a trustee, impartial and fearless to do the right thing for all the stakeholders. That is corporate governance. It can be ensured only by example. You cannot legislate it. You cannot prescribe it.'

Ishaat Hussain

The Tatas wanted the TCS IPO to be fair not only for the new shareholders of TCS but also for all the shareholders of Tata Sons. The team drawing the allotment scheme of TCS shares had completely omitted the shareholders of Tata Sons. They were under the impression that since shareholders of Tata Sons, through Tata Sons, were owning 100 per cent of TCS, they would be in the same position, either by owning TCS directly or owning TCS as a 100 per cent subsidiary through Tata Sons. However, Soonawala did not find that to be a fair decision. He could see a discounting factor creeping into shareholders of Tata Sons when TCS' assets would be moved one stage further down. Tata Sons' shareholders would be entitled only to a part of TCS profits as dividends and needed to be compensated for this discount. He suggested that shareholders of Tata Sons must participate in this IPO and become direct shareholders of TCS. Accordingly, an offer for sale of 3.26-crore shares was made to Tata Sons, giving them the first right to buy TCS shares at cost price. All shareholders exercised their right, except Tata Trusts, which held 66 per cent of Tata Sons. Being public charities, they were not legally permitted to buy shares. Over the years, criticisms had multiplied that the tax-exempt status which charitable trusts in India enjoyed was being misused. The government came hard on trusts by prohibiting tax-exempt charitable trusts from holding equity stakes in new companies after 30 November 1983. In case of any other family-controlled business, there was a possibility that some member of the family would have gobbled up those shares by writing out a cheque of that amount. However, at that time there was no threat of those shares being taken by anyone. They would have remained with Tata Sons.

Subedar went back to the drawing board to discover a way out for Tata Trusts to lawfully benefit from the IPO. 'I reflected and concluded that in this kind of a situation we can gift shares to the trusts,' he recalled. According to the prevailing law, a company could offer assets to any charitable institution as gifts and be eligible for tax exemption. The trusts had the right to buy 6.5 per cent of TCS shares. Tata Sons decided to gift the entire allotment to Tata Trusts. On 31 March 2003, Tata Sons' balance sheet reflected nearly ₹8858 crore as borrowings.[13] By cashing part of its holding in TCS, Tata Sons could have reduced its leverage and increased future borrowing capacity. However, it decided to let go of that value for being fair to its largest shareholder (Tata Trusts), which in turn could use the funds earned through dividend or sale for charity that would benefit the core stakeholder of the Tata Group—the society. When TCS got listed, the trusts sold part of their stake and realized ₹5000 crore in cash. It was twenty-five times the annual dividend income they received from Tata Sons in those years. A substantial amount was added to the corpus fund of Tata Trusts in a legal and fair manner because Tata Sons believed in wealth creation, not just wealth maximization. It wasn't just a gift of shares to the trusts, but a great gift of goodness to society.

This wasn't a one-off situation. Historically, Tata Sons prioritized the interests of Tata Trusts. When the same person wore various hats (as chairman), he found a common way for all three stakeholders (Tata Trusts, Tata Sons and Tata companies). The moment there was a bifurcation (of roles between the Trusts and Sons), there had to be much more communication between them and the operating companies. This was the case during the later years of J.R.D. Tata as chairman and after Ratan Tata stepped aside as chairman of Tata Sons. 'In Tata Sons, we are at an intermediate level within the group. We have the trusts above us. When we think of shareholders, we think of them with one more facet, which is charity,' shared Subedar. The trusts reciprocated by accepting retention of profits in Tata Sons to be ploughed back in businesses for facilitating growth. Historically, Tata Sons never attempted to dilute the majority stake of the trusts. It is the uniqueness of its model, which is rarely discussed. Any other holding company would look to raising equity within itself from time to time to get much-needed funds for growth. Since Tata Trusts were not permitted to invest in equities, , their holding would get diluted if Tata Sons were to make a rights issues. After the managing agency years, the trusts' holding had come down from 85 to 66 per cent. Hence, to maintain the trusts' majority and ownership and uphold the principle of trusteeship that formed the basis of the Tata Group structure, in a hundred years, Tata Sons never made an issue of capital, barring one rights issue in December 1995. This was quite unprecedented in global corporate governance history. During our conversation, Gopalakrishnan metaphorically described the philosophy of corporate governance at Tata companies.

> We try to run it as though we are the moon and not the sun. That it is somebody else's energy, the consumer, community, and shareholders, whose *tejas* [effulgence] that we are reflecting, rather than our board. I'm sure we are not always successful.

'How was J.R.D. Tata's style of corporate governance? What was it like having him chair the board meetings?' I asked Hussain who has worked with four chairmen over thirty-five years—from J.R.D. to N. Chandrasekaran. He reminisced,

> Many directors want to go into the boardroom to bash up the top management. They are like the leaders of the opposition! That is not the role of a director. The single most important job of the board is to have the right CEO in place—with the right values and execution capabilities. I learnt my lessons about corporate governance from J.R.D. He was so courteous that I just cannot tell you. I was a young guy, but he would treat me like an adult and allow me to share my view point. That was not only true for me, but for everybody. He was extremely transparent, consulted people, and carefully

chose whom he brought on to his board. He did not want group-think. He always wanted diversity of people, thoughts and styles.

I was amazed at the continuity of thought, when another Tata leader, a generation apart, and who never worked with J.R.D. in person, held the same principles of governance. 'You need people on the board with the same value systems,' observed Mukundan Ramakrishnan, MD of Tata Chemicals, among the youngest to hold the top job. 'That doesn't mean you need people who are part of a clique. The need for diversity, candour, open discussion and transparency is vital. All these literally govern the way the organization goes,' he emphasized. It was the Tata ethos consistently reflected in governance practices over a quarter-century. Doongaji provided an apt conclusion when he said, 'At the Tatas, we are not just compliance-oriented, we are culture-oriented. Our governance compliance is in response to the inherent culture of the Tata Group.'

CHAPTER 6

DECODING INDIA'S NUMBER ONE BRAND

'Tata Group symbolizes trust, the highest levels of corporate governance and doing good for the community. Those three fundamental pillars of the Tata brand will remain unchanged.'

Harish Bhat

There is immense diversity in the usage of the Tata name and Tata brands across Tata Group companies. For ease of understanding, Tata companies can be divided into three distinct categories. First, Tata companies that distinctly identify themselves with the Tata brand—Tata Steel, Tata Motors, Tata Chemicals, Tata Communications or Tata Power. Second, Tata companies with an individual identity—Trent, Titan, Rallis, Voltas, Vistara or Taj Hotels. Most of these called themselves 'A Tata Enterprise' as part of their brand promotion and communication. Third, Tata companies that are joint ventures with international partners—Tata Sky (with Star TV), Tata Hitachi or Tata Cummins. Tata company product and service brands can be classified into two categories. First, products and services with the Tata prefix—Tata Indica, Tata Swach, Tata Mutual Fund or Tata Salt. Second, products and services with an independent identity—Tanishq, Westside or Fastrack.

There are diverse reasons for different names, some historic, others market-driven. Companies that had long been known through their abbreviations such as TISCO or TELCO were changed to Tata Steel and Tata Motors respectively in the noughties, partly for creating a common Tata identity, and partly for highlighting the change in business focus. Then there were companies founded with a distinct name. For example, Titan, which was a joint venture between Tata Industries and the Government of Tamil Nadu, with the latter holding a slightly larger stake than the Tatas. In Titan—'Ti' stood for Tata Industries while 'tan' for Tamil Nadu. There were market-driven considerations as well. 'For a lifestyle product like a watch, Titan was considered to be a nice sounding brand name, which has been proven in the market place,' observed Harish

Bhat, the Tatas' brand custodian. In case of Trent, founded in 1998, it was a joint decision between Ratan Tata and Simone Tata, former chairman of Trent, that the new retail enterprise should not use the Tata name directly, as the group was venturing into an area it had never worked before—retail departmental stores. Hence, the name Trent (short for Tata Retail Enterprise) was selected. Companies such as Taj and Rallis have been in existence for nearly a century and have developed a strong identity of their own in respective customer segments. The top leadership believed that changing their name would have been regressive. For similar reasons, global acquisitions such as JLR and Tetley retained their original names across international markets where they commanded immense goodwill. Other overseas acquisitions that were not customer-facing brands were renamed for greater organization-wide uniformity. The example of Tata Chemicals' operations in Africa, Europe and America was a case in point.

Despite this diversity, the identity of India's number one brand has emerged from its culture. Every brand has a story associated with it, which is as vital in communicating the essence of the brand. The main story behind the Tata brand has been the story of its founder—Jamsetji Tata, who established this business house 150 years ago with the vision, 'In a free enterprise, the community is not just another stakeholder in business, but is in fact the very purpose of its existence.' It is this image of the founder with fire in his eyes and a dream for the future that was seen in his portraits in the chamber of every single Tata leader I visited. His busts at the entrance of Bombay House and TCS House in Mumbai, or full-length statues in scenic surroundings at the Tata Motors plant in Pune or the Tata Steel plant in Jamshedpur are reminders of his vision for the Tatas. 'Jamsetji brought to this brand the founder's mentality of keeping community centre stage, of trust, of ensuring that we are pioneers. I think brands that retain their founder's mentality are brands that tend to do very well,' emphasized Bhat.

Of course, Tata companies also aspire for profitable growth. They are market leaders in more than fifteen different categories—whether Titan in watches, TCS in software, Voltas in room air conditioners or Taj in hospitality. Satish Bhalchandra, divisional manager at Tata Motors, shared an interesting facet—the reputational benefits of the Tata brand for its employees. He recollected an instance when someone from the nearby village came to V.D. Mehrunkar, then head of HR at Tata Motors, and gave him a big invitation card. When Mehrunkar asked him what it was, the gentleman replied that it was his son's marriage invitation card. Under his name, it was written in big bold letters that he worked in the Tata Motors canteen. Satish shared with great enthusiasm during my visit to the plant:

> People take a lot of pride in publicly sharing that they work in the Tatas' canteens! In fact, the Tata reputation has helped several Tata Motors employees start their political careers and occupy positions as municipal corporators, MLAs and even the mayor of Pune, while working at the Tata Motors plant. Interestingly, Girish Bapat, Pune's guardian minister, worked at Tata Motors for twenty-seven years.

Vivek Talwar, an architect by training, serves as the chief culture officer at Tata Power. When I asked him, what attracted him to the Tata Group, he said, 'There is certain respect that I get for the group I work for. The simplest example is my Tata Power identity card. Several times, I have flashed my card and the security allows me into the airport. The guy who is standing behind me flashes his company's card and he is asked for a government ID. Flustered, this guy pleads, "But you just allowed him to go?" There is a power to the Tata brand, and that comes from its core values, which are understood by everybody.'

Facets of a fabulous brand

In 1997, Interbrand, a brand consultancy valued the Tata corporate brand[1] at ₹3720 crore. By 2017, it consistently topped the brand league in India with a valuation of ₹73,944 crore, a twentyfold rise in as many years. It equalled

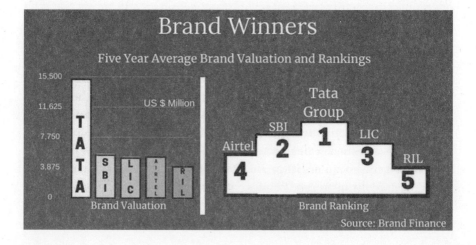

the valuation of the next two brands put together. Another leading brand consultancy company—Brand Finance, valued the Tata brand in 2007 at ₹51,300 crore. By 2017, its valuation had increased to ₹87,353 crore, and was the most valuable brand in India. Over the last two decades, most Indian and international brand-tracking surveys ranked the Tata brand at the highest levels. It was more visible and had more positive connotations than any other Indian company or industrial group.

What contributed to this universally popular brand identity? Six key brand attributes emerged.

Trustworthy brand. A senior Tata Steel executive once had a conversation with the chairman of SAIL (public-sector steel company) on the possibility of a joint collaboration between the two competitors. 'You have a federal stand as far as the government is concerned and Tata Steel has the mining expertise. Can we join hands and bid for coal blocks?' he proposed. 'I am agreeable to this. If I join hands with the Tatas, no questions will be raised even in the Parliament. Such is your reputation,' replied the SAIL chairman. The Tata executive was elated at the acknowledgement of the trust factor associated with their brand.

K.R.S. Jamwal, executive director at Tata Industries, recalled how Ratan Tata used to conclude every annual general meeting with the slide—'Lead, Never Follow'. The two core facets of the Tata brand were thus effectively captured in its motto 'Leadership with Trust', where one underpinned what the companies should be doing (leadership) and the other underpinned how they should be doing (with trust). Over 150 years of its existence, a constant vision of Tata companies consisted of the community being at the centre stage, and trust being the undercurrent of its businesses. Consumers at both ends of the economic spectrum were willing to associate and identify themselves with the Tata product and the company. A study by Tata Steel revealed that 75 per cent of premium customers were willing to pay for its products because of the Tata brand. Professor Narayandas, senior associate dean at Harvard Business School, attributed this to the trust in the Tata brand. 'Trust is priceless,' he underscored. The person buying a packet of Tata Salt, was getting the promise of a high-quality product, just like someone buying an apartment from Tata Housing or jewellery from Tanishq. Trust was the core brand promise. The belief across customer segments was that 'I am getting a good deal for what I am paying because it is a Tata product'. The product and service quality were interlinked to this core brand promise of trust.

Pioneering brand. A vital attribute of the Tata brand has been its pioneering spirit. The Tatas were the first to establish a steel mill in India, a power company in India, five-star hospitality in India, and an IT services company in India. Tata companies were the first to provide branded salt in India, first to curate branded jewellery in India and the first to sell retail steel in India. The pioneering nature of the brand is well-recognized. We'll see the making of many of these pioneering products and services in subsequent chapters.

Ethical and socially conscious brand. R.K. Krishna Kumar, former director at Tata Sons, who also served as MD of leading Tata companies, including Tata Tea and Taj Hotels, shared:

> In my fifty years with the Tata Group, I have interacted with various authorities in the Central and state governments, forest department, police and civil services, taxation and fiscal authorities. The moment they see the Tata visiting card, their attitude changes, they are very significantly altered and corrected, when making the demand.

Abanindra Misra, chairman of Tata Sponge Iron, shared a humorous incident that happened many decades ago.

> A colleague in the collieries and I had to go to a police station because one of the metal-towing dumpers was involved in an accident. The vehicle was seized, and my colleague was requesting the inspector to release it. The senior inspector entered and listened to our arguments. He asked, 'Where do you come from?' 'We are from Tata Collieries.' Then he fired his junior, 'Why do you argue with them? They will go all the way to the chief minister but will not give you a penny. You are wasting your time trying to extract something from them.' Quite furious he told us to take the vehicle and leave.

This attribute of ethics and social consciousness that the Tata brand represents, has resonated well with the Indian youth who are far more passionate about those causes than perhaps earlier generations. Several Tata companies have made efforts to proactively engage with them on such causes without sounding preachy. Tata Tea was one such company. Its catchphrase '*Har Subah Sirf Utho Mat. Jaago Re!*' (Every Morning Don't Just Get Up, Wake Up) was used to create a positive impact with its advertising budget. From 2007, it targeted several social issues, including women's empowerment, voting, student pressure and corruption. Themes such as '*Khilana Bandh, Pilana Shuru*', '*Chhoti Shuruat*', '*Soch Badlo*' aimed to bring about a positive change in society. Over the years, the Jaago Re! campaign as a social-marketing initiative appealed to crores of Indians. Over twelve-lakh Indians signed their pledge against corruption and for voting in elections. Those issues received huge attention from people after the brand endorsed them.[2] It was one of the few brand campaigns that ran for a decade. It not only made Tata Tea an iconic brand, but also boosted the Tatas' brand perception as socially responsive and committed to nation building.

Patriotic brand. Post the 26/11 terror attacks on the Taj Mahal Palace Hotel, Mumbai, in 2008, Ratan Tata avowed, 'We may have been knocked down, but not out.' At a time when the victims were grieving, the ordinary Mumbaikar was agitating, and Indian masses were determined on retaliating, the Taj Group of Hotels communicated a message resonating this spirit. It ran a brilliant three-part communication campaign 'Taj Forever', which aimed at healing, moving forward, and communicating to the world that 'Taj is forever'. The first part emphasized defiance. 'It really hurt us that our flagship hotel was targeted. We were so emotional about it, and that was the message we tried to communicate by publishing defiant messages,' observed Deepa Misra Harris, then senior vice president of global sales and marketing. The second part of the campaign contained healing messages to people who were injured and affected by this tragedy. The final part of the campaign emphasized that the hotel was renovated and Taj was once again ready to welcome its guests. It was a common resolve that the tower wing should be opened in record time. Within just three weeks of the attacks, it did reopen. The powerful message by the Tatas to the world was that Taj and India were not going to be bogged down by such acts of cowardice.

Fighter brand. For long years, the Tata brand was perceived as risk-averse. However, in the last two decades, the brand has emerged as a fighter brand. On the inorganic front, it challenged the largest global companies and established global brands and hoped to win in every marketplace it entered—whether through Tetley or JLR. On the organic front, it turned the tables on formidable competitors. Despite being one of India's first indigenous AC manufacturers in the 1950s, Voltas lost substantial ground post-liberalization when it had to compete against every global brand that entered the Indian market—Hitachi, Panasonic, Samsung, or LG. Being relegated to the sixth position in the industry and bleeding from severe losses in the early noughties, Voltas rose from the ashes through innovative, energy-efficient products and an expansive distribution network across 9750 outlets pan-India to become India's number one room air conditioner brand in 2014.[3] Once again proving itself as the fighter brand.

Global brand. Venkatadri Ranganathan, chief operating officer at Rallis India, had just landed in Atlanta, USA. The first thing the security officer asked him was, 'Are you are from India?'. He nodded. 'Have you got some dal?' the officer queried. 'No, I am hardly staying for one week. So, I don't have dal,' Venkatadri replied. 'Where do you work?' was his next question. 'Tatas,' he replied. 'Oh, TCS! You guys are intelligent,' the officer said with a beaming smile. Explaining to him that he wasn't in TCS, but Rallis was inconsequential. He had responded to similar queries during a previous visit to Ecuador. When he mentioned the name Tatas, the Ecuadorian officer said, 'You guys are making the $2000 car!' Ranganathan was amazed that the Tata brand had gained such global recognition through its products and services.

In the last two decades, an additional attribute added to the Tata brand identity has been its global identity. It is no longer an Indian brand. With 65 per cent of group revenues from overseas operations, the Tata brand has become global. Mukund Rajan, former brand custodian at Tata Sons, highlighted the critical success factors for building a strong global brand. 'We must invest in service to the community and ensure we get our performance right up there with the best in the world in each of the overseas markets. That's when you'll have a Tata brand that has the same kind of currency it enjoys in India.'

This was evident in TCS' employment practices in China where 97 per cent of the 3000 associates it hired across six global delivery centres were local Chinese. The Chinese people know the Tatas through TCS, which was among the top ten global service providers in China, had delivered high-quality services and also created jobs in the domestic market. The same was its approach in the USA. While TCS earned 50 per cent of its $19-billion revenue from the US market, it was also among the top two job creators in the USA, having recruited more than 12,500 employees between 2012 and 2016, and invested $3 billion in employment, nationwide STEM education programmes, academic partnerships and endowment. The governor of Louisiana had praised TCS engineers for their vital role in providing software for emergency services during Hurricane Katrina. A similar focus was visible through Tata Chemicals' welfare projects for 30,000 community members through the Magadi Foundation in Kenya at an annual expense of ₹100 crore and socio-economic contribution as the UK's largest industrial employer with 40,000 employees on its rolls through Tetley, JLR and Corus. *The Economist* commended the Tata approach, which did not believe in 'kill, cure or sell' philosophy of conglomerates like GE and its leaders such as Jack Welch. In the 1980s, Welch had earned the dubious moniker 'Neutron Jack' for laying off employees while leaving buildings intact. The word 'neutron' was in reference to the neutron bomb which supposedly had a similar effect. In contrast, the Tatas believed in nation building, employment creation and technical skills training even in their global ventures.[4]

Unity in intention, action and communication

Corporate communications and engagement with media are often rife with less than transparent behaviour and communication. Any statement can move markets and the choice of words is most important. Reflecting on his experience of balancing the roles of brand custodian, chief ethics officer and group spokesperson, Rajan shared:

> Barring issues of what should remain confidential and what is price-sensitive, I have not felt at any time any kind of scrutiny or pressure that there is any compromise between what one would do ethically and what one would do as official spokesperson or communicator on behalf of the group.

Several leaders across Tata companies referred to the 'newspaper test' as their benchmark in good corporate governance. This meant that anything a leader is contemplating or communicating to colleagues should be done with the assumption that it could potentially appear on the front page of national newspapers the next day. And if it did, would it pass public scrutiny? 'If it does, then you are on safe ground. That's the way it is with the Tatas. We have never felt that there is anything in our conduct that would not pass public scrutiny,' underscored Rajan.

For a long time, the Tata brand was known through the image of J.R.D. Tata. In those years, J.R.D. and the Tata Group were synonymous. It was for this reason that company-level problems in the 1980s did not impact the Tata brand as people looked up to J.R.D. and his impeccable credentials. Over two decades since, Ratan Tata focused on creating a brand that would be known for its products and services, for business excellence and innovation. It wouldn't be linked to the charisma of a particular leader. It was for this reason that occasional turmoil in boardrooms, whether at Tata Sons or individual companies, and arraignments against senior-most leaders, did not much affect the Tata brand. Between 2016 and 2017, when there was a change of guard at Tata Sons, the Tatas' brand strength index score in fact improved significantly. Its brand rating was upgraded from A+ to AA+ by Brand Finance. This validated Ratan Tata's efforts to transition the Tata brand from an individual-centric to an institution-centric identity.

CHAPTER 7

WEALTH CREATION, WITH A DIFFERENCE

'The core purpose of the Tata Group is to make money. The question is how do you make that money? And what do you do with the money you make?'

Ishaat Hussain

As per the fundamentals of economics, the four factors of production—land, labour, capital and enterprise—should provide factor payments in the form of rent, wage, interest and profit. While the Tata Group has been acknowledged for its pillars of strength, namely culture, structure, governance and brand, has it created wealth for its shareholders? Hussain shared:

> If I didn't make money, we wouldn't be here. Even the founder always maintained that 'to the extent that you can afford', everything that you do, including making money, should be good for society. Society includes a large body of stakeholders, including the providers of capital. That broadly is our approach. The means to us are as important as the end.

A commonly held perception has been that the Tatas do not talk about shareholders and their interests as much as other companies. 'Is it true?' I asked Gopalakrishnan. 'It is. But we don't ignore them either,' he admitted while providing an insight into the focus of discussions inside Tata boardrooms. 'If I look at the discourse of what is discussed at board meetings, in terms of priority, five stakeholders get roughly equal importance: employees, community (including supply chain partners), shareholders, lenders (banks and financial institutions), and government.' 'Isn't that very unusual,' I asked. In an American company, shareholders and lenders would get disproportionate importance. 'But in an Indian company, the government's views, and employee and union issues also emerge. So, the discourse at the Tatas is very much socialistic. They have a corporate form that is capitalism, but their intent is socialism. We are the world's best socialists. What Karl Marx said, we are doing all the time. But we look like capitalists,' he emphasized.

The capitalists wouldn't be convinced by this argument. So what if the Tatas are owned by charitable trusts that spend over ₹1000 crore every year for social well-being, in addition to an equal amount spent by Tata companies through corporate social responsibility (CSR)? What's in it for shareholders who invest their precious money in Tata companies? Do they get their fair share? 'Show me the money, lots of it, and now' is the clear expectation of the Milton Friedman brand of economists, who believe that the 'business of business is business'. Some analysts have even compared India's largest conglomerate with America's multinational conglomerate—Berkshire Hathaway (BH) that is led by the fabulous investor Warren Buffet as chairman and chief executive. If BH could be worth $390 billion in fifty years, why did the Tata Group reach a market value of only $145 billion in 150 years? I posed a similar question to Hussain. He was appalled. He said:

> Do they know that between 1958 to 1992, Tata Steel was not allowed to expand at all? That Tata Motors could not produce more than 30,000 trucks a year, despite a production capacity to make ten times that number? The Tatas had the largest insurance company, the second largest bank in the private sector, and were pioneers in aviation. All these companies were nationalized. We just *weren't* allowed to grow. How can you expect a comparison with BH, who never had to go through the Licence Raj, and operated in a free capitalist society for the last fifty years, which we didn't? Let us compare BH with the Tatas during the post-liberalization era. I don't think we will be far behind.

It was a valuable suggestion. I embarked on a comparison of Tata Group with leading Indian business houses and global conglomerates on the benefits shareholders received by investing in them. Shareholder returns and wealth creation to investors by Tata companies had been discussed much less in the media. Whilst handpicked companies like TCS and Titan were mentioned by emphasizing solid returns, the benefits of investing in the group were seldom highlighted. Our analysis showed some eye-opening numbers on the investor front.

Comparison with BSE Sensex and Nifty Indices. A simple review of shareholder returns across Tata Group showed that over a twenty-six-year horizon (1 April 1992 to 31 March 2018), the group outperformed the market and other well-known conglomerates in India and abroad. This was particularly important given that the companies analysed had lasted various economic, business and political cycles while they continued to be leaders in their sectors. Given the Tatas' diversity, we identified sixteen companies that best represented the group's presence across most sectors and decided to equally divide an investment of ₹1 lakh in these businesses beginning 1992.[1] These included: Tata Steel, Tata Motors, TCS, Indian Hotels, Tata Power, Tata Chemicals, Tata Communication, Tata Elxsi, Tata Metaliks, Tata Sponge Iron, Tata Investment Corporation, Tata Global Beverages, Titan, Trent, Voltas and Rallis. By 2018, the invested ₹1 lakh would be worth roughly ₹40 lakh. During the same period, a BSE Sensex investment would be worth ₹10.26 lakh and the Nifty would be worth ₹10.73 lakh. In other words, the investment across Tata companies would yield the investor 15.15 per cent on an annualized basis[2] after reinvesting dividends, while the benchmarks would yield only 9.47 per cent on a similar measure. Another common performance metric to highlight returns to shareholders, focuses on the Return on Equity (RoE).[3] Investments in the top three Tata companies through TCS, Tata Motors and Tata Steel had an average RoE of 34.17 per cent from 2000 to 2009 and 24.6 per cent from 2009 to 2017, which were remarkably high in the Indian large-cap sector where RoE over 15 per cent was considered sound.

Comparison with large Indian conglomerates. While India witnessed several notable conglomerates over the years that have benefited shareholders, the Tata Group stood ahead of comparable-sized companies[4] post-liberalization. Notably, after the global financial crisis of 2008, most conglomerates stood on an even keel and Tata Group returns ever since were extraordinary. The period beginning January 2009 saw the Tata Group provide total returns (CATSR) of 28.24 per cent as against 19.45 per cent of the Aditya Birla Group and 9.77 per cent of the Reliance Group. In other words, an investment of ₹1 lakh in January 2009 equally across the selected Tata companies would be

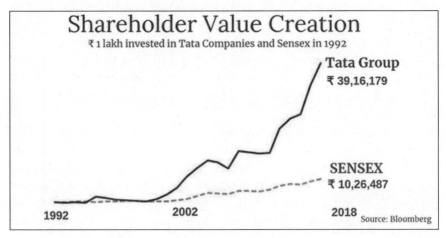

Shareholder Value Creation
₹ 1 lakh invested in Tata Companies and Sensex in 1992

Tata Group
₹ 39,16,179

SENSEX
₹ 10,26,487

1992   2002   2018   Source: Bloomberg

worth ₹998,200 (10x the initial investment) in March 2018. The same would be worth almost 5x and 2.5x in the case of Aditya Birla Group and Reliance Group respectively.[5]

Comparison with large global conglomerates. The Tata Group also outperformed developed market peers in Asia, America and Europe, especially given that domestic volume contributes only a third of its revenues. Annualized total shareholder returns[6] over a twenty-six-year period from 1 April 1992 to 31 March 2018 for Mitsubishi (Japan) were 5.2 per cent, for GE (the USA) 5.9 per cent, for Siemens (Germany) 10 per cent, for Berkshire Hathaway 14.2 per cent and for Tata Group 15.2 per cent.[7]

Comparison with Berkshire Hathaway. Hussain's premise that the Tata Group's returns were probably higher than BH post-liberalization had been vindicated. It could be puzzling as to why BH was brought into this comparison. Differences are many, but similarities can also be observed. Importantly, only over a long period of time—both allocate capital in several industries; build consistent sustainable capacity in the companies; reinvest profits back into their businesses to stably grow the business; operate in relatively less disruptive businesses that they have helped stabilize with time and developed a 'moat' around them and; decisions made around the array of choices directly affect the performance of the group's results. On that front, Warren Buffett has been praised over his decision-making, selection of acquisitions and constant push towards the ideologies that back the interests of the company and the group as a whole that have helped BH deliver stellar returns and in the process made him a multibillionaire with a net worth of over $80 billion. The Tata Group exceeding shareholder returns of BH over a twenty-six-year period, during which regulatory shackles were gradually removed in the Indian economy, was indeed a significant feat, and spoke volumes about their financial forethought.

The findings laid to rest concerns over the capacity of Tata Group companies to create shareholder wealth. Shareholder returns, returns on equity and scale achievement over time have made the Tata Group a compelling case to keep an eye out for in the investing world. Moreover, they have validated the commercial success through the Tata way of business. As Prakash Telang shared, 'We firmly believe that we can make reasonable profits by not compromising on our principles.' Along with their consistent focus on people and planet, the Tatas have been successful in sustainable profit-making. Through its key pillars of strength, Tata companies had excelled in the creation of wealth, not just for shareholders, but for all stakeholders.

Let me end with an anecdote that communicates the Tata vision behind the creation of wealth. In the late 1980s, J.R.D. was addressing a gathering at Jamshedpur during the inauguration of Tata Steel's new blast furnace. During the course of his talk, he explained the meaning of dedication.

When Tata Steel completed fifty years of its existence in 1957, we had Prime Minister Jawaharlal Nehru coming over here and dedicating the Jubilee Park to the people of Jamshedpur. Whenever, I go to Jubilee Park, I see children playing. When I interact with them, I see a smile on their face. That smile is the true meaning of dedication of anything we create for Tata Steel. Today I am dedicating the blast furnace to the people of Jamshedpur because I

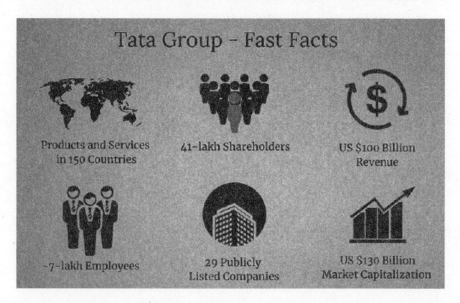

Tata Group – Fast Facts

Products and Services in 150 Countries

41-lakh Shareholders

US $100 Billion Revenue

~7-lakh Employees

29 Publicly Listed Companies

US $130 Billion Market Capitalization

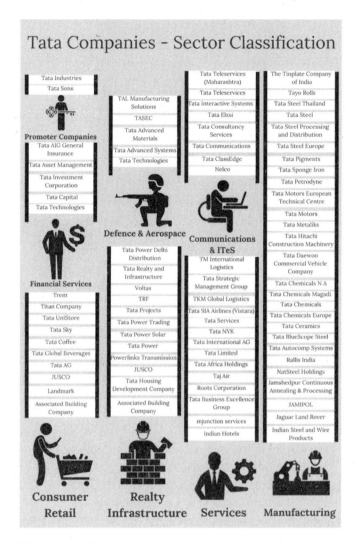

Tata Companies - Sector Classification

would like the wealth this furnace creates to be very similar to the smile of the innocent children at the Jubilee Park.

N.K. Sharan, now vice president at Tata Sons, was an eyewitness to this event. He was then a young engineer in his early twenties. Three decades later, while sharing his journey with the Tata Group during a conversation at Beldih Club in Jamshedpur, the connection between the furnace and the smile of children was fresh in his memory. 'That was to my mind, one of my first lessons on what the Tatas think about when they create wealth.'

CHAPTER 8

IN SEARCH OF EXCELLENCE: FROM EXISTENTIAL CRISIS TO THE ZENITH OF QUALITY

'If we don't renovate the plant totally, ten years from now, Jeh, you and I will be standing outside the gates selling tickets to people to come and see the steel museum!'[1] Jamshed J. Irani, then joint MD of Tata Steel confessed to J.R.D. Tata. He had a hearty laugh, but grasped the seriousness of the situation. It was the mid-1980s. India was still under Licence Raj. Government control on private enterprises was substantial, to say the least. India was in a way handcuffed to modernization because of government policies.

To better appreciate the context of what Irani mentioned to J.R.D., let's look back at the first six decades of Tata Steel's evolution. Before that, a word of appreciation is due to Jamsetji's vision. On receiving Lord Hamilton's support for his steel scheme in 1900, he sent a cable to Tata and Sons from London itself, instructing that they should get licences for iron ore, coking coal and fluxes. These captive mines gained by Tata Steel right from inception remained its greatest advantage, especially during its formative years, when the company witnessed two world wars under the Raj, and later when it faced a centralized government system with socialist leanings.

The initial sixty years of Tata Steel can be divided into seven phases. Phase I (1912–18) was marked by World War I. The company received impetus for its production and profits due to wartime demand. Phase II (1918–24) consisted of a period of intense steel dumping in India. Tata Steel suffered heavy losses and worked hard for a massive turnaround under the leadership of Dorabji. Phase III (1924–35) was marked by tariff protection and fourfold capacity expansion at Jamshedpur to 660,000 tonnes per annum. Phase IV (1935–40) was a period of boom and prosperity and coincided with the commencement of World War II. Phase V (1940–48) was marked by intense wear and tear of equipment to meet wartime production requirements. Tata Steel provided 30 lakh tonnes of steel for purposes connected directly or indirectly with the war.

It had even lived up to its commitment of providing steel for the war efforts at pre-war rates. The US and the UK companies made no such commitments and profiteered immensely during the war. In post-war years, the imperial government imposed standardization of prices between Indian steel and imported steel in India. As a result, the Tatas ended up subsidizing imported steel to the tune of ₹40 crore, an amount they could have otherwise used for much-needed plant modernization. Their goodwill gesture to help the Raj in its hour of need had been disregarded.[2]

Phase VI (1948–56) was marked by the early years of Indian independence. The socialist approach of the Congress party in power led to several pricing restrictions on private companies. Despite heavy wear and tear to its machinery, Tata Steel had to keep its expansion proposals in abeyance for want of funds due to the niggardly policy of the government. Phase VII (1956–67) was marked by a capacity expansion 'approved' by the government under its licencing policy to 1.2 million tonnes per annum (Mtpa). It was also the time of the upsurge of the public-sector steel plants. Consequently, Tata Steel's market share fell from 75 per cent at the start of World War II to 25 per cent by 1967.[3]

Working under the government's 'watchful eyes'

During our conversation, Irani particularly reminisced the days of the 1960s and '70s. Steel could not be imported because of prohibitive import duties, the lowest being 125 per cent. The domestic production was heavily controlled on financial and manufacturing fronts. Between late 1960s and late 1970s, Tata Steel's chief engineer had put up fifty plans for modernization of the Jamshedpur plant. Not one of them was accepted by the government or the Tata Steel board.[4] The primary question being—where are we going to get the money? In fact, at one time, Tata Steel wanted to put up a very small unit and required ₹17.50 crore in foreign currency. But rules would not allow the company to spend its own money to get foreign exchange. These were the kind of financial restrictions till early 1980s.

The manufacturing front wasn't any better. Everything was controlled by the government. Under the MRTP Act, 1969, the government instructed most companies, especially in the private sector, what to make, how much to make and whom to sell. The law left little freedom for decision-making, leave aside innovation or expansion, to individual company leadership. A Joint Plant Committee (JPC) with representatives from the management and labour engaged in price- and quantity-related discussions with the government on an annual basis. As chief metallurgist, Irani was responsible for those negotiations with the government. A typical meeting involved a visit to the director general of technology (DGT) to bargain for a price increase. The archetypal arguments for requesting a rise in the price at which the company could sell its products to the market involved justifications such as rise in the costs of manpower, coal and water. This was followed by a request to the government to graciously permit an increase in the price of steel. After inordinate deliberations and arguments, the DGT would sanction half of what was requested. Over a period, the steel industry representatives, which included Tata Steel and other public-sector steel companies, realized that they should ask twice of what is required, as the government invariably approved half of what was asked for!

This continued for more than a decade. Irani lamented that Tata Steel was held back at 2 Mtpa production. It was not allowed to modernize because the public-sector steel plants were coming up at Bhilai, Bokaro, Durgapur and Rourkela. Just because Tata Steel existed from before Independence, it was 'allowed' to survive, with the threat of nationalization always hanging over it like the sword of Damocles. It was in this backdrop that Irani joked about the Tata Steel plant soon becoming a steel museum. But J.R.D. took it upon himself to get the requisite board approval. A complete ₹4000-crore modernization plan in four phases running to the turn of the century, was finally accepted by the board and the government.

It was around this time in 1988–89 that a delegation of Indian industry leaders through the Confederation of Indian Industry (CII) was invited to Japan to study quality-related best practices that had contributed enormously to Japan's success in achieving world-class levels of industrialization. Notable were interactions with the Japanese Union of Scientist and Engineers (JUSE). Irani, part of the delegation, spent a couple of months there studying the plants and made neat notes that have been since preserved. He returned from Japan with two lessons. First, a core group must be created to drive quality management across the organization. Second, this core group must report to the managing director. It must be a top-driven quality-management initiative, not left to delegation. He insisted that the finance people from the company should go to Japan and study how a plant is built, and then scrapped within a period of a dozen years to build another one, a concept alien to India. This was at a time when Tata Steel was trying to resuscitate a plant that was built by Dorabji, over half a century earlier! In those years, Dorabji had the blast furnace set up by the Americans, the steel shop by the Germans and the coke ovens by the Welsh. Interestingly, till the mid-1990s, Tata Steel possessed the country's oldest blast furnace, lit in 1911. Though scheduled to shut down several decades earlier, it survived for over eight decades. According to a local tribal belief, it would never shut down and continue to bring prosperity to the company because a tribal woman worker had given birth to a child there when the foundation was laid!

The first phase of modernization at the Jamshedpur steel plant was completed by 1991.[5] This long-awaited freedom that came with the economic liberalization that year brought in its wake several challenges, which the Indian steel industry was not ready for. The most critical being an open market that would bring in international competitors. In fact, a group of senior industrialists campaigned against imports to protect the Indian steel industry. The situation at Tata Steel was no better. An internal note on the strategy of the company described early 1990s as the company's 'baptism by fire'.[6] While it had the distinction of being India's largest private sector company in a duopolistic market, it also had the blemish of being one of the most expensive steel producers in the world. Several leading consulting companies called it an inefficient operator in a sunset industry. Some others suggested that the Tata Group should sell Tata Steel and exit the industry as it may not be able to face international players in a new competitive system.

There is a popular story indicating the prevailing mindset of Indian industry. Bharat Wakhlu, who retired as group resident director for Tata Sons in 2014 after three decades with leading Tata companies, primarily Tata Steel, recollected his personal experience. In the early 1990s when the price of steel shot up, Tata Steel started selling part of its scrap steel in the open market. It emerged that the company made more money from the sale of scrap than it made from selling certain grades of prime steel. When he brought this to the notice of a senior manager and suggested that the company should make efforts to reduce process-scrap generation by improving process quality levels, he was told that the company was making great money through selling scrap, and hence it wasn't a problem![7]

This was a mindset problem. Irani recollected the 1970s when he was in charge of product quality at Tata Steel. In those years, if any customer had the temerity to complain about quality, he would issue an order to starve him for six months. 'Don't give him anything,' he would thunder. After all, Tata Steel had contributed to some of the most iconic infrastructure projects in independent India. Whether it was Calcutta's Howrah Bridge that was built from 17,000 tonnes of high-tensile steel, 30,000 tonnes steel used to build one of the largest dams in India—the Bhakra Nangal on the Satluj—or 20,000 tonnes to build the largest port in India at Kandla, it was all the Tatas' steel. The planned city of Chandigarh, the dams at Hirakud, Vaitarna–Tansa and on the Tungabhadra, the locomotive works at Chittaranjan and the coach factory at Perambur had one commonality. They were all built from the Tatas' steel. Interestingly, in the 1930s, 72 per cent of India's steel requirements were fulfilled by Tata Steel alone. And it wasn't limited to India. In 1942, the armoured cars used in World War

II were fitted with bulletproof plates and rivets made by Tata Steel. Christened 'Tatanagar' and built at Jamshedpur entirely with Indian technical know-how, these were used extensively by the British Indian Army at the North African front. Several army personnel had reported how Tatanagar's sturdiness saved the lives of men under shellfire and bombing. 'Indian craftsmen can be proud of their Tatanagars,' they complimented. With such an illustrious track record, the company and its leadership were in no mood to listen to the quality complaints of a diminutive customer. Several months later, this ill-fated customer who had been, shall we say, denied supply, would come literally on his knees saying, 'I didn't really mean to complain, please renew my supplies.' It was only then that his supplies would resume. That was the type of almost improper control exercised on customers. The prime reason for this intimidating attitude was that despite operating at 100 per cent capacity, market demand was always more than Tata Steel's production. The government never permitted capacity expansion, and so the need for steel was always more than the production in India. Steep duties prohibited steel imports. The industry was living behind this protected wall. It was the same for other products—whether chocolates or television sets. Whatever was made in India in those years sold like hot cakes within the country because no imported material was allowed. As soon as imports became popular in the post-liberalization period, all those companies that had survived on the crutches of government protection, collapsed.

Change with changing times

To appreciate the imperative for change and the apparent resistance to change, it is important to understand the background of Tata Steel. In its first eighty years of existence from 1907, it moved from 1 lakh tonnes to 20 lakh tonnes annual production capacity. Of which, the journey from 10 lakh to 20 lakh began only in 1958, which was facilitated by a ₹52-crore World Bank loan, the largest granted to any country in Asia at that time. Since there was no steel industry in its formative years, the company was manufacturing all kinds of steel products. With no other industry to support the steel industry, Tata Steel had all ancillary facilities, which contemporary plants do not have. It had its own foundries for making castings, its own machine shop, fabrication shops, and paint shop. So much so that in the earlier days, the British employees working at the plant needed soda water, and for them a soda water-making machine was also available! In short, Tata Steel was a behemoth.[8] The 'focus on your product' management strategy was not possible in those times. The company's energies were dissipated in addressing challenges that were peripheral to the core objective of steel making.

In 1970s, the emphasis was more on quality control by inspection. It was felt that ensuring quality is the job of the inspector. If any improvement is required in the processes, the industrial engineering department was in charge. In those days, Taylor's system of division of labour was still in vogue. When newer plants were set up in late 1988, the company realized that it must strengthen the processes and engage employees through greater training. It would have been cheaper for the plant manufacturer to send a few experts to teach Tata Steel employees about the new equipment. However, at Irani's insistence, Tata Steel's board agreed to send 120 of its best employees to Britain to get complete exposure to the new technology and equipment that were being brought into the plants. People's involvement was vital in this new journey. A joint body to promote quality was also formed by the management and the union. In those days, Japan was on the rise and Quality Circles (QC) through the involvement of employees were considered as one of the reasons for Japan's success. Tata Steel adopted the QC technique to improve quality in some departments. Initially people were sceptical that this Japanese concept will not work in India because it hadn't worked in America. The Japanese are so disciplined, and our people lack high levels of commitment. But, it worked. To improve adoption, interdepartmental competitions were held, and those who won awards were sent to participate in national and international competitions.

However, some people were sceptical about the various quality initiatives. They felt that for improving quality, extra time must be invested. Who will pay for this extra time? Misra recollected an incident. In 1989, when he was assistant superintendent in the foundries division, a person from his division came to him and said:

> If you want me to spend time in quality circle, then you give me time off. I can't do it beyond duty hours. And if I do it within duty hours, my productivity and incentive are affected. Secondly, I do not get paid according to the efforts I have put in in improving quality. If the product became better, so what? You don't pay me extra!

These were genuine concerns of a blue-collar worker because the incentive scheme was designed only on rejection and acceptance, but not on improvement. Misra confessed that it took quite some time in convincing people about the importance of quality. The employees needed to see its requirement from the customer's point of view. The problem with the suggestion management scheme was that the person who gave the idea received the award, and not the implementer. Then why would he be interested in implementing it? To balance this increasing demand for greater recognition, the company started declaring 'person of the month' in every division. It was required to display this on the noticeboard for each month along with the reasons for his selection. Tata Steel was changing with changing times. This was reflected in popular perception. A 1989 CII report recommended that steel products should not be marked as 'Made in India' because of the country's poor reputation for quality. Instead, Tata Steel should mark its products as 'Made by Tata'.

Heading this Tata empire with its pan-India and even international appeal was an octogenarian chairman grounded in his style of leadership and his quest for learning. Govindarajan Jagannathan, who later became the chief of total quality at Tata Steel, shared a personal experience at Jamshedpur in March 1991 when he was the chief value engineer. Every year, Tata Steel celebrates the Founder's Day on 3 March. In those years, Tata Steel used to organize an exhibition of success stories. As the head of value engineering, Jagannathan was asked to showcase how the company had achieved improved performance at reduced cost. The first visitors that day were the board of directors of Tata Steel who had gathered for the board meeting at Jamshedpur. Since the VIPs were coming to see the exhibits, each department head was asked to represent his or her stall. Right after the inauguration, J.R.D. arrived. He was patiently going through various stalls and curiously observing and hearing success stories. When he came to the stall on value engineering, he was more than curious. At eight-six, he was carefully observing all exhibits and listening to Jagannathan's narration with apt attention. As it was time for the board meeting, Russi Mody, then MD of Tata Steel, reminded him that they had only five more minutes to go back to the board meeting. J.R.D. looked at Mody and said: 'Russi, you know, I had learnt about electrical engineering, metallurgical engineering and mechanical engineering, but I have not heard about value engineering. This seems to be very interesting. I want to learn more from this young man here. Can I come a few minutes late for the meeting?' For the next twenty minutes, J.R.D. questioned and deepened his appreciation for the subject.

A landmark year for India, for Tata Group, for Tata Steel

The year 1991–92 was significant for India as the New Industrial Policy was tabled in the Parliament. In 1981, J.R.D. had appealed to the government to free the economy and see the difference. It took a major economic crisis to heed the appeal. The year 1991 was also significant for the Tata Group as J.R.D. passed on the baton of leadership to Ratan Tata as the chairman of Tata Sons. In the subsequent year, Irani took charge as the MD of Tata Steel from Russi Mody, who served at the helm of affairs from 1974 to 1993. A J.N. Tata Scholar for his MSc in metallurgy from Sheffield University (UK), Irani had received a gold medal for his PhD. After a brief stint at British Steel, he joined Tata Steel in 1968 at J.R.D.'s invitation, who was impressed with his achievements. Over the next quarter-century, Irani rose up the ranks.

New leadership at both levels brought in a renewed focus on transforming Tata Steel and bringing forth its latent capabilities in quality and business excellence, just as it had done in the fields of labour harmony and community development. Ratan Tata made several visits to Jamshedpur to enthuse and energize the senior team to turn the tide, and achieve what was considered hitherto impossible. Tridibesh Mukherjee, former deputy MD at Tata Steel, recalled one such series of interactions that he had with Ratan Tata in his very first year as chairman. These underlined the hands-on style of his leadership that had a substantial impact on Tata Steel.

It was July 1992, when Mukherjee, then senior general manager (operations) at Tata Steel, attended the company's AGM for the first time. He was delighted to be a part of the select group invited to dinner that evening at the Taj Mahal Hotel by Ratan Tata, and reached the venue on time. However, instead of felicity, the environment in the room was sombre. He saw directors with grave faces, some with their heads in their hands. Something was amiss. Informally dressed in a light green shirt, Ratan Tata punctually arrived at the venue. After exchanging pleasantries, he started speaking from his heart.

After the previous year's Union budget, steel imports to India had been liberalized. Consequently, the Jindals, the Ruias and the Mittals had announced the setting up of ultra-modern steel plants in Karnataka, Gujrat and Maharashtra. The South Korean steel giant POSCO wanted to set up a large plant in Odisha. Ratan Tata was very supportive of the liberalization process, new investments, including FDI, and was confident that the Tata Steel team would cope with the new set of challenges. During dinner, he shared with the top team the glorious past of the Tata Group, and that Tata Steel was a blue-chip company of the group and of India. In the past, it had made profits even under very difficult circumstances. But in the first quarter that year, the company had hardly made any profit. In those years, it wasn't mandatory to publish quarterly results or release analysts-focused presentations. It took time for Mukherjee to figure out the implication of the phrase 'hardly any profit'. Actually, Tata Steel was staring towards posting a loss of ₹180 crore for the first time in eighty years. Ratan Tata wondered if the top team at Tata Steel would let this happen.

All those sitting around the table of the Hibiscus Room at Taj Mumbai had only one answer—Tata Steel would do it. Since Mukherjee was running operations, Ratan Tata presented a challenge before him—to accept a cost reduction target of ₹500 per tonne of steel manufactured. It was 7.5 per cent of cost, a substantial target to achieve in less than nine months. That too at a time when the cost of everything that steel plants used had gone up, including raw materials that came by rail to Tata Steel, as railway freight had gone up. The target sounded impossible. It needed a miracle.

That night, Mukherjee made several trunk calls to his colleagues in Jamshedpur, and told them that he had accepted the challenge from the chairman on behalf of the team. He returned to Jamshedpur at 9 a.m. on a Sunday and drove straight from the airport to the meeting room of the Tata Steel guest house. Ten of his colleagues had assembled there, most looking edgy and defensive. Many of them had ideas, and yet they were full of inhibition as no other company in the world had achieved such a steep cost target in such a short span of time. However, the inspiration to prove their eighty-year-long heritage got the better of them and before midday, they decided on an action plan. The overarching objective being that no initiative should even remotely jeopardize the safety of employees. At that time, Tata Steel ran in three well-defined and watertight silos—the raw material division, the marketing and sales division and, the works at Jamshedpur. The target was so stiff that everyone had to innovate, break away from the past and devise a new way of thinking.

In October that year, Ratan Tata came to Jamshedpur. In a packed boardroom, before the senior team, Mukherjee presented the action agenda. The focus was to benchmark performance parameters with the best in the world. 'If they can achieve, so can we,' he said. While there were many missing pieces in the jigsaw, the team was determined to achieve the target. Ratan Tata was happy and encouraged them to proceed as planned. He came again in January 1993, and this time he chaired a cost meeting that lasted till 2 a.m. In that meeting, Mukherjee presented the graph that indicated that for the first time in several years, the cost would come down instead of going up. With supreme satisfaction, he announced that the cost will come down by ₹350 per tonne that year. Ratan Tata wasn't impressed. He said, 'Doc, you don't have to make another promise. Your promise is with me. Your reputation and your prestige is at stake!' It wasn't a firing, but a challenge to an aspiring team to achieve the unachievable. The entire team was there, and they unitedly committed to achieve the target before the end of the financial year, March 1993. The approach worked, the attitude to do what hadn't ever been done had taken root in this dynamic team, innovation became their mantra and they achieved the target in the next two months.

Mukherjee underscored his early learnings at Tata Steel. 'I learnt the importance of setting targets and teasing out innovative ideas, in implementing such ideas, in breaking away from the cage of inhibition, in uniting divided groups. I also realized that a target may not motivate everyone, but will impact the emotionally charged.' To get the best out of people, leaders must address two challenges: setting a target and emotionally charging the teams. Unsurprisingly, instead of a loss of ₹180 crore, Tata Steel made a substantial profit that year.

Top-down commitment, bottom-up change

As MD, Irani's top priority was to implement and internalize the concept of total quality management (TQM)[9] across the company. He literally bombarded the entire plant with this approach. A special campaign was launched with the capital letter Q in golden colour on a blue background depicted across the Tata Steel campus. While the lower-case 'q' depicted product quality, something that the labour was aware of, 'Q' stood for total quality. It took many months to imprint this clarity in the minds of 75,000 employees through mass communication campaigns and large number of training sessions. After all, we are talking about India's largest private sector steel company! To complement this process, implementation of ISO 9000 standardization process was also started. It began with peripheral divisions such as bearings, then moved on to customer-facing divisions, and was eventually mandated for all eighty-six divisions of the plant. To reduce costs on external assessors, the company devised its own TISCO standards based on ISO 9000 and trained its own in-house assessors. By 2000, the ISO 14000 environmental management standards were also implemented across the company.

Irani put together a team of dynamic youngsters to champion the cause of total quality across the plant. He selected high-performing candidates from various departments to be a part of this cross-functional team. Many times, he would be told by the divisional heads that certain managers couldn't be released for the TQM work because they were almost indispensable for the functioning of their divisions. He would often retort, 'That's why I want such people, who can't be released.' The message of the top management's commitment to quality was becoming loud and clear within the rank and file.

Management initiatives, unlike technology changes, are difficult because they impact human behaviour. Implementing a new technology is relatively easy. Accepting a new idea and making it a part of your daily life is relatively difficult. It requires sincerity of purpose and intensity of efforts to tweak the DNA of an organization. When the TQM initiatives began at Tata Steel, the company was already in business for over eighty years. Changing a successful organization is difficult, even more in times of prosperity. If the company is sick or passing through a difficult time, then people are mentally tuned to some surgery. But if the company is doing well and people are asked to change, it is more difficult.

Irani knew this. While he had initiated the TQM projects and got together a passionate team of quality champions, little would happen sitting in Bombay

House till the grass-roots leaders at the Jamshedpur plant were convinced of the need to change. They needed to think the way he was thinking. Sometime in the mid-1990s, he called S.K. Benjamin, president of Tata Workers Union, to his office in Jamshedpur. He said, '*Benjamin Saab, aap aur aapka poora team Japan jaiye aur vahan dekhke aayiye ki vo log kya kar rahe hain.*' A fifteen-day tour was organized for the entire union leadership. They visited leading companies and their plants in Tokyo and Osaka, including that of Nippon Steel, Japan's largest steel producer. They understood what those companies were doing, the safety, upkeep and quality standards, and the levels of productivity. It was a rare example of an Indian company exposing its union leaders to the best in the world. When they came back, it was extremely easy to talk to them. The change which Irani wanted to unleash, became easy for him. In subsequent meetings, the union representatives were fully supportive of all company initiatives. In fact, the union leadership team would share anecdotes of what they had learnt during their visit to the Japanese steel plants. This participative style of taking everybody on board for a massive change was a great lesson in emerging India.

From quality to business excellence

In the early 1990s Tata Steel was looking for an integrated model for business excellence. In those days three frameworks were popular. The Deming Model from Japan, the Baldridge Performance Excellence Framework from the USA, and the European Foundation for Quality Management (EFQM) Excellence Model. Tata Steel adopted the Baldridge Framework. To recognize excellence, the company also instituted two awards—one in the name of J.N. Tata, and another in the name of an acknowledged metallurgist—S. Vishwanathan, former general superintendent at Tata Steel. On 14 February every year, the company started celebrating 'Quality Night'. During the programme, the best departments were awarded the J.N. Tata Award for total quality and the S. Vishwanathan Award for maximum improvement over the previous year. The best quality improvement projects were also recognized.

Around this time, Tata Sons instituted the J.R.D. QV Award based on the criteria under the Malcolm Baldridge National Quality Award, the one that Tata Steel had already adopted a couple of years earlier. Tata Steel decided to tune itself towards it as the model integrated all the processes for excellence in business. In 1996, it submitted its first application for the award. Given its size and diversity, it documented a little about all its processes in diverse areas, including mining, bearings, ferro-alloys, and the core steel strategic business unit (SBU). When the evaluation results were presented, Tata Steel had received 201 out of 1000 points. Irani and the entire senior team were crestfallen. They couldn't accept that despite their consistent efforts on total quality for more than five years, they were much behind the curve. Sharan recalled the meeting after the J.R.D. QV team presented its findings to the Tata Steel senior management. At that time, Irani said:

> We have two options today. One is to tell you [assessors], that your findings are ridiculous, and we don't believe you. You haven't understood our business. The other is that we accept your findings, introspect ourselves, and see what we can do. As a leader of this company, I am choosing the second option.

Most seniors at that time almost pounced upon the TQM team that the fault lay with them. Probably, they did not present the company's case correctly and that the application submitted for the award may have been defective. While the TQM team members were disappointed, it was an opportunity for introspection. Misra, then senior divisional manager for TQM, recollected his conversation with the team. He observed that the company had been on this total quality journey in an organized way for five years. 'If we cannot win the award in the next five years, then it would be a decade since we began this journey. If we don't make it in a decade, then something is wrong with us, we are not doing it right.'

A behemoth in action

Rising to the occasion, the company again embarked on its quality journey with renewed rigour. To better understand the new TBEM process, Irani himself attended a two-day training programme at the newly formed TQMS. Inspired by the MD's commitment, all vice presidents followed suit. In the ensuing months, Tata Steel introduced several focused initiatives to improve quality, productivity and safety. Customer-centricity became the buzzword. The slogan that resonated across the plant was 'Customer First, Har Haal Mein'. The company benchmarked each of its functions with the best in class. Its customer complaints management process was benchmarked with Modi Xerox, credit management with Citibank, operational excellence and innovation with GE, safety with DuPont, and retail distribution with several FMCG companies. Prominent billboards at the plant and in Jamshedpur also had a new message that reflected the company's transformational journey. Instead of the traditional catchphrase 'We also make steel'; they now read, 'Cost, Customer and Code'.

In the next TBEM assessment in 1997, with 443 points Tata Steel was the highest performer in the group. Suddenly, the perception of the senior management towards its TQM efforts changed as Tata Steel was now even ahead of Tata Motors and Tata Honeywell, which were considered more up to date. Tata Steel received a token plaque for its achievement. It was a rectangular one with titanium polish. Irani kept it on his table as recognition of the company's success. So thrilled was he at this achievement that he would not allow anybody to touch it because that might leave behind some fingerprints on the titanium shine. He would proudly show the plaque to every visitor. Misra recollected that he had even seen him polishing it with his handkerchief to maintain the shine! Irani was exhilarated with this recognition of Tata Steel's potential.

In 1998 and 1999, the company did even better with 510 and 582 points respectively. It was the highest score; head and shoulder above other Tata Group companies. Between January and November 1999, Tata Steel implemented the enterprise resource planning (ERP) platform by SAP. Many consultants discouraged SAP implementation stating that the company's dispatch would be interrupted for a month. Firdose Vandrevala, then vice president of marketing and sales, was unconvinced of the argument. He said that even if we have to close for a month, we are ready, but SAP has to be implemented. We want our customers to see us as a transparent company, and benefit from the ERP system. While SAIL implemented SAP a decade later, Tata Steel was the first in the industry to implement it across the entire value chain, and probably the fastest SAP implementation in India at that time.

The turn of the millennium brought the tidings that the company had been striving for—Tata Steel became the first company in the Tata Group to win the J.R.D. QV Award. It had crossed the threshold of 600 points that was required to win the award. The Steel SBU at Tata Steel had scored 616 points. A decade of hard work and commitment to TQM and business excellence had finally borne fruit. At a glittering ceremony on 29 July 2000 in Jamshed Bhabha Theatre of the National Centre for Performing Arts (NCPA) in South Mumbai, Ratan Tata presented the trophy to Irani, to a standing ovation. In a tribute to Tata Steel, Ratan Tata said: 'If somebody had asked me five years ago as to which is the company in our group least likely to win the award, I would have unhesitatingly said Tata Steel. Yet here we are, celebrating that they are the first company out of all to reach the 600 mark!' Not only had Tata Steel won the award, it had also achieved the highest employee satisfaction values in the steel industry, tripled labour productivity between 1995 and 2000, and reduced procurement cost by over 40 per cent.[10]

The millennium brought in unprecedented recognition for the company. In November 2000, the CII conferred the coveted CII-EXIM Bank Award for Business Excellence on Tata Steel. It was the third company to receive the award after Hewlett-Packard and Maruti Udyog. Tata Steel also received the Prime Minister's Trophy for being the 'Best Integrated Steel Plant' in India. It was acknowledged as Asia's first-ever integrated steel plant. While the company acknowledged its approach 'Customer First, Har Haal Mein' to this outstanding success, there were important management lessons from this journey. Irani underscored two of them.

> Firstly, it is possible to improve. We don't have to keep on pointing to our forefathers that they did things in a particular way and we can't do it better. Secondly, unless you change, you are dead. You can always get good equipment, but you must have the will to change. Our people, including our union, had that will to change.

Scaling higher peaks

The year 2001 was another inflexion point in Tata Steel's transformational journey. The first was a transition in top leadership. Irani concluded his term and passed on the baton to B. Muthuraman, a Tata Steel veteran since 1966. In his years at the top, Irani had transformed the company from becoming a 'steel museum' into one of the finest in Asia. Between 1992 and 2001, the company expanded its capacity from 2 to 3.4 Mtpa production capacity, and reduced its labour force from 78,000 to 48,000.[11] This spoke volumes of the levels of productivity and efficiency that had been introduced into the ecosystem during the 'Irani decade'.

International recognition came in the very year he stepped down. In July 2001, World Steel Dynamics (WSD) ranked Tata Steel as the No. 1 world-class steel maker. It was ranked ahead of giants like Arcelor, Europe (Rank 2), POSCO, South Korea (Rank 3) and Nippon Steel, Japan (Rank 10). Peter Marcus, the founder and editor of WSD, visited Jamshedpur earlier that year and evaluated the company on diverse factors.[12] In a report on the Indian steel industry published in May 2001, Marcus identified Tata Steel as India's only world-class steel maker. In a record of sorts, Tata Steel was ranked in the top spot for 2004, 2005 and 2006. Sajjan Jindal, chairman of JSW group, acknowledged the strengths of Tata Steel when compared to its peers:

> Control over raw materials, a highly skilled operating team, fully integrated plant, Tata brand equity, mixed product profile, and cheaper access to capital being AAA credit rated company. While we pay an average of 17 per cent, they pay 12 per cent, which is even below prime lending rate.[13]

External recognition kept the motivation high, and Tata Steel implemented many focused initiatives. A series of lectures by Harvard Business School Professor Robert Kaplan on balanced scorecard[14] initiated the company on that method. Another addition was the Japanese approach of Total Productive Maintenance (TPM),[15] which was extremely good for improving the reliability of the steel plant units. To engage those in the service departments and functional divisions, the company introduced Six Sigma,[16] an initiative pioneered by GE in 1995. In 2002, Tata Steel adopted 'Vision 2007' to celebrate its centenary year. One of the major targets was to become an economic value added (EVA) positive[17] company by then. This required the company to achieve a PAT of ₹1000 crore, twice of what it had achieved in the previous financial year, which was itself a historic first. The task was daunting. But aspirations were superlative. In the very next financial year, the company achieved its objective of becoming EVA-positive, four years ahead of schedule. It joined the league of a handful of steel plants in the world that added to shareholder value. All others eroded it.[18] By 2004, Tata Steel crossed the 700-points level in the TBEM assessments, the first in the group to do so, and that too within four years of winning the award. With 707 points, its steel SBU won the 'Leadership in Excellence' Award. At a ceremony at the NCPA on 29 July 2004, a special plaque was presented to Tata Steel to mark this milestone achievement. Ratan Tata commended their consistent commitment to business excellence. By now, it had become the lowest-cost producer of steel in the world!

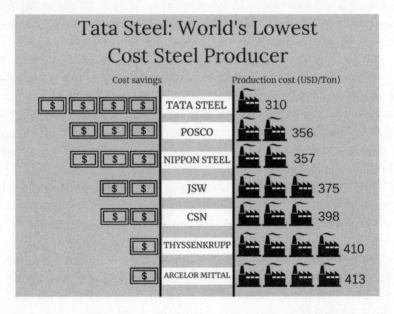

Towards the pinnacle of international quality

What next? This was the question on everybody's mind that evening when Tata Steel achieved what no other Tata company had achieved, or for that matter, no other steel maker in India, at that point of time. Sharan , then chief of business excellence, was with the senior leadership on stage—Muthuraman, Mukherjee, and A.N. Singh. He recollected the conversation he had had with Muthuraman after the programme. The obvious target was to work towards achieving 800 points. For that, the company had to do something radically different. For this, Sharan requested the MD's permission to explore the Deming Prize. Revered like the Nobel Prize in the world of quality, the Deming Prize is one of the highest awards for successful implementation of TQM by individuals and institutions across the globe. Sharan believed that Deming Prize would take Tata Steel to the next level. Besides it would also give an edge to Tata Steel to compete with Japanese companies that were entering the Indian market. Instantly, Muthuraman said, 'Yes, go ahead.' Sharan admitted, 'This is one thing that is absolutely phenomenal in the Tata leadership—if the subordinates bring some idea to experiment, the leadership will just say, "Yes, go ahead."'

On initial exploration, the company realized that while the objectives and principles were the same as TBEM, Deming's methods were different. For greater clarity, Sharan visited JUSE in Tokyo, met Professor Y. Ando and invited him to come to Jamshedpur as a consultant. Professor Ando came and performed an initial diagnosis to understand the situation. Looking at the size of Tata Steel, he suggested that his senior, Professor Noriaki Kano from the Tokyo University of Science be invited. Sharan promptly wrote a letter to Kano. He received an interesting reply— 'For Professor Kano to come to Jamshedpur, the CEO of Tata Steel must come to Tokyo and request him.' The professor was keen to understand his eagerness and sincerity in the implementation of the Deming Model. Sharan showed the letter to Muthuraman. Spontaneously he said, 'Write to him that I will come to Japan and request him personally.' In the meantime, Hemant Nerurkar, then chief operating officer, was going to Tokyo on official work. Sharan wrote to Professor Kano, 'A very senior executive is coming to Tokyo. Will it be fine if he comes and requests you to come to Jamshedpur?' He replied seeking clarification on the designation of Nerurkar. After satisfying himself with the seniority, he finally met Nerurkar at the Hilton Hotel in Tokyo. Professor Kano eventually came to Jamshedpur to study the company on its Deming aspirations.

After a year of preparation, the initial diagnosis at Tata Steel was done in 2005. After the diagnosis, the assessors met Muthuraman and the senior team. During that interaction, he asked the team of assessors when they could challenge the Deming Prize. The assessors were all veterans, with the average age being sixty-five years. Among them was Professor Ejuka from Tokyo University. He commented that Tata Steel must work hard to become a quality organization. He told Muthuraman, 'You don't understand the profound meaning of quality. It may take at least three years before you can even apply for the Deming Prize'. A 700-point company as per TBEM assessment, Tata Steel was extremely confident of its eligibility. This comment was a jolt; heartbreaking to say the least. It put a big question mark on whatever the company was doing for over a decade. Yet, the senior management in all humility accepted their observations, and was committed to improve and work towards the goal.

The company embarked on a well-knit company-wide customer-centric approach to quality, an area that was highlighted as a weak point in the Deming assessment. It also began working towards making its shop floor workers functionally and digitally literate, and focused on the socio-economic development of the underdeveloped communities around Jamshedpur, an area of concern highlighted by the Deming team. While the senior and middle management people were thoroughly trained on the principles of data-driven TQM, Muthuraman read up all the available literature of international companies that had won the Deming Prize, especially Toyota, which is acknowledged for its superiority in this domain. To empower and implement the Deming way across a 38,000-strong workforce took Tata Steel three years. In 2008, it was ready to challenge the Deming Prize.

For ease of assessment, the total steel plant was divided into six applications representing various business and supporting functions—flat products, long products, iron making, raw materials/mines, shared services and corporate functions. To win the award, the company had to perform as per Deming standards on each one of them. A group of fifteen assessors came to Jamshedpur in September 2008. For each of these six applications, the company was assessed separately by that group. Misra, then vice president at Tata Steel, recalled the punctuality and discipline of the all-Japanese team. 'You had to start in time, finish in time, and your presentation had to be very precise. I was once marked by the assessors that you have exceeded your time by 30 seconds!' That was the level of their conscientiousness. Unlike their Western counterparts, they would not socialize in the evenings. Parties were a strict no-no. Throughout their fortnight-long diagnosis, they were looking for actual evidence for every process. The visit concluded with a special one-on-one with Muthuraman and the senior leadership of the company. Three weeks later, through an early morning call from Japan, Muthuraman was informed that Tata Steel had won the Deming Prize. It was the first integrated steel company in the world to have won the award.

If one were to look back at its journey from 1988, when the company faced existential crisis and Irani mentioned about the Tata Steel plant becoming a museum, the company had made phenomenal progress in just two decades, while remaining grounded in its culture and multi-stakeholder commitments. To attribute the success to the collective efforts of the entire Tata Steel fraternity, Muthuraman, in the Tata tradition, took along with him to Tokyo—Raghunath Pandey, then president of the Tata Workers' Union. On behalf of the 35,000 strong Tata Steel family, the MD and union president accepted the award at an impressive ceremony on 12 November 2008. It was possibly the best gift the company could give itself on completing 100 years as India's leading steel maker.

Between 2001 and 2009, during Muthuraman's tenure, the company had grown from 3.4 to 5.4 Mtpa production capacity (India operations), and the profits (PAT) had grown ten times—from ₹553 crore to ₹5201 crore. This was also the period when the company had gone global by acquiring leading steel companies such as NatSteel in Singapore (2004), Millennium Steel in Thailand (2006), and Corus, the Anglo-Dutch giant (2007). These had increased its global production capacity to 25 Mtpa, an eightfold growth in eight years. In October 2009, Hemant Nerurkar took charge as MD. He had joined the company in 1982.

Ever since the company won the Deming Prize, it had set its eye on the Deming Grand Prize, considered the summum bonum of a company's quality journey. Instituted in 1969, it could be applied to by companies that had already won the Deming Prize. However, the applicant must wait for three years or more (including the award year) after it had received the Deming Prize. The focus of evaluation under the Deming Grand Prize was on significant process improvements since winning the Deming Prize. While quality improvement initiatives focus on efficiency, i.e. doing things right, strategy focuses on doing the right thing. Combining these two with innovation was the real challenge before the organization. To strengthen its customer focus, Tata Steel embarked on three programmes concurrently. These included customer value management, retail value management and customer product optimization. This was the time when the world was just recovering from the financial crisis. India too had been affected, though in a limited way. However, there was scepticism within the company that when the financial results had not been encouraging, did it make sense focusing on an award? The argument given by the proponents of the customer-centred TQM approach was that if we had not proactively worked towards these initiatives, the situation could have been worse. While working towards the Deming goal, the company continued to perform exceedingly well in its TBEM assessments. In 2010, the Tubes division of Tata Steel won the J.R.D.

QV Award. In 2011, Tata Steel Wires division and Ferro Alloys and Minerals division won the award. Tata Steel had the record of the maximum number of its divisions, strategic units and subsidiaries winning the award since inception.

Confident that it had made a quantum leap in organization-wide process quality, Tata Steel applied for the Deming Grand Prize in 2012. The same procedures were repeated. A team of assessors came from Japan and evaluated the processes on-site. They were convinced of Tata Steel's deservedness. On 14 November 2012, Tata Steel was awarded the Deming Grand Prize in Tokyo. It had once again created history by becoming the first and the only integrated steel company in the world to win this award. It was only the twenty-second company in the world to receive this award since its inception in 1970. Some of the others in that league were Toyota Motor, Nippon Steel, and Komatsu.

The building blocks in the journey towards excellence

In search of excellence, Tata Steel's journey began from existential crisis and culminated by attaining the zenith of quality. Three key insights emerge from its experience.

Firstly, all its initiatives were people-centric. Especially the Deming approach, which depended on 100 per cent bottom-up involvement. In the process, 100 per cent of the company's employees were trained. Operators were empowered to solve problems and not depend on a higher-up. If required, the company was willing to train them, but they had to do their job with total commitment. People started understanding the importance of their limited job on the larger business. It wasn't limited to boardroom strategy development.

Secondly, you needed to make the proverbial 'elephant to dance'. Any steel or heavy manufacturing company is very siloed. Tata Steel worked very hard on cross-functional teams. The importance of the internal customer was drilled down to the last employee. You need not be the marketing person with a front-facing role. If you are on iron making, you are the customer of raw materials and supplier to steel making. Every employee on the shop floor must not only meet his objectives, but also foster collaboration.

Most importantly, one had to be very clear that the company was doing quality for business. TQM for business; Deming for business. It was not an academic exercise for self-fulfilment, but a means to an economic end. The output and outcomes had to get reflected in the top- and bottom-line performance. This was very evident in the financial performance of Tata Steel. Between 2006 and 2016, Tata Steel touched ₹16,000 crore in cumulative savings through TQM-based improvement.

CHAPTER 9

TATAS' FIRST 100-BILLION-DOLLAR COMPANY; INDIA'S MOST VALUED

'With honest and straightforward business principles, close and careful attention to details, and the ability to take advantage of favourable opportunities and circumstances, there is a scope for success.'

Jamsetji Tata

The late Russi Lala was an eminent journalist and a biographer of the Tata Group. The credit of documenting several historical facts and stories connected with Tata companies goes to him in substantial measure. Author of several books on Tata companies, trusts and leaders, he was also a trustee at Tata Trusts for many decades. To tap into the distilled essence of his understanding of the Tata Group, he was once asked by a young Tata manager: 'What are the one or two things, which you feel make the Tatas different from any other corporate?' After thinking for a moment, he said, 'First is, not being self-centred. Looking for others' benefit in every decision made. Second is, the human touch in every decision.' After some time and thought, he continued, 'I will add one more thing—pioneering. Whatever business we do, we try to be a pioneer in it.'

The Tata Group has been a pioneer in several industries since its inception. It set unique standards in products and processes, transforming established business models, and redefining prevailing industrial structures that had devolved due to systemic limitations or self-serving and apathetic approaches of existing players. Over the years, this pioneering spirit converted itself into a quest for innovation of all types and at all levels within leading Tata companies. In a conversation, Gopalakrishnan elaborated his understanding of the role innovation can play in an organization:

Innovation is all about creating a distance between yourself and your competition and being better at it. It can come through product, but it can also come through the business model. Having a great product where the business model is not distinctive or having a business model without a distinctive product can be infructuous.

For most people, innovation is about doing something nobody in the world has ever done before. But innovation can also mean something that is difficult to replicate. It may mean first time in the world, or first time in that part of the world, or first time for the target customers. Just as Six Sigma delivers efficiency and lower operating costs, strategic planning delivers direction and budgets, and marketing processes deliver brand recognition, innovation delivers differentiation.[1] It could be product, service, or process differentiation. It could also be differentiation through an innovative business model like the global offshore delivery system introduced by TCS in the late 1970s, which marked the beginning of the globalization of the Indian IT industry. IT companies such as Infosys, Wipro and several others came later and emulated this model. The journey of TCS from being a small division under Tata Sons to the most valued company in India is a legend of contemporary times.

At crossroads of existence—to be or not to be

It may be hard to believe that a company that contributes nearly two-thirds of the Tata Group's present-day profits, was once on the verge of shutting shop. The year was 1978. TCS' four-year partnership with Burroughs Corporation had just ended. In those years, Burroughs was among the largest mainframe computer manufacturers in the world. Its joint venture with TCS had opened the doors for the Tatas' fledgling division to many international business opportunities. After the separation, TCS had to function as an independent company. Forty-three of its key employees were transferred to Tata Burroughs as per Tata Sons' decision. Tata Burroughs, a joint venture between Burroughs Corporation and Tata Sons, was to focus on selling and maintaining Burroughs equipment in India. TCS, an operating division of Tata Sons, was mandated to create a new market for its software services. It was a difficult phase in TCS' decade-long history It had to begin its game afresh at 'love-all' and restart the hunt for international clients and partners to sell its services, with a team of computer engineers who hardly had any idea about sales and marketing. Until then, business from Burroughs had comprised over 90 per cent of its overseas earnings. Its once faithful partner was now its internal competitor—Tata Burroughs.[2] That's TCS for you, four decades ago. Fast-forward forty years, and you have a company that is the largest IT employer in India with nearly 400,000 employees, $19.09 billion in revenues and $100 billion in market capitalization. With 289 offices across forty-six countries and 147 delivery centres in twenty-one countries, TCS is present across five continents.[3]

'TCS was not sure which way to go when I took over,' recalled Faqir Chand Kohli, former deputy chairman of TCS, about the days in 1969 when he was brought into TCS on a year-long deputation. With a workforce of ten consultants and 200 operators, TCS' main responsibility was to manage the punch card operations of TISCO. Kohli had joined the Tata Electric Companies (TEC, now Tata Power) in 1951. In 1964, Tata Electric first started using computers, way ahead of its time. The first computer was installed at the Tata Institute of Fundamental Research (TIFR), for its operations and stores management. 'In 1968, we installed what was at that time called "online computer", of course with the government's permission without which it wasn't allowed. It was used to control power generation and the flow of power through the transmission lines,' he shared. At that time, the UK, France, Germany and Japan were all using analog systems. Tata Power was the fourth utility company in the world to use computing. The other three were in the USA. Kohli's rise at Tata Power had been meteoric. In two decades, he rose from chief load dispatcher to deputy general manager.

From serving the Tatas to serving India

J.R.D. Tata, on the advice of his brother-in-law Colonel Leslie Sawhney, established a small interdisciplinary team of qualified people as Tata Group's in-house data-processing unit in 1962. An initial investment of ₹50 lakh and a rented IBM 1401 were its key resources.[4] In 1968, while planning for the imminent and authoritarian MRTP Act, TCS and three other units[5] were incorporated as operating divisions of Tata Sons with twenty senior executives from various Tata businesses. Subramaniam Ramadorai, former vice chairman of TCS, recalled, 'In those days TCS was a Silicon Valley start-up . . . with India's brightest people and with no dictated agenda.' Kohli's exposure to computing and commendable performance in Tata Power was responsible for his almost forced deputation into TCS as general manager by P.M. Agarwala, then director-in-charge of TCS. Resisting his transfer to TCS, Kohli is believed to have told J.R.D., 'I don't know anything about computers.' To which J.R.D. shot back, 'Well, no one in India knows anything either.'[6] Kohli's heart was in Tata Power; he aspired to lead the company someday. However, having a task cut out for him at TCS, he got into the act, almost instantaneously. With no trail to follow and no benchmark to emulate, TCS had to build the market from scratch.

'There was no question of having customers. We had to build consumers and educate them about the use of computers,' admitted Kohli. Its first breakthrough came through a contract from the Central Bank of India to automate its inter-branch reconciliation process. A noteworthy execution brought orders from fourteen other banks. Projects from Unit Trust of India, Bombay (Brihanmumbai) Municipal Corporation and Delhi Transport Authority followed.

TCS set an internal goal that Tata Group companies would not account for more than 10 per cent of its revenues. 'We were into management consultancy from day one, but we just did not want to give a report and walk out. We wanted to provide a solution to clients, and it happened that you needed software to provide that solution,' reminisced Kohli.[7] By 1972, he had set the vision for TCS and requested Tata Sons management to permit him to return to his first love Tata Power and electrical engineering. But they wanted him to stay with TCS. He obliged, and the rest is history. It can be said that Indian electrical industry's loss was India's embryonic IT industry's gain. The journey was far from smooth. The challenges for Kohli and his team had just begun.

After nationalization of banks by the Indira Gandhi government in 1969, there was declining business with banks as the Centre did not want computers in India. It believed that computerization would lead to mass unemployment. It is contextual to mention a fact that few know. It was TCS that had developed the now ubiquitous permanent account number (PAN) system for the income tax department way back in 1977. Impressed by the output, the company was given an assignment to computerize the total processing of income tax. However, Charan Singh, then finance minister, decreed that there would be no computerization in the finance ministry as it could create unemployment! If implemented then, India would have been far ahead of several countries through a fully computerized tax administration system.

It was around the late 1960s when Kohli got elected on the esteemed IEEE board of directors, headquartered in the USA. Before leaving, he presented his concerns before J.R.D. with respect to the lack of business opportunities for TCS in India, and averred that it may have to be closed soon. However, he used his frequent visits to IEEE, almost every quarter for two consecutive years (and at no cost to the Tatas, he emphasized), to explore business prospects in the USA. He would always visit Detroit, the headquarters of Burroughs Corporation (BC). At that time, Burroughs wanted a healthcare software that would be packaged with their computers.[8] Kohli convinced them that BC and TCS could work together. BC was convinced and the two signed what can be called the first IT outsourcing contract of India for $24,000. Surprisingly, TCS didn't have a single Burroughs machine then. It was a giant leap of faith to deliver the software package without compatible hardware. But TCS went ahead and developed the whole system on an available ICL computer (acquired from Life Insurance Corporation when its communist unions had prevented its use perceiving a threat to their jobs). TCS built an ingenious filter to transfer the system from ICL to a Burroughs computer. BC was impressed. TCS had successfully completed its first software export project. 'We never looked back thereafter,' he said. In 1974, Kohli was made the director-in-charge for TCS.

India had missed the Industrial Revolution (due to British Rule) and the microelectronics revolution (due to the socialist mindset of the post-Independence Indian governments). Kohli predicted during a function at the Computer Society of India in 1975 that India had another revolution waiting for it—the IT revolution. 'Primarily, it requires the capability to think clearly and this, we (Indians) have in abundance. We have an opportunity on an equal basis, even to assume leadership. If we miss the opportunity, those who follow us will not forgive us.' Kohli ensured that the opportunity was not missed. Later, he even advocated developing appropriate courses to develop human resources for high-end chip design and testing. As a result, India became home to a thriving chip design and testing industry.

Unlike most companies that first establish themselves locally, and then go global, TCS focused on the international market from the beginning. This was due to lack of adequate demand in the domestic market, poor computer infrastructure and naive technological knowhow. Kohli blamed the lack of belief of the Indira Gandhi, Morarji Desai and Charan Singh governments in computer technology for this. The scenario improved only during the Narasimha Rao government. From a macro perspective, the knowledge gained by Indian developers through overseas IT projects during the 1970s and '80s, brought tremendous learnings to India, widely benefitting the Indian IT industry.

In the 1970s, Kohli could foresee the decline of Burroughs business and felt the need to acquaint his TCS team to IBM machines. Eventually, the team gained so much proficiency in software building on both frameworks that TCS accepted a US-based bank consortium's project to migrate their software from Burroughs to IBM. In the mid-1980s, when several companies were migrating from Burroughs to IBM, TCS capitalized on its dual expertise and grabbed those opportunities. As it delivered more and larger migration projects, Western customers noticed the company's custom software development capabilities as well as its abilities in performing complex systems integration and packaged application implementation.[9] As a result, migration services accounted for a large portion of its international revenues.

In the mid-1980s, the company spotted C++, then a new programming metaphor. It sent its personnel overseas for getting trained. When they returned to India, a hundred more were trained domestically. A couple of years later when there was a huge demand for C++ in the market, TCS was right on top with its people trained and ready to deliver. By the late 1980s, the company was the largest consultancy outfit in India, bigger than the next ten software companies put together. It was working on over 500 projects at various stages of development in forty countries.

Acknowledging the company's capability of spotting technology trends ahead of the curve, Kohli had once observed, 'TCS tracks technology as it is developed worldwide and starts working on it twenty-four–thirty-six months before it is actually commercialized in the international market.'[10] While these timelines reduced in the years ahead, its first-mover advantage provided a strategic lead on several occasions, including Y2K solutions. Kohli's spade work in travelling to the West and building connections, created a brand name not only for TCS, but also for India. This recognition eventually opened doors for numerous Indians to work abroad and set up companies in Silicon Valley. India's image in the West from the land of snake charmers and elephants was transformed to a land of brilliant software programmers. N.R. Narayana Murthy, co-founder of Infosys, India's IT bellwether and a close competitor to TCS, often acknowledged Kohli as the pillar of TCS and the leader of the Indian IT industry. Nandan Nilekani, Infosys chairman, believed that TCS had pioneered the Indian software industry and played a seminal role in the global acceptance of Indian software capabilities.[11]

During a conversation at his office on one of the top floors at the Air India Building located in the plush Nariman Point business district of Mumbai, the nonagenarian Kohli, often called the 'Bhishma *Pitamah*' (grand sire in the epic Mahabharata) of India's software industry, shared insights into his six-decade-long association with the Tata Group. Hailing from Peshawar, Kohli completed his graduation in physics from Punjab University in Lahore, and did his postgraduation from Massachusetts Institute of Technology (MIT), USA. Despite an offer to pursue PhD at the prestigious MIT, he returned to India in 1950 to assist his family who had relocated to Lucknow, after being pushed out from Peshawar (where his family had a prosperous business) due to their Hindu identity.

'My family was in distress and I didn't want to leave them alone,' he admitted.[12] Despite the trauma of migration, he was committed to contribute significantly to India's future and not just make a living for himself. Often described as the Henry Ford of IT services, Kohli-led TCS moved software development from artisan-like activity to an industrial assembly line of a software factory.[13] By the time Kohli stepped down from executive responsibility at TCS in 1998, over two lakh Indian programmers were driving the global IT revolution. Not just that. In the 1990s, IT and computer sciences became the numero uno career choices for engineers in India. Of the million students that wrote the IIT-JEE every year, 50 per cent joined the IT industry. In a way, Kohli and the top leadership at TCS can be credited for creating enormous employment opportunities for the Indian youth, an invaluable service to the nation.

An industry-defining business model

In 1974, TCS imported the first Burroughs machine (B1728) to India. At that time, it had cost the company $300,000, with an equal amount of import duty. It was an enormous yet worthwhile investment for TCS (partly funded through a bank loan). Working on the latest system opened new avenues for TCS. In the same year it signed an agreement with Burroughs to provide software expertise both in India and overseas through the first-ever IT software and services outsourcing contract project. This provided TCS an opportunity to send its team overseas for systems software installation. Ramadorai called this strategy of doing part software development in India and software implementation on site as the beginning of the Indian outsourcing model. In subsequent years, TCS began using an on-site-offshore model of IT delivery. This involved expatriating certain developers to the client locations overseas and engaging another team locally in India to assist the client.

At that time, three approaches of delivering software exports were available. The first one was contract programming, also referred to as 'body-shopping'. In this case, the software exporter (like TCS) hired individuals on a contractual basis for software development at the client's premises (like Burroughs) overseas. The client was responsible for the developers' salary, travels and local housing throughout their stay. The exporter received a commission for supplying the client with programmers having the relevant expertise.[14] In the early 1970s, the deficiency of engineers for the expanding computer industry in the West, abundance of unemployed Indian engineering graduates, and a growing international reputation of Indian software engineers provided an opportunity for body-shopping. Indian firms such as TCS were forerunners in sending Indian engineers overseas to do software programming.[15] Thousands of Indian professionals were sent to the USA to work on project sites. An interesting study revealed that a third of the students who graduated from the

IITs between 1973 and 1977 had settled abroad. By 2000, some 25,000 IIT alumni were settled just in the USA.[16]

The second approach of delivering software exports was on-site project management. In this case, the exporter took total responsibility of project delivery. The company sent its own programmers to the client's location, bearing all costs. This approach had inherent advantages as programmers worked in close coordination with the client. N.M.K. Bhatta, former delivery head, identified three of them—better capture of client requirements, final output as per client expectations, and greater empathy from clients. However, there were disadvantages for the software exporter. These included escalated costs due to high living expenses overseas, cultural differences between programmers and the client's employees, lack of work–life balance for programmers as they stayed away from home for months on end, restrictive US visa rules for Asian expatriates, and lack of adequate IT infrastructure on the clients' premises.

The third approach to global IT delivery was offshore development. In the 1970s and '80s, Indian software industry matured. Increasing client confidence on Indian capabilities and quality standards enabled Indian firms to move their work offshore. The maturity came with an ambition to move up the value chain and deliver complete solutions from India instead of remaining mere subcontractors. TCS made a concerted attempt to move away from on-site work towards offshore. In 1988, it set up its first IBM centre in India with a ₹10 crore worth IBM mainframe 3090 computer at Madras (now Chennai) and targeted all IBM customers and research labs to come to India. This gave a real stimulus to TCS' offshore business. The offshore model had great advantages for TCS and other software exporters from India. It was highly cost-effective, provided better work–life balance to programmers, ensured greater adherence to initial requirements with limited real-time changes, and better coordination and coaching of employees. Global clients doing business in the USA and western Europe preferred Indians and gave Indian firms more business because of greater compatibility with English language than competitors from China and the Philippines. The glitches with the outsourcing model were that occasionally the software development digressed from initial requirements. Handling client expectations from a long distance, installation of the software and training of the client's employees were problematic. Many aspects of the final delivery, such as installation of the software and training of the clients' employees, were not possible offshore.

During our conversation at the TCS House in Mumbai, Jayant Pendharkar, then head of global marketing, elaborated on the many challenges and complexities of managing international IT projects.

IT projects are fairly complex. The duration of delivery may range from three months to several years. Therefore, during project execution, many things change—people, expectations, environment, and even technology change. Clients are not able to capture their requirements well and even if they do, their requirements keep changing. So we have to be flexible enough to cater to these changes, and ensure that we don't end up making a loss.

There were people-related issues too as they form the core of any service enterprise. Despite extensive training, new issues crop up on-site.

The projects handled on-site are not taught in colleges as they are state-of-the-art in nature. Most often, these have to be learnt on the job itself. Moreover, expectation management is a challenge. The client may not want young programmers, but they are the ones with experience in the latest technology. The clients want senior people, but their skills might be outdated.

In fact, the young 'programmers' that TCS sent for overseas projects were not code writers, but highly qualified engineers and computer science experts from leading Indian institutions, especially the IITs.

To leverage the advantages and overcome the limitations, TCS evolved an on-site-offshore model of software delivery, now-popular as the Global Network Delivery Model™. This model ensured that project activities were split between the client and TCS. The client-facing activities were on-site and the non-client-facing services were done offshore in India. A small team was maintained at the client's site during the project delivery stages. Of course, there was no real-time connectivity between the continents in those years. Software codes were sent by airmail between engineers on-site and offshore on tapes and discs! A small change meant a week's delay. When the Internet became mainstream in India in the early 1990s, regulatory restrictions limited quick sharing of information and progress with clients. Offshore companies in India were connected to high-speed Net but through low-speed local cable lines. A long-overdue policy change in 1998 effectively ended a monopoly on Internet-service-provider (ISP) gateways and allowed India's private sector to offer high-speed Internet bandwidth to the IT industry. This gave the benefit of real-time communication. Tata Communications, another Tata company, played a major role in this sector. The impact of TCS' global delivery model, state-of-the-art technology[17] and the enabling ecosystem was visible in the gigantic jump made in the share of revenue from its offshore model from 10 per cent of total revenue in 1988 to 71 per cent by 2005.

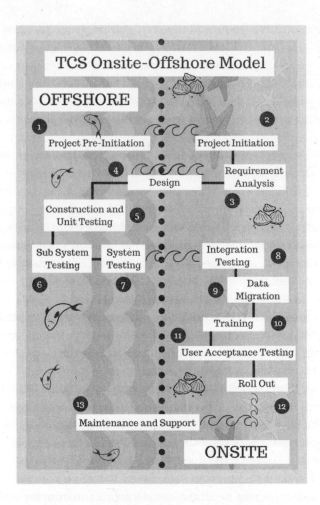

From cost to quality to excellence—the TCS way

> 'In TCS, we have an important global partner that can be trusted to deliver.
> They combine deep domain and technical knowledge with a global delivery
> model that brings tremendous value to our customers.'

Bill Gates

The TCS model's cost-effectiveness and convenience was widely appreciated by
clients and even competitors within India, who were coming up in large numbers
to participate in the IT services revolution. The model's popularity was primarily
because of its cost benefits. Manpower costs accounted for nearly 80 per cent
of software development projects. For example, a typical Indian programmer

earned $7000–20,000 as compared to his US counterpart who received a salary between $60,000–100,000.[18] The other reason was the complex work-visa process in the USA, which often acted as a hurdle for getting people on-site. These were compelling reasons for overseas clients to shift software development activities to India and other emerging economies. The *McKinsey Quarterly* estimated that the US companies saved 58 cents for every dollar spent on business services that were offshored.[19] Over the years, TCS' model received wide acceptance across industries, especially the financial services industry. Financial multinationals, including Bank of America, Standard Chartered, Merrill Lynch, Morgan Stanley and the ING Group, embraced this model to benefit from substantial cost savings and high-quality solutions in much shorter time.

Indian IT firms enjoyed great success in the 1980s due to manpower cost differential. Infosys and Wipro, which emerged as TCS' key competitors, were founded in 1980–81 and headquartered at Bangalore. As the forerunner in the Indian IT industry, TCS continued to grab the lion's share of business. However, the company soon realized that overseas clients were not just looking for the lowest cost. They also focused on quality and support. TCS held on to this insight and embarked on its quality journey with strict adherence to its delivery schedules. Over the years, its definitive delivery commitment made it stand out in the West and earn repeat projects.[20] In later years, 'Experience Certainty' became its catchphrase.

A milestone in its project execution history was a ₹40-crore contract signed in 1989 with the Swiss Securities Clearing Corporation (SEGA) to create a real-time securities settlement system for the Swiss market. It was the single largest contract bagged by an Indian software firm until then. TCS clinched the contract despite competition from Arthur Anderson (now Accenture). The project of delivering a world-class system to a mature financial market was completed within the budget and on time. Seventy per cent of the work was done offshore in India, thereby validating the success of the TCS model. It brought great laurels to the company. Ramadorai recalled SEGA as a classic example of an extremely complex and tough deal touching millions of customers. The confidence of delivering it under all odds and bringing together the best competencies were the company's greatest achievements. It gave the company huge confidence to go for big-ticket high-quality projects.

Success with SEGA brought several pricey projects to TCS. It won projects for setting up the National Stock Exchange (NSE) systems in 1993 and dematerialization systems for the National Stock Depository Ltd (NSDL) in 1996. This was extremely fulfilling for the company for two reasons. First, it won the contract against global leaders such as Digital Equipment and Hewlett-Packard. Second, the project won accolades for being the fastest implementation of a depository system in the world. TCS had come up on the world stage through sheer performance, quality and delivery.

Over the next two decades, it delivered some of the most prestigious and complex projects the TCS way. Some of these included engine design for GE Aircraft (1996), automation of the Johannesburg Stock Exchange and the Canadian Depository System (2003), Enterprise Resource Planning (ERP) system for Indian Railway Catering and Tourism Corporation (2006), Passport Seva Project for processing Indian passport applications (2008), Telecom state-wide area network systems integration projects for Chhattisgarh, Tamil Nadu, Bihar and Andhra Pradesh (2009), and software platform for the Indian Income Tax Department (2013). All systems built by TCS had the bandwidth to handle data flow for decades, thereby ensuring successful and seamless operations.

The pride of delivering a high-quality system is reflected in a conversation between Ramadorai, then MD of TCS, and a visitor. In May 2004, when the Vajpayee-led NDA lost the general elections, there was a lot of panic; stock markets crashed by 25 per cent in just two days. This was also the time when TCS was getting ready to launch its IPO. The visitor remarked to Ramadorai that the emerging scenario would be quite worrisome for the company. But Ramadorai wasn't perturbed. Instead, he expressed delight because the BSE and NSE systems had been designed by TCS a decade earlier. Despite the stress of crashing markets and millions of transactions, the systems had excelled in performance and managed the increased scale. This was a tribute to the capability and ingenuity of TCS engineers.

In an oft-cited article on business strategy by Professor Porter from Harvard Business School, strategy is explained as being all about improving operational efficiency by productivity, and quality by remarkable management tools such as partnering, total quality management, benchmarking, and re-engineering.[21] A similar approach was visible at TCS. However, it customized long-held management concepts that were the stronghold of manufacturing companies for its IT services business. It focused on managing the supply chain of TCS recruits such as Toyota or Ford did for its parts. It talked of inventory management of its engineers and the logistics of deploying them like Dell did for its hardware products. It used ERP to deliver their software, the way Reliance or Tata Steel did for its petrochemicals and steel products. It treated software as products and employees as assets. 'In terms of management theory, it was a truly remarkable framework that untangled the spaghetti of managing a services company,' remarked Shivanand Kanavi, former vice president.

Natarajan Chandrasekaran, now chairman of TCS, observed that the TCS model of software delivery and quality was perfected over the years in partnership with clients such as General Electric, American Express and Prudential Insurance.[22] Such client partnerships brought immense learning. For example, in the 1990s, TCS established a dedicated offshore development centre (ODC) for GE at SEEPZ in Mumbai. Under Jack Welch, GE had integrated the Six Sigma approach as central to its business strategy. Inspired by their example, TCS imbibed a culture of quality benchmarking, and mandated that every project manager in the company should be a Six Sigma black belt.

Experiencing 'one TCS', globally

What began in the 1970s as a business imperative due to labour arbitrage,[23] transitioned a quarter-century later into strategic and process imperatives such as optimization and digitization of diverse business processes with a focus on quality and time-to-market advantages. By the turn of the millennium, when leading multinationals from the USA and Europe established their presence in emerging economies like China and countries in eastern Europe and Latin America, TCS established bases in some of those countries to provide support to long-standing clients. Following the 9/11 terror attacks, when the US government imposed restrictive visa policies, there was increasing concern about a potential backlash against Asian outsourcing due to the heightened security sensitivity. Furthermore, the demand for IT personnel was skyrocketing in India, the cost of Indian engineers was being driven up, and India was losing its cost advantage.[24] At such a time, TCS focused on establishing regional centres in Hungary for Europe and Uruguay for Latin America. Called 'near-shoring', it became the new buzzword in the industry. These centres offered in-demand capabilities, with language and cultural sensitivities. The near-shore centres in New Jersey and Phoenix (the USA) provided convenient access to clients in their own time zone, and familiarity with local business environment. The global delivery centres (GDCs) in India and China provided highly efficient offshore services and deep technical expertise not available elsewhere.[25] In all these places, TCS did not go for local partnerships and franchises, but established greenfield projects and created its own employee base, and replicated the model established in India. Whether through near-shoring or GDCs, TCS ensured that its international clients experienced 'one TCS'—a uniform standard of service, irrespective of whether they were served from Mumbai, Mexico or Malaysia. For this, it established the Global Network Delivery Model (GNDM) in 2002, a customer-centric engagement model based on an Integrated Quality Management System (iQMS). The distinction of GNDM was its one global service standard. Fifteen years later, with nearly 400,000 employees from 131 nationalities across forty-six countries, it continued to facilitate a globalization of the TCS workforce. 'It was as if everyone was working in the same building,' observed Ramadorai.

Given the globalized nature of the IT industry, and the constant fluctuations in policy and immigration regimes in different countries, Ramadorai put in place a clear strategy. In the short-term, he believed in total compliance with all regulatory issues. In the medium-term, the company was ready with global delivery centres to finish projects in case of restrictions on visas and people movement. 'In the long-term, we should look at the potential of WTO negotiations for globalization of services,' he emphasized. Professor Pankaj Ghemawat, now at the Stern School of Business, New York University, had worked closely with the senior leadership of TCS during the 'Ramadorai years'. He observed a similar triple-horizon approach to innovation at TCS. The company employed 60 per cent of efforts to derivative innovation (continuous improvement, twelve months horizon), 30 per cent to platform innovation (next generation platforms, one–two years horizon), and 10 per cent to breakthrough innovation (disruption, two-plus years horizon). It consistently followed a structured approach to innovation, a critical success factor in the fast-moving IT industry. Over the years, TCS also established innovation labs and dedicated ODCs across India and forty-three countries. More than 2500 TCS employees worked in R & D, asset creation and innovation, with a consistent annual investment of 1.5 per cent of the total turnover on research and innovation. This amounted to ₹1770 crore in 2017.

Creating value through customer-centricity

> 'If you are not meeting clients, you are not hearing anything. It is important
> to know what clients think of you, what they think of the future.'

> N. Chandrasekaran

'In TCS, the customer is the king. If a customer asks for a report on Friday evening stating that he wants it on Monday morning, the employees would work through the weekend to deliver the report. If ever there is a conflict between the employee and the customer, the decision will be in favour of the customer. That's the attitude and culture of the organization,' observed G. Jagannathan, former global head of business excellence. Yet, employee attrition at TCS was at 11–12 per cent, lower than the industry average of 14–15 per cent. Contrary to companies such as HCL that believed in 'employees first, customers second',[26] TCS had always been a customer-centric organization and had mastered the art of B2B customer relationship management. As a result, more than 90 per cent of its business was repeat business, an outcome of its high-quality delivery and long-term relationships with clients built over several years. S. Padmanabhan, former chief human resource officer at TCS, made another insightful observation:

> Many people who worked on the clients' side several years ago as junior or middle-level managers grew to become CIOs and CEOs. We keep in touch. Nobody compromises in value and delivery, but the network helps. Wining, dining and partying is not our culture. Relations are built on mutual respect and value.

TCS had fully digitized its customer relationship management process. Handling customer complaints was built into the project management system, with red alerts sent to senior-level managers when complaints were not resolved in time.

The senior-most leadership of the company exemplified its customer-first approach. Chandrasekaran (fondly called Chandra) created tremendous value by keeping his focus on customers. He started as an intern at TCS in 1987 while pursuing MCA at the Regional Engineering College, Tiruchirappalli, and eventually led several projects in Europe and the USA, effectively spending a decade overseas. Travelling across the globe and working in multiple industries convinced him about the importance of understanding customers' requirements and delivering them in time and in totality. In his years as the CEO of TCS, he was known for travelling across the globe for three weeks every month to meet global clients. On average, he personally interacted with 400 clients a year.[27] In 1977–78, Hewlett-Packard president John Young had shared the term 'management by wandering around' to Tom Peters and Bob Waterman, as HP best practice. Three decades later, the TCS leadership mantra could be described as 'management by flying around'!

Humour aside, customer-centricity was the compelling reason for the top leadership's global outreach. It also provided a vital opportunity to ideate with staff and country managers across the globe. The benefits became evident. In 2001, TCS was bidding for a $100 million deal with GE Medical. A key aspect of the deal was the vendor's ability to deliver globally. Abidali Neemuchwala, now CEO at Wipro, was then the global head of business process services at TCS and reported to Chandra. In the SWOT analysis he presented to Chandra, he identified lack of non-Indian employees on the company rolls as a weakness. During the presentation rehearsals, Chandra jested, 'Abid, why don't the France and China team leaders present their parts in French and Chinese.' On the D-Day, an all-American audience in Milwaukee didn't understand a word of French or Chinese. But they didn't ask any questions on TCS' global expertise either. The message that even with Indian employees, the company had gained a strong understanding of global markets and even global languages, was strategically communicated. TCS won and became the first Indian company to bag a $100 million deal.[28]

'Customer first' at TCS wasn't always about working with large multinationals in developed economies. There was a constant endeavour to explore newer geographies and sectors. In late 2007, Chandra and V. Ramaswamy, then director at TCS, were running together as part of their daily routine. Out of the blue, Chandra observed that TCS should explore the opportunity of serving small and medium enterprises. Ramaswamy laughed, remarking casually that in that case TCS would lose its shirt and pants in servicing small enterprises. He was quite happy consulting for US clients. The team thought that Chandra had forgotten all about it. In February 2008, he invited the entire senior team to a presentation where he outlined a vision of TCS serving the SME market and customers at the base of the pyramid. As if to challenge his preconceived notion, he nominated Ramaswamy as its head. Ramaswamy met small and medium enterprise (SME) entrepreneurs across India. The Tata brand opened its doors. A conversation he had had with a Gen X entrepreneur in Coimbatore was representative of customer needs on the ground. He recalled, 'One guy in Coimbatore told me, "First I upgrade the antivirus. Then the PCs become slow. Then I must upgrade Windows. And after that the local Mr Fixit says I have low RAM. I know Lord Ram. What's this Low Ram!"'[29]

Subsequent discussions with Chandra led to the insight that the offering would have to be sold like electricity, with a pay-as-you-use model. The billing was to be like the telecom industry. This led to the birth of the iON platform, an IT-as-a-service business model that delivered on-demand business capability[30] and functioned as a 'build-as-you-grow' and 'pay-as-you use' ERP hosted on the cloud. By 2018, it had diversified into e-learning through its platform 'academic hub' and had grown to become one of the largest digital assessments and examination platforms. Over 80 per cent of high-scale examinations across 607 cities in India were conducted through its digital infrastructure.

During a TCS board meeting a few years later, when Professor Clayton Christensen, guru of 'disruptive innovation' and a board member at TCS, suggested that TCS must disrupt itself and explore the SME businesses, Chandra said, 'We've already done that!' Of his experience with TCS, Professor Christensen said, 'With other companies where I am a board member, I do my homework so that I can contribute. With TCS, I sit in the meeting with a writing pad so I can learn.

Creating the first 'all-women IT centre' in Saudi Arabia

Customer-centricity also meant thinking unconventionally and within the socio-economic context of the geography in which the company was operating. In September 2013, TCS was pitted against four competitors to set up a BPO centre in Saudi Arabia that would service clients such as Saudi Aramco and GE. Known for its restrictive practices against women, the deeply conservative Islamic kingdom had only 13 per cent of its women in the native workforce. During a discussion with the BPO team, Chandra suggested, 'Why not set up an all-women centre?'[31] The idea was instantly appreciated. Not only did the company win the contract, the pioneering initiative gave TCS a competitive advantage with social acceptance. With a 76–24 per cent equity partnership by TCS and GE respectively, the TCS All-Women Centre began at Riyadh in 2014. Probably among the first BPOs to set up shop in Saudi Arabia, it was the first one in the region to employ only women.

In the initial days, to get families on board, TCS invited fathers, brothers, husbands and other family members to accompany their women for interviews at the centre. They would be given a quick tour of the centre to demonstrate the company's commitment to keep it an all-women workplace. TCS ensured that even janitors and support staff in the campus were women. 'In cases where services of a man are required, announcements are made, so women employees can put on their abayas and niqabs—or leave the room,' shared Neeraj Srivastava, TCS regional director for Saudi Arabia and Bahrain.[32] To acclimatize first-time employees to the dos and don'ts of working in an office environment, over 610,000 cumulative hours of intensive training sessions were conducted. The centre worked with leading Saudi universities and educational institutes to build specialized training programmes that helped in job creation and employment opportunities for women in the kingdom.

By 2015, when Amal Fatani, a distinguished academic and promoter of women's empowerment in the kingdom was appointed as the centre head, it was no longer a BPO, but had become an integral part the TCS's global delivery network. The highpoint of the centre was a special visit by Prime Minister Narendra Modi on 2 April 2016 during his two-day bilateral visit to Saudi Arabia. After spending forty minutes at the centre interacting with women and even obliging for selfies, he said, 'The energetic atmosphere that I witnessed here today sends a strong message to the rest of the world. I congratulate TCS for their efforts in training talent in India and globally and making tomorrow's professionals equipped for the digital world.' In two years since its commencement, the centre had reached a milestone of hiring 1000 women professionals of which 85 per cent were Saudi nationals.

Unparalleled success, unequalled leadership

On 25 August 2004, TCS finally went public and became a dream script for everyone's investment portfolio. In the months leading to the IPO, Ramadorai underlined the TCS approach to value creation that was in alignment with the Tata way of business. 'The pressures from the stock market to be driven by quarterly goals will increase, but TCS remains committed to a philosophy that judiciously combines short-term interests with long-term ones,' he said.[33] In the subsequent years, the company lived up to this vision and remained a darling of the market and winner of the Standard and Poor's BSE IT Index with returns to retail shareholders at around 28 per cent CAGR. In simple words, this meant that if an investor had invested ₹1 lakh in 2004 in the TCS share at the issue price of ₹850, his investment in 2018 would be worth ₹16,47,058. This was a phenomenal return of 312 per cent over fourteen years. Moreover, it gifted shareholders with 1:1 bonus shares not once but thrice in 2006, 2009 and 2018. As a result, one share bought in 2004 would have multiplied into eight shares by 2018. Besides remarkable capital appreciation, TCS was known in the market for its dividend payout. On average, the company had paid ₹321 as dividend for a single share.

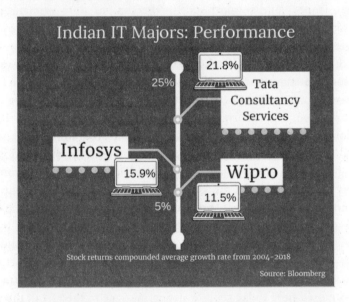

The day 19 April 2018 was momentous for the Tata Group, TCS, and its 550,651 shareholders. At the stroke of 10.30 a.m., India got its first IT company with a $100 billion (₹6.7 lakh crore) market capitalization, more than that of its other four rivals combined.[34] TCS was catapulted to an elite club of sixty-four companies in the world with 100 billion in market capitalization. This mark was special as it exceeded the GDP of 128 countries of the world, including Sri Lanka, Kenya and Luxemburg. The TCS market cap was 25 per cent higher than all 559 stocks listed on the Pakistan Stock Exchange combined. In proportionate terms, TCS contributed 62 per cent of the Tata Group's total market value of ₹10.79 lakh crore. The other twenty-nine listed companies together accounted for the remaining 38 per cent. It emerged as the most valued firm in India accounting for 4.43 per cent of BSE's total market cap[35]—a truly befitting gift in its golden jubilee year and the 150th year of its largest shareholder—the Tata Group. It was truly the making of a legend, a dream story of an in-house data processing unit becoming India's most valued company.

A dream team

In the fifty years since its formation, the company had only four CEOs. The contribution by each CEO was exceptional though contextual. Kohli gave the company a direction, fought scepticism, and through personal credibility gained international assignments. He recalled Nani Palkhivala, who was chairman of the executive committee of TCS for several years, spending an entire week overseas with Kohli to interact with customers and communicate the credibility that TCS brought with the Tata brand. Under their watchful guidance, the company grew from ten consultants in 1969 to 14,000 by 2000. Through a visionary initiative 'Top 10 by 2010' Ramadorai made TCS one among the top ten global consulting companies by 2009. During his tenure, the revenues multiplied twenty-five times from ₹1084 crore in 1998 to ₹27,813 crore in 2009. He expanded its global footprint to forty-two countries, including newer geographies such as Latin America, eastern Europe and China. The employee base also expanded tenfold to 143,000. During the 'Chandra years', TCS' consolidated revenues grew 4.2 times to ₹1,17,966 crore, and it became the second most valuable IT company in the world. The employee base increased nearly three times to 387,000 employees, and the company was rated the world's most powerful brand in IT services in 2015 and recognized as a global top employer by the Top Employers Institute across twenty-four countries. Unlike most CEOs that credit their pedigree from leading business schools in India and overseas, Chandrasekaran never attended a management programme. His rise to becoming the first non-Parsi, non-Tata-family chairman of Tata Sons (in February 2017) can be credited to the technical, management and leadership skills he learnt on the TCS treadmill.

Referring to the extraordinary contribution of Ramadorai and Chandra to TCS, Kohli reflected, 'I was looking for people who will build the industry for this country. I don't take any credit for their success.' On identifying great talent for TCS, he said, 'Your knowledge makes you a leader, as also your assessment of the qualities of individuals. And you will have the ability to assess others' qualities only when you yourself are a top-class human being.' Sharing his vision for the future, Chandrasekaran believed that digital—a combination of mobility, cloud, social, analytics and big data—was the biggest trend and must be harnessed. Kohli, at ninety-four years, had a more patriotic vision for TCS@50 and the IT industry. 'The IT industry should not be only an outsourcing industry. It should be addressing software requirements of the entire country and not just the software consultants in the US,' he stressed.

Fifty years ago, when the TCS story began, Accenture, Apple, Cisco, Compaq, Dell Microsoft, Oracle and Sun did not exist. Neither were technologies such as C, Java, LAN, Linux, Microprocessor or the World Wide Web invented. That's indicative of the power of the vision of J.R.D. and Kohli in building a company from scratch in an underdeveloped economy, which fifty years later became the world's second largest IT services company. TCS' role in pioneering the Indian IT industry gets further heightened as four of the top ten IT service providers in the world are from India.[36]

As the popular saying goes, 'Rome wasn't built in a day', the history of TCS and its industry-defining practices can be captured using three 'I's—insight, innovation and inspiration. Its business model provides important learnings that can be classified into five distinct phases. In the 1970s, it redefined the image of Indian software programmers. In the 1980s, it redefined software exports. In the 1990s, it redefined the quality paradigm in the IT industry. In the noughties, it redefined global software delivery. In the 2010s, it redefined the financial potential of an IT company while creating value for multiple stakeholders. For the global IT industry, TCS has been a pioneering and path-breaking 'disruptive business model'.[37]

CHAPTER 10

INNOVATION: TATA GROUP'S MANTRA FOR THE TWENTY-FIRST CENTURY

'No institute of science and technology can guarantee discoveries or inventions, and we cannot plan or command a work of genius at will. But do we give enough thought to nurturing the young investigator, to providing the right atmosphere and conditions of work and full opportunity for development? It is these things that foster invention and discovery.'[1]

J.R.D. Tata

Prakash Telang joined Tata Motors as a Tata Administrative Service manager in 1972. A peer of Professor Kasturi Rangan (my mentor at Harvard Business School) while studying at IIM Ahmedabad, Telang reminisced his early years at TELCO. We were sitting at the Tata Motors guest house in Pune, overseeing the picturesque lake, Sumant Sarovar, named in memory of TELCO's legendary leader—Sumant Moolgaokar. A manmade lake containing effluent-treated water, it was envisaged by Moolgaokar way back in the 1960s and constructed at an expense of ₹15 lakh. Nearly fifty years later, it continued to be a birdwatcher's delight with rare species regularly flocking to its banks from as far away as Tibet. With 150,000 trees planted in the vicinity, the place is a green oasis in Pimpri-Chinchwad—Pune's industrial area. Moolgaokar had empowered Vasant Kulkarni, manager (construction), to accomplish his vision of greening the whole area.[2] Under his guidance, the company's chief horticultural officer, B.D. Sharma, ably executed the plan in a barren neighbourhood. In those years, no tree could be cut on the factory premises without the chairman's written permission, which he never gave. It had to be transplanted.

With nostalgia writ large on his face, Telang went back to the 1970s. 'Innovation has now become a buzzword. But even in those years, Moolgaokar had started a growth division with the objective of doing something new all the time.' Given the learning opportunities, Telang, then in his twenties, opted to work in that division. 'We were expanding the TELCO plant in Pune and setting up a manufacturing facility for which we needed assembly conveyors, testing machines, furnaces, materials and equipment. We used to make most of them in the growth division.' He fondly recollected how Moolgaokar used to come to the Pune plant on Saturdays and interact with young members of the growth division. 'So, young man, what is the new thing that you are going to show me this time?' would be Moolgaokar's regular question to them. That sense of challenge, placed before them by the top leader to continuously innovate, ensured a high level of motivation. 'How can we do something that is required for the organization?' was the question topmost in their minds. At the same time, it wasn't innovation at any cost or of any quality. Moolgaokar had an eye for doing everything correctly. So, when the machine piping was not done well or if the wiring was slightly inclined, he would not even look at the machine, just walk away.

'These are the kinds of standards that he built into us in those formative days. We learnt quite a lot from a leader of his stature,' reminisced Telang, who became the Tata Motors' MD in 2009. 'We didn't call it "innovation" in those days, but innovativeness has always been a part of the Tata Group's sanskaar, its way of thinking,' observed Gopalakrishnan. 'In recent years, we have adopted the global practices associated with encouraging innovation in the group, and these have added more power to the spirit of innovation that has been such an integral part of the Tata way of doing business.'

Tata Motors' little elephant

A vital endeavour in Tata Group's innovation journey has been the creation of a culture within companies. The senior leadership play the biggest role to facilitate this. Let's continue with the example of Tata Motors to understand this better. Being in a product-based industry, their innovations have primarily been product-centric. From 1998 to 2008, Tata Motors has seen three incredibly innovative products that were firsts in the industry and in India. The top leadership had a unique vision for each of them. For example, in 1998, when Tata Indica, India's first indigenously manufactured car was launched, it was a culmination of Ratan Tata's vision to put India in the exclusive group of countries that had an indigenously designed and engineered car.

Half a decade later, a similar vision formed the basis for the super-successful commercial vehicle Tata Ace. An industry first, this mini-truck series revolutionized the light commercial vehicle (LCV) segment in India for last-mile connectivity. Ravi Kant, then vice chairman of Tata Motors, recalled how the idea of Ace first emerged.

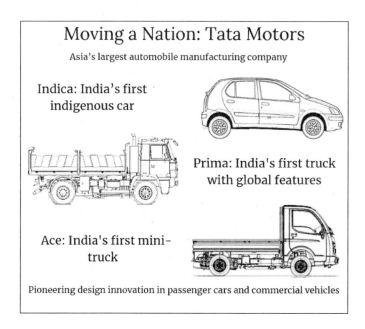

Moving a Nation: Tata Motors

Asia's largest automobile manufacturing company

Indica: India's first indigenous car

Prima: India's first truck with global features

Ace: India's first mini-truck

Pioneering design innovation in passenger cars and commercial vehicles

Sometime in the early years of the millennium, when we were doing a review of where we were and what requirements would emerge in the future, one of the key ideas which surfaced was that road development would bring goods and services even to remote villages. To facilitate that, we needed small trucks or buses.

It was the time when the Golden Quadrilateral and the Pradhan Mantri Gram Sadak Yojana projects had commenced in a big way under Prime Minister Atal Bihari Vajpayee. This led to demand creation of two types of commercial vehicles. The heavy trucks for the highways, and the smaller 'mini-trucks' for intra-city and rural usage. Tata Motors decided to focus on both. However, the execution strategy was different. It developed the heavy trucks by acquiring Daewoo Commercial Vehicles in South Korea. Thus, one arrow of Tata Motors' growth strategy pointed overseas, and how they could get into global markets. This led to the design and development of the now-popular Tata Prima truck with a 40-tonne capacity.

The other arrow pointed at the mass market in India for which a different kind of vehicle was required. The senior management was in favour of proactively exploring a smaller commercial vehicle as its demand was historically less cyclical compared to large vehicles. The idea of a 'cheap, nasty and rugged vehicle for India' was sealed during a strategic review meeting of the Tata Motors executives with Lord Kumar Bhattacharya of the Warwick Manufacturing Group in the UK.[3] In our conversation at the Tata Motors guest house in Pune, where most of these grand projects were envisaged and discussed, Girish Wagh, now head of the commercial vehicle business, reminisced the early days of ideation of the Tata Ace. The young team of engineers headed by Wagh, then just thirty years old, was given the mandate to explore customer requirements at lower end of the market.

Understanding customers' tangible and intangible requirements was possible only by spending a lot of time with them and experiencing the pains they went through with a product. Three weeks in the field interacting with target customers provided interesting insights to the team. 'I used to move around with three-wheeler drivers and ask them about the kind of product they need. All of them used to ask for the four-wheelers and give very rational and functional reasons,' shared Wagh. The typical reasons were capacity to overload, greater stability, and ability to go longer distances. 'I used to probe further to get the intangibles. When you spend the whole day with them, you build trust and they feel confident to confide in you.'

One such three-wheeler driver told Wagh that he was driving his father's vehicle, as his father had developed a spinal cord problem due to constant vibrations experienced while driving. 'Can you make something, which will have less vibrations?' he asked. A lesser-known ergonomic requirement was thus captured. Another truck driver in Ahmedabad complained of competition from three-wheeler commercial vehicles that could deliver faster and at much lower costs. He wanted a truck half the size of the market leader in the heavy commercial vehicles—Tata 407.[4] Wagh travelled with another three-wheeler owner near Coimbatore for the entire day. He kept enquiring the reasons for his preference for a four-wheeler. While at first he gave the usual reasons, at the end of the day when they both came back to his starting point, he took Wagh aside and said, 'If I have a four-wheeler, I will get better marriage proposals in the village.' Wagh was startled at this revelation. In the subsequent weeks, several drivers repeated this motive. This was something he and his team had never thought of—the family and matrimonial prestige associated with a four-wheeler in the hinterland! 'This was a very deep emotional reason, which we wouldn't have known without spending time with them. It was important that we find these insights because they would become enduring reasons to buy the product later,' he observed.

By the time the team returned to the Pune plant, over 4000 truck and three-wheeler operators from rural and semi-urban areas had been interviewed. The feedback was clear. The three-wheeler owners aspired to own a four-wheeler but couldn't afford it. The four-wheeler owners wanted a vehicle at the cost of a three-wheeler but didn't want to downgrade themselves due to the lower prestige associated with driving it. They were looking for a last-mile-distribution vehicle that had low maintenance costs, higher driver safety, and better driving comfort. At that time, the sub-four-tonne market was dominated by three-wheelers with Bajaj Auto, Mahindra and Mahindra, and Piaggio as key players. No one in the industry had thought that four-wheeler trucks could fit into that space. A sweet spot for a new product offering emerged at Tata Motors.

On one of those days when Ratan Tata had come to the Pune plant for project review meetings, Wagh and his team decided to share their findings with him. It had been a long day for Tata. He had been doing standing review meetings on the shop floor continuously for seven hours. Wagh and team were the last of the reviews, and he appeared tad tired. When Wagh started talking about their learnings from the field and the opportunity for a new product for mass market consumers, he saw Ratan Tata's eyes light up. He went through the entire presentation with utmost attention, and at the end, said, 'This appears to be a very good opportunity. This is something we need to do and I am ready to support it with whatever is required.' He made this comment in the presence of a large group and demonstrated his commitment to the rank and file. The entire senior team at Tata Motors understood his vision for this new product, which was for the base of the pyramid market, hitherto not envisaged by the competition.

K.R.S. Jamwal, executive director at Tata Industries, called the Ace an example of classic Ratan Tata thinking. Having assisted him on strategy-related matters concerning Tata companies in the years when Tata Ace was in the making, Jamwal had closely watched him craft strategies. 'He was a person who looked a lot at data and numbers. Some of the best ideas come from a person who looks at things differently. We could see him derive insights about a different view of the world.' Without such insights, companies typically tend to be just a follower. They wait for someone else to identify the opportunity and then quickly copy that. That's what the competition did after the Ace was launched—they jumped on the bandwagon.

While the value proposition and positioning of Ace was itself an innovation, the Ace journey from idea to market was one of the many firsts for Tata Motors. Due to massive losses faced by Tata Motors in the previous years caused by recessionary trends in the commercial vehicle business, the product development budget for Ace was kept at an all-time low of $50 million, one-eighth of that for Indica. For comparison, the average budget allocated by multinational companies for developing a single auto-platform was $500 million. Interestingly, it was also the first time at Tata Motors that a new product development project was given to an extremely young team, and cross-functional teams were formed for product development.

The team decided to keep the target price of Ace at ₹2 lakh. This was the upper limit at which three-wheelers were currently available in the market and would make it an attractive proposition for three-wheeler drivers to progress to a four-wheeler. To attract a price-sensitive customer looking for long-term economy, the Ace would be able to deliver goods at the cost of ₹6.70 per tonne per kilometre as compared to the segment average of ₹8.54. Its powerful engine designed in-house and comfortable interiors would provide flexibility to the driver to run trips of up to 500 km per day without stops for refuelling.[5] This meant that a round-trip drive between Mumbai and Pune could be completed within a day. Moreover, at a time when three-wheelers were banned on expressways and large commercial vehicles were not allowed within city limits, Ace would become the only vehicle in India allowed on every road. For this, the team decided to meet certain emission standards and crash safety regulations.[6]

While there were innovations in designing and manufacturing, there were innovations even in sourcing and marketing. It became the first product of Tata Motors to use e-sourcing and outsourced over 80 per cent of parts from 120 suppliers. This was far better than its own average of outsourcing 60 per cent parts from nearly 400 suppliers for commercial vehicles. The suppliers were given design and cost targets, and they too innovated to deliver as per specifications. Tata Motors used a multilingual marketing approach and positioned Ace as India's first mini-truck. The ad campaign referring to Ace as *Chhota Hathi* was a thumping success, especially in Tamil Nadu, where Ace came to be popularly called *Chinna Annai* (little elephant), based on TV commercials. A new dealership network was set up to improve access for small-time entrepreneurs who would be driving the vehicle themselves. To make it cost-effective, sales-only outlets[7] were set up by Tata Motors dealers. Within 100 days, over 300 new distribution points came up across India. Tata Motors Finance Ltd, the company's financing arm, even offered financing options to make purchase easy for first-time buyers.

In May 2005, the Ace was finally launched at a market price of ₹2,25,000. The vehicle became a resounding success. In the first year itself, it sold nearly 100 vehicles every day, and far exceeded company expectations. By 2007, over 100,000 units were sold, the first cargo-carrying commercial vehicle in India to achieve that record. Given the demand, production had to be shifted from the existing Pune plant to a special plant constructed for Tata Ace at Pantnagar in Uttarakhand. Prasann Kumar Chobe, former head of the Pantnagar plant, recollected the occasion when Ratan Tata visited the plant and interacted with the young team, many of whom were locals. As per their tradition, they wanted to touch his feet in respect, but he would not allow them. Instead, he embraced them.

The tremendous response received by Ace encouraged Tata Motors to launch over a dozen products built on the Ace platform. This included the Tata Magic series, which focused on last-mile passenger travel. A decade later, the Tata Ace family of products had sold 20 lakh vehicles, making it one of the most successful products of the company ever. With 85 per cent market share, it became one of the most preferred choices of Indian entrepreneurs and small businesses. It enabled new businesses, generated employment and stimulated entrepreneurship, and was seen in the hills, crowded cities, and on small-town roads. Over the decade since its launch, one in every five commercial vehicles sold in India across 1600 showrooms was from the Tata Ace family. It eventually established a global footprint through sales spanning twenty-eight countries across South Asia, Africa and the ASEAN. Impressed by its performance during the trials, Ratan Tata had given the name Ace. The vehicle lived up to its name.

Visionary goals and passionate teams

'Everyone is catering to the top of the pyramid. The challenge we've given to all our companies is to address a different market. Pare your margins. Create new markets.'[8]

Ratan Tata

Both Tata Indica and Tata Ace had a pattern. To borrow the term from *Built to Last* by Collins and Porras,[9] Indica and Ace were 'big hairy audacious goals' (BHAG). The top leadership's commitment to achieve the end objectives made all the difference. Therefore, the first characteristic of the culture of innovation at Tata Motors was to have visionary goals that could lead to game-changing innovations. It wasn't game-changing in terms of gaining market share and fabulous financials alone, but also at a superordinate level—placing India on the automobile engineering and production map, or addressing the base-of-the-pyramid requirement for last-mile-delivery vehicles.

The next step in building an innovation culture was to put in place a team of passionate and highly committed individuals, with a belief in BHAG. This was complemented by altering existing organizational structure and hierarchies that could hinder innovative thinking. Wagh reminisced Ratan Tata's proactive participation in empowering teams. He often told them that he would like to be part of the problem-solving process. Through his involvement and appreciation, he created an environment, where there was no fear of failure. This was a vital element for building the culture of innovation. This is probably counter-intuitive to how efficient organizations work. They typically have well-defined goals and targets, and people get paid based on how much they have achieved. However, to do something that was never done before, they needed a different approach.

Let's see how this happened with the help of a real example. The story of the origin of Tata Nano is well known. The disruptive and unprecedented innovations involved in the making of Nano are well documented by most leading business schools globally. At the peak of the rainy season, Ratan Tata was travelling in his car. At a traffic signal, he saw a family of four perched precariously on a scooter. As the signal turned green, he was hoping that they wouldn't slip, but they did. That's when he thought of a better mode of transportation for the Indian masses.

> Most innovators are intense observers. They carefully watch the world around them, and as they observe how things work, they often become sensitized to what doesn't work. As they engage in these types of observations, they begin to connect common threads across unconnected data, which may provoke uncommon business ideas.[10]

This was a key skill of disruptive innovators shared by Dyer, Gregerson and Christensen in the context of Ratan Tata's powerful insight gained just by observing a family of four on a scooter that rainy day in Mumbai.

While this is one part of the story that is often reported, the other lesser-known one is that Ratan Tata had been contemplating an affordable means of transportation since the year 2000—three years before he first mentioned the idea in an interview to the *Financial Times* in Germany. Over the years, the idea became concretized through discussions with the senior team—a mode of transportation that is affordable for families belonging to the lower strata of society. The final specifications emerged as all-weather, safe (Euro IV compliant) and affordable. The price of ₹1 lakh was also given as a casual reference during that interview in 2003. However, the media stuck to it, and Ratan Tata accepted it as a challenge.

Let's go back to the year 2005 when Wagh was nominated project director for Tata Motor's small car project, now popularly called Tata Nano. He recalled how Ratan Tata proactively participated in the evolutionary progress of the project. During these interactions, he did not act as the chairman, but as a team leader of an innovation in the making. He could easily have delegated these nitty-gritty steps to the senior leadership at Tata Motors, yet he was on-site to calibrate and celebrate every small development. A good example of this was when the engine of Tata Nano was redesigned thrice. When the first engine prototype was ready, Tata personally came to the Pune plant and drove around in the mule cart (an agricultural version of what a car would eventually be). He was not happy with the power of the engine and suggested that the team needed to work further. Benchmarking the design with an established segment is easier as the target can be pegged against where the competition is or what the customer expects. But, it was quite a challenge for the team to design the engine for a car that had no parallel in the world, and which was attempting to create a segment of its own. At such times, Tata himself wore the hat of the customer and made the judgement on what would be acceptable. The team worked for six months and prepared the prototype for a bigger engine. He again came to Pune and tested it. He appreciated the improvement but wanted more changes. Again, the team worked for six months and improved the output. Finally, when he drove around in the mule cart with engine version 3.0, he was satisfied. Through this iterative and participative approach, Tata as the leader created working principles. This involved appreciating what was done well. For what didn't meet expected performance levels, he encouraged the team to stretch and do even better.

R. Venkataramanan, now managing trustee at Tata Trusts, served as vice president in Ratan Tata's office for nearly a decade. In our interaction, he recalled that Ratan Tata would test every new car that came out of the Tata Motors stable. He would patiently listen to the engineering team's logic on various design features, but would ultimately tell them, 'Try to put yourself in the customers' shoes and see what he wants. He doesn't care how you get it. It is the engineering team and the company's job to ensure that happens.' The customers' experience ultimately mattered for the success of any product or service.

'A very important source for innovation is the customer himself. When senior leadership meets with customers and understands their problems, a lot of innovation happens,' observed Sanjaya Sharma, then CEO at Tata Interactive Systems (TIS), and a lifer at the Tata Group. He narrated the example of an entirely new product category that TIS designed for their customer—Credit Suisse, which wanted to drive traffic to their corporate website. They thought that putting learning modules on their corporate page would make it interesting for people. 'Nobody puts learning objects on the corporate website. And, if you put learning objects on the corporate website, you can't expect people to spend more than a couple of minutes on that,' observed Sanjaya. Based on this specific requirement of the client, TIS designed 'learning nuggets', short capsules of information aimed at enhancing managerial acumen and building soft skills to deliver behavioural change. This solution was a radical departure in the e-learning space and was an answer to the problem of information overload where attention and time remained scarce commodities. TIS compressed twenty-minute computer-based learning modules into 100-second learning nuggets that were interactive, multimedia-enabled and animated. 'We found that the client did get a very good response to our solution, and traffic moved to those learning nuggets on their corporate website,' concluded Sanjaya. This innovation was a clear outcome of listening to the customers' problems and thinking creatively. Thus, customer-centricity is a core tenet of the innovation journey, irrespective of the industry.

Removing fear of failure

In 2006, Wagh met Ratan Tata at Bombay House. It was the time when Tata Motors was setting up the Tata Nano manufacturing plant at Singur, West Bengal. Accompanying Wagh was M.B. Kulkarni, construction-in-charge for the factory. During the meeting, he explained the topography of the land to Tata. The 1100-acre land allocated for the factory had a frontage of the Kolkata–Delhi highway of around 3.5 km. There was also a small rivulet flowing through the area. When he saw the topography, Tata observed that the highway was at a height of 13–14 feet from the ground level, whereas the construction team was planning to fill the factory land only up to 7 feet. The difference in the height could lead to problems. Kulkarni submitted that their team had analysed flooding data of the previous twenty-five years and arrived at that conclusion. Given that filling 1100 acres of land would require a huge amount of sand or fly ash, these decisions required approvals at an earlier stage. Tata gave his approval and the construction progressed as planned. By 2007, the land filling was done to the height of 7 feet and the construction work began. The foundation of the plant had come up to the plinth level, several feet above the ground level.

It was the peak of the monsoon season, and there were heavy rains in the region in September–October 2007. One evening before the team left the plant at Singur there was heavy flooding. That night, somebody opened the sewage gates to release water from the rivulet to avoid flooding and damage to irrigation. Consequently, the entire plant got flooded. The next day when employees came to the factory they saw a 'lake' instead of the plant site! The water had risen far above the compound walls. The police and security were moving around in boats! So, the team decided to revise the construction plan and raise the plinth levels. For this, a lot of reworking had to be done, which involved extra time and resources. Wagh informed Kant, then MD, who suggested that the two of them come to Mumbai and explain the changes to Ratan Tata. This made Wagh extremely apprehensive. He instantly recollected Tata's observation a year ago about the difference between the height of the highway and that of the factory land. What would his reaction be now that their decision had backfired?

The change would involve crores of rupees and a delay in the proposed timeline of the product launch. With palpable anxiety, Wagh presented the changes, costs and time requirement to Ratan Tata. He heard them patiently and asked just one question, 'From where did water come into the plant?' After hearing the details, he finally said, 'Good, go ahead.' Wagh and Kulkarni couldn't believe their ears. They had anticipated a sound thrashing given that they had miscalculated the requirements despite the group chairman pointing out his concern. But he was composed, and focused on action rather than regrets. Unable to believe his reaction, at the end of the meeting, Wagh went up to him and confessed that he was nervous for not abiding by the chairman's suggestion given a year ago. In response Tata said, 'Yes, I remember what I said. But that's okay. I see that you have learnt from this experience. Whatever you are doing now is the right thing, so please go ahead and do it.' This was a classic example of removing fear from failure at the highest levels of the organization. For a project of this magnitude, this was a very high-scale failure. It cost a lot of money, and four months' loss of time. However, Ratan Tata's approach was very different. He was keen to promote the truthfulness and genuine intent of his team. 'How can you have the fear of failure when you have this kind of support!', acknowledged Wagh.

Ragunath Mashelkar, the eminent scientist, had once compared innovation to a child. It needs a mother to take care of it on a continuous basis. It also needs a father to ensure that timely resources are provided. At times, when it is unwell, it also needs a paediatrician to provide remedial medication. Organizational leadership must don all three roles and create an environment that fosters innovation. This can be called organizational innovation. When such a work culture gets embedded into the company ethos, people are inspired to think laterally and experiment with ideas. Organizational innovation can lead to process innovation. Questioning the status quo and exploring newer processes ultimately lead to product and service innovation. This has been the experience of several Tata companies. Arup Basu, president of new businesses and innovation at Tata Chemicals, shared his perspective. 'If innovation must happen in a sustained manner, we need to democratize it. It can no longer be at the top. It must be top-down as well as bottom-up. This can happen only through the right culture, right processes and right strategy.'

Celebrating innovation

The opening of the Indian economy marked the beginning of innovation as an integral part of Tata companies. Tata Sons encouraged Tata companies to adopt innovation as a strategic approach to global growth through a three-pronged strategy:

i. Better communication and recognition of innovative ideas and efforts;
ii. Facilities for learning from other companies; and
iii. Support for collaborative research and partnerships with academic institutions.

While business excellence was the binding glue of the Tata Group, innovation became the mantra for each Tata company to distinguish itself in its industry and to create a niche for itself through its products, processes or services. Several Tata companies invested in establishing R & D centres across the globe to stay abreast of the latest technologies and innovations.[11] Ranjit Joshipura, deputy general manager for innovation at Tata Sons, highlighted the multi-company pollination at the Tata Group as its greatest strength that could be leveraged for making innovations happen. 'Given the unique configuration of the Tata Group with over 100 companies, you have a huge intellectual property floating around, which needs to be harnessed.'

Ravi Arora, now vice president of innovation at Tata Sons, recollected a landmark 2006 visit to the USA that reinforced the group's passion and commitment to innovation. A group of twenty top leaders from Tata companies, including CEOs and CXOs, spent ten days at leading US companies known for their core competence in innovation. These included 3M, Intel, Microsoft, and Hewlett–Packard. The visit concluded with a day-long interaction with innovation guru Professor Christensen from Harvard Business School.[12] In one of the interactions after the team returned to India, Ratan Tata asked them about their key learning. One of the simplest things they learnt was to celebrate innovations by Tata companies. This wasn't happening despite achievements by group companies. In 2006, the group kicked off an annual event to recognize innovation and celebrate the successes and struggles of the group's innovation endeavours, now called Innovista.

To build on the momentum, Ratan Tata envisaged a body that would fuel the wheels of innovation across group companies. Accordingly, the

Tata Group Innovation Forum (TGIF)[13] was set up in 2007 to integrate the Tata culture with innovation-focused process orientation. Managed by Tata Quality Management Services (TQMS), it was headed by Gopalakrishnan. The impact of TGIF and the efforts of TQMS could be seen from the fact that from 101 innovation projects submitted by group companies at Innovista 2006, the number expanded to 5000 projects by 2017—a fiftyfold increase in a decade. The projects submitted to Innovista are those implemented within Tata companies. A very innovative 'Dare to Try' Award is also given to teams that have made audacious attempts at innovation but couldn't achieve the expected results. A jury of 400 senior leaders from across Tata Group companies evaluate these 5000 projects through a robust process. The shortlisted entries are presented at four regions across India and three cities across the globe. The five to six winning entries from each semi-final are brought to Mumbai for the finals. In a day-long event on 20 April, sixty teams make presentations in parallel tracks. The jury consists of the who's who of India Inc. They ask searching questions to the participants before deciding on the awards. On 21 April, the top twelve teams are given the Innovista award by the group chairman. In my interactions, one of the TQMS members compared Innovista with the Filmfare Awards. Like Filmfare celebrates Bollywood stars, Innovista celebrates the Tatas' innovation stars!

Barriers to innovation

A constant conflict with respect to innovation is the pressure to balance short-term financial output with long-term investments. How to manage this? Most Tata companies follow a three-wave approach. Wave zero is about quarterly and yearly results. These are important from the shareholders' perspective and provide funds to invest in the future. Wave one is about incremental innovation that builds on existing products, such as launching new variants for existing products and exploring new segments. For example, Tata Global Beverages markets a brand of drinking water called Tata Water Plus fortified with nutrients, such as copper, which helps support bodily functions, and zinc, which helps strengthen the immune system. While it looks and tastes like normal water, it is a solution to the deficiency of these minerals in many Indians. Harish Bhat, brand custodian at Tata Sons, called the wave one products those that can build on top of a company's existing portfolio and where investments may not be that significant. Yet, it does require investment and focus.

The most far-reaching innovations come under wave two. These are disruptive innovations, new categories of business or new methods of approaching existing categories. 'In any budgeting or business planning that we do, we always keep aside funds for wave one and wave two,' observed Bhat. 'The Tata Group leadership has always encouraged us not to sacrifice the later waves for the sake of the current year, and to invest for the future.'

A fine example of wave two innovation is the budget hotels brand—Ginger. Launched under Roots Corporations, a Taj subsidiary, Ginger Hotels was promoted as a Tata Enterprise. Formerly planned as IndiOne, the name Ginger was selected by Ratan Tata as a fresh and out-of-the-box name. Initiated under the leadership of Krishna Kumar, then vice chairman of Indian Hotels, and inspired by Professor C.K. Prahalad's concept of 'bottom of the pyramid', Ginger catered to a new concept of 'smart business hotels' without frills and fuss. It targeted the 2-crore business travellers and tourists who could not afford luxury and star hotels and looked for economy hospitality services—a major gap then existing in the sector. Ginger emerged as an example of business model innovation. It provided contemporary and functional facilities at one-third the tariff of similar offerings in high-end hotels. Launched on 25 June 2004, all Ginger Hotels were strategically located close to central business districts. The latent demand for such an offering and the trust in a Tata enterprise were evident from the fact that the first Ginger at Whitefield in Bangalore was booked out for two years on the day of its launch.[14] With direct competition from unbranded mom-and-pop kind of hotels, Ginger scored on three critical factors: affordability, hygiene and security. Within five years of its launch, the South Asian Travel Tourism Expo named Ginger the 'best budget hotel chain' in India. By 2018, Ginger became the largest pan-India budget brand hotel with over forty properties across thirty locations, especially lesser-known destinations.

While several Tata companies have been innovation trailblazers, several others need to catch up. During my interactions with many leaders at Tata Sons, a common observation was a greater need for commitment to innovation at the top levels of Tata companies. While employees at the junior and the middle levels are gung-ho about innovation, the senior leadership's commitment and appetite for risk is seldom lacking. Thus, strategy feeding the innovation engine is a gap that needs to be fixed. Many companies still feel that innovation is 'good to have' and not 'must have'. This transition from 'good to have' to 'must have', where companies must innovate to survive is vital. While TQMS and TGIF strongly recommend to Tata companies' leadership that they must include innovation as part of their strategy roadmap in their annual strategy document and have targets and objective KRAs around innovation for their entire company and hierarchy, these are not mandatory.

Venkataramanan shared a personal observation from Ratan Tata's visit to the Google headquarters in 2012–13. To make a difference to customers or the market, Google emphasized on making an exponential difference. Marginal improvements of 10 to 15 per cent were not enough. Ratan Tata was impressed with Google's innovation strategy that unless an idea—product or service— was a game changer that was a 10x multiple of what it was today, they weren't interested in supporting it. Ratan Tata believed that such an orientation had to be incorporated in the culture and DNA of every organization. Nearly half a decade earlier, speaking at the J.R.D. QV Award ceremony in 2007, he had communicated a similar vision on innovation for the Tata Group, and the creation of an enabling ecosystem:

> What I would like to see is innovation that perhaps leads to disruptive technologies that basically comes from creating an environment that allows our people to dream, giving those people the encouragement to convert those dreams into reality, motivating those people to make that happen, and not to slap them down because it has not been done before.

He wanted Tata companies to move beyond the initial steps in innovation undertaken as part of TBEM, and play a much larger, transformative and pivotal role in the future.

Drivers of innovation at Tata Group

> 'Pure research has to happen, but even more important is to come up with innovative models to ensure that what we have is available to all. We need different kinds of innovation based on access.'[15]
>
> N. Chandrasekaran

What can other companies learn from the Tata Group about innovation? What makes Tata companies innovative? What are the core drivers of innovation at Tata companies? Five clear insights emerge. Let me elaborate on these with relevant examples.

Firstly, Tata companies want to provide consumers with best-in-class products. An innovation is typically in response to a solution that the consumer is seeking. The consumer may be seeking the solution vividly or in a subliminal way. Either way, it must be a solution that fulfils the consumer's needs.

Titan's products are a good example to elaborate this. College-going youth in India were looking for a brand of watches that matched their lifestyle and dressing sense, and communicated their attitude. Fastrack was a solution to that latent need of a youthful consumer. Another example is Raga. This brand of watches for the Indian women almost look like pieces of jewellery. They were a solution to a need that Indian women were seeking but wasn't fulfilled by Western-looking watches available then. Raga was a perfect accessory with saris and beautiful Indian dresses and looked elegant with traditional Indian jewellery. The Mia line of jewellery by Tanishq is another example of satisfying a latent need of the modern young working women for fashionable yet affordable jewellery. All the pieces in Mia are crafted in 14-karat gold, making the collection durable and lighter on pocket, and yet providing superior finish, wide variety and striking designs. Mia was acknowledged as a great example of design innovation, process innovation, branding innovation and sales innovation—all rolled into one.

The second driver of innovation has been the Tata Group drive to constantly do something new, which adds to the category or industry. They wish to be thought leaders and idea leaders across industries. So, if the Nano was an innovation in the car category or Tata Water Plus an innovation in the beverages category, it was driven by this desire. Tata companies are not happy being a participant in an industry. They would like to be leaders, not just in terms of market share, but also in terms of doing something different and being the first mover.

Tata Steel's Pravesh brand of steel doors and windows is a fine example of category addition. Blending the elegant looks of wood and the inherent strength of steel, Pravesh doors were waterproof and termite-proof. They emerged as a relevant innovation for rural areas, but were also used in Bombay House for its utility, durability and visual appeal. The example of industry-level addition is evident at 500 of Tata Steel's exclusive retail stores where the company provided not just construction/maintenance products and home aesthetic products, but also the service of installing them as per customer specifications. It not only sold steel for making a shed, but also built the shed for the consumer, who was spared the time and effort of engaging different agencies. From 2008, it introduced completely customizable modular wardrobes, extensive range of smart and stylish furniture, and became one-stop shops providing end-to-end customer service. It empowered Indian consumers to expect a superior retailing experience while shopping for steel, a first in India's largely unorganized retail steel space.

Let's take another example: Tata Sampann Besan, which was introduced for health-conscious food connoisseurs. An important product of Tata Chemicals' consumer product business, besan (gram flour) is traditionally used in Indian households to make fried snacks such as pakoras and *fafdas*. While deep-frying increases the deliciousness of the food item, it also brings along health hazards. Increasing health awareness among urban consumers stimulated the company to research about reducing the oil content of fried products without altering the taste. Various analyses were performed at Tata Chemicals labs to understand the physical, chemical and material properties of besan. After several rounds of testing, the results showed that a lower particle size of besan led to a 20 per cent reduced oil absorption than common market brands. This led to the introduction of a differentiated 'low oil absorb' besan with a reduced oil uptake. The product became popular.

The third key driver of innovation is the focus on mass market. A lot of Indians want products that deliver good value but are unable to pay for them. This is the segment that Tata companies have increasingly focused on in recent decades. Tata Global Beverages' Tata Agni Tea or Titan's Sonata brand of watches focus on making good products of reliable quality accessible to consumers at a price point affordable by consumers at the base of the economic pyramid, which is a very large segment in India.[16] This objective is achieved by engineering services in a way that they bring value to consumers at the price they want to pay, such as in the case of Ginger Hotels. It can also be achieved by dramatically new designs or product ideas, such as in the case of Tata Swach, which deserves some elaboration.

The story of Swach began as the 'Sujal' water filter developed by TCS at the Tata Research Development and Design Centre (TRDDC) in Pune with 85 per cent purifying capability. Sujal was extensively distributed as part of the company's CSR initiative in providing drinking water in the hinterland and during disaster rehabilitation. A 2006 visit by Gopalakrishnan to TRDDC led to the commencement of a journey of transforming Sujal into a fast-moving consumer durable for the mass market. According to a WHO and UN study, 80 per cent of diseases and 33 per cent of deaths in India were caused by unsafe drinking water. An estimated 500,000 children below the age of five years died every year due to diarrhoea. Nearly 85 per cent of people in small towns and villages hardly used any water-purifying methods. To cater to this segment, during one of the first meetings, Gopalakrishnan threw an unexpected challenge at the team led by Sabaleel Nandy, a young TAS officer, 'Could they try for drinking water what Thomas Edison had done for lighting through his electric bulb?' The team thus received a mandate to create a 'bulb-like' water purifier that had to meet four distinct requirements: must use natural materials; can be used by homes having no electricity or running water; must be portable and easy for the consumer to buy and use; and must provide bacteria free water of international standards.

While the basic product was provided by TCS, the advanced product development process was led by Tata Chemicals. The use of nano-silver and nano-coating technology led to the design of a product that achieved the mandated 99.99 per cent purity levels acknowledged by international laboratories in the UK and the Netherlands. Despite the estimated capex of ₹9 crore, the team effectively delivered within ₹1.5 crore.[17] It partnered with the precision equipment manufacturing division at Titan for making the production assembly equipment for the filter. All these enabled Swach to create a new benchmark in the low-cost offline water-purifier market. The product was priced at ₹1000 per unit, which was 50 per cent less than HUL's Pureit and Eureka Forbes' Aquasure. The cost of the replacement filter cartridge was ₹300. This combination made Swach the lowest cost water purifier in the world with a cost of 10 paise per litre for pure drinking water. Citing Swach, Professor Alhstrom from the Chinese University of Hong Kong observed that by concentrating on bringing lower-end disruptive innovation to the market, firms can do untold good for consumers, particularly those in developing economies, while creating sizable new businesses that facilitate economic growth.[18]

Rallis, a subsidiary of Tata Chemicals, had a huge network of 30,000 retailers. It was roped in for the distribution of Swach. It complemented Tata Kisan Sansar, Tata Chemicals' own distribution network that was spread across 23,000 villages with a reach of 23-lakh farmers.[19] Two other Tata companies— Tata Business and Support Services Ltd and Tata Teleservices Ltd—provided call centre and toll-free number facilities for Swach customers. By 2013, more than 10-lakh units of Swach were sold across twenty states of India, of which more than 80 per cent were first-time users. Several national and international awards also poured in. Swach also became a platform for six Tata companies to work synergistically by providing research, design, manufacture, distribution and aftersales service facilities—an unprecedented initiative, which itself was an innovation. It demonstrated the collective power of the Tata Group.

The fourth key aspect of innovation is creating a culture. The examples of Tata Swach, Tata Ace and Titan Edge illustrate how leading Tata companies and their top leadership worked towards creating a culture that encouraged innovation by a younger generation of employees, who were empowered to deliver without the fear of failure. This is the driver that most senior leaders emphasized on during my interactions. In our conversation, Syamal Gupta, former director of Tata Sons, stressed that the core of innovation is creating an enabling organization culture. 'Innovation cannot be delivered just by establishing innovation centres. It has to be embedded in the DNA of the company,' he said as he reminisced his fifty-year-long association with the Tata Group. Six common features can be observed in the innovation culture of most Tata companies. These include:

Mission: A mission to redefine industry standards and benchmarks
Expertise: An internal team of experts

Team and leadership: A young and dynamic cross-functional team led by an enthusiastic people manager

Top-management involvement: Top-level involvement, removal of rigid organizational hierarchies to ensure free flow of ideas and their implementation

Stakeholder synergies: Greater synergies through collaboration and long-term relationships with supply-chain partners

Financial prudence: A budget to ensure optimal utilization of resources, yet no cap on ideas and genuine experiments

Finally, and most importantly, underpinning all these is the desire within the Tata Group *to be pioneers in India, pioneers for India*. Pioneers are individuals who set new boundaries and venture into hitherto unexplored avenues. The example of Tata Salt is apposite. In the early 1980s, the Government of India in collaboration with UNICEF was actively promoting the use of iodized salt to counter iron deficiency, especially in children. In 1984, goitre, a disease caused due to iodine deficiency, had reached endemic proportions. Prime Minister Indira Gandhi approached Tata Chemicals to address this rising concern. The company took it up as an opportunity to serve communities in need. It launched a nationwide movement of salt iodization, with India's first-ever iodized salt—Tata Salt. Over the years, Tata Salt created a strong emotional connect with customers, and was often ranked as India's most trusted food brand in later years. An entire generation, including myself, grew up listening to the popular jingle '*Namak Ho Tata Ka—Tata Namak*' on Doordarshan. When I had visited Mithapur, the salt town established by Tata Chemicals, I could not but miss the big board at the entrance of the factory that read: '*Hum Desh Ka Namak Khate Hain, Hum Desh Ka Namak Banate Hain*' (We are faithful to our country, we make the salt of India).

By 2016, more than 70,000 tonnes of Tata Salt were sold in 3000 towns through 16.6 lakh retail outlets reaching 13.5 crore households and 60-crore Indians each month. It was the market leader commanding a share of 24.7 per cent of the national branded salt category. The stupendously selling Tata Salt made Tata Chemicals reach more consumers in India than any other Tata company. Capturing the essence of the Tata Salt story, Gopalakrishnan observed, 'Taking a common commodity, such as salt, packaging it and making it India's largest food brand, and developing a whole ecology of a business system around it is a huge innovation that we tend not to focus upon, because we take it for granted.'

Whether steel, hospitality, power, aviation or IT, India has witnessed the pioneering spirit of the Tata Group ever since it was founded 150 years ago. That spirit has remained the unseen foundation of innovations galore at the House of Tata.

CHAPTER 11

THE EMPIRE STRIKES BACK?

'At the Tatas, we believe that if we are not among the top three in an industry, we should look seriously at what it would take to become one of the top three players—or think about exiting the industry.'

Ratan Tata

It was 14 August 2001—eve of the fifty-fifth anniversary of India's independence. The country was listening to the presidential address by K.R. Narayanan, which was being telecast on Doordarshan from New Delhi. Over 1400 km away in Mumbai, a dramatic announcement was made at the annual general meeting (AGM) of TELCO (now Tata Motors) by Ratan Tata. He offered to step down from the chairmanship of the company owning responsibility for the ₹500-crore loss suffered by TELCO that financial year. It was the biggest ever loss reported by an Indian company until then. Moreover, it had come just four years after TELCO had achieved the feat of becoming the first Indian company to achieve revenues of ₹10,000 crore. The dramatic offer from Tata came after a section of agitated shareholders asked difficult questions to the board for the company's dismal performance at a stormy AGM.[1] Seeing the commitment of Tata Group's senior-most leader, the shareholders were pacified and rejected his offer.

The AGM was a turning point for TELCO. It began a process of introspection within the company, which had enjoyed impressive profits since its founding in 1945 by J.R.D. Tata. In its five-decade history, it had never missed giving a dividend. So much was the confidence and command that TELCO enjoyed in the Indian markets, that it charged a healthy margin on top of its costs. Customers were not only willing to pay that price, but were also ready to wait for several months on a wait list to buy a TELCO truck. Then what happened suddenly? Was it the huge investment of ₹1700 crore that TELCO made in the new passenger car business,[2] which culminated in the launch of the Indica two years earlier? Let's go back seven decades and trace the journey of India's largest commercial vehicle company.

Placing a nation on wheels

The TELCO story began in September 1945 when Tata Sons acquired for ₹25 lakh the East Indian Railways' derelict Tatanagar workshops at Jamshedpur with the intention of manufacturing boilers and steam locomotives for the railways.[3] J.R.D.'s vision was to build a first-of-its-kind engineering complex in India. Busy with TISCO, he assigned the responsibility of TELCO to Sumant Moolgaokar, a mechanical engineer from Imperial College, London. J.R.D. recognized the spark in Moolgaokar while the latter was working as a director at ACC. He insisted that he take charge of the new venture and was made director-in-charge of TELCO in 1949. Over the next four decades, Moolgaokar elevated TELCO to be one of the finest, largest and most successful private-sector companies in India.

With Britain was not keen to part with its technology, TELCO collaborated with Krauss Maffei of West Germany in 1952 for the manufacture of locomotives. Between then and 1970, when TELCO discontinued its locomotive line, it manufactured 1156 locomotives and 5000 railway wagons. The upgradation of Indian Railways, which was the government's top priority was substantially achieved in the 1950s itself. A government decision to prohibit vehicle assembly by foreign companies in India opened a new business avenue for Indian companies. The Tatas explored the opportunity of manufacturing diesel trucks fully realizing that the sole reliance on the locomotive business wasn't desirable. Government monopoly in locomotive purchase and its power to control prices to its advantage would leave the company susceptible to uncertainties. As J.R.D. was exploring collaborative opportunities, an unanticipated prospect presented itself. In the post-World War II years, the battered German industry was exploring for collaborations beyond European borders. Daimler-Benz and TELCO explored a proposal to jointly manufacture diesel road vehicles. Delighted at a possible collaboration that could catalyse Indian industry, J.R.D. and his team went to Geneva for negotiations. After much discussion, the chairman of Daimler-Benz accepted a revised proposal prepared by the Tatas in May 1954.

While the new partnership was joyfully conceived, there were fears that the venture could be stillborn, thanks to India's bourgeoning bureaucracy. With trepidation, J.R.D. and Moolgaokar approached industries minister T.T. Krishnamachari in Delhi. He went through the proposal, and instantly gave permission for the undertaking. The caveat was that within four years TELCO would be considerably indigenized. The two were thrilled at the minister's response as they never expected such instant approvals. This marked the beginning of the fifteen-year collaboration between the Tatas and Benz during which 179,000 Tata Mercedes-Benz vehicles rolled out of the Jamshedpur plant. In September 1960, the company's name was changed from Tata Locomotive and Engineering Company to Tata Engineering and Locomotive Company, marking a clear shift in the company's business primacies. Not only did TELCO live up to the indigenization precondition set by T.T.K., but even before the conclusion of the contract with Benz, Moolgaokar planned for independent engineering capabilities for TELCO. From June 1969, when the collaboration concluded, the Tatas were ready to begin manufacturing the Tatas' diesel vehicles with the 'T' replacing the Benz symbol on the rear of its trucks. In the 1971 war against Pakistan, 45,000 Tata trucks were used by the Indian army to travel to areas at altitudes up to 15,000 feet in bitter cold. The ruggedness of the vehicles could be estimated from the fact that roads were non-existent in some of these places.

Moolgaokar's master plan had started to unfold in 1966, when a 500-acre plot of land was acquired in the Pimpri-Chinchwad industrial area near Pune for building a second TELCO factory. However, from 1966 to 1979, when TELCO's Pune plant was being built, not a single truck was manufactured. J.R.D. supported Moolgaokar, by now the vice-chairman of TELCO, during the painful gestation years. He once said, 'I knew that Moolgaokar was building not just a factory, but an industry.' Moolgaokar's vision wasn't just assembling trucks but manufacturing them. He was building a fully integrated plant with capabilities to design and manufacture advanced machinery and equipment to even make parts of the truck. The heart of the plant, then and now, is the Engineering Research Centre (ERC). When the construction was complete, the Pune plant was considered an 'industrial jewel' by observers. The then chairman of Volvo, the Swedish auto giant, after visiting the Pune plant had said, 'I am stunned that such a set-up could be constructed by Indians. It is of a quality that we rarely see even in our part of the world.'[4] A new chapter had begun in the TELCO story in the 1980s.

A global first for the Indian automobile industry

India's economic liberalization led to the arrival of global car giants such as General Motors, Fiat, Ford, Honda, Hyundai and Toyota into the Indian passenger car market. In 1993, at an event of the Automotive Component Manufacturers' Association of India in New Delhi, Ratan Tata first suggested the probability of an industry-wide collaboration to manufacture an 'Asian car' as a project to further Indian pride. Surprisingly, response from the industry was lukewarm. In an interview to *Outlook*, Ratan Tata recalled two vital reasons why TELCO decided to venture alone in the passenger car project.

> Every car company we spoke to wants a joint venture in which they would have ownership. That would have meant two negatives for TELCO. One, the joint venture would have been off TELCO's books. Two, history shows that after a product is established, the partner wants to increase its stake to a majority holding.

Moreover, in the early 1980s, TELCO had successfully developed a range of commercial vehicles, including the popular 407 and 709 series. This was followed by the Tata Sierra in 1991, which was the first sports utility vehicle (SUV) to be designed and manufactured in India. In 1992, the Tata Estate was launched on a pickup platform. In 1994, the Tata Sumo was rolled out as a multi-utility vehicle. Its name was an acronym of TELCO's former chairman—Sumant Moolgaokar. In 1998, TELCO launched the Tata Safari. This remarkable record of developing its own products and the talent pool of over 300 young engineers at the company's ERC, emboldened Ratan Tata to independently venture to manufacture the first indigenous Indian car at TELCO.

His vision for the car was practical and customer-centric: 'We'll have a car with the Zen's size, the Ambassador's internal dimensions, the price of a Maruti 800 and the running cost of diesel.' Whether it was the estimated investment of ₹1700 crore, requirement of 3885 components, 740 dyes and 4010 product fixtures, or a comprehensive distribution network suited to Indian requirements, the underlying vision remained the same.[5] The project was entirely executed on CAD (computer-aided design) applications. Though its first attempt at manufacturing a car for the passenger segment, TELCO benchmarked itself with world-class solutions—collaboration with Hitachi for engine management systems, agreement with Nachi-Fugikoshi for robotic welding,[6] dyes for the body from Miyazo of Japan, and Durr of Germany commissioned to upgrade the second-hand Nissan paint shop acquired in late 1996.[7] Besides, French engineers helped develop the 1300cc four-cylinder engine. To match international design standards, TELCO selected IDEA, the Milan-based design house, for the exterior and interior styling. This was achieved in collaboration with ERC Pune.

Unlike its counterparts in East Asia—Malaysia's Proton, which was helped by Mitsubishi, and the Koreans, who were helped by American auto majors—TELCO had chosen to develop both the engine and the body in-house with the help of international consultants and experts. This unprecedented and radical approach discomforted many analysts.[8] It didn't end with independent production but extended to sourcing. At that time, the auto component manufacturing industry in India was highly fragmented with a poor reputation for quality. TELCO floated Tata AutoComp Systems as a joint venture for providing quality parts for the auto industry in India. Given its very first entry into the passenger car industry, it developed an indigenous supply chain of 300 vendors for providing 1360 parts for Indica. This created over 12,000 jobs.

Having been a market leader in the commercial vehicles space, where customer pressure was far less compared to passenger cars, TELCO worked towards institutionalizing the focus on delivering customer satisfaction across the organization. It began in mid-1998, when the existing range (Sierra, Estate, Sumo and Safari) was clubbed together under a new marketing division that preceded the launch of Indica. A team of young and dynamic individuals with the passion for marketing a new car was formed. Forty-four new dealers were selected in 1998 for the Indica distribution network for their customer orientation and passion for customer satisfaction.

The ultimate testimony to the faith of Indian consumers in the Tata brand and its products was seen from the fact that 115,000 fully paid orders were booked within seven days of its launch, a feat that was then a first in the history of the Indian automobile industry. When the first Indica rolled out of the Tata Motors plant on 14 December 1998, it marked the advent of India's first fully indigenously made car in a record time of thirty-one months and at one-sixth the cost of international peers. The media went gaga over Indica when displayed at the Auto Expo 1998. With an attractive price, good styling and the economy of diesel, the car had a successful launch.

The dark gloomy days at the turn of the millennium

The ecstasy of being a pioneer was marred by unexpected complaints about Indica from several quarters. There were glitches of high noise and vibration levels in the car, besides performance of the engine and issues with the fan belt. Many of these were traced to the bought-out parts. Some auto experts observed that the Tatas got parts of the car right, but not the entire car.[9] Given the high quality standards associated with Tata products, customers had high expectations, which were met partially. The media too didn't take kindly to the car's performance. There was anxiety in TELCO's leadership corridors. Had the company taken the right decision by investing in a passenger car project? Notably, it was the largest-ever investment made by the Tata Group in a single project until then. Within a year of its launch, the chairman was advised to sell the newly formed passenger car division following the poor response to Indica.

Officials from the US-based Ford Motor Company came to Bombay House and evinced interest in the car business. Praveen Kadle, then CFO at TELCO, recalled that after discussions in India, TELCO's senior leadership was called to the Ford headquarters at Detroit for further discussions. Kadle, who accompanied Ratan Tata to Detroit, recollected, 'For nearly three hours, we discussed the sell-off with Ford officials but were meted with humiliating treatment.' 'Why did you start the passenger car division at all when you do not know anything?' they questioned the senior team led by Ratan Tata during the meeting. 'We will do you a favour by buying your car division.'[10] Sombre after the Detroit discussions, Ratan Tata returned with his team to New York that very evening.

Many of TELCO's loyal commercial vehicle dealers also believed that the company had made a blunder by venturing into the passenger car business. Ravi Kant, then executive director at TELCO, mentioned how the company had made a conscious effort to diversify into the passenger vehicle business primarily because the commercial vehicle industry was highly cyclical. It wasn't a fad to start a new business from scratch. The East Asian crisis of 1997 had jolted most businesses to avoid putting all their eggs in a single basket. Hence, even though TELCO was a market leader with more than 50 per cent market share, it was geographically and demographically focused on India and predominantly on the commercial vehicle business. The cost of complying with new emission norms and the increasing weight of competition were further putting pressure on the company's operating margins. Inopportunely, even before TELCO could fully implement its diversification strategy, its worst fears came true. Besides the poor response to Indica, around 1999–2000, the commercial vehicle market in India shrunk by 40 per cent. TELCO had piled up huge stocks with dealers, and products remained unsold for two years. These led to staggering losses. The unprecedented situation shook everyone in the company.

During our conversation at his Bombay House office, Kant confessed, 'Whenever there is a successful organization and this kind of thing happens, it hurts your pride.' But the top leadership and the entire company decided not to give up, and instead use this adversity as an opportunity. Three distinct phases were planned as part of the recovery strategy. Phase one was intended to stem the bleeding. Phase two to consolidate the company's position in India. Phase three to go outside India and expand operations internationally.[11] Though these were planned as two-year phases each with a target of turning around fully within six years, they were executed in parallel.

Setting the house in order

With the belief 'what's cut can grow back; what's eroded is gone forever', the senior leadership spearheaded the 'cost erosion' exercise at TELCO. Between 2000 and 2002, TELCO managed to contain cost erosion of a whopping ₹600 crore. No item or process was considered sacrosanct. Every nook and corner were explored to squeeze costs. Kant gave full credit for this bold initiative to the younger employees of TELCO. Most senior executives within the company were convinced of reducing costs, but proposed a 0.5 to 1 per cent reduction. It was the younger employees at the middle-management level who indicated this bold target of 10 per cent reduction in costs during a breakfast meeting at TELCO's Pune plant. 'You have years ahead of you at this company. If you make this company strong, you will be the beneficiary,' Kant told them. They were encouraged to convert the ideas into a clear strategy and make a presentation before him and the senior leadership the very same afternoon. The presentation was an eye-opener for TELCO's top leadership. They were convinced that 10 per cent cost reduction was indeed achievable. They lent their full support. The dynamic team was asked to synergize with their counterparts across functional areas from the Lucknow and Jamshedpur plants of TELCO and consolidate the action plan within a fortnight. 'If we had tried to go only through the top, we might not have succeeded as well,' Kant quipped. Moreover, inter-plant interactions had never happened earlier. There were people within TELCO who had worked for twenty-four years in Pune or Jamshedpur, but had never once visited the other plant.[12]

For many decades, TELCO had operated in a seller's market with a cost-plus margin mindset. While it benefited in the post-LPG era, it soon started feeling the heat of competition. The market was gradually determining the prices of the products. Competition was slowly turning the tables in favour of customers. It was gradually becoming a buyer's market. A market leader such as TELCO had to adapt to the nuances of cost management and transition from engineering excellence to business excellence. The latter was proactively facilitated by implementing the TBEM processes.

One of the key elements of the cost erosion exercise was cost reduction through value engineering of core components and benchmarking with competitors. The material costs constituted 65 per cent of the target cost erosion plan. 'Everybody had a cost erosion target built into his area of work and we saw a cascading effect take hold,' recalled Telang, then senior vice president (manufacturing), who was also the 'cost-erosion champion' and in charge of the entire initiative. Over 1200 cross-functional teams and more than 900 self-directed teams of employees played an important role in cost reduction and quality improvement. The exercise institutionalized several best practices that would stand in good stead in the years ahead. Not surprisingly, the entire group cheered TELCO's achievement when its commercial vehicles division won the prestigious J.R.D. QV Award in 2005, having crossed the prestigious 600 mark in the rigorous TBEM evaluation.

To optimize on manpower costs, TELCO introduced a voluntary retirement scheme, leading to a reduction of nearly 5000 employees in two years. On the working capital front, vehicle inventories were reduced from six months to six weeks, and receivable days were reduced from three months to a fortnight. Credit to several dealers was stopped. This strategy was a huge success in working capital management.

On the external front, price negotiation of all bought-out components was aggressively done with suppliers, besides introduction of a vendor rationalization programme. This was also the time when TELCO introduced e-sourcing. Eventually, it became one of the largest companies doing e-sourcing in India. TELCO also divested all non-core activities by forming subsidiary companies.[13] The excavator division was spun off as Telcon (now Tata Hitachi Construction Machinery). The machine tool division was spun-off as TAL Manufacturing Solutions Ltd. TELCO also sold its non-core business stakes in joint ventures with Mercedes-Benz, Bridgestone, IBM and Asahi Glass. As a result, the cost of debt for the company came down from 12 to 5.5 per cent. All these contributed 25 per cent of the cost reduction targets.[14]

At TELCO's AGM on 20 July 2003, two years after the ominous AGM in 2001, Chairman Ratan Tata made two significant announcements. The first was that in the past two years, TELCO had swung its performance by ₹1000 crore, and had made a profit of ₹500 crore. The company was declaring a 40 per cent dividend for its shareholders, at a time when two of the world's three top auto firms were suffering haemorrhaging losses. The shareholders were jubilant as the chairman had lived up to his commitment. The other announcement was that on the eve of TELCO's golden jubilee, the company was being renamed 'Tata Motors'. Clarifying to the shareholders about the change of name, Tata said, 'Engineering per se is not our business; it is a capability that we have. The new name defines the business we are in.'

India first

Having achieved targets of phase one far beyond expectations, phase two of its turnaround strategy now came in centre stage. The focus was consolidating its position in commercial vehicles and passenger vehicles across India. The thrust was given to quality and features to improve product competitiveness. Research showed that segments in which Tata Motors had been traditionally strong, i.e. medium trucks were declining. This segment also had the greatest amplitude of cyclicity. Newer segments where it was not so strong like light commercial vehicles and buses were growing in demand. These segments were less cyclical in nature. The defence business was also opening up and was steadier compared to the others. Competition was intensifying and customer expectations were rising. Describing the uniqueness of those times, Kant's oft-quoted statement was, 'Customers expect European quality at Chinese prices!'

This was the time of unprecedented infrastructure growth across India. The Golden Quadrilateral Project to connect the four metropolitan cities, the secondary road network to connect the state capitals with important towns, and the Pradhan Mantri Gram Sadak Yojana to connect the rural hamlets with existing roads were initiated by Prime Minister Atal Bihari Vajpayee. This led to identification of two new segments at both ends of the spectrum—the light commercial vehicles (LCVs) and the heavy commercial vehicles (HCVs). Tata Motors was weak at both ends. The outcome of focused efforts in this direction led to the introduction of Tata Ace for catering to the LCV segment in 2005. Tata Novus and Tata Prima launched in 2005 and 2008 with international collaboration, were Tata Motors' offerings in the HCV segment. With 130 models of light, medium and heavy vehicles, Tata Motors consolidated its position as the unquestioned leader in the commercial vehicles space with a market share of nearly 65 per cent. Competitors Mahindra and Mahindra and Ashok Leyland were lagging far behind.

On the passenger car front, let's complete the Indica story. After unproductive discussions with Ford in 1999, Ratan Tata returned to India. Determined to prove the mettle of India's leading automobile company to succeed even in the passenger car segment, he called an emergency meeting at the Taj President Hotel in Mumbai. There was detailed analysis of the snags in Indica, and the design flaws and quality glitches that needed rectification. The priority was solving problems of customers who had already purchased the car. For this, Tata Motors set up retro-fit camps across India where 45,000 cars were repaired. Over forty parts were replaced free of cost for all Indica customers. Moreover, senior managers from the company interacted with customers and patiently listened to their complaints and provided solutions. In the car market, the damage caused through word-of-mouth criticism can be enormous. Tata Motors had already suffered a setback in the first six months after the launch of Indica. It did not spare any effort to win over loyal customers by solving their problems in every way possible.

In parallel, the team worked on a new version of Indica. It created a new design, eliminated all quality problems, and collaborated with suppliers for altered parts. The new Indica V2 was launched in January 2001 with the catchphrase 'even more car per car'. This time around, they had got it all right. The customers were delighted. In less than eighteen months, V2 became the fastest-selling automobile in Indian history by clocking sales of 100,000 cars.[15] It crossed the 100,000 mark in volume faster than Maruti 800, Zen, Matiz and Uno, the top-selling cars of those times. It soon captured a market share of 24 per cent and emerged among the top three models in the compact car segment (hatchback) after Maruti and Hyundai. By 2004, it was India's second-largest-selling hatchback. Through peaks and troughs, Indica's success was an outcome of collective work at Tata Motors. The collaborative efforts of young self-directed teams proactively supported and guided by senior leadership was its success formula. While sharing the Indica story at an event in New Delhi, Ratan Tata had said, 'Together, we can make things happen; we just need to do it.'

The fabulous response encouraged Tata Motors to launch several new models and variants aimed at specific target segments. Tata Indigo catering to the mid-size segment (sedan) was launched in 2002. Marina, Xeta, Dicor and the second-generation Vista were all built on the insights gained through Indica's indigenous design and production. By 2007, the millionth car on the Indica platform had rolled out from the Pune plant.[16] Indica and its variants constituted over 14 per cent market share in the passenger car segment (with competition from Maruti Udyog and Hyundai Motors) and 20 per cent market share in the utility vehicles space (with competition from Mahindra and Mahindra and Toyota). Within five years, Tata Motors had been reasonably successful in consolidating its position in India.

Going global

The time was ripe to fly beyond the seas on the east and the west of the Indian peninsula. Phase three of Tata Motors' turnaround strategy was international diversification. The objective was twofold. To identify key markets and segments overseas to improve competitive position, and to identify inorganic growth opportunities for increasing market share. Ratan Tata elaborated on the group's global strategy, 'We want to expand into geographies where, as a group, we can have a meaningful presence and where we are able to participate, as we have in India, in the development of that country.'[17] Having suffered from the cyclical nature of the trucks business in India, Tata Motors wanted to go into other geographies that didn't follow the same economic cycle. 'While the cycle in India is going down, in some other country it may be going up. That way, we can reduce the impact of downturns,' observed Kant. One of the prime motives to explore international markets was to de-risk its business model.

The company adopted a focused strategy to target a dozen countries in economic stages one and two[18] as priority markets for its existing products, rather than carpet bombing its products in seventy countries, which had been its earlier strategy. For targeting countries in developed economies belonging to economic stages three and four, inorganic growth was the identified strategy. In 2003, Tata Motors' international business accounted for ₹400 crore out of a total revenue of ₹9100 crore, a mere 4.4 per cent. With a target of generating 25 per cent of its revenues from international business by 2007, Tata Motors soared to spread it wings beyond India.

On 27 September 2004, Ratan Tata rang the opening bell at the New York Stock Exchange (NYSE) to mark the listing of Tata Motors on the world's largest bourse. It became the first Indian company in the automobile and engineering sectors to be listed on NYSE, and the eighth Indian company across sectors.[19] This was an important step in its global ambitions. How difficult was this given the governance standards expected in international markets and developed economies, I asked Kant. 'We thought they were different. But when we started reading the fine print, we discovered that we already met more than 80 per cent of their requirements. It was a question of filling that gap of 20 per cent to meet the NYSE requirements,' he acknowledged.

The Korean 'konnection'

With the ₹465-crore acquisition of Daewoo Commercial Vehicle Company (DCVC) in March 2004, the global ambitions of Tata Motors had finally begun. Founded in March 1967 as Daewoo Industry Company Ltd., Daewoo Corporation had risen to become South Korea's second largest business group by 1997. However, hit hard by the Asian financial crisis, the company went bankrupt by the year 2000. In April 2002, General Motors bought Daewoo Motor, part of the Daewoo Group, at a bargain price of $1.2 billion. The bus business was sold to a Korean competitor. What was left for sale was DCVC, the truck business. Unlike its bankrupt parent Daewoo Motor, DCVC was a profit-making company. Around April 2003, KPMG, the leading consultancy firm, informed Tata Motors that DCVC was available for bidding.

'We acquire a company only if it gives us a new technology, new markets, new products, new customer bases or a new product development capability. The deal must also make financial sense,' observed Kadle, then CFO at Tata Motors. DCVC fit most of these criteria. One of the major synergies in acquiring Daewoo was its predominant presence in the HCV segment that Tata Motors wanted to develop in a big way. It had ninety-three models in diverse categories with presence in select East Asian geographies, including China where Tata Motors had little or no presence. It would provide Tata Motors with a market to sell its medium and light commercial vehicles, a segment in which Daewoo had limited presence, even though it possessed an annual production capacity of 20,000 vehicles.

Having been shortlisted as the top ten bidders, Kant led a multi-functional team to South Korea. This was unlike the usual mergers and acquisitions (M&A)[20] practice of the finance and admin teams spearheading the due-diligence process on-site. He wanted the Tata Motors executives who were likely to run the Korean business, if acquired, to see for themselves the plant and the ecosystem. During their interaction with the DCVC employees, the Tata team got the feeling that the Korean company was keen to be acquired by an American or European bidder. They considered it a matter of prestige not to be acquired by a company from a developing economy. DCVC's militant labour union was also notorious for expressing its displeasure through violent means. During the acquisition of Daewoo's car division by General Motors, the union members had invaded the upscale hotel in Seoul where the announcement was scheduled to be made.[21]

Kant believed that acquiring the company would be truly successful only if it was done by winning the confidence of the management and the unions. The team decided to acquaint their Korean counterparts with the Tatas' credentials. Given the barriers of language and culture, the entire dossier—the bid, the company material and a DVD on the Tatas—was translated into Korean and shared with them within seventy-two hours. All through their presentations and interactions they sought to impress Daewoo about their international exposure and partnerships, and the fact that the Tatas were the sixth largest manufacturer of commercial trucks in the world, with a history of quality and customer-centricity. On the softer side, they were exposed to the Tata values, decades-long employee welfare practices, and the Tata ethos of charity and social responsibility.[22]

The twin package of ability and nobility of the Tata Group and its passionate communication in the local language impressed not only the senior leadership, but also the unions and the local government in South Korea, who were impressed with the high standards of corporate governance of the Tata Group, an issue with many family-owned companies in South Korea. The managers and the union were now willing to be acquired by an Indian company. In March 2004, when the acquisition was completed at $102 million, it was the fastest major acquisition ever in South Korea. With the formal acquisition, Korea's second-largest truck maker with a 26 per cent market share, became a wholly owned subsidiary of Tata Motors.

All through the acquisition process, Ratan Tata encouraged the team to see itself as a Korean company, and not as an Indian company in Korea. Expressing his delight at the largest acquisition by any Indian company in Korea, he said, 'Korea is a shining example of what can be achieved with diligence and dedication, and I am sure we will learn a lot from operating in South Korea.' Guided by the chairman's approach, Kant shared the company's integration process, 'The operation would be run basically by Koreans. That would give them a sense of pride.' This he believed would communicate to the Korean managers and employees that the Tatas are not just buying assets, but a running company that they want to grow. Kwang-Ok Chae, the president of DCVC, was appointed CEO of Tata Daewoo Commercial Vehicles (TDCV), the new entity. To create a sense of identity with the parent company, TDCV sent its union leaders to visit Tata Motors plants in India. It was an eye-opener for the Korean employees. They realized that the Tatas were a much larger and much grander group than they had anticipated, and that too with a history and a heritage.

In an interview, Ratan Tata recalled an interesting instance during his visit to the TDCV plant, 'The first day I visited the plant, I was asked to eat in the workers' cafeteria. I was appalled by that thought, because I thought I'd have to eat in silence, not speaking the language. Although the language wasn't spoken, through collaborative interpretation on both sides, it became clear that they wanted to know whether we would fund some employees for visiting Buddhist sites in India. Once we got over that, we were all part of the same clan. The top management of Daewoo was very pro-Indian, very keen to visit these religious sites themselves. Many of the workers did so too.' He found it amusing that the Tatas had no major trouble dealing with the Korean unions as they considered the Tatas to be a Buddhist company and India to be a Buddhist country.[23]

Tata Motors instantly roped in Daewoo to work on its ambitious 'world truck' programme. Daewoo had been working on a similar project independently, and the collaboration hastened the progress on the new platform by nearly two years. Their strength in integration of vehicles was combined with Tata Motors' competencies, manpower and resources.[24] In January 2008, Tata's 'world truck', named Prima, was successfully launched first in South Korea, and then in India.

By 2006 itself, TDCV had earned enough profits to repay the entire loan of $51 million taken for the Daewoo acquisition. Instead, it used $10 million to acquire a plot of land adjacent to the plant for future expansion. This once again indicated the Tatas' total commitment to Korean interests. The Daewoo acquisition and integration changed the perception and attitude towards Tata Motors around the globe. Kant shared how by 2006 when he took over as Tata Motors' MD, the company regularly received offers to buy some company somewhere in the world. 'But we were not in any hurry,' he smiled.

More joint ventures and collaborations

An interesting offer came their way in 2005. Spanish bus maker Hispano Carrocera was in financial difficulties. A reputed bus and coach manufacturer with 25 per cent market share in Spain, and sales networks in Europe and countries outside Europe, Hispano fit in well with Tata Motors' growth strategy. The company had no bus division of its own and lacked technology to manufacture top-end buses. The deal would be a win-win opportunity and give Tata Motors access to Hispano's design and technological capabilities to fully tap into the growing potential of this segment in India, Spain and other export markets. In February 2005, Tata Motors acquired 21 per cent stake in Hispano at ₹70 crore.[25]

In May 2006, it entered a joint venture in Latin America. This was the Brazil-based company—Marcopolo—a global leader in bodybuilding for buses and coaches. The 51:49 joint venture was to set up a new manufacturing facility as Tata Marcopolo in Dharwad (Karnataka) with a total investment of ₹200 crore and an employment potential of 6500 direct jobs. By 2009, the Dharwad plant was ready to roll out 30,000 units annually to cater to India's growing need for world-class, fully built buses for intra-city and inter-city transportation with international standards of comfort, quality and safety.

In December 2006, it formed yet another 70:30 joint venture with Thonburi Automotive Assembly Plant in Thailand. With an equity of ₹120 crore, the venture facilitated Tata Motors' entry into the world's second-largest market for pickup trucks (after the USA). Subsequently, Tata Motors bought out the stake of Thonburi, and used the Thai facility as the base to make and sell trucks in the Asia–Pacific region.

In line with Tata Motors' inorganic growth strategy, the new ventures targeted specific markets for niche products. While Hispano was for higher-end vehicles, Marcopolo was for medium-range vehicles and Thonburi for pickups. Even as India and the world thought that Tata Motors had made a global mark, the best was yet to come.

The empire strikes back

On 12 June 2007, Ford Motor Company announced its plan of selling two of its prestigious brands—Jaguar and Land Rover (JLR). Ratan Tata got an informal brief about this and discussed the opportunity with the senior leadership. Kant had consistently maintained that the only way Tata Motors could enter the US markets was through M&A. 'If I get an opportunity, I will look at it very actively,' he often said. The steep costs of establishing a brand and developing products that met expectations of consumers from developed markets were key barriers for a company such as Tata Motors to grow organically in those economies. Ford's announcement was probably that long-awaited opportunity. Tata Motors began a nine-month due-diligence process.

Ford Motor Company, America's second-largest automaker (after General Motors), had acquired Jaguar for $2.5 billion in November 1989 by making offers to Jaguar's US and UK shareholders. Founded in 1935, Jaguar had a history of producing 'beautiful fast cars'. It also had a sporting heritage and had produced winning racing cars at major sports car endurance races. In its seventy-year long history, it had gone through a series of changes in design and ownership before it landed in the Ford stable. Land Rover (LR) was regarded as a British icon ever since it was founded in 1948. It was considered the gold standard in off-road vehicles. Having been the mainstay of army and police vehicles in several countries, LR successfully merged luxury with ruggedness to produce a formidable and powerful vehicle for all terrains. In its half a century of existence, it belonged to diverse owners till it was acquired by BMW in 1994. Ford acquired Land Rover from BMW in the year 2000 for $2.7 billion, and the Rover trademark in 2006. It was previously licensed to MG Rover Group of the UK. Although LR remained profitable, Ford, then the world's third-largest automaker, never managed to make money from its investment in Jaguar. It was forced to sell the two UK-based companies so that it could concentrate on its own loss-making core car business in the USA. LR and Jaguar sold about 300,000 vehicles between them and were probably a distraction for Ford's larger turnaround effort in its parent US market. What precipitated Ford's decision to sell the two brands were unprecedented losses—$2.67 billion in 2007 and a record $12.6 billion in 2006, for which Jaguar was supposedly the biggest contributor.[26] Over time, due to several reasons, Jaguar had developed a poor reputation. There was a popular joke around it: 'You never bought one Jaguar. You bought two, because one was always in the garage!'

Ford knew that there was no way they would sell the more profitable brand (LR) and keep Jaguar with them. It insisted that if any investor or company wants to make an offer, it must be for acquiring both the brands. Several private equity (PE) firms from the USA and the UK, expressed interest in purchasing the brands from Ford. JP Morgan's PE arm, whose bid was led by former Ford chief Jacques Nasser, and a consortium of Apollo Management and Mahindra and Mahindra from India were the other key bidders, besides Tata Motors.[27]

In May 2007, Cerberus had purchased Chrysler for $7.4 billion. Thus, the market sentiment was that PE investors had a stronger chance. But the over 16,000 employees at JLR held a different opinion. The unions were opposed to PE investors buying JLR. Their experience was that such investors closed pension schemes, stripped assets and made the labour force redundant. The unions also insisted that the acquiring company could not close any of the three factories related to JLR. Lord Kumar Bhattacharya, founder of the University of Warwick Manufacturing Group, strongly opposed a sale to PE investors. He believed that if Ford could not make Jaguar profitable, private equity certainly could not.[28]

As for Tata Motors, it had several reasons for seriously proceeding with the JLR acquisition. Firstly, both were great brands, though Jaguar had a mixed reputation. Ford had hugely invested in both brands to improve quality and create a pipeline of new products. The acquiring company would benefit from these investments. Secondly, JLR had advanced manufacturing plants. Thirdly, JLR dealers were highly committed to the brands. During due-diligence process, Ratan Tata and Ravi Kant met long-standing dealers of both brands. They were impressed that despite their dismal performance over the past years, dealers had immense faith in the power of JLR as brands. Most importantly, the JLR acquisition would provide Tata Motors with a strategic opportunity to acquire iconic brands that had a global presence. This would increase its business diversity across markets and in product segments where it had no presence since inception.

The Indian and international auto markets were keenly watching and were intrigued with Tata Motors' interest in acquiring luxury car brands. All along, the company had been known for designing and delivering value-for-money cars, trucks and buses that were meant to provide great functionality. Acquiring a luxury car maker meant entering a very different market segment and catering to a very different geography. Moreover, JLR was far bigger than Tata Motors.

What was the strategic thought process that went on behind the scenes? I asked Ishaat Hussain. He emphasized Ratan Tata's strong belief that luxury cars were probably a very good business to be in. 'If you want to be in the luxury car market, the only way you could do it was by making a global acquisition,' he confessed. A former vice president in the group chairman's office, who had the opportunity to see the acquisition process at close quarters, shared, 'One of the reasons of going to JLR was that their premium SUVs were a product extension of the Tata Safaris. If we were to get to that product in-house, it would have taken us years.' Arun Gandhi, director at Tata Sons and man Friday for global acquisitions, provided a sneak peek into the commercial benefits of the JLR deal:

> We had realized that Ford was in a such a dire cash trap that they had to sell something. At that point of time, we could possibly acquire the brands at a good price. On the technical side, JLR acquisition would help the Tatas use its R & D capabilities for bringing quality to cars made in India.

The low-cost Tata approach and the high-tech JLR operations would provide great synergies and make the Tatas a global brand.

The D-Day was 2 June 2008. Tata Motors announced that JLR had been acquired at $2.3 billion (₹9200 crore). Ford was raising money to ensure its own survival and had sold the brands for several billion dollars less than what it had paid to acquire them. 'Having learned about pensions in the UK from the Corus transaction, I made Ford put an additional $600 million into JLR pension funds,' quipped Gandhi. The purchase consideration included the ownership of Jaguar and Land Rover, with perpetual royalty-free licences of all necessary intellectual property rights, manufacturing plants, design centres and a worldwide network of national sales companies. The Ford Motor Credit Company was to provide financing for JLR dealers and customers for a year, while Tata Motors entered advanced negotiations with auto finance providers in the UK, Europe and the USA.[29]

JLR employees, the UK unions and the governments in India and the UK supported the deal. British Prime Minister Tony Blair reportedly acknowledged the acquisition being in Britain's interests because the Tatas had a track record of managing people and communities, and were respected by people of several countries. Gandhi recalled how the Tata brand and Tata ethics came to play during the acquisition:

> When we signed the agreement, the Ford director told me that 'we are doing this transaction with the Tatas because we know that you will fully comply with the agreements. We were not so sure what the other parties interested in acquiring this business were proposing to do, and whether they would ultimately comply with our agreements'.

Following the acquisition, newspapers ran headlines such as 'The Empire Strikes Back', 'Jaguar Is Now an Indian Beast' and 'Tatas Rule Britannia'! Some had more tongue-in-cheek comments— 'So what if the Queen of England still has the Kohinoor, the diamond and most famous jewel taken from India during colonial times? The Tatas now have Jaguar and Land Rover, the icons of British luxury.'[30] The British citizenry felt discomforted that India, a former colony, had acquired two of Britain's most iconic brands. In a conversation with MBA students at Stanford University, Ratan Tata remembered the fiery and vocal reactions from Brits expressing their displeasure. 'When Ford had not been able to make a profit with JLR, what was Tata, with no experience in the premium car segment going to do?' some said. Many others felt that the Tatas would shut down the plants in Britain, move them to India, and convert Birmingham/Coventry plants into a real estate project. Another spicy rumour was that the Tatas were going to have Tandoori chicken restaurants all over the Midlands! But the Tata approach was very different from what they had expected. The Brits would soon realize the Tata way.

Recall the Detroit discussions between Ratan Tata and Ford Motor Company in 1999, when the latter had humiliated the Tatas for venturing into the passenger car business? Within a decade, the situation had come around a full circle—from the Tatas approaching Ford to bail them out by acquiring Tata Motors' passenger car business to Tata Motors bailing out Ford by acquiring their luxury car business in the UK. In fact, Ford chairman Bill Ford thanked Ratan Tata, saying, 'You are doing us a big favour by buying JLR.'[31] Many dubbed it 'sweet revenge'.

In the initial days after the acquisition, Ratan Tata personally addressed employees at JLR plants. Most were expecting that he would assert his leadership and give them an action plan for the way ahead. Instead, he told them, 'We are looking forward to extending our full support to the JLR team to realize their competitive potential. JLR will retain their distinctive identities and continue to pursue their respective business plans as before.' He further said, 'It is our intention to work closely to support the JLR team in building the success and pre-eminence of the two brands.' The Brits realized that JLR would remain British in identity. Only the ownership had passed on to an Indian conglomerate. David Smith, the acting CEO of JLR, was nominated as the new CEO. The Tatas believed he was best suited to lead the business as he had twenty-five years of experience with JLR and Ford.

Ratan Tata's commitment did not end with speech-making. Gandhi recalled that Tata often spent time on the shop floor at JLR plants in the UK. For the first time, workers saw the owner on the shop floor. They had never seen a Ford director there. In fact, relations between the unions and Ford had historically been tense. In 2004, production at Land Rover's plant in Solihull was halted by strikes over pay. When Ford threatened to withhold investment, workers agreed to change working practices. But the Tatas were different. As an outcome of this, quality improvement and workers' engagement reached a new high.

... And the global financial gloom descended

On 15 September 2008, three months after the Tatas' acquisition of JLR, Lehman Brothers, a global financial services firm, and the fourth-largest investment bank in the USA, filed for bankruptcy. Many others soon followed. It was the beginning of a global financial crisis that affected almost every continent. Decline in consumer wealth was estimated in trillions of dollars. The interconnectedness of nations in a globalized world, and its negative fallout were visible in full measure. This indirectly contributed to the European sovereign debt crisis that began in the last quarter of 2009 and affected most nations of the European Union. It became apparent that Tata Motors couldn't have picked a worse time to make an acquisition of this magnitude. With the collapse of the mortgage market in the USA and the subsequent financial crisis, anyone who had cash was no longer in the mood to lend it. With severe liquidity crisis, the demand for luxury cars in Europe and North America—JLR's two biggest markets—hit its nadir.

Already burdened with a debt of ₹21,900 crore, Tata Motors was forced to put more money into JLR after it failed to secure financial aid from Britain in the crisis scenario. It spent an additional ₹4500 crore to keep the struggling brands afloat. This was an awkward position for a company that had been virtually debt-free. 'We were bleeding. Banks were not giving any money. And we needed money,' recalled a senior Tata Group executive. For the year ending 31 March 2009, Tata Motors posted an annual loss of ₹2505 crore, compared to the profit of ₹2168 crore in the previous year. The JLR unit made a pre-tax loss of ₹1800 crore.

The UK's department for business, enterprise and regulatory reform eventually agreed to underwrite a £340-million loan to JLR given by the European Investment Bank and another £450 million from another group. However, the guarantees came with stiff riders, including, among other things, a seat on the JLR board, the right to choose its chairman and vetoes on investment and employment issues. This would have made the Tatas almost lose control. They rejected the offer and secured a £500-million loan from a consortium of Indian banks, including State Bank of India and Bank of Baroda. With this experience, the Tatas decided to retreat from loans given by the UK and European government-linked financial institutions.[32]

Tatas achieved what Ford couldn't

Tata Motors adopted a threefold strategy for dealing with the crisis and turning around JLR: cash management, cost control, and new product development. It was reminiscent of the efforts Tata Motors had made between 2000 and 2006 to turn around the parent company with great success. It was now replicating the strategy at a global level. It hired KPMG and Munich-based Roland Berger Strategy Consultants to advise on cost-cutting and cash-flow management at JLR. Their mandate was to make JLR profitable. The globally renowned consulting companies suggested the formation of cross-functional teams to manage liquidity and contain costs at various levels within the business. The implementation efforts were successfully spearheaded by a young team, just as it was done in India in 2001. The anticipated savings were an astoundingly high amount.[33]

On the labour front, the company undertook a multi-pronged strategy to manage costs. One was to send several hundred employees on a sabbatical. Secondly, the permanent workforce was rationalized by 32 per cent and the labour force was trimmed by 2000. In February 2009, the company also managed to negotiate with thousands of workers on a pay freeze (until 2010) and a shorter four-day working week to avoid compulsory job losses during the financial crisis. Salaried staff also agreed to a three-hour extension of the working week to forty hours and a pay freeze. The deal with its workforce saved about £68 million for the company.[34] Several other cost-saving initiatives were implemented with success.

To complement its cost-management efforts, Tata Motors divested stakes in group companies. In September 2008, it sold a 1.3 per cent holding in Tata Steel to Tata Sons for ₹485 crore. In November 2008, the board approved a ₹4145 crore rights offer. All proceeds were channelled to make JLR profitable. Ratan Tata and Ralph Speth, CEO of JLR from February 2010, travelled across the USA meeting dealers and accepting feedback on JLR brands. Based on their inputs, Tata Motors invested in R & D for newer, more fuel-efficient and contemporary models. At 14 per cent of its annual revenues, its R & D investments were much higher than industry standards of 5 per cent. These efforts paid off when the global economy revived. Much of the success in the post-crisis scenario came from newer markets such as Russia, China and Latin America. China, a country that had provided just 1 per cent of JLR sales till 2005, contributed over 20 per cent of its sales a decade later. To capitalize on the demand, efforts were made to expand dealerships in China, where luxury car sales became stronger than Western markets.

By 2017, Jaguar tripled its sales compared to 2009 and the JLR revenue topped by $34 billion (₹2.31 lakh crore) within the consolidated Tata Motors revenue of ₹2.74 lakh crore. With 2600 dealerships in 170 countries, JLR employed 35,000 people globally of the 79,500 employees within the Tata Motors Group. Considered to be the largest employer in the UK's automobile sector, JLR often ranked in the top five 'best employers to work for' list in the UK. Tata Motors' success in acquiring and eventually turning around JLR surprised analysts and investors alike. In 2008, many critics had commented that Tata Motors was making an expensive mistake by acquiring JLR, which had little synergy with Tata Motors' mass-market image. Past examples of similar acquisitions that weren't successfully integrated prompted many of these doomsday scenarios for Tata Motors. The Daimler–Chrysler merger that had happened a decade earlier in May 1998, where a high-end brand was combined with a set of more mass-market brands, was a case in point. One of the reasons for failure was that US-based Chrysler's employees always perceived it as a takeover with major decisions taken by Daimler headquartered at Germany. Consequently, many employees left Chrysler in the initial days post-acquisition.[35] Ultimately, Chrysler was sold to a PE fund in 2007.

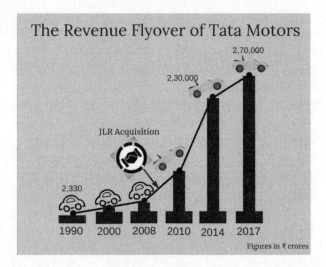

The Tatas handled the acquisition very differently by granting autonomy to managers in England. Speth pointed out that synergies between JLR and Tata Motors were limited to processes. 'The business and science of luxury cars is completely different from that of mass vehicles,' he said.[36] Though JLR was a wholly owned subsidiary of Tata Motors, it consistently kept the brand identity of JLR distinct. It did not try to impose its culture on JLR in any significant manner. The Tatas' hands-off policy of achieving integration was executed with great finesse and success. In later years, Ratan Tata remarked that Speth had done a terrific job of leading the team of people. In the long term, JLR helped Tata Motors improve its financial results when the company's commercial vehicles business was yet again going through a cyclical downturn and some of its passenger cars were underperforming in Indian markets.[37]

Leadership secrets to global success

'The critical challenge to a global company's leadership is to engage itself with its people at the same level of intensity and seriousness as with capital investments or business strategy.'

Satish Pradhan

Sharing his insight on the success of JLR, Gandhi said, 'The real success of JLR is because of the suggestions and time that Mr Tata himself gave. His involvement and vision changed JLR's fortunes.' During our conversation, Professor Krishna Palepu, senior associate dean at Harvard Business School, highlighted Ratan Tata's conviction that JLR kind of opportunities don't come often. 'He believed that these are amazing brands that were let down by previous owners. The way to restore them was to give a lot of freedom to people who were stewards of those brands.'

The JLR acquisition portrayed the Tata Group as an entity willing to take tremendous risks. These were not blind risks, but calculated ones. The acquisition was for the long-term, independent of the financial crisis. It was executed with clear vision and conviction, immense courage and systematic implementation. It wasn't a reckless approach to extract maximum value from a venture. Attributing the long-term success of the JLR acquisition to the Tata culture, Gandhi said: 'We have not had a single legal battle with Ford under any of the original agreements. It is the Tata code of ethics—keeping our word under all circumstances—which has been the key to our success in all transactions that I have done for Tata Sons.'

In a letter to shareholders in 2009, Ratan Tata had written, 'I feel strongly that in later years we can look back on the JLR acquisition and say to ourselves that this was a very worthwhile strategic acquisition and one which has brought us considerable technology and global presence.' A decade later, his words proved to be prophetic.[38]

CHAPTER 12

WHEN CRORES OF TEABAGS CARRIED THE TATA NAME INTO WESTERN HOMES

'We are no longer an Indian company; instead we are a global company that was born in India and will continue to have strong roots here.'

Ratan Tata

From the beginning of recorded history, India has been an outward-looking global economy with a consistent trade surplus. In 1 AD, India's share in world GDP was 32.9 per cent, the highest among all countries of the globe. This was three times of all European countries put together and twenty times that of Russia.[1] For 1700 years thereafter, India remained the world's largest economy. It was the colonial rule between 1700 and 1947 that acted as the biggest drain on Indian resources and severely impacted our economy. During this period, India's contribution reduced from 24.4 per cent to 4.2 per cent.[2] Post-Independence, the country's leadership adopted the soviet model of development, which further reduced India's contribution to 3.1 per cent by 1970. It was only at the turn of the last millennium that Indian economy finally started opening up. After 250 years of economic exploitation and fifty years of experimentation, India was offering itself another chance.[3]

Economic liberalization brought in major changes in outlook among leading Indian companies. They were becoming increasingly concerned about customers, product quality and brand—key prerequisites for facing competition. There were others too who secretly canvassed for protection. Ratan Tata was one industry captain who welcomed competition. He believed that economic protection for Indian firms was detrimental to customer interests, and selective opening of the economy was subjective. 'The most painful way is to open up (the economy) fully. The strong live and the weak die. There is bloodshed, and out of it emerges a much leaner industry, which tends to survive.'[4]

Just as in the previous four decades, fiscal and monetary authorities stepped in to intervene in the macroeconomic scenario. But this time it was for creating an enabling environment for internationalization of Indian companies. The draconian FERA (Foreign Exchange Regulation Act), which imposed strict regulations on payments and dealings in foreign exchange[5] since 1973, was replaced by the liberal FEMA (Foreign Exchange Management Act) in 1999. Between 1999 and 2004, foreign investments by Indian companies that were capped at $15 million increased to 100 per cent of the acquiring company's net worth. Unlike earlier, a company could also invest or acquire businesses overseas in sectors unrelated to their business in India. By 2007, RBI increased the cap on total overseas direct investment by Indian companies to 400 per cent of their net worth. To provide greater financial support for global investments and acquisitions, and to provide greater business to domestic banks, Indian companies were also permitted to borrow from Indian banks for global investments and acquisitions. Having lived through the Licence Raj nightmare, Indian companies were delighted at these developments.

Ratan Tata believed that for a long time the Tata Group had been very inward-looking, seeing only India as its market. Part of the reason was foreign exchange restrictions. 'Now that these restrictions have been eased extensively, we should be looking at growing overseas in a serious manner. I don't mean just exporting our products, but looking at acquisitions, alliances and things of this nature.' In fact, 'international business' was one of the key items on Ratan Tata's strategic plan for the Tata Group drawn up in the 1980s. This proposal saw the light of day only after he became the chairman of Tata Sons. Goaded by their leader's vision, leveraging benefits of a new economic ecosystem within India and seizing opportunities emerging on the global horizon, most Tata Group companies embarked on their globalization journey. Their paths were different, their destination same. Let's see what happened in this fascinating journey of adventure, audacity and acquisitions.

Tatas' tea company

What is the world's top drink—the most consumed beverage? Of course, water. What comes a close second? It's tea. A popular legend connects the discovery of tea to Chinese Emperor Shen Nung around the year 2737 BC. Considered to be a 'divine healer', Shen Nung insisted on drinking boiled water for good health.[6] Once while travelling to a far-off place, when his servants were boiling water for him, dried leaves from a nearby camellia (tea) bush accidentally fell into the water. On drinking the hot 'beverage' with a pleasing aroma, Shen Nung discovered that it was refreshing and had a great flavour. He endorsed it as a medicinal beverage across China. It was only 3000 years later, around 300

AD when tea became a daily drink in China. His work *The Classic of Tea* by Lu Yu, was the single most influential work on the cultural significance of tea. It was strongly influenced by the Taoist faith and was central to culture in eighth-century China. Not only was tea drinking described as a religious ceremony, but there were also guidelines on the appropriate state of mind for the tea drinker, and the atmosphere in which tea should be drunk![7] Around 900 AD, it travelled to Japan and gradually became part of the formal Japanese ceremony. In 1660, tea brought in by sailors from China was introduced in London. For nearly a century thereafter, it remained a beverage for the aristocrats. It was only later around 1750, when England started trading with China for large quantities of tea that it became affordable for the average Brit.

Tea travelled all over the world; but when did it come to India? There are two interesting stories associated with the advent of tea in India. The first one is of a British soldier who found the *Camellia sinensis* (tea plant) on the banks of the Irrawaddy river in Burma (present-day Myanmar). Pleased with its taste, he introduced it in Assam. Another story is that when trade relations between the British and the Chinese started to weaken in the eighteenth century, the British East India Company began experimenting with tea cultivation in India, using imported seeds from China. The first successful cultivation was undertaken in Assam in 1838.[8] Another account traces the first experiment of growing tea plants in the Nilgiris in 1832, and the earliest record of commercial tea planting to Kerala around 1875.

Why am I giving this long introduction about tea? It's for two reasons. Firstly, the experiments that happened 180 years ago in Assam and the Nilgiris have turned out to be so successful and popular that India has become the country with maximum production and consumption of tea in the world, even beating the original discoverer—China. Secondly, I am sharing this tea tale because I am going to explore the fascinating story of how Tata Tea became the world's second largest tea company.

Tata-Finlay Ltd, Tata Group's tea, coffee and spices business, was established in May 1963 as a joint venture with James Finlay and Company, a Scottish firm that first came to southern India in 1897. In December 1982, James Finlay and McLeod Russell divested their holdings in the company and Tata Tea was born. With fifty-three estates and over 26,000 hectares under cultivation, Tata Tea became the largest tea grower in the world. Its subsidiary—Tata Coffee—was the largest coffee plantation company in Asia. Even during the days of the Licence Raj, Tata Tea was the owner of the largest instant tea factory in the world (outside the USA) located at Munnar in Kerala, and the world's largest exporter of instant tea.

The company became successful on its proposition of 'from tea bush to tea cup'. Krishna Kumar, former MD of Tata Tea, explained this core competence.

> We had large tea estates where tea was grown fresh. Within sixteen days of manufacturing it reached the consumer. Companies that bought tea from auctions didn't have this advantage. The auctioned tea itself would have been four months old. From the auction, it would be taken to the packaging factory for blending. All this would take another three months for our competitors. The consumer was not getting fresh tea from them. On that hinged our strategy.

To further enhance its promise of freshness and take on the competition, the company pioneered an out-of-the-box solution in 1984. Percy Siganporia, former MD of Tata Tea, called it the plantation poly-pack solution,[9] wherein tea was packed on the plantation itself using flexible packaging (poly-packs). Till then, tea was sold in cartons, which affected its freshness. Most multinationals quickly latched on to this innovation and introduced their own poly-packs.

The Tata *taazgi*

From a predominantly tea-plantation company in the early 1980s, Tata Tea ventured into branded tea in the late 1980s. The company leadership realized that despite having over fifty tea gardens across India, they had the tea but not the brand. Cyclical price fluctuations had made the commodity end of the business loss making. The real profits were being made by the Unilevers of the world who had very few gardens, but were buying their bulk tea in auctions and selling them in pouches. Darbari Seth, then chairman of Tata Tea, and Krishna Kumar believed that Tata Tea should transition from trading to branding in the long haul. It should be a marketing company, a consumer-led company, for which it needed its very own and well-known tea brands. Front-end investment in business rather than the back end made sense in a market that had stood still at the rate of population growth.

Knowing well the pulse of the Indian consumers and their tastes, Tata Tea's product strategy focused on providing customized brands of tea to suit regional preferences, especially the un-serviced segments. Accordingly, the Brahmaputra brand was sold in north and west India, the Chakra Gold, Kanan Devan and Gemini brands were sold in south India, Tata Tea Leaf for Jharkhand and a specific dust tea variant for Odisha. In later years, the company introduced specific brands to target different segments across the economic spectrum. Tata Tea Gold with richer blend and aroma targeted the high-end. Tata Tea Premium for the mid-market segment. The Agni brand was for price-conscious consumers. It was also most crucial for the company as 60 per cent of the market belonged to the sub-₹100 category.[10] These and many other brands were sold pan-India through a distribution network of 600,000 outlets, predominantly in the urban cities and towns. It used over 80 per cent of its tea production for its own branded tea products. The customer promise across brands was the same—taazgi (freshness), thereby capitalizing their ownership of the entire value chain—from sourcing to distribution, which ensured taazgi for the customers. In the early 1990s, one of their ads on Doordarshan became extremely popular with the jingle 'Anu Taazgi Dede' (Anu, give me freshness), where hundreds of men are dancing with mugs in their hands and asking film star Anu Agarwal for freshness. She dances to their tune and sings 'Tata ki Chai Lele' (Have Tata Tea)!

While tea is an inseparable part of the morning routine of nearly a billion Indian households, the importance that Tata Tea brands hold in consumers' minds can be understood through an anecdote. Harish Bhat, former chairman and MD of Tata Tea, recollected an insightful experience during his uncle's death ceremony in Mangalore. The ceremony, performed on the thirteenth day since a person's death, involved giving the priests who perform that ceremony, a favourite product of the departed. 'I was surprised to see that my uncle had specifically instructed his sons that the gift to be given to the priests during the ceremony would be packs of Tata Tea Gold. That was the brand he loved during his life,' shared Bhat. In fact, he showed me photos on his cell phone of the priests with packs of Tata Tea Gold. 'If a person liked Tata Tea so much during his life, the brand must have impacted him in some manner,' concluded Bhat, now brand custodian at Tata Sons.

The fall of the Berlin Wall in Germany in November 1989 was a watershed moment indicative of the breaking down of barriers between the erstwhile blocs of the Cold War era. For Krishna Kumar, it symbolized the removal of trade restrictions across geographies. A year later, post-economic liberalization in India, the market situation indeed started changing. Hindustan Unilever (HUL), Tata Tea's prime competitor in India, had nearly 40 per cent market share (twice that of Tata Tea) and prominent brands such as Brooke Bond, Taj Mahal and Lipton. There were seven other national brands, including Goodricke, Duncans, Hasmukh and Wagh Bakri that accounted for 15 per cent share in India's packet tea market, besides several regional brands. There was strong likelihood of many global brands entering India, thereby creating greater competition. Many of them were exploring acquisition of tea gardens within India. This would enable them to provide the same value proposition of freshness as Tata Tea. Loss of the Russian business and uncertainties in the domestic market prompted major tea companies to reassess their strategies.[11] That is when Tata Tea ventured to make acquisitions within and beyond the shores of India. In the early 1990s, it established its international business division to consolidate export operations and explore innovative methods of selling tea to Russia, Uzbekistan and Kazakhstan. By then, it had acquired Consolidated Coffee, Asia's largest coffee producer. In 1996, it made its first overseas acquisition of the Watala Tea Estate in Sri Lanka. With 1100-crore kilos of high-quality tea leaves, and higher levels of productivity, it was a promising deal.

Tryst with Tetley

Now let's fly 7000 kilometres from India to Britain. Tetley and Company's tryst with tea began in 1856 in London, then the centre of global tea trade. The company expanded from the tea supplies business to blending and packing of tea. By 1888, the company began exporting Tetley Tea to the USA. An interesting incident happened in 1908, which led to the invention of the now famous 'teabags'. New York tea merchant, Thomas Sullivan, started sending samples of tea to customers in small silken bags, to avoid expenses associated with tins. The recipients thought that the tea was to be brewed with the bags into the tea pots, instead of emptying the contents. So successful was this accidental innovation that in 1939, the idea was brought to Tetley in the UK by one of its American representatives. The company capitalized on it and gradually mainstreamed teabags across markets and eventually introduced them in the UK in 1953. Nearly half a century later, the Tetley Teabag became the largest source of its income.

By the late 1990s, Tetley had become the world's second largest tea brand (after Lipton) with an annual production of 20 billion teabags. It blended, packed, marketed and distributed tea globally with three distinct markets—the UK and Ireland, the USA, and other commonwealth countries contributing to 54, 26 and 20 per cent of its revenues respectively. Given that it did not have its own plantations, it sourced tea through auctions from countries in Africa, Asia and Latin America. Due to differences in consumer palates, and uncertainty in availability of specific variety of tea leaves because of monsoon-related vagaries in different countries, Tetley's final blends were made from up to forty different varieties of tea from over 10,000 tea estates.[12] The Tetley brand, which accounted for 85 per cent of the company's global sales, was positioned as a premium brand in developing markets and at the higher end of the mass market in matured markets. Besides teabags, its product portfolio consisted of instant tea, flavoured tea, decaffeinated tea, green tea and herbal tea. It annually produced nearly 2000-crore teabags.

Tata Tea's first association with the Tetley brand was in 1992 through a joint venture with Lyons Tetley of the UK. Tetley was impressed with the quality of tea it had purchased from Florida-based Tata Tea Inc., a fully-owned Tata subsidiary set-up in 1984. Tata Tea was keen to enter into an agreement to supply instant tea to Tetley's operations in the USA. The new company Tata Tetley Ltd based in Cochin, manufactured teabags for export to eastern European and Middle Eastern markets.

By 1995, Krishna Kumar was Tata Tea's MD. In our conversation, he emphasized his convictions that changed the course of the company over the next five years.

> It was on track of becoming a consumer-driven company in India. But I soon realized that no company can remain successful or even survive if it remains a pure Indian company. A global world was unfolding. We realized that our marketplace is the world. But how do we get there? It was very difficult to launch our own brands and fight MNCs because it entailed huge investments.

Around that time, Kumar heard that the owners of Tetley wanted to sell their brands. He found a promising opportunity he had been long looking for.

The Tetley brands had continued to change ownership since their inception. By 1994, Pedro Domecq, a Spanish liquor company, was bought out by Allied Lyons, the owner of the Tetley brand for £739 million. The two entities merged to form Allied Domecq and became the world's second largest spirits company (after Canada's Seagram Group). By 1995, Allied Domecq decided to focus on the liquor business and divest the Tetley brands. It was an opportunity Kumar had been waiting for. He was supported in this adventure by senior leaders from Tata Sons.

The benefits of an acquisition were evident. If acquired, Tetley would provide Tata Tea distribution access in developed markets across thirty-five countries, including western Europe and North America. Tetley's expertise with brand and marketing and Tata Tea's strong base of plantations in India and Sri Lanka would be symbiotic and integrate the entire value chain. The two brands would also complement each other—Tata's mass-market brand portfolio and Tetley's premium brands. This was the greatest advantage for Tata Tea as building brands in developed countries was an enormously complex and cost-intensive exercise, especially for a company from the developing world. It would also give Tata Tea ownership of an established international brand to compete with HUL in India. Kumar was thoroughly convinced that Tata Tea should proceed with the due-diligence process to acquire Tetley. An opportunity of this kind was unlikely to arise again.

During our conversation, he recalled the attempt by Tata Tea to bid for Tetley.

> For making that bid, we had to remit money from India. Those were the days of foreign exchange restrictions, but we received strong support from the Reserve Bank of India and the Government of India, particularly the commerce ministry. They understood that this acquisition would be good for an Indian company and for the country. At ₹1500 crore, if accomplished, it would have been the first and the largest cross-border acquisition in the history of corporate India.

Tata Tea went through the normal process of a cross-border acquisition— gaining acceptance from the seller, and finalizing mutually agreeable terms on price and payment. Tata Tea's team was stationed at London during the due-diligence process. However, there was a problem. 'Tetley was three times the size of Tata Tea. We didn't have the resources for an outright purchase. So, we structured bond-based acquisition financing. However, this was not acceptable to the sellers. I failed. Tetley was acquired by somebody else,' shared Kumar with a tinge of regret in his voice.

Tetley for Tata

> 'In a world where brand strength is a crucial business success factor, the acquisition of the Tetley brand will provide Tata Tea with a valuable and worthwhile global opportunity.'

> Ratan Tata

Tetley's new owners were not keen on long-term ownership. In February 1999, Kumar, by then vice chairman, was informed by Arthur Anderson, leading consulting firm, that Tetley's owners were keen to sell the brand. Tata Tea and Tata Sons had long considered the benefits of acquiring Tetley. It was the only global tea brand not owned by consumer conglomerates such as Unilever and Nestle, and hence was a relatively easy acquisition target. The second opportunity to acquire Tetley was truly a godsend. Kumar recalled the Tatas' efforts to proactively pursue the acquisition.

> We worked very hard for a long time, put together a plan and resources, and got Tata Sons to support Tata Tea in making the acquisition with full backing of the Government of India. In that entire episode, I must have met everyone, except Prime Minister Atal Bihari Vajpayee. I met the commerce minister, finance minister, secretary to the government, and the RBI governor. The Tata name acted like a passport wherever I went. The RBI and the government did not doubt our integrity. They could have said no. It was not like today when you can make an acquisition without difficulty. Everyone understood the purpose behind our endeavour and supported us.

In June 1999, Tata Sons gave the green signal to Tata Tea for making a bid to acquire Tetley. A team headed by Siganporia, then deputy MD at Tata Tea, proceeded to London for due diligence. Arthur Andersen was appointed as financial advisers.[13] An intense due-diligence process clearly indicated that Tetley's expertise in tea buying, blending, packaging, cutting down inventory, sourcing and distribution was far superior to that of Unilever. The skill sets gained from Tetley, post-acquisition, would help Tata Tea's Indian operations to compete with Hindustan Unilever, the market leader.

A key member of the Tata team was Arun Gandhi. Partner at N.M. Raiji and Company, a chartered accountancy firm in Mumbai and auditors of Tata Tea, Gandhi was an expert in M&A. He recalled his experience of leading the first cross-border acquisition by an Indian group,

> At that time, remittances by Indian companies were restricted to certain times the company's net worth. The rest of the amount had to be borrowed locally. Structuring the transaction, looking at tax implications, compliance with FERA were challenges I worked on. We had to make an application for such an acquisition to RBI, which was also done, and permission received.

After nearly an eight-month-long due diligence, the Tatas gave their final bid for acquiring Tetley in February 2000. This time, its offer was fully backed by financing. Hooray! It was accepted by the owners. The Tatas beat competing interests from Nestle, the Swiss food company. The final acquisition price for the worldwide Tetley Tea business (including their private label tea business in the USA), amounted to £271 million (₹1900 crore). The acquisition was financed with £70 million in equity (including an issue of global depository receipts listed on London Stock Exchange) and the remaining through debt instruments. The equity investment in Tetley was routed through a special purpose vehicle in the UK called Tata Tea (Great Britain) Ltd. Tata Tea subscribed £60 million in the equity of its new subsidiary. The balance £10 million was subscribed by Tata Tea Inc.[14] Rabobank International acted as the adviser as well as the sole lead arranger for the transaction. Rana Kapoor, now MD of Yes Bank, and then head of Rabobank's India division, played a vital role throughout the deal. Rabobank underwrote £181 million of the total debt component. 'All securitization is based on Tetley's operations. Tata Tea is totally insulated from it. Its exposure is limited to the equity component,' stated Soonawala, then vice chairman at Tata Sons, at the time the acquisition was completed. He expected no strain on Tata Tea from the purchase. The two companies would retain independent identities to ensure Tata Tea's financial security.

The Tetley deal was hailed as the first-of-its-kind in the world. At the time of the acquisition, Tata Tea, a $200-million company, was world's largest integrated tea company with an annual sale of 250-crore tea bags. It had acquired Tetley, which was nearly four times its net worth. Many called this 'the audacious acquisition of a global shark by an Indian minnow'.[15] Not only was it the largest cross-border acquisition of an international brand by India Inc. but also the first instance of an Indian company resorting to a leveraged buyout (LBO)[16] to acquire an entity much larger in size. Gopalakrishnan called the use of the LBO model to fund the acquisition a business model innovation in times of stiff forex regulations. 'A funding model practised elsewhere was picked up and fitted into the Indian context in a manner that offered the least risk,' he observed.[17]

The Tetley acquisition brought about a sea change in the global perception about Tata Tea. 'Earlier we were seen as the underdog trying to stand up to Unilever. Now we are an MNC in the FMCG segment,' quipped Siganporia after the acquisition.[18] In an interview to *Economic Times* in 2001, Kumar shared a long-term vision for the Tatas' beverage business.

> I see us fusing all these entities into one super global company; seamlessly operating as one entity, deriving all the efficiencies of integration and imparting the necessary aggression in the marketplace to gain market share. It will be a very successful global tea company, owned by the Tatas.[19]

The post-honeymoon blues

During our conversation, Kumar observed, 'The challenge for us was not only about how to acquire Tetley, but also how to incorporate the practices of Tetley, combine them with ours and get world-beating standards in operation.' The post-acquisition integration of two legendary companies wasn't one without challenges. Homi Khusrokhan, former MD of Tata Tea, who took charge in the year after Tetley's acquisition, jovially compared the integration phase with the adjustment phase in a marriage, which starts immediately after the honeymoon. He identified several challenges Tata Tea faced in effectively integrating two companies from two continents with two different cultures.

The most evident challenge was one of cultural integration. Given that the acquirer was a smaller company than the one acquired, and that too a former colony, made many Tetley employees uncomfortable in the early days. For example, Tata executives complained about being kept waiting when visiting Tetley's UK head office reception centre, despite being the senior partners! Tetley people complained about being run by a company that was predominantly India-centric, with limited knowledge about Western markets.[20] Acknowledging the seniority and experience of the Tetley employees, and to prevent mass resignations, Tetley employees were given substantial retention packages. Thus, key managerial talent at Tetley continued to run the Tetley business. Tata Tea also appointed Boston Consulting Group to help integrate Tetley's operations with its own in purchase of loose tea, blending and marketing. From a structural perspective, a supervisory board consisting of executive directors from Tata Tea and Tetley was set up. Under the board's direction, a steering committee oversaw the integration. Cross-functional teams consisting of members from both companies were formed to study and suggest integration and efficient management of eight key business processes, including product and new market development, procurement and logistics.[21] The entire Tata Tea buying and blending team was also trained in Tetley methods and quality standards so that the two companies could seamlessly operate in these areas, especially when Tetley bought 80 lakh kg of Indian tea every year.

The other key challenge was managing an acquisition that was heavily ring-fenced with a 3:1 debt/equity ratio.[22] Khusrokhan observed that in such a scenario, banks had a say in what was being done. Therefore, in the early days, Tata Tea restricted its role to an advisory one: monitoring, guiding and watching over Tetley's operations. By the end of 2001, an encouraging performance by Tetley led to greater equity investments by Tata Tea and Tata Sons. Some of the high-cost debt incurred on the acquisition was brought down to 1.37:1 by March 2003. This was also the first year when the board of Tata Tea (Great Britain) Ltd, the 100 per cent owner of

Tetley, approved a maiden interim dividend of ₹30 crore. By 2005, the debt/equity ratio reached the desirable 1:1 level. Accordingly, Tata Tetley Ltd. merged into Tata Tea on 1 April 2005 and became a unit of the company. Tata Tea's vision of a single operating company with global presence and operations had been achieved. By then, it realized several benefits. 'Tetley has given us access to knowledge, and globally benchmarked processes, which in turn, has enabled the company to manage the transformation to branding that much faster,' observed Siganporia. The way forward was volume growth through entry into newer geographies, growth through value-added and flavoured tea, and inorganic expansion.

A global beverage company

'The Tata Group thinks from century to century, and not from quarter to quarter.'

Harish Bhat

Empowered with the experience gained through the successful acquisition and integration of Tetley with Tata Tea, the latter's acquisition spree continued. In October 2005, Tetley US Holding, a subsidiary of Tata Tea, acquired the California-based Good Earth Corporation, a maker of green tea and herbal tea. In June 2006, Tata Coffee, another subsidiary of Tata Tea, acquired the US-based Eight O'Clock Coffee Company (EOC), from Gryphon Investors for ₹1015 crore. A month later in August 2006, Tata Tea achieved its second global milestone. It acquired a 30 per cent stake in enhanced water maker, Energy Brands Inc., USA, (Glaceau Vitamin Water), for $677 million. At that time, it was the largest overseas acquisition by an Indian company. Recalled Gandhi, who was by then a director in Tata Sons:

> An Italian family owned the company. We saw value in the business and acquired a stake. Within less than a year, the family interests were sold to Coca-Cola Company for $4.1 billion. We had a choice, whether to continue with a minority interest or sell our stake. We decided to sell it rather than be a minority shareholder with Coca-Cola.

Ratan Tata had always maintained a clear mandate for Tata companies. In an interview he once stated, 'Our policy has been that we won't be passive investors; we always go for equal partnership. If the pressures are strong, we have them (joint venture partners) buy us out or we buy them out.' Coca-Cola acquired the Tatas' stake for $1.2 billion (₹4920 crore). Tata Tea and Tata Sons made a profit of $523 million (₹2144 crore) on the deal in just nine months.

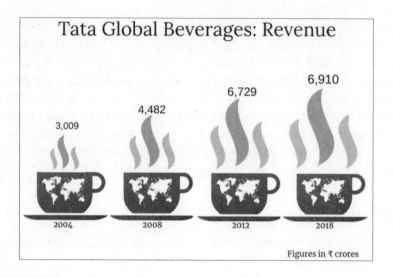

Tata Global Beverages: Revenue

3,009 — 2004
4,482 — 2008
6,729 — 2012
6,910 — 2018

Figures in ₹ crores

In a span of six years, Tata Tea had spent $1.2 billion to acquire several companies across the globe to expand its product portfolio and enter developed markets. Domestically, it achieved its long-cherished dream of defeating HUL, its closest rival. For more than a decade since 2007, the Tata Tea market share hovered between 19.2 to 21.4 per cent compared to HUL's 18.6 to 20 per cent. Compare this with its market share of a mere 3 per cent compared to HUL's 80 per cent in 1974. Tata Tea had come a very long way and become a force to reckon with in Indian and global markets. Moreover, it had a workforce of about 60,000 permanent employees—a distinct feature in the tea industry where competitors mainly employed only contract labourers.[23]

Kumar's vision of Tata's global beverage company came true when Tata Tea became Tata Global Beverages and was introduced as such to shareholders at the AGM in July 2010. The new company with a global management structure encompassed all acquired companies and joint ventures and was one big cohesive group of brands, including Tetley, Tata Tea, Tata Coffee, Eight O' Clock Coffee, Himalaya and many others. It had become the most globalized company in the Tata Group with 70 per cent of its revenues coming from international operations, and more people around the world drinking Tata Tea than using Tata vehicles, Tata steel or even TCS software! By 2018, every single day, 4.5-crore cups of Tetley tea were consumed across the globe, making Tata Global Beverages the world's second largest tea company.

CHAPTER 13

JOINING THE RANKS OF WORLD'S MOST GEOGRAPHICALLY DIVERSIFIED CHEMICAL COMPANIES

An oasis in a desert of despair[1]

The Tatas' foray into the chemicals industry marked its very first acquisition—the Okha Salt Works (OSW). Kapilram Vakil, grandson of Nanabhai Desai, the first Indian justice of the Bombay High Court, had returned from University of Manchester with a chemical engineering degree around 1918. Despite many offers in Britain, he opted to join Tata Sons as chief consulting chemist. After serving several Tata projects both in India and overseas, and exploring avenues to start a venture in the chemicals sector, Vakil left Tata Sons in 1923. His efforts in reconnoitring the Gujarat shoreline for prospective opportunities attracted the attention of Maharaja Sayajirao Gaekwad, the visionary ruler of Baroda. To create jobs and economic development in an area that was lagging behind in his kingdom due to harsh global situations, Gaekwad invited Vakil to undertake the development of salt and alkali industries in Okhamandal, the northwestern tip of the Gulf of Kutch. He was given 1700 acres of land free of cost. In September 1926, Okha Salt Works was born as an outcome of Vakil's untiring entrepreneurial efforts. The eminent industrialist Walchand Hirachand was the chairman of the firm and Kapilram Ltd the managing agents. Till then, manufacture of salt and salt-based products was a monopoly of foreign companies. However, his enterprise was not going to be a dream run. A combination of factors, including the impact of World War I on the Indian economy, the vagaries of nature in the desert region, and British legislation, turned the venture into a loss-making unit. Despite these insurmountable troubles, within a decade of inception, OSW emerged as the largest manufacturer of sea salt on the Indian subcontinent.

It was becoming increasingly difficult for Vakil to independently sustain his enterprise. Once again, he looked up to Maharaja Gaekwad for financial help and guidance, especially because he was keen to expand from salts to alkalis. At that time, V.T. Krishnamachariar, the Diwan of Baroda, wrote to the Tatas if they would be interested in assisting a project of national importance.[2] Nowroji Saklatvala, then chairman of Tata Sons, showed keen interest and encouraged Vakil to prepare a comprehensive plan for setting up the chemicals plant. This was a time when India produced no industrial chemicals and depended on imports for basic soda compound inputs that were used in textile, glass, paper and soap industries. The proposed venture would hence be highly relevant to Indian industry. The estimated expense of ₹1.2 crore for setting up the new plant and township, and acquiring OSW's existing set-up was discussed and debated by a team of experts at Tata Sons, along with Vakil. The plan was finally accepted by J.R.D. Tata, the new chairman. OSW can thus be called the first major acquisition by Tata Sons. Vakil was paid ₹11.5 lakh for the acquisition; he continued to lead the new venture. J.R.D. listed the group's new venture—Tata Chemicals, considered the biggest chemical works in India at that time—on the Bombay Stock Exchange in March 1939, on the eve of World War II. But, it wasn't before a decade and a half thereafter that Tata Chemicals achieved stability.

The impact of World War II was felt when the ship carrying the material to set up the plant was torpedoed and sunk. Thereafter, a combination of complex circumstances, including limitations of a fledgling economy after Independence, import dumping, natural calamities, and labour unrest, took a severe toll on the Tatas' plans for the success of its model chemicals township and plant at Mithapur (meaning 'city of salt' in Gujarati). Zola Deutsche, an American consultant, told J.R.D. that he was in the wrong place and in the wrong business. The sooner he got out of it, the better for him and the group. But J.R.D. refused to give up. The Tatas were convinced that alkalis and chemicals are the 'germ cells of industry'. They believed that through this company, they were helping India with the means to become a modern industrial state. The enormity of efforts and the doggedness displayed by the Tata leadership to make a dream come true can be understood from a statement J.R.D. made, 'Of all the companies with which I have been concerned, none has had to overcome so many difficulties, compounded with bad luck, as has been the lot of Tata Chemicals.'

'Cometh the hour, cometh the man,' it is often said. The year of India's independence brought to Tata Chemicals' Mithapur plant a twenty-seven-year-old lad who eventually became synonymous with the growth and success of Tata Chemicals over the next forty-five years. He was Darbari Seth, a Pathan from the North-West Frontier Province (now in Pakistan). Seth had completed his chemical engineering from the University of Cincinnati and gained brief experience with Dow Chemicals in Holland. He joined Tata Chemicals at the insistence of a former professor in January 1947. Given his dynamism, he was identified in the early 1950s and subsequently groomed by J.R.D., and made in charge of the Mithapur plant by 1956. His ascent in the organization from a chemical engineer to the chairman is a fascinating journey grounded in hard work and a never-say-die attitude. Although a victim of partition horrors, he was a proud Indian with a vision. He worked towards making Tata Chemicals not only India's premier chemical enterprise but also one of the largest integrated salt works and chemical complexes in the world. During his years at the helm, the company's market cap increased 900 times—from ₹5 crore to ₹4600 crore.[3]

Gopalakrishnan called the chemical industry the software industry equivalent of the twentieth century. Vakil had once observed that a nation's industrial prowess could be gauged by the quantity of sodium compounds it consumed. Expectedly, for most part of the century, the chemicals industry was a fast-growing one, attracted large research expenditure and fascinated people with its technology. Having succeeded in becoming one of India's leading chemicals company, Tata Chemicals was desirous of making a mark on the global stage, and continued to explore opportunities beyond Indian shores. It had first made attempts to build a soda ash plant way back in 1971 in Argentina, and an alumina smelter project in Venezuela in 1990. Both were wrecked by government red tape. Liberalization brought its own set of problems making the company vulnerable to global competition and imports. So Tata Chemicals' mantra for the 1990s was 'defend, consolidate and grow'. By 2004, when Khusrokhan joined as executive director, the company was ready to spread its wings across the global markets.

The world's most geographically diversified soda ash company

'When you are stuck in India, you face the heat of overseas-based competition on your home turf. Why not go out and fight them on their home turf?'

Homi Khusrokhan

Tata Chemicals' very first global venture was the acquisition of 33 per cent stake in Morocco-based chemical company, Indo Maroc Phosphore S.A., for a consideration of ₹133 crore. At that time, India imported 50 per cent of the world's production of phosphoric acid and Morocco accounted for over 40 per cent of global trade in acid. The investment, which came with board representation for Tata Chemicals executives, provided valuable phosphoric acid supplies for its fertilizer plant in Haldia. Tata Chemicals' leadership was keen to diversify both—sources of supply and markets for its products to beat economic cyclicity, a common problem in B2B markets. Over the years, the company had expanded and classified its products into 'LIFE' categories. Living Essentials (agri) included items used in everyday living—iodized salt, protein-rich pulses, nutraceuticals and water. Industry Essentials (chemicals) primarily consisted of industrial supplies such as soda ash and soda bicarbonate, key ingredients in glass, detergent, pharmaceuticals and industrial chemicals. Farm Essentials (fertilizers) comprised crop nutrients such as urea and phosphate fertilizers. These contributed 6, 48 and 46 per cent respectively of the company's consolidated revenues by mid-noughties.

Tata Chemicals' first major target had its story intertwined with India's chemical industry in some measure. In early twentieth century, four British chemical companies became extremely successful: Brunner Mond, Nobel Explosives, British Dyestuffs, and United Alkali. In 1926, these four were amalgamated into a giant called Imperial Chemical Industries (ICI) with 33,000 employees.[4] Not known to the common masses given its B2B focus, ICI group of companies was the largest multinational company operating in India until the late 1970s, even bigger than its well-known British peers—HUL and ITC. One of these four—Brunner Mond—was divested from ICI in 1991 and acquired by Soda Ash Investments, a consortium of PE investors, including Wayland Investments and Barclays Bank. True to a typical PE mandate, the consortium's key focus was to milk the company[5] at the best price, whenever the opportunity arose.

Brunner Mond was not only a market leader in the UK's soda ash business with manufacturing locations in several countries, but also had a hidden gem—the Kenya-based Magadi Soda Company (MSC) as its subsidiary. Established in 1911, MSC had access to trona (a naturally occurring mineral that contains sodium carbonate compounds) from one of the purest surface deposits in the base of Africa's Great Rift Valley at Lake Magadi, 120 kilometres south-east of Nairobi. The self-renewing trona deposits at Magadi were the second largest in the world, and formed a key ingredient in the manufacturing of soda ash. (Trona converts into soda ash when heated and purified.) Prasad Menon, then Tata Chemicals MD, had been prospecting opportunities for collaborating with and eventually acquiring Brunner Mond since 2001. While he received a cold shoulder during many an interaction at international industry events, the proverbial doors finally opened in December 2005. Within three weeks and with Menon leading the team at the negotiating table in London, Brunner Mond became a Tata Chemicals subsidiary. A two-decade veteran at ICI, Menon had tried hard to negotiate an acquisition only for MSC, but as in most international M&As, it was a package deal for ₹798 crore. Tata Chemicals had gained a 63.5 per cent stake in Brunner Mond from Wayland Investments and

Barclays Bank, and the remaining stake was gained through a mandatory open offer. The acquisition was funded through internal cash balances.

The deal not only brought Tata Chemicals into the $1-billion club but also established it as the world's third-largest soda ash producer, with a total capacity of 3 million tonnes (over three times its pre-acquisition capacity). It also gained access to markets in Germany, France and Africa in addition to its Asian presence. A year before Jamsetji Tata set up the Empress Mills in Nagpur in 1874, Chemist Ludwig Mond entered into partnership with industrialist Sir John Tomlinson Brunner to form a chemical manufacturing firm, Brunner, Mond and Company in Cheshire (northwest England). Little was it known that more than 140 years later, their destinies would converge! Incidentally, ICI, the former owner of Brunner Mond had attempted to cripple Tata Chemicals in its formative years. The story had come full circle when Tata Chemicals acquired two of ICI's former companies. Ironically, ICI's identity ceased by 2008. A series of highly leveraged acquisitions negatively impacted the conglomerate, which was eventually acquired by the Netherlands-headquartered specialty chemicals company Akzo Nobel.

In any acquisition, integration of both entities is the real challenge. In this case, there were not one, but three entities spread across three continents, nurturing three exclusive misunderstandings. R. Mukundan, now Tata Chemicals MD, recalled them.

> Mithapur was worried that with Kenya brought in the India operation would be scaled down since it wasn't as cost competitive.[6] In Magadi, the worry was that the purchase has been made to eliminate the competition it was posing to Mithapur. In Britain, the worry was that they came as a baggage with Magadi and would be disowned later.

Once again, the Tatas' approach to cultural integration came into play. Even before the acquisition, it won the confidence of the Brunner Mond employees by committing to protect their pensions, a priority for British workers. Post-acquisition, it launched Project Fusion, a strong integration plan with a clear intent of meeting business objectives. The 100-day integration process with time-bound targets was implemented through cross-functional teams in Britain, Kenya and India. Even before senior executives from the UK and Kenya came to Mumbai as part of Project Fusion, Tata Chemicals had issued communication guidelines for its executives to mingle with newer colleagues: avoid terms such as 'acquisition' and 'ownership', and instead speak of 'coming together' and 'parentage'; and avoid the use of 'you' and 'us', and instead always use 'we'.[7]

Khusrokhan, who took over from Menon as MD of Tata Chemicals, had gained substantial first-hand experience with the Tata–Tetley integration (when he was Tata Tea's MD). In the Tata scheme of things, the senior leadership at Brunner Mond was given charge of running the operations, while Tata Chemicals focused primarily on financial control. For longer-term synergies, a Global Chemicals Advisory Council to guide strategy and policies, and a Business Heads Council to coordinate operations, sales and marketing, were formed with representation from three companies. The challenge with the Kenyan workforce was of a different nature. Historically, they had not been treated well by Indian traders in East Africa. They carried a similar notion about the Tatas. Menon realized that the only way to expose them to Tata values would be to bring them to India. Five of the senior-most leaders from Magadi were brought to Mithapur and Mumbai. That was it. In Menon's words 'they came, they saw, they were converted'.

The Tata Juggernaut rolls on to another continent

While Tata Chemicals was courting Brunner Mond, another chemicals major 12,500 kilometres away, in New Jersey, was also wanting to acquire that company. They felt slighted when Tata Chemicals acquired the company they had long cherished to own. General Chemical and Industrial Products (GCIP) was one of the world's leading chemicals company founded in 1884. Its facility at Green river in the state of Wyoming, USA, was one of the largest soda ash facilities in North America, with an underground trona mine that spanned 55 square miles. The trona dated back 5-crore years when the Green River Basin harboured a 1554 sq km lake. With evaporation over time, the lake left a 20,000-crore tonne deposit of pure trona between layers of sandstone and shale. The estimated recoverable trona ore reserves were approximately 60-crore tonnes, enough to meet global demand for approximately 100 years! GCIP annually mined more than 45-lakh tonnes of trona ore to produce about 25-lakh tonnes of one of the finest quality of soda ash in the world. Moreover, the cost of producing soda ash from trona at the Green river basin were amongst the lowest in the world.[8] It was a dream facility for any soda ash manufacturing company.

In March 2005, GCIP's leadership came to India with a proposal to acquire Tata Chemicals. They met Menon and Mukundan at Bombay House and expressed their thoughts. The Tatas politely declined their offer but expressed interest to work collaboratively. Two years later, Tata Chemicals made an offer to acquire GCIP to Harbinger Capital Partners, a PE fund which had acquired GCIP in 2004. They declined. The Tatas made two more offers, the one in December 2007 being the most attractive—$950 million. While Harbinger was considering an IPO for GCIP, the Tatas' offer was too attractive to decline. Khusrokhan and Mukundan were invited for discussion at a notice of just two days. They promptly agreed and landed in New York on a Monday morning to initiate the process. After six weeks of due diligence, Tata Chemicals proposed a final offer for $1.05 billion on 28 January 2008. Harbinger declined. Seeing the Tatas' intense interest in acquiring GCIP, the PR fund leaders thought that a little more haggling would bring forth a better price from the Tatas. Mukundan, and his ninety-member team had worked hard to come to the fair price. He was not ready to bargain. 'To my mind, you must know your walk away point in a deal. It doesn't matter if it's a dollar more or less. You have to step out of the room and say—my game is done.' As Mukundan was leaving for Mumbai, the Harbinger leadership called him again at the airport and asked him to stay back for negotiation. He refused stating that this was not the Tata way of doing business and that his company wasn't willing to bargain for $5–10 million for the deal. Realizing that they had negotiated up to the hilt, Harbinger called back five minutes later, and confirmed the billion-dollar (₹4000 crore) acquisition of GCIP by Tata Chemicals over a call with Mukundan at the JFK International Airport.

It was a historic day for Tata Chemicals. With this acquisition, the company had risen to become the second largest producer of soda ash (after Solvay) in the world, with a consolidated annual production capacity of 5.5 million tonnes. A debt-free company, GCIP gave access to Tata Chemicals to markets in North America and Latin America, Europe, and Far East Asia. The key advantage of the acquisition was access to natural soda ash, which was at half the cost of production of synthetic soda ash (extracted from common salt). It was also environmentally friendly and used less energy in the production process. Tata Chemicals now had access to two of the world's largest and lowest-cost natural soda ash reserves.[9] In just three years from 2005 to 2008, Tata Chemicals' revenue from soda ash increased from 18 to 49 per cent, and revenue from international operations for its chemicals business jumped to nearly 65 per cent. Between 2000 and 2008, Tata Chemicals' revenues increased eight times. It was no longer a company dealing in inorganic chemicals. It became a provider of holistic solutions in the global chemicals sector. Charting the road ahead after a slew of acquisitions, Khusrokhan shared Tata Chemicals' vision.

There comes a time in the history of companies when they stop thinking in traditional compartments such as domestic and international. The vision we have is not to be the largest soda ash company in the world, but the world's premier soda ash company. That means having the best people, the best processes, the best customers and, of course, giving the best possible returns to our stakeholders.

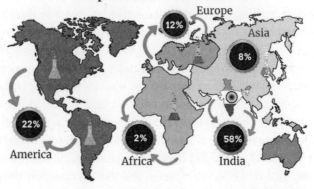

Tata Chemicals: Geographic Dispersion of Revenue

Figures as in 2017

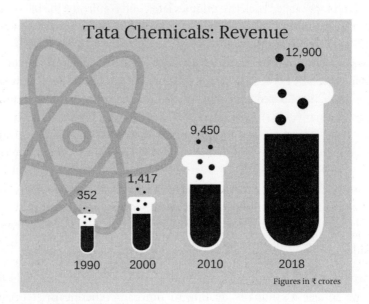

Tata Chemicals: Revenue

1990   352
2000   1,417
2010   9,450
2018   12,900

Figures in ₹ crores

The vision and its fulfilment

On Tetley's acquisition, Ratan Tata had said, 'It is a bold move and I hope that other Indian corporates will follow.' Since then, there was no turning back. India Inc. did follow the Tatas' example and acquired over 400 companies across domains during the same period. Yet, the biggest global acquirer from India was Tata Sons. From the mid-1990s to 2003, Tata Group acquired on average one company every year. In the decade since the turn of the millennium, Tata Group acquired over thirty-six global corporations, investing nearly $30 billion. Before it began its global journey in 2000, the group earnings were about $9 billion. Within ten years, Tata Sons' net revenue was eight times larger at $70 billion, of which two-thirds came from overseas operations.[10]

Share of International Revenues

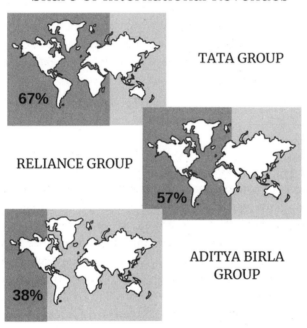

As envisaged by Ratan Tata two decades earlier, the reforms of 1991 led to a considerable restructuring of the Indian industry, which emerged from it leaner, more efficient and competitive. In some ways, the Indian experience followed the Japanese and Korean tradition of enterprise development policies, which may have lessons for other developing countries.[11] In the process, with operations spread across eighty countries in just a decade, the Tata Group truly became India's first and largest multinational conglomerate.

CHAPTER 14

A CHORUS ABOUT CORUS

'I hope that a hundred years from now we will spread our wings far beyond India, that we become a global group, operating in many countries, an Indian business conglomerate that is at home in the world, carrying the same sense of trust that we do today.'

Ratan Tata

Since the mid-1990s, Tata Steel was exploring another site for setting up a greenfield steel plant. The Jamshedpur plant was reaching saturation, and the leadership believed that an additional plant in another location would help achieve the company's organic expansion plans. The first site identified was Gopalpur in the Ganjam district of Odisha. It emerged the best of fifteen locations on the east and west coast due to its strategic location on trunk rail and road routes and its proximity to iron ore mines. Its claim to fame was that it had sent Prime Minister Narasimha Rao to the Parliament in 1996. With Tata Steel's investment, it was slated to be the biggest industrial plant in India.[1] With great efforts Tata Steel got the land and by 1998 had invested over ₹130 crore in developing it. However, the site suffered from severe water shortage. Lack of access to port and installation of railway lines, both of which were the responsibilities of the Odisha government made the site unfeasible. The company decided to look for another place. Having done business in Odisha for nearly a century, Tata Steel had established its credentials. Hence, the prospective site was identified at Kalinganagar in the Jajpur district of Odisha. It was allotted an area of 3741 acres of land for which payment was made to the government. The factory was initially planned at a cost of ₹15,000 crore and slated to start production by 2010.

In January 2005, Tata Steel moved a team to Kalinganagar to oversee plant construction. With great enthusiasm of building India's largest greenfield steel plant, the company had anticipated to reach production of 15 Mtpa by 2015. Little did it know that trouble was awaiting Tata Steel. In the very first week at Kalinganagar, scores of people belonging to the local tribes gathered at the plant site to protest construction. They alleged they had received lower than market-rate compensation for their land from the government and hence would not let Tata Steel build the compound wall to demarcate the area. In the madness that ensued, thirteen tribal people lost their lives in local police firing. What was meant to be a harbinger of commercial success for Tata Steel, became a liability.

Tata Steel did not give up. While the issue got entangled in local politics and tribal rights, the company continued to invest in community and tribal development around Kalinganagar. Not only did Tata Steel support a new rehabilitation policy for the tribal population by the Odisha government, but also went further. Hussain highlighted that Tata Steel built a school and a twenty-bed hospital at Kalinganagar for the tribal population. The company also created colonies for people belonging to thirteen villages near the site, established skill development centres and gave preference for jobs to native people. Over the years, the villagers were convinced of the Tatas' genuine intentions and willingly moved away from the land.

In November 2015, Odisha Chief Minister Naveen Patnaik inaugurated Tata Steel's new Kalinganagar plant, a decade after it had been planned. He acknowledged that the plant with 3 Mtpa capacity would create direct employment opportunity for 3000 people and indirect employment for 22,000 people. Highlighting the Herculean efforts to restore normalcy at Kalinganagar, T.V. Narendran, now MD at Tata Steel, recollected how several people had written off the project just like the Nano plant at Singur. 'We ignored the naysayers, went to work on the ground and slowly, bit by bit, got the project back on track.' This did not come without its associated costs. The extra payout and time overrun saw the cost of project go up nearly 75 per cent to ₹26,000 crore. In 2025, when the plant reaches its terminal capacity of 12 Mtpa and becomes a bigger plant than Jamshedpur, the investment would swell to ₹50,000 crore, over three-and-half times of the original estimate.[2]

In 2005, Tata Steel signed another agreement with the Chhattisgarh government to set up a 5.5 Mtpa plant in Bastar at a cost of almost ₹20,000 crore. However, that plan never saw the light of day. It was shelved several years later citing delay in land acquisition as the primary reason. Moreover, Tata Steel could not prospect an iron ore mine near Bastar because it was allocated in an area infested with Naxal activities. Were such organic expansion plans commercially tenable for Tata Steel in the long run?

Tata Steel's global adventures

The constant concern of senior leaders at Tata Steel and Tata Sons was that given the complexity of the Indian steel industry, the red tape in getting permissions, and issues of land acquisition in the hinterland, it would not be able to reach its growth goals domestically—neither through organic nor inorganic means. Opportunities for domestic acquisitions in the steel sector hardly existed. At such a time, Ratan Tata's vision to see the Tata businesses in a global context inspired Tata Steel to venture beyond Indian shores. Proximity made East Asian countries the first target market. NatSteel headquartered in Singapore became the very first international acquisition. In August 2004, Tata Steel signed an agreement to acquire Singapore's largest steel company for ₹1313 crore in an all-cash transaction. The acquisition process was completed by February 2005. It not only added an additional capacity of 2 Mtpa to Tata Steel's 4 Mtpa, but also gave access to six markets—Australia, China, Philippines, Malaysia, Thailand and Vietnam.

In April 2006, Millennium Steel became the second global acquisition by Tata Steel, adding another 1.2 Mtpa to its steel production capacity. It was Thailand's largest manufacturer and distributor of long steel products with over 90 per cent of sales generated from domestic consumption. With its consolidated production capacity doubling in just two years, Tata Steel jumped from the fifty-sixth to the twenty-eighth position in global ranking. 'These first regional acquisitions let us test the waters of M&A and taught us how to run a transnational business, to understand the cultural issues and to integrate larger organizations,'[3] observed Koushik Chatterjee, now CFO at Tata Steel.

A chorus for acquiring Corus

Tata Steel wasn't satisfied with the scale it had achieved with Asian acquisitions. One of the main reasons for its increasing growth appetite was the anticipated increase in demand for steel—both domestically and globally. India's per capita consumption of steel was 40 kg, far below the global average of 185 kg. Domestic consumption was expected to grow substantially due to the strong GDP growth projections, and a ₹14.4 lakh crore infrastructure investment planned between 2007 and 2012 by the Government of India.[4] In a 2005 strategic review, Tata Steel's board agreed that the next stage would have to be a strategic alliance or takeover. The company had the right mix of being the world's most profitable steel company and was in Asia's fast-growing markets with access to raw materials. That's when it received signals of interest from the Anglo-Dutch steel giant—Corus. It was during a meeting on 24 November 2005 to explore collaborative opportunities, between Ratan Tata, B. Muthuraman, Tridibesh Mukherjee—the top leadership of Tata Steel—and chairman Jim Leng and Managing Director Philippe Varin of Corus, when the latter observed, 'Corus and Tata Steel have capacities of 20 and 5 million tonnes respectively. Both have approximately the same market value and similar product lines. Can we not put our businesses together in some meaningful way?' That was when the idea of acquiring Corus first occurred to Ratan Tata.[5] Tata Steel had engaged with Corus since 1992 in coke making and blast furnace facilities improvement. It was also one of the few big steel makers with its own abundant coal and iron ore reserves. If the Corus acquisition did materialize, one of its strategies would be to produce raw steel at a low cost in India, then ship it to Corus' first-rate mills to make finished products.[6] Whatever the strategy or structure, Ratan Tata was clear about one thing—the identity of Tata Steel would have to remain intact. A foundation of the Tata Group, the company had been symbolic of and synonymous with India's industrial development.

Formed in 1999 through a merger of British Steel Corporation[7] and Koninklijke Hoogovens, Corus had a production capacity of 19 Mtpa, and ranked among the top ten steel-producing companies in the world. It had sixteen manufacturing locations across Europe and North America, besides thirty-three distribution centres. Around this time, Netherlands-based Mittal Steel, one of the world's largest steel producers by volume and turnover founded by Lakshmi Mittal from India, had merged with Arcelor of Luxembourg, world's largest steel producer in terms of turnover, becoming ArcelorMittal— the world's largest steel maker with a combined manufacturing capacity of 109.7 Mtpa, nearly four times the size of its closest competitor—Nippon Steel from Japan. Following the merger, the global steel industry stock market index rose by nearly 24 per cent more than the overall index for all world stocks.[8] Emphasizing the role that these developments played on Tata Steel's decision to explore a global partnership with Corus, Hussain observed:

> After merging with Arcelor, Mittal had grown to over 100 Mtpa annual capacity, and we were at 8 Mtpa. We looked at the threat—if you want to remain a relevant player in this business, you must get to at least 25 Mtpa. That is what Corus would help us do. It was a defensive move in a globalizing context.

The Corus deal, if accomplished, would catapult Tata Steel to the position of sixth-largest producer of steel in the world. Besides giving it an instant presence in major global markets and in value-added products serving automobile and construction sectors, the combined entity would save ₹2025 crore in production, procurement, financing and other synergies in the first three years after acquisition. From a strategic perspective, it would ring-fence Tata Group's flagship company from a potential takeover threat, especially when Tata Son's ownership of Tata Steel was around 35 per cent, and global consolidation in the steel industry was increasingly becoming the order of the day. Corus would de-risk the Tatas' Indian business between high-growth emerging markets and price-stable developed markets. But this would come at enormous financial commitment of accomplishing a deal ten times larger than any previous acquisition by Tata Group.[9] Thus, problems of the Indian steel industry and consolidation of the global steel industry were prime factors that made the Corus deal a must-explore opportunity. A former vice president in the group chairman's office recollected the situation faced by Tata Steel at that point.

> We were having huge challenges in setting up our plants domestically with clearances running into more than ten years. If we went with Corus, we would have an existing 21 Mtpa capacity readily available. Where on earth would you get that on day one? It is the ability or time required to get that much capacity at that particular point of time, which offered a tremendous opportunity for us to be global.

The audacious acquisition begins

After a lot of parleys between the two camps, in October 2006, Tata Steel confirmed its interest in acquiring Corus, and proposed a $7.6 billion (₹34,200 crore) bid at 455 pence a share in cash. What began as a negotiated deal turned into a full-blooded corporate war when Companhia Siderurgica Nacional (CSN), a resource-rich Brazilian company entered the fray in November 2006 with an indicative bid of 477 pence a share. Ratan Tata picked up the gauntlet and marshalled a team of experts to work for the Tatas. Rothschild, the investment banking and advisory firm, was roped in along with representatives from ABN Amro, Deutsche Bank and Credit Suisse.[10]

Arun Gandhi, the chief strategist of the deal, acknowledged that acquiring Corus had huge challenges because it was a listed company. 'For the first time, India and the Tatas were going overseas to look at a listed company. Given the size of the transaction, this wasn't done before by anybody,' he acknowledged. How did the impossible finally happen?

Gandhi described the view he gained from the cockpit throughout the exciting acquisition process. 'After CSN's offer, we made a statement that the Tatas are still interested and are considering the matter. We did not want the market to sell shares to CSN.' The core team put together by Ratan Tata for this unprecedented deal consisted of Gandhi, Muthuraman, Chatterjee and Hussain. On Sunday, 10 December, a collective decision was made to present a counter-offer at 500 pence per share. On Monday, 11 December, even before Gandhi woke up at London, CSN had made a counter-offer at 515 pence. The process was getting supremely competitive and extremely exhilarating. He had very limited time to make another statement for the markets. But even before the London Stock Exchange opened at 8 a.m., Gandhi confirmed the

Tatas' interest to pursue the deal, just to ensure that the shares were not sold to CSN at 515 pence. To avoid this ping-pong kind of situation between two bidders, the UK's panel on takeovers and mergers (PTM) decided a nine-round bidding process between the Tatas and CSN, a first in the UK's M&A history. The panel selected 30 January 2007 as D-Day. It had to be a day and time when stock exchanges in India, Brazil and London were closed. This is because the performance of either company during the bidding process could have huge repercussions on the share prices of the three listed companies in their respective countries. On 30 January, bidding was to start after 4.30 p.m.[11]

Gandhi was in the Tata lawyer's office in London and the Tata team led by Ratan Tata was at the Taj Mahal Palace Hotel in Mumbai. CSN was in their lawyer's bidding room. Both lawyers' offices were electronically connected with the PTM. After both parties made their bids for a round, the PTM would inform them about the higher bid and confirm whether either would want to enter the next round. They had an hour to decide and make a fresh bid. It sounded like a scene from a movie! Gandhi shared the insight he gained from reading the bidding documents.

> In my view, I had possibly read the requirements better than CSN. I understood that only the last round of bidding really mattered. If between two offers you were higher, you had to pay only five pence more than the opponent's bid, not what you had bid.

The bidding began from 515 pence, and Gandhi went up five pence every time CSN's bid was higher than the Tata bid. After every round, Gandhi interacted with Ratan Tata and team on the hotline. On two occasions they even changed phone numbers to ensure total secrecy. A stage came when the Tata team in Mumbai asked Gandhi, 'Why are you going up only by 5 pence?' They were upset that he was not being aggressive enough. 'I could not tell them my game plan. They did not know my strategy till after the event,' quipped Gandhi. At every round, the bidders were required to provide a certificate to the PTM that they were ready with the cash, lest there were payment problems after the bid was won. 'I had kept my bankers in the office to give me a cash certificate after every round,' recalled Gandhi. 'Of course, not in the room from where I was bidding,' he laughed. 'That one night I must have borrowed several billion dollars!'

In the last round, the bid price reached 595 pence. CSN had no clue about the Tatas' maximum offer. Gandhi did not know theirs. The ninth round was over. CSN's final bid was 603 pence. Gandhi, on behalf of the Tatas, had bid 608 pence (close to the maximum limit internally set by the Tatas). Tata Steel clinched the deal at $12 billion (₹53,500 crore). It created history by making the largest-ever acquisition in Europe, and that too by a former British colony! It was as if history had come a full circle. Nearly a century ago, Jamsetji Tata had requested Lord George Hamilton, then secretary of state in British India, for the government's cooperation in starting India's first steelworks. A 100 years later, in the centennial year of Tata Steel, it acquired one of the largest steel companies of England. Ratan Tata and team were thrilled to acquire a company four times its own size. India was jubilant with headlines across newspapers showering praises on the Tatas for being the first multinational Indian conglomerate.

The acquisition was structured as a 100 per cent LBO funded through cash resources and loans raised by Tata Steel and a special purpose vehicle (SPV) – Tata Steel UK. The debt was raised on the cash flows and the assets of Corus and repaid through its future earnings. Thus, Tata Steel's assets were ring-fenced in case of a default. The acquisition also brought in an additional workforce of 42,000 employees of Corus. This was in addition to the 3000 employees of NatSteel and 1000 employees of Millennium Steel that had joined the Tata fold in previous years. The total strength, including the domestic labour force for Tata Steel, was now 87,000. Integrating such a diverse workforce was for sure a complex task. Gandhi recalled the agreement with the trustees of the Corus pension fund. 'They finally agreed for the transaction as we had proposed, where we were borrowing money against the assets of Corus, which were their security also. They agreed because of the Tatas' name and ethics.' By November 2007, a strategy and integration committee was formed with equal representation from the Tatas and Corus. In the Tata tradition, it was decided to retain the top management members of Corus in their existing positions. Philippe Varin continued as the CEO of Corus, a position he had taken over in 2003. A new board was formed that consisted of Ratan Tata and Jim Leng, chairman of the Corus Group, besides other members.[12]

A good deal for Tatas?

B. Muthuraman, then MD of Tata Steel, chided analysts who were apprehensive that the Tatas had gone for an expensive deal and paid proportionately more than what Mittal had paid for Arcelor in the previous year. In an interview to *Business India* he said, 'What analysts are seeing is the present, they are not taking the future perspective. If organizations also start taking short-term views, we will all be hedge funds.' To emphasize the global vision of Tata Steel, Muthuraman outlined key benefits and synergies from the Corus acquisition. Firstly, it came with a capacity of 20 Mtpa at a cost of little more than half of what a similar greenfield site would.[13] The Tatas' attempts at starting greenfield ventures at Kalinganagar and Bastar had thrown up far more challenges than ever imagined, besides skyrocketing the costs of production. Secondly, Corus would give Tata Steel access to high-quality, focused and developed European markets. Many Corus products aimed at top-of-the-range customers in areas such as aerospace, electronics, motor manufacturing and diagnostic equipment, and commanded 10–20 per cent more on price.[14] This would complement Tata Steel's strong retail presence in low-cost, high-growth Indian and South Asian markets. There was a potential to rise from the current combined capacity of 25 Mtpa to 40 Mtpa by 2012. This would take Tata-Corus to the world no. 2 position.[15] Thirdly, Corus had highly developed R & D capabilities with 950 researchers that would support Tata Steel's advanced R & D facilities leading to technology transfer and cross-fertilization between companies that were specialized in different areas of the value chain. The Tatas would gain ownership of over eighty patents assigned to the Corus Group by the United States Patent and Trademark Office, a significant addition to the nine patents awarded to the Tata Group.

Muthuraman also believed that the management and work culture at Corus was similar to Tata Steel. Both emphasized on continuous improvement and were committed to business ethics. This would help in integrating the two gigantic entities.[16] Ratan Tata acknowledged that the people integration at Corus was very complicated. 'There was the Dutch element, there was the English element, and the Indian element—and each one was very protective of their culture, their turf and their seniority.' While there were complexities galore, and humongous efforts ahead, for the top leadership to make this acquisition work to mutual advantage, the Corus deal had made Tata Steel—India's first Fortune 500 company, and a force to reckon with in the global steel industry. The stagnating markets in parts of the developed world and the significant capacity expansions in China loomed large in the years ahead.[17]

Do all acquisitions succeed?

'In the immediate next year after we acquired Corus, it made £300 million more profit than what we had estimated,' recalled Gandhi. It was celebration time when first full-year numbers of Corus were added to Tata Steel. The consolidated profit was up three times to ₹12,350 crore and revenue increased by 415 per cent to ₹1,31,534 crore. The board recommended 160 per cent dividend. Unfortunately for the Tatas, that was the first and only year to rejoice the acquisition. In the second year after the Corus acquisition, economic recession swept global markets. In the year 2007–08, the European steel industry's output fell by 31 per cent. Due to the commodities crash that followed, Tata Steel Europe's operations could neither justify nor service the huge acquisition cost. Corus, which had reported sales of $18 billion (₹79,488 crore then) and a pre-tax net profit of $1 billion (₹4416 crore) in 2007, reported a net loss of ₹6724 crore ($1.08 billion) by 2015.[18] In the nine years since acquisition, Corus delivered a profit only once. What had gone wrong in what looked like a marriage made in heaven? Most observers considered it to be a classic case of geopolitical and legislative factors destroying value in a promising acquisition. An eyewitness to the Corus chronicle, Gandhi observed that in an international acquisition, you have to worry about the local laws and practices, pension funds, political and legislative situations and geopolitical equations.

One of the main reasons severely affecting the growth and profitability of Tata Steel and in fact all steel manufacturers in Europe was the easy availability of low-priced Chinese steel. Karl-Ulrich Kahler, former CEO of Tata Steel Europe, emphasized that the UK government had consistently ignored the Tata Group's requests to protect it against Chinese dumping. The UK was one of fourteen countries that had been blocking EU plans to impose tougher sanctions on cheap Chinese steel imports. While the USA raised its tariffs on steel imports from China from 266 per cent to 522 per cent, the EU imposed provisional tariffs of 16 per cent for Chinese steel used to manufacture cars and appliances and in construction.[19] On the other hand, China's ministry of finance continued to provide tax rebates for steel exports. By 2015, China's global steel exports reached record 112.4 million tonnes, nearly 50 per cent of global steel production, causing a global steel glut, which plunged European producers into crisis. Chinese steel, though sold at a loss, forced Tata Steel to halve prices on some of its products to remain competitive. Stephen Kinnock, Member of Parliament from Port Talbot, location of Tata Steel's largest plant in the UK, blamed the troubles of Tata Steel to the UK's 'China First' Policy. He said:

They have done a number of deals with the Chinese government for investments to come into various large-scale projects. As a quid pro quo, the British government is looking the other way—or actively supporting China—in its strategy for trading in global markets. In this case, it is steel.[20]

It didn't end with that. In 2008, the British government passed the Climate Change Act to drastically reduce carbon emissions. Accordingly, energy-intensive industries had to pay a mandatory amount per unit of carbon emissions produced. This was a form of a green tax. With electricity amounting to one-third of manufacturing costs, the green tax added to the woes of the steel industry. In comparison, according to Eurostat, power tariffs in Germany and Spain were two-thirds of that in the UK. In France and Finland, it was almost half. The UK's wholesale gas price was more than three times that of the USA. Compared to this, the Chinese steel manufacturers operated in a regulatory environment where there was no pressure with respect to carbon emissions, thereby making Chinese steel 40 per cent cheaper. Superior quality raw material, higher transportation costs, and expensive distribution, marketing and sales infrastructure further contributed to high costs of manufacturing steel in European mills. The employment costs, including wages and salaries, social security and pension, accounted for nearly 20 per cent of the revenue at Tata Steel UK, as compared to 11 per cent at Tata Steel India. Moreover, there was an oversupply of steel globally, and demand had not lived up to expectations. Some like the automobile industry had substituted the use of steel with that of aluminium, further impacting demand. Expensive business costs, weak demand, and the strong value of the pound against other European currencies made exports difficult for Britain's largest steel company.

Ratan Tata effectively summed up the geopolitical changes at the Annual Conference of the EXIM Bank in 2016.

At the time Corus was acquired by Tata Steel, China was building enormous steel capacity, which it was absorbing for its own growth. No one in Europe saw the impact of what would happen if China started dumping steel on the world market. Nor did many people understand the absolute effect of the collapse of the European economy and the problems relating to the Euro . . . . The key problems of English facilities were that they were under-invested and over-manned. If we want to continue to be in that business, we have to cut back on the size and scale of that operation and make them profitable.

In an unusual yet practical move, in March 2016, Tata Steel put its British operations up for sale. The investment firm Greybull Capital agreed to acquire Tata's Long Products Europe division in Scunthorpe, (northern England) at a symbolic sales price of £1. To sustain the loss-making division, Greybull arranged for a £400 million investment and financing package. While it was keen to sell the remaining plants, it couldn't get the right buyers for the British plants. Most buyers were keen on purchasing the profit-making Dutch plants of Corus. With a 9000-strong workforce, Tata Steel's Dutch operations had consistently made profits despite the global gloom. It had maintained profit margins at about 3 per cent in its worst days, albeit down from around 30 per cent in 2007 at the peak of the steel boom. By December 2016, Tata Steel had entered into an agreement with the trade unions that it would keep the giant steel plant at Port Talbot in South Wales and other parts of its steel business going in Britain until 2021, preserving as many as 11,000 jobs. In return, the unions made substantial concessions, including an agreement in principle to close their generous pension plan and replace it with a new one that would require employees to pay more for their future retirement.[21]

In 2015, when production began at Tata Steel's Kalinganagar plant, Europe accounted for nearly 60 per cent of its consolidated revenues, Indian operations were a third and the rest came from its operations in southeast Asia. Tata Steel India, however, accounted for 80 per cent of the company's operating profit on a consolidated basis. Ever since the global financial crisis, Tata Steel was sustaining its loss-making global operations using cash from its profitable operations in India, besides help from Tata Sons. This contrasted with the situation in Tata Motors, where the JLR operations set off the losses incurred by the Indian operations due to cyclical changes. Gandhi observed that the oft-criticized $2-billion JLR deal had increased to a market value of $18 billion within a decade. On the other hand, the Corus acquisition took place in a very bullish period. During the year-long negotiations, Gandhi had been to London almost every alternate week. There were occasions when he was in London as his wife was in the hospital battling a serious ailment. 'What inspired you?' I asked. 'Commitment of the people in the Tata Group,' he replied. He highlighted several unknowns that can affect such global acquisitions:

> You have a situation where the British are living longer. Their life expectancy has increased from eighty-two to eighty-two-and-a-half years. Consequently, the pension liability goes up by ₹900 crore. Now, a decade ago, I did not know that Brits will live six months longer![22] One should not be looking at such transactions in hindsight with a 20:20 vision after 10–12 years. Any

transaction, if one had the astrological knowledge, would have possibly been dealt with differently.

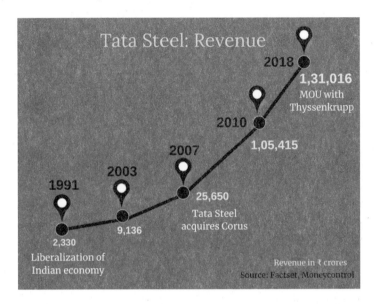

Just about the time I concluded writing the book, Tata Steel deconsolidated Tata Steel Europe (Corus) from the Tata Steel Group through a 50:50 joint venture with ThyssenKrupp, a German multinational conglomerate. The deal was touted as the biggest consolidation in the European steel market since the acquisition of Arcelor by Mittal Steel in 2006 and Corus by Tata Steel in 2007. Tata Steel ThyssenKrupp headquartered in the Netherlands would be Europe's second-largest steel maker after ArcelorMittal with 48,000 employees across thirty-four sites, production of about 21Mtpa and revenues of around 17 billion euros. The venture would create additional value of around 5 billion euros for both Thyssenkrupp and Tata Steel due to joint synergies.[23] Subject to clearances, the merger would be complete by December 2018, and would reduce Tata Steel's debt burden by ₹20,000 crore. This could even be complemented by a divestment of Tata Steel's businesses in South-East Asia valued at ₹3500 crore as part of its strategy to exit non-scalable businesses and turn focus to domestic market.[24] Needless to say, the cyclicity of business can always bring the story a full circle!

CHAPTER 15

HITS, MISSES AND LESSONS

Raymond Bickson, then MD at the Taj Group of Hotels (part of the Indian Hotels Company Ltd), was attending a board meeting in one of the most expensive hotels in Italy on Lake Como. He was having dinner with the owner and fourteen international guests. There was a lot of noise outside and one of the guests remarked in jest, 'What kind of a noisy hotel do you run here!' The owner replied, 'Don't blame us. Blame Raymond!' Bickson gave him a confused look, 'How am I responsible for the noise in your hotel?' The owner laughed, 'Raymond, it's an Indian wedding. They've rented the entire hotel!' There was laughter across the dining table. The message was clear. Affluent Indians could now afford the best hospitality facilities anywhere in the world.

To tap these growing numbers who wanted Indian menus and experiences at international destinations, Taj started to collaborate with leading hospitality chains in markets where it had no properties. In 2006, it entered into a strategic alliance with South Korea's Shilla Hotels and Resorts; and inked a marketing alliance with Japan's Okura Hotels and Resorts in 2007.

Coming to know of these international collaborations, Manny Berbere, owner of four palace hotels in Switzerland, called Bickson and expressed interest to form an alliance with Taj. 'Manny, why do you want to collaborate with Taj?' Bickson asked. The response helped him realize the potential of Indian tourists at world-class destinations.

> In the summertime, there are so many Bollywood movies made in Switzerland. My palace hotels are filled with Indians who want to see where these movies are made. So, I have Indian chefs to cater to many Indians coming to Switzerland. It's a market that I want to tap further into with Taj.[1]

Given this immense potential, Taj made acquisitions across important source markets.[2] In 2005, it acquired the Pierre, one of the top five hotels in New York, at an estimated cost of $50 million from Four Seasons. The forty-four-storeyed five-star hotel that opened its doors to guests in 1929 (on the eve of the Great Depression), had a fantastic location on New York's renowned

Fifth Avenue in midtown Manhattan facing the Central Park. Along with 201 rooms, forty suites and twelve grand suites, Pierre also had eighty service apartments run by a cooperative, most of which were owned by uber-rich celebrities such as Viacom chairman Sumner Redstone, Harrod's owner Mohamed al-Fayed, couturier Yves Saint Laurent, and talk show host Larry King.[3] This prevented an outright acquisition of the property, and the Tatas proceeded with a thirty-year lease. According to the agreement, along with the rooms, Taj also had to service these apartment residents. This acquisition came after losing out on two others, including the Intercontinental Hotel where Taj lost out to Donald Trump, former hotelier and now president of the USA.[4] Gandhi recollected the learning he gained during the negotiations with the unions, 'The New York unions are very strong, particularly in the hospitality industry. We had to learn how to deal with them and understand the benefits for medical relief, holidays, and overtime, which was very different from our Indian experience.' He gave the example of an elevator operator at the Pierre whose only job was to stand there and wish the guests good morning and good evening. Another employee's sole role was to find the right buttons to replace the missing ones on the shirts and jackets of hotel guests and residents. 'We say unions are bad enough in India. Actually, they are not. But they are no different in New York,' quipped Gandhi. Since the takeover, many employees and senior managers visited various Taj hotels in India to experience first-hand Asian, and more specifically, Indian hospitality, and bring back the learnings to their jobs at the Pierre.

Taj further expanded its presence in the USA through two more acquisitions—Ritz-Carlton in Boston and Campton Place in San Francisco. Deepa Misra Harris, then senior vice president of sales and marketing, explained the logic.

> If we have a presence in source markets, the guests there will know and experience our brand. So when they come to India, they would prefer Taj. The more you grow in your source markets, the easier it will be to retain market share in India.

This was a major concern as competition in India had reduced the company's market share to 12 per cent. Key domestic competitors included the Oberoi Hotels, the Leela Group and ITC's Welcome Group of Hotels. International players, including Marriott, Four Seasons and Hyatt, were also establishing properties in key locations. To retain its lead in the domestic market, Taj expanded from sixty-two hotels and 7900 rooms to 17,000 rooms and 137 hotels in a single decade. At the same time, the Indian market grew from 62,000 rooms to 140,000 room. With the number of hotel rooms in India tipped to expand to 500,000, Taj aimed at expanding its base to 50,000 rooms to maintain its market share at 10–12 per cent.

The 2008 financial crisis was the villain for many an industry. The hospitality industry too wasn't spared. Taj had acquired most of its properties at the peak of prosperity and paid exorbitant prices for some investments. Following the crisis and the Mumbai terror attacks, valuation of properties and room rents dipped. Many expansionary decisions were slowed down to ensure consistent financial viability. To strengthen properties in India and South Asia, Taj's core markets, and set off losses in foreign markets, Taj even had to divest from several international properties. In 2014, the 100-room W Hotel in Sydney (acquired in 2005) was sold for ₹180 crore. In 2016, the Taj Boston was sold for about ₹850 crore.

In the same year, Taj sold its stake in the British luxury hospitality group Belmond Ltd (formerly Orient-Express Hotels) for ₹450 crore. The company had acquired an 11.5 per cent stake in the NYSE-listed company in 2007. Orient-Express had nearly thirty properties across the globe with nine key properties in Italy alone. These were some of the best hotels in the world with a set of rooms where the minimum rate was $1500 a night. It also had its own tourist trains and cruises, and would have been a game changer from Taj perspective on an international scale. However, the ownership structure of Orient-Express was such that a certain percentage of its shares was owned by its wholly owned subsidiary, which was wholly controlled by the directors of Orient-Express. In American lingo, this situation is called the poison pill being in the hands of the directors, who never wanted to cede control. On two occasions the Tatas made an acquisition bid and wrote to the board. But the board rejected their offer. Gandhi shared with a tinge of regret:

> Before proceeding with an offer, we acquired some shares to have a foot in the door. We were aware of the poison pill situation. But we thought the directors would be far more attentive to shareholders' interests. Unfortunately, they rejected our offers not because they were deficient or detrimental to shareholders' interests, but to protect their personal positions as directors with all perquisites.

Having realized that the Tatas would not be able to progress with the acquisition, Taj sold its stake in 2016.

Taj Group of Hotels: Revenue

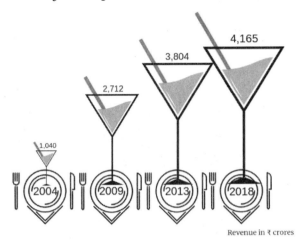

Revenue in ₹ crores

In 2014, when a new leadership team took charge at Taj, most new developments were planned through the asset-light management contract route, where new properties would be managed by Taj under its brand. In exchange, Taj would receive a commission of about 7 per cent on revenue generated. Despite withdrawal from marque international properties due to global recession, Taj's international strategy did have a positive impact on its revenue. In the dozen years after liberalization, revenue contribution from outside India increased from 5 to 35 per cent.

Was globalization mandatory for all Tata companies?

I asked Hussain this very question. 'Ratan Tata's vision for globalization is often misunderstood,' he said. 'The world is globalizing and therefore we should look at our businesses in a global context. That was the point he made.' When the economy was opening, he encouraged Tata companies to look at supply chains in a global context and sell products by expanding the existing scope of the market. 'If you have the managerial capabilities and can find the finance, you may go and buy a good asset abroad. However, if you come to the conclusion that my source in India is the best and my products are only meant for India, let that be your decision. Therefore, it was a way of thinking, rather than a diktat to go abroad,' recalled Hussain. 'To some extent, he did say that if you want to grow fast, then you have to probably go abroad, because in India there are far too many obstacles.'

Voltas: India's Leading AC Brand

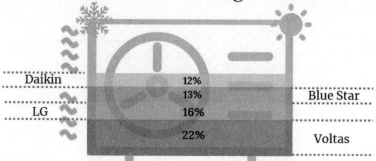

Daikin	12%
	13% Blue Star
LG	16%
	22% Voltas

Figures represent market share as in 2017

Hussain gave the example of Voltas, a Tata company he led as chairman. After a lot of internal discussions, the Voltas board concluded that the company did not have managerial capabilities and the finances at that point in time to go abroad. Nonetheless it had a very strong brand and products in India and hence stuck to the Indian market. But it focused on global sourcing with 60 per cent coming from China. 'Hence, globalization is not only acquiring assets abroad, your supply chain can become global.' In 2006, Voltas launched its new brand positioning with the catchphrase 'India ka Dil, India ka AC'. A decade later, it was India's market leader in room air conditioners with annual sales of a million air conditioners and over 20 per cent market share beating South Korean biggies LG and Samsung.[5] With only 4 per cent of Indian households owning air conditioners, compared to 70 per cent in China, the future growth potential is huge.

It's not that the Tatas always acquired others and never ceded ground. Lakmé is one example. 'Simone Tata used to lead that business. She realized that the company would neither be able to take on international giants nor have the money to buy one,' acknowledged Hussain. Lakmé was sold to Hindustan Lever in 1996 for ₹200 crore.

After 1991, many Tata companies transitioned from an international to a global strategy. The former involved exports of surplus production, as was done in the case of Tata Motors for many decades. The latter was an integrated growth strategy with three key aspects:

i. Accessing material, financial and human resources from the best and most competitive parts of the globe.
ii. Acquiring customers and accessing markets that constitute future profitable growth from anywhere in the world.

iii. Connecting these two through best-in-class processes and facilities to create the best value for customers leveraging global supply chain, suppliers, partners and locations.

The Tata way to mergers and acquisitions

'It is the approach of the people who run an organization that holds the key; how adaptive they are to changes that have an impact on them. It is here that the process of an Indian company going global truly begins.'

R.K. Krishna Kumar

National integration. In the first decade of the millennium, through three major acquisitions (Tetley, Corus and JLR, all in the UK), the Tatas became the UK's biggest manufacturer and largest employer with 40,000 workers, just ahead of British Aerospace. If one were to include TCS, this number would rise to 45,000. The common fear among most Brits was that the Tatas would strip out technology in the acquired companies and ship it home, and even lay off workers in thousands by transferring production to low-cost locations in India. Contrary to these conjectures, the Tatas not only retained the original names and brands, but even added numbers to the workforce it inherited through these acquisitions. For example, the workforce at Halewood car plant where JLR's Evoque is made, was doubled to 3000 within two years of acquisition. The brands Jaguar, Land Rover and Tetley that have been admired by Brits were retained and sold as premium brands in India alongside Tata Motors and Tata Tea products. The Tatas effectively projected an image of a professionally run conglomerate, independent of nationalistic overtones. The group ran acquired companies on sound principles rather than on prejudiced patriotism.[6] India's culture and business principles were far better reflected in this approach to integration.

Community integration. Historically, the Tata way of business focused not only on exploiting commercial opportunities in countries where the group invested but also playing a developmental role in those countries by connect themselves with the society and environment, with ties to the government, or culturally, so as to enjoy the same degree of trust that they do in India. This approach contrasted with that of the previous investors of the acquired companies. Most of them were PE investors, who despite belonging to the native country, were primarily focused on milking their investment and gaining short-term profits. In contrast, the Tatas were strategic long-term investors. Their strategy in the acquired companies moved from a purely quarter-to-quarter outlook to a vision of five to ten years.

Employee integration. Cultural and human integration form a vital part of any successful M&A. In each of their acquisitions, the Tatas initiated customized integration programmes based on unique requirements and circumstances. Elaborating on the HR aspects in a successful integration, Satish Pradhan, former Group CHRO at Tata Sons, observed, 'A global compensation programme has to be flexible enough to address unique nuances and, at the same time, should have a common underlying principle. A company needs to develop and inculcate a comfort level of working with a multi-ethnic workforce in multi-geography settings.' This was very evident in all acquisitions, whether with native Kenyans of the Magadi Soda Company or with native Koreans of the Daewoo Commercial Vehicle Company. In fact, Bloomquist and Deville, former leaders of GCIP that was acquired by Tata Chemicals, were taken aback when they were asked to stay and steer the organization. It was in stark contrast to the American way of M&A. They recalled their previous experience of how old managements were typically terminated post an acquisition. The speed with which old offices were closed and employees packed off was considered a proof of effective decision-making and a matter of pride for the acquiring company's senior leadership. But the Tatas were different.

The Tata way of leading companies after an acquisition was often described as 'light-touch' and 'hands-off' approach. It had the following characteristics as seen in key acquisitions:

i. *Look at the acquisition as a partnership rather than an acquisition.* Place confidence in the existing management and work with them. The number of Indian managers working on-site is limited, with those stationed in the acquired company primarily focusing on knowledge transfer and systems integration to ensure seamless operations over time. Despite obvious cultural differences, the Tatas won the Koreans' confidence at Daewoo with this approach.

ii. *Not seek total structural integration with the parent company.* For example, Tata Chemicals' acquisitions in Africa, Europe and the USA were independent international divisions. Same was the case with Tata Steel and Tata Motors. Even while changing names of the acquired companies, the Tatas displayed high levels of sensitivity and empathy. For example, when Kenyan employees were uncomfortable accepting a foreign name for Magadi Soda Company, Tata Chemicals proactively engaged with them, did a survey and got opinions from various representatives. This approach endeared the company to the native people who eventually accepted the name 'Tata Chemicals Magadi'.

iii. *Co-create a vision for the enlarged organization.* Avoid issuing diktats based on the acquiring company's prevailing practices. Instead, create shared change through cross-functional performance and process improvement teams. This builds mutual trust in the partnership between two organizations and in the target-setting process. 'If the vision exercise isn't shared or if the process isn't participative, then the acquired organizations' willingness to be part of the future action plans and the consequent accountability will be much lower,' observed Koushik Chatterjee, who proactively led many of Tata Steel's global acquisitions.

iv. *Retain identity of original brands,* especially premium brands with worldwide presence and acceptance. This was evident in Tetley and JLR brands flourishing even a decade after the acquisitions.

v. *Focus on a uniform performance culture, not on a single organizational culture.* Acquaint the acquired company's employees with Tata ethos and heritage enshrined in the TCOC, and expose them to best practices promoted through TBEM. This was done through presentations by long-standing Tata employees, and through exchange programmes where employees of acquired companies were brought to India to experience the ecosystem at Jamshedpur, Pune or Mithapur. As Kale et al. observed, 'Structural separation and operational autonomy deliver results only when an acquisition understands the parent's values.'[7]

This approach wasn't easy, was prone to several risks, was time-consuming, and required immense maturity from senior leadership on all sides. Yet, over a period of fifteen-plus years, the Tatas were fairly successful in implementing it with visible long-term outcomes and impact. The Tata approach to global acquisitions in terms of cultural integration, branding and customer focus could be called pragmatic. The acquired global brands were nourished for the long-term and no attempts were made to implement drastic changes.[8] Through their strategies and practices, the Tatas effectively created a template of benevolent integration and of encouraging growth with continuity post global acquisitions. To critics of the Tatas' 'light-touch/hands-off policy' post-acquisition, Kant wisecracked, 'In companies we acquire, we keep management independent, but accountable. "Hands-off" is not the same as "left alone", it does not mean we are not involved.'[9]

Learnings from the Tatas' globalization chronicle

Looking back at the Tata Group's globalization journey, Ratan Tata effectively summarized the key learnings.

> We succeeded with globalization for branded products that have global markets, but not in enterprises that produce commodities. Our efforts to infuse cash, and our endeavour to build and grow companies we acquired paid off in several cases. Although some of our acquisitions may not have met initial expectations, I feel the group as a whole is now stronger because of its broader pursuit and awareness of world markets.[10]

It is public knowledge that among the Tatas' globalization moves, some have been highly successful such as Tetley and JLR, and some have not, for example, Corus and Taj. But none can deny that the group's ambition and achievement of transforming a set of Indian companies into a global giant, is without a parallel in the emerging world. Samsung is the only example that comes close.[11] Unsurprisingly, some even called the Tatas—the Asian version of America's General Electric.

There are two key learnings that emerge from this ambitious achievement. Firstly, Tata companies leveraged the Tata brand for facilitating these big moves. None of the individual companies would have been able to do it on their own without the Tata backing, in terms of financing, negotiations, and building trust with executives of the acquired companies. These were strengths derived from affiliation to the Tata Group—managerial, technical, financial and reputational.[12] For example, Tata Sons' overseas offices assisted Tata companies with business development and external relations in key geographies through a team on the ground. For the acquired companies, it was Tata Group that was acquiring them and not just Tata Motors or Tata Tea. For all those reasons, the Tata brand and Bombay House was critical. When an emerging market company acquires an advanced economy company, the top leaders move on to work in another multinational. But in the case of the Tatas, most of them stayed because they admired the Tata Group and its vision.

Secondly, different companies had different imperatives for going global. Some of them did well by balancing their focus on India versus the world. A senior professor at Harvard Business School, who had closely studied the Tata Group for over two decades, shared a conversation he had had with Ratan Tata nearly twenty years ago. The dialogue focused on the oft-asked question as to why Tata Group was spending precious resources chasing markets outside when the rest of the world was coming to India. To that, Ratan Tata gave an insightful answer backed with an analysis of the economic opportunity and the Tata identity:

> If India is growing at 10 per cent, the addressable space for us [the Tatas], given our values, is not the entire 10 per cent. We can probably take 6 per cent, as the remaining 4 per cent are a set of opportunities that will require us to compromise on our values and we are not willing to do so. Hence, our effective growth rate for India is far lower than India's growth rate. If we want to grow, like our Indian counterparts, we must grow abroad. We can't grow just in India.

A similar reply was given by J.R.D. Tata way back in 1986 in an interview to Pritish Nandy.

> . . . From the days of Jamsetji Tata, we had tried to stick to our norms of corporate behaviour . . . Everyone in the Tatas is proud that we do not succumb, whatever may be the circumstances. We would rather do without a project than bow and scrape and bribe.[13]

That was before the Indian economy was liberalized. Ratan Tata's response was after the liberalization. However, the Tatas' approach was consistent.

These were examples of industry captains uncompromising on the group's core values. If that meant thinking more expansively, they were willing to do that. Probably, that was at the heart of the Tatas' imperative of pursuing global growth—to make sure that the group could grow without having to chase all opportunities, whether they fit the Tata values and culture or not.

CHAPTER 16

THE MAKING OF A TITAN

In July 1984, the Tata Group and the Tamil Nadu Industrial Development Corporation (TIDCO) established Titan Watches Ltd as a joint venture with each holding 26 per cent shares. France's Ebauches and Japan's Citizen Watch Company were technical collaborators. Tata Group stalwart Xerxes Desai led the venture out of a small room at the Taj West End Hotel in Bangalore.

R.M. Lala connects the group's foray into horography, the art of watchmaking, to a chance meeting in the mid-1970s between I.M. Mahadevan, an IAS officer, who came for help to the Desai-led Tata Press, for converting his computer-generated tapes into a printed book. During that conversation, he suggested to Desai that the Tatas should consider manufacturing watches as an area of diversification. While Desai and the group leadership liked the idea, the scheme remained dormant till early 1980s when Mahadevan took charge as the chairman and managing director of TIDCO. That's when a unique business collaboration between a private business group and a government-led industrial undertaking began.

A couple of years earlier, the Government of Andhra Pradesh-led Allwyn Company had already entered the watch business. Having achieved significant success with the its refrigerator business in the 1970s, Allwyn collaborated with Japanese company Seiko for their new watch business. The titan in India's watch market at that time was Hindustan Machine Tools, popularly called HMT. A Government of India enterprise, it was started in 1961 at the instance of Jawaharlal Nehru and partnered with Japanese watchmaker Citizen. Interestingly, Nehru named the first HMT watch 'Janata'. Most people of that generation would fondly recollect receiving an HMT watch on a special occasion. Such was the demand for HMT watches in those years that people had to wait for days to buy them, with many of its models available at a premium in the grey market. For nearly three decades, HMT ruled the Indian market with its catchphrase 'Desh Ki Dhadkan'. Till 1991, it had nearly 90 per cent market share. However, opening the markets to private competition and global players changed this scenario forever.

In mid-1980s, the Rajiv Gandhi government had begun to ease rules for private-sector companies. It allowed private industries to tweak their product mix within the quantity approved under the Licence Raj. This was a policy change that helped the fledgling Titan. Backed by investments for an integrated manufacturing facility at Hosur, Titan stormed the Indian market with its analogue electronic quartz-based technology in April 1987. At a time when the market was dominated by mechanical watches, Titan's trendy designs were preferred by customers compared to bulky HMT watches. Until then, watches in India were considered a functional product, simply used for telling the time. Titan is credited for revolutionizing the way Indians thought about watches by converting the watch from a utilitarian timekeeping device to a fashion accessory. Renamed Titan Industries in 1993, and Titan Company in 2013, the company became the fifth-largest watch manufacturer in the world by 2018. It had nearly 1450 exclusive stores with 19 lakh square feet of retail space in 266 towns, and a presence in over 11,000 multi-brand outlets that also sold its products. This ranked it among the largest retail companies in India with nearly 60 per cent market share of watches. At the back end, it had twelve state-of-the-art watch and component manufacturing and assembly plants. Some of these even manufactured components that were exported to Swiss watchmakers. So, let's see how Titan broke the Tatas' jinx with consumer-facing businesses and built a super successful customer-centric retail business.

Transforming a timekeeping device into a fashion accessory

All over the world, watches are either a fashion statement or a style statement. Only at the very low end of the market they are used as a timekeeping device. A watch is much more than just a timekeeping device. It is in some ways a marker of time and coming of age. In those years, we got our first watch on completing Class X or upon entering college. The next would be on getting a new job or on getting married or on a promotion. Even on retirement, people were given watches as a parting gift. Effectively, a watch is connected with the most important stages of our lives, thereby making it a serious accessory with an important role and a deeper significance. The watch is an extension of our personality. And not to forget, generations have passed on watches to each other. It's a matter of pride to wear your father's watch. Like mothers pass on jewellery to their daughters, men have been passing on watches to their sons. In some ways, a watch is eternal, just like the time it communicates. This has been the personification of a watch that Titan has consistently communicated in the last three decades.

Prior to market entry, Titan had thoroughly analysed buying preferences, market and technology trends, manufacturing options, and strategies of global players.[1] Till the time Titan launched its watches, it was a seller's market. Titan believed that it should be a consumer's market and that they should get a choice of styles on a par with international trends. Its designs and themes were so diverse that on one end it included watches that were an ode to the sensuality of chocolates and on the other there were ones inspired by astronomy. Nearly 500 new designs were created every year at Titan's design studios. The mere act of providing a lot of choice and categorizing the products for looks such as dressy watches, formal watches, casual watches, and more, gave a cue to the consumers that different watches can be used for different occasions and needs. It changed the perception of the consumer about the utility of the product by transforming the nature of the Indian watch market through concept marketing rather than product marketing. It also emphasized on the idea of gifting watches for weddings or to close family members on different occasions by glorifying it through targeted communication. Most of the initial ads of Titan focused on the theme of a watch as a thoughtful gift for someone special.

Its idea of launching exclusive retail stores like 'The World of Titan' showcased the brand and its products in a glorified manner. Till then, watches were mainly sold through multi-brand outlets without much displays. The World of Titan outlets created experience centres rather than mere showrooms with hostesses welcoming the customers. It was the first-of-its-kind experience in an era when India was not yet bitten by the consumerism bug. Titan went beyond the looks of the stores and focused on retail training. The store managers and sales representatives would politely engage with customers and understand their requirement and purpose of purchase.[2] They would also cue them towards, 'Are you looking for a casual-wear watch or for a wedding gift?' Titan's initiative catalysed the watch trade. Most retailers selling multi-brand watches felt that if Titan could do it, why not them? They upgraded their stores to look better and showcased their products more stylishly and prominently. The other important aspect for Titan was to be present in all relevant places, including those where people did not come to buy watches but other stuff, thereby attracting new consumers. Titan showrooms were opened at malls, department stores and more.

Bhaskar Bhat, Titan's MD, was a founding employee of the company who joined the business when it was just known as the Tata Watch Project. He acknowledged that the Tata name was used by Titan to enter the market in the 1980s. 'Titan Quartz from Tata was how we launched Titan.' For many years it was positioned as a Tata company. 'That gave us the legitimacy, especially with associates, dealers and bankers. Once people know it's a Tata company, a whole lot of doors open for you.' However, consumers may not be happy with the trust factor alone. They would want good-looking watches and a brand that has an appeal. While the Tata name played a big role in giving Titan the reputation of being a trustworthy brand, the company worked hard to meet other expectations of consumers. The output was impressive, and the Indian consumer gave a thumbs-up to Titan's cost-effective, low-maintenance, and attractive-looking wrist watches.[3] The company set striking benchmarks in design, quality and retailing. For instance, it launched five times the number of watch models than HMT. 'We were the first to have a national selling price, something unheard of in those days,' recalled H.G. Raghunath, CEO (watches and accessories) at Titan.[4]

Understanding the consumer for delighting her

'The customer is much more than a stakeholder—she is what the entire ecosystem of an organization has to revolve around.'

Bhaskar Bhat

During its formative years, Titan gained a solid understanding of consumer requirements. These insights formed the building blocks of its steady evolution and elevation as a market leader. The firsts among consumer expectations were product usage and quality. Consumers expected a branded product from a reputed company like Titan to have a certain level of usage comfort and experience. Another driver was the packaging. Does the product come with a good outer packaging and a stylish carry bag? Given that almost 40 to 50 per cent of watches are bought for gifting friends and family, consumers expect that stores have adequate gift-wrapping options. Those should be good-looking so that the one presenting the gift feels comfortable. Providing a choice of paper would be even better. The second area of satisfaction is the buying experience during the purchase process. Were they able to get the product of their choice within the price band they had in mind or according to some advertisement they had seen? Here, the quality of assistance provided by the front line staff at the store played a significant role. The billing process, ease and comfort in completing the transaction are equally important parts of the consumer's experience. The right ambience within the store is important as well. Pleasant fragrance wafting in the air and soft background music make for a joyful buying experience as opposed to a transaction-led activity. Then, there are issues outside the store that affect buying experience. At one stage, Titan realized that the greatest source of customers' dissatisfaction was parking problems while getting to their stores. So, availability of parking or valet parking became important.

It didn't end with the purchase. Post-purchase service, also called after-sales service, was equally vital. Once a consumer bought a product, she expected it to be serviceable conveniently and quickly. Similarly, when they came for service, how were they handled? Was their problem addressed? Were they satisfied with the completeness of the solution? The company believed that for a lifestyle product, every element of the consumers' experience must be thought through—the product and the buying and servicing experience. Titan focused on delighting consumers on all three parameters. These formed the heart of customer satisfaction in the retail business. Bhat admitted:

> We believe by adopting customer-centric practice, we can build competitive advantage. Something like customer first is not visible to a competitor. It's only in transactional behaviour that people talk about such things—'You know when I went to Titan, I was treated like this. It was really a sensitive sales process.' Our desire is to be different from the rest in this customer-first approach. For us competition therefore is less important.

Having understood the heart of customer satisfaction, the test is to understand and keep pace with her constantly changing and evolving expectations. The first challenge for success in a retail market is the ability to get a pulse of the market at the time the change is happening, not after it has happened. Identifying gaps before everybody else does could be considered the first requirement for becoming a strategic innovator.[5] Titan realized that it needed to be contemporary and consistently updated. It couldn't let it slip. The other aspect was that consumers' expectations were steadily growing. 'My watch should be longer-lasting, and my glass should be scratch-proof.' So, while the product life cycle was coming down, i.e. Indian consumers were buying watches more often or probably discarding watches more often, their expectations of quality and their newness quotient were going up all the time. They also expected more features for the same or lesser price. The broader expectation was, 'I need more value for my money.' 'This meant that we needed to perennially work on enhancing something on the product front so that it met their expectations, or at least didn't fall short of it,' observed Ajoy Chawla, now senior vice president of strategy. The third challenge was on the retail purchasing experience.

Consumer expectations were not limited to the product category but were benchmarked against practices outside the category. For example, a very good clothing store offered a thirty-day, no-questions-asked return policy, then why not for watches? Titan realized that its performance benchmarks were being set outside the category. 'We have to work much harder to ensure that our retail stores are not just the best in the watch category but are as good as shoes or garments, or cosmetic or department stores. We need to constantly look out for new retail benchmarks,' Chawla admitted. Bhat believed that from communication to buying experience and from usage experience to after-sales service, everything needed equal attention from the organization. Nothing could be left to chance.

Titan watches for every age, stage and image

Right from its early years, Titan gained substantial market leadership in India by keeping pace with evolving consumer preferences and introducing a series of brands to suit specific customer segments. A decade into its existence, Titan introduced the Sonata range of watches as a value-for-money brand for the lower end of the market. 'When you deal with such a large and culturally diverse market, it's better to go in with multiple brands rather than a single one,' Desai had observed justifying the company's multi-brand strategy.[6] Within six months of its launch in March 1997, Titan had sold 500,000 Sonata watches, accounting for 20 per cent of the company's growth in that year. To establish the Indian brand overseas, Titan also forayed into the international market in the mid-1990s. With offices in London and Paris, it entered a dozen European markets with steel quartz watches. Despite a combination of European designers and a London-based advertising agency, it didn't succeed.[7] The cost of building a brand in Europe was prohibitively high. However, Titan products were well received in the Middle East and the Far East countries despite competition from 300 other brands. Regardless of the ups and downs, Desai was very confident of Titan's business model and its future strategy. 'We simply have to do, whatever we are doing better. Decrease costs, build up the brand, distribute, set stretch targets and bring in considerable refinement in the manner we manage the business.'

The Government of India had committed to lifting all restrictions on imports of watches by 2002. Analysts were concerned whether Titan would be able to withstand foreign competition when leading international brands entered Indian markets through official routes. Till that time, of the two crore watches sold each year, nearly half were through the grey market. Most believed that Titan's brand and distribution network would be its greatest advantage when competition peaks in the organized market. But Desai was not the one to rest on the company's past laurels. In 2002, Titan launched Edge, the slimmest watch in the 'universe' that was a precision-engineering marvel. It was an outcome of a challenge thrown at the company by Desai himself—whether Titan had the capacity to make the world's thinnest watch, and thereby create an identity of superior quality and manufacturing excellence before its international peers. Recipient of a national award for excellence in R & D in electronics, and certified by Chronofiable SA, Switzerland, Edge was produced indigenously after four years of intensive R & D. It had a total slimness of just 3.5 mm and a wafer-thin movement of 1.15 mm. For a comparison, most watches average between 6 and 10 mm in thickness.

Recollecting the Edge story, Bhat emphasized that the idea was not motivated purely by economic objectives.

> It was an idea for pursuing prestige, of being considered among the best watchmakers in the world. We were aware that we have engineering capabilities in India, which could be compared with the best. If we can bring them together, provide resources and inspire them, we can come up with a world-class idea.

The outcome was a close collaboration between Titan's design studio, the production department, and the R & D team. 'We gave our team the freedom of latitude and the freedom to operate. Thus, Edge was driven more by passion, and not by profits.'[8] Needless to say, not only did Titan survive global competitors in Indian markets, it grabbed nearly 50 per cent of the market share with the second player well behind at around 20 per cent. In the next decade, it continued to woo its consumers by launching newer brands for different segments—whether it was Nebula for women in 2004 or the Xylys brand, a Swiss-made range for the premium market in 2006.

The Titan way of wooing customers

> 'A watch is very complex to make and is perhaps the only thing that has to work twenty-four hours, like the human heart. Yet, the look and feel of a watch are what make people buy it.'[9]

> Bhaskar Bhat

Constantly listen to customers. 'Our most important agenda is to continually unearth customer dissatisfiers and literally delight them. For us, the customer is at the centre of all activities. Everything she wants; we woo her and we sell to her,' shared Bhat during our conversation at Titan's head office that overlooked the lush gardens of Hindustan Aeronautics on Bangalore's Old Airport Road. Titan relied on its customers to help the company become better at customer centricity. The presence of robust processes to continuously listen to customers and track their articulated and latent needs and aspirations was an important process at Titan. A good example was Fastrack, an idea that was dormant since 1987. It was only in 2003 that the company realized that the preferences of young customers were changing. They no longer wanted their father's brand. This idea had a huge potential and Fastrack broke away as a sub-brand. By 2018, it was the fastest-growing brand at Titan and was often acknowledged as India's largest youth brand. It included not just watches for the youth, but also fashion accessories such as sun glasses, bags, wallets, belts and women's bags sold across eighty-three towns through 164 exclusive Fastrack showrooms.

Similarly, Raga came out of such an understanding that women in India don't merely want to wear a smaller version of men's watches, which was a norm for decades. They wanted watches to match their dresses. Raga was introduced in 1992 as a watch for the modern Indian woman who transcends roles with poise and panache. To give women consumers their distinct identity, Raga had no male version. The process of constantly listening was also applicable to its distribution network, which was the first point of contact with the final consumers. It would provide first-hand authentic insights on what consumers were looking. Titan's foray into large sporty watches was an outcome of this feedback. In its journey towards premiumization, Titan collaborated with several high-end international brands at various points of time to market their products in India. It started with Tommy Hilfiger in 2004. Police, Timberland, and FCUK followed. This strategy too paid off with high-end watches accounting for one-fourth of its business even during tough times.

Constant improvisation and product innovation. Titan based its product improvement on customer feedback and requirements. The company observed that customers were looking for longer-lasting batteries, scratch-resistant glasses and waterproof watches. It is obvious that Indian consumers don't use their watches in the most appropriate manner. Water penetration into the dial as perspiration or rainwater featured as a regular problem. A lot of these insights dominated product improvisation. In other instances, a separate class of products was introduced to meet an emerging need. The introduction of its HTSE (high-tech self-energized) collection was an outcome of the feedback that eco-friendliness was a big trend among millennials, and the company should capitalize on that. In July 2011, ten styles of the HTSE collection were launched by ace shuttler Saina Nehwal. The threat from digital devices and the increasing popularity of miniaturization of technology triggered Titan's move into the smartwatch category. In January 2016, it launched JUXT, a smartwatch developed in collaboration with Hewlett-Packard. Juxtaposing tech with style, JUXT could be paired with Android and iOS-based smartphones with equal ease. The conceptualization, R & D and commercial launch was completed in just twelve months. Titan had improved its own record with Edge and HTSE, which had taken forty-eight months from conceptualization to launch.[10] 'In this new world order of business, the ecosystem of a corporation will not be a mere circle but a digital-cum-brick-and-mortar sphere. In both these areas, the customer will reign supreme,' acknowledged Bhat.

Building a prestigious brand. One of the core reasons for the success of Titan has been its focus on building a sense of prestige associated with its brand. In the retail industry, customer pride is very vital. Satisfaction is typically linked to a mental image they have about the brand they are wearing. If that image about Titan is constantly enhancing, the consumer would feel proud to wear its products. This imagery aspect was critical to Titan's C-SAT (customer satisfaction in corporate lingo) strategy. In the initial years, Desai partnered with Ogilvy and Mather, India's leading ad agency to create a niche for Titan's ad campaigns. Harish Bhat fondly recollected how Desai readily agreed to the use of Mozart's twenty-fifth symphony as the signature music for Titan. It was the marketers' intuition in Desai that convinced him that in a country where very few people followed or listened to Western classical music, this tune would transcend culture and gain mass popularity. This little-known tune soon became Titan's identity in most urban Indian households. It gave an imperial feel to the brand's identity.

A series of creative ads followed year after year and built on the multifaceted identity of Titan and its products. For example, the advertisement of Titan Edge with Aamir Khan as the brand ambassador had the catchphrase 'more attention than you can handle' to emphasize the prestige associated with wearing a Titan Edge, the world's slimmest watch. Along with a sense of pride, the company also promoted watches as an accessory for every occasion and for every dress. Different watches even for events within a day—formal watches for work and traditional watches to go with Indian wear for the evening family programme. Through a series of ads for nearly five years in the early years of millennium, Titan proactively promoted the concept of matching a watch with every dress, with Bollywood star Aamir Khan as the brand ambassador. Millennials tend to wear different watches with different dresses as compared to the Gen X style of the same watch for every season. While Titan may not have built that consumer behaviour, it surely capitalized on it and proactively promoted it by giving consumers several reasons to buy a new watch for every season. In later years, Titan launched gold watches under its Nebula brand to fulfil consumer needs at the peak of the consumer pyramid.

Provide a delightful retailing experience. Having internalized this distinction in the consumer's psyche, Titan organized its retail stores into discrete zones. There were zones for classical products, fashion and sporty products, premium products, men's products, women's products, and separate sections for kids' accessories. In each of them, the displays followed a slightly different approach in terms of colours and design. Categorizing products into those styles created a look within the stores and enabled customers to conveniently look at different offerings within a category based on pricing and styles. This further enhanced buying experience.

Another industry-first by Titan was the introduction of its Helios chain of watch stores that brought together over thirty-five top international brands of watches such as Movado, Kenneth Cole, Versace, Tag Heuer and many more, under one roof. It benefited consumers by providing over 2200 watches of these international brands, and service for those brands in a world-class setting. Harish Bhat, former chief operating officer of Titan's watch business, identified this one initiative as having benefitted not just the customers, but several other stakeholders in varied ways, while creating value for the company. 'Helios raised retailing standards within India. Prior to their launch, there were no showrooms to match the quality levels of these international brands . I would like to think that Titan Helios has benefited the retailing industry within India,' he observed. By 2018, there were fifty-seven Helios stores across twenty-seven metro cities of India.

Delight customers even after sales. Titan's dealer networks reported that customers don't throw away their old watches. Many customers would come to Titan showrooms with their HMT watches or those of other brands. Titan capitalized on this insight and launched an exchange offer for several years encouraging customers to get their old watch and take a new one as an exchange offer. It generated into a successful marketing programme. When that outlived its utility, the company introduced end of season sales. Yet, it knew the importance of establishing a strong service network as most Titan customers expected access to repair services at the place they had bought the product. Accordingly, Titan tried to put up a service centre in almost every store where a Titan product was sold. At a time when customers were taken for a ride in the name of aftersales service, Titan followed the '3R philosophy'[11]— repair hurt feelings, repair the watch and repair the damage caused to the company's reputation through a watch malfunction. Chawla observed:

> The service network has to keep pace with the growing population of watches, not just their demand. The population of watches determines the servicing

needs because people keep their watches for five or ten years. They don't
throw it away. If nothing else, they come for a battery change, strap change
or plating. So, we have a large service network.

With an annual consumption of 4.3 crore watches, the need for service was
incontestable. By 2018, Titan provided the largest network of exclusive service
centres—716 watch-care centres in 277 towns across India.

During our conversation, Professor Narayandas, independent director on
the Titan board, made a pertinent observation, 'In the presence of a dominant
player like HMT, Titan was able to come from nowhere and leverage the quartz
and digital technology to achieve market dominance in India. That required
talent. The Tata Group has the power of attracting the best talent.' By providing
a unique value proposition through innovation based on differentiation,
cost leadership, segmentation and reach, Titan created immense value for
its customers. This was consistently nurtured through the Titan Innovation
Council, a cross-functional team of senior and middle management to create
ideas and spread the innovation culture across Titan.

Interestingly, former chairman and managing director of HMT, N.
Ramanujan had worked out a joint venture with Titan to leverage its growing
popularity when Desai was the MD. Surprisingly, the government turned
down the proposal.[12] By 2017, the Titan brand portfolio owned over 60 per
cent of the domestic market share in the organized watch market. It annually
sold 1.3 crore of the 4.2 crore watches bought across India. On the other hand,
HMT shut down its watchmaking business in 2016 after making average
annual losses of ₹200 crore for several years. Allwyn, the other competitor
who had started watchmaking in 1981, became defunct by 1995. Despite being
a pioneer in the Indian watchmaking industry, HMT was unable to match
the speed of innovation and organizational transformation required in the
competitive times of the new millennium.

Winning a woman's heart

'There's more to customer focus than creating products that satisfy our
customers. We treat them like kings and queens; we want them to come back
to us.'

Bhaskar Bhat

A decade into its existence, Titan ventured into an industry that was hitherto
unexplored by the Tata Group—gold and branded jewellery. Inspired by the

Western model where watches and jewellery are sold together by renowned international brands, Titan launched its own jewellery brand called Tanishq ('Tan' meaning body; 'Ishq' meaning love, both in Hindustani language) in 1995. Being second in size only to the Indian food industry, and with a market size of ₹50,000 crore then, it provided a promising opportunity. Titan's first steps in the jewellery market were in the late 1980s. It ventured into the business to earn valuable foreign exchange that would help its watch business import critical components. It manufactured and sold jewellery in Europe and the USA under the brand name 'Celeste'. However, due to an economic downturn, the demand for jewellery in those continents declined. So Titan decided to venture into the Indian markets as it had by then invested substantially in factory, resources and manpower. Moreover, India often ranked first (alongside China) as the country with the maximum gold consumption in the world. The country's annual gold consumption was between 800 to 975 tonnes. Capitalizing on this opportunity, Tanishq began its domestic journey in 1996 with the first Tanishq store in Chennai.

However, it was far from a smooth ride. There were several missteps that cost them heavily for nearly five years. Instead of 22-karat[13] gold jewellery that was popular in India for centuries, Titan attempted to change consumer behaviour by launching 18-karat gold and diamond jewellery, that too in delicate and largely Western designs. It believed that the less expensive and scratch-proof 18-karat jewellery would enable consumers to buy more and larger pieces. Having successfully transformed the watch market to quartz technology, the company leadership believed that it would be able to turn around the Indian customer and build an appetite for 18-karat jewellery. However, one major point that Titan missed was that in India, unlike in the West, jewellery was not purchased only for personal consumption. It was purchased for religious reasons, and also for investments that would be given as gifts to a daughter during her marriage. For both reasons, the 22-karat 'purer' version of gold was an obvious choice. It took several years for the company to realize and accept this aspect of the consumers' psyche. In the meantime, cumulative losses from Tanishq had mounted to ₹150 crore. In early 2002, Titan engaged McKinsey to draw up a feasibility study about its business and brands. One of McKinsey's key questions was, 'Tell us why the jewellery business shouldn't be shut down.'[14] Bombay House was consistently nudging Titan to reconsider their 'adventure' into a new industry that hadn't provided them with any financial returns. However, Ratan Tata left the final decision to Desai, who was a titan of India's retail industry in his own right. That year proved to be the inflection point in the Tanishq story.

After extensive consumer research and internal discussions, at the turn of the millennium, Tanishq came forth with 22-karat gold and diamond jewellery with exquisite Indian designs. To compliment this move, and what later proved to be its master stroke, Titan introduced the 'karatmeter', a spectroscopic device that used X-rays to provide an accurate and non-destructive means of testing the purity of gold. Titan brought this simple laboratory equipment to all Tanishq stores. Any customer could use it to test the quality of their jewellery at no cost. The outcome was quite unbelievable. Scores of urban women started pouring into Tanishq stores in leading metro cities to test the quality of their gold ornaments. Most were shocked beyond measure because 60 per cent of the jewellery tested was below the caratage their family jeweller had assured them.[15] This led to a considerable loss of faith in traditional family jewellers and significant confidence in the scientific assurance provided by Titan's karatmeter. The karatmeter was a process innovation, which almost created a social revolution. It enabled Tanishq in gaining a foothold in the Indian jewellery market, and altering the structure of an industry that was predominantly fragmented.

Lower prices, Indian designs, superior craftsmanship, assurance of purity, guaranteed quality and proactive dealing with customers became Titan's success mantra in its jewellery business. It kept design at the centre of its DNA and launched the asset-light franchisee model for expanding economically. Over the years, two-thirds of its sales were through the franchised stores. In the first decade, Tanishq was largely a small-format store. It gained mastery in the 2000 square feet retail business. As one analyst observed, 'There is no better company than Titan when it comes to understanding where to place its stores, how much rental to agree to, and how to staff its stores.'[16] Within half a decade of its new strategy, over 15 lakh customers were visiting Tanishq's stores across India each year. By 2010, it complemented these smaller stores with large-format company-owned stores. At the peak of the marriage season shopping, it inaugurated a 20,000 square feet glitzy showroom on Usman Road, Chennai's main jewellery market. This was followed by a massive 25,000 square feet Tanishq store in the plush western Andheri suburb of Mumbai in 2011. Bollywood superstar Amitabh Bachchan was the guest of honour. The consumer insight Titan gained was that the average ticket sizes and average consumer spending at these grand stores were much larger. A 20,000 square feet store thus provided greater sales than ten stores of 2000 square feet size. As a result, Titan launched these large-format stores across most metro cities in India.

Harish Bhat was a part of the team that Desai put together to turn around Tanishq. He recalled that experience as professionally transformative.

> A business turnaround is heart-wrenching, but it is so fulfilling to achieve. It taught me that if you get to the right fundamentals, do what is correct by the consumer and by the business, and if the market opportunity is ahead of you, you'll always find a way of turning around a business and make it successful.

The turn of the century brought increasing change in attitudes of working women. This was a period when women in India had started balancing tradition with modernity. They wore professional-looking jewellery to work and traditional ornaments for personal occasions.[17] Through its wide range of products, including Amara, Uttara, Inara and Mirayah, that were inspired from designs of flowers and constellations, or those based on astrology, Tanishq catered to requirements across price bands, thereby expanding its reach and scale. To cater to the requirements of working women, in 2011, it launched a new sub-brand— Mia, which created simple yet elegant pieces at value for money prices. At the other end of the spectrum, it targeted the much-in-demand wedding jewellery segment, which constituted half of the total jewellery market sales in India. In 2017, it launched another sub-brand—Rivaah, a wide range of beautifully handcrafted wedding jewellery for brides that was designed and conceptualized by Titan's design team in Bangalore. Rivaah celebrated the culture of thirteen bridal communities across India by offering region- and tradition-based designs. From the *shankha pala* that was a must for Bengali brides, to *chandan* and *jadtar* jewellery for Gujarati brides, from the *guluband* for a Sikh bride from Punjab to the *oddiyanam* with the image of Goddess Lakshmi, a must for the Hindu bride from Tamil Nadu, Tanishq had it all. To exhibit the gorgeous work of its skilled artisans, Tanishq designed and created several exquisitely crafted jewellery pieces for top Bollywood films—*Jodhaa Akbar* (2008) and *Padmaavat* (2018), which featured the grandeur of the art, culture and heritage of the Rajput–Mughal era.

Though considered tough, Tanishq tried its best to understand and win the Indian woman's heart. The outcome of its efforts was visible in the company's performance. In the first decade under the leadership of Bhat, who took over from his mentor Desai in 2002, Tanishq clocked an annual revenue of ₹7000 crore by 2012. Not just that, it had created 14,330 designs for customers in that single year. While Desai was the visionary behind Tanishq, Bhat is credited for converting that vision into a thriving and profitable business.[18]

The company showed immense working capital discipline to counter the low margins in the jewellery business resulting in ₹1000 crore surplus cash each year. Moreover, in a largely cash-based industry, Titan instilled a sense of transparency. It scrupulously followed government regulations on documenting large transactions with customer PAN card details for purchases above a threshold limit. Highlighting the nature of competition Bhat observed, 'Other jewellers don't do it. So you end up attracting certain kind of customer and not a certain other kind of customer. People entering a Tanishq store know that they can't get away without showing their PAN card for high-value purchases.' In recent times, when brands such as Nirav Modi and Gitanjali have come under the scanner for questionable financial and business practices in the branded jewellery industry, the example of Tanishq stands out as a benchmark. The company has publicly committed to a set of 'ten Tanishq promises' that obligate high standards of quality, integrity and purity to every consumer.

Within twenty years of its inception, Tanishq became India's largest branded jewellery retailer with a pan-India presence of 243 showrooms in 147 towns and a total retail space of 9.71-lakh square feet. By 2018, of Titan's total sales of ₹15,656 crore, the watches and accessories division contributed ₹2126 crore and the jewellery division contributed ₹13,036 crore. The organized segment constituted 10 per cent of the ₹250,000-crore jewellery market in India. Tanishq had a 4 per cent market share of that 10 per cent making it the largest player in the branded jewellery market. The remaining 90 per cent was catered to by 400,000 independent jewellers. Titan also retained watch market leadership with over 55 per cent market share—and with only thirty in every 1000 Indians owning a wristwatch. Both businesses had huge headroom for growth in the years ahead.

India's retail giant continues to expand

Often described as 'restive by nature, maverick at heart and forever in search of the next big idea', Titan continued to venture into newer areas of the Indian retail sector. In 2007, it was the ₹3000 crore prescription eyewear retailing business. The idea first surfaced while the Fastrack team was exploring sunglasses as an accessory for its millennial customers. Dominated by dozens of unorganized players and a few branded ones such as Lawrence and Mayo, Titan found an opportunity to bring to play its expertise in entering an unorganized sector and using brand power and performance power to delight customers. Customers were charmed with choices that were uncommon in a traditionally managed industry. Within a decade, Titan's eyewear division had set up nearly 500 stores across India, gained substantial market share by becoming India's largest optical retail chain, and pleased over 60-lakh customers in a business that had high margins.

After eyewear, Titan's next target was the highly expensive, underserved, unorganized and under-penetrated ₹2000-crore perfume market in India. In 2013, it launched its 'Skinn' brand of fragrances to widen its footprint in the personal lifestyle segment. Made and bottled in France (to avoid alcohol bottling regulatory hurdles in India), the fragrance was designed in-house and created by six world-renowned master perfumers. Available for him and her, Titan sold Skinn at World of Titan stores, key departmental stores and through e-commerce.

In 2017, Titan added another promising customer-facing retail business to its basket. This time it was the Indian ethnic wear. Taneira, its youngest brand was a collection of authentic handwoven saris, handpicked from over twenty states across India. Over 3500 unique pieces priced from ₹2000 to 2.5 lakh were curated at two Taneira stores in Bangalore that offered the convenience of a full-fledged 'style studio'. A 2012 survey indicated that 80 per cent of India's 24-crore households purchased at least one sari a year. At ₹25,000 crore, the sari market was five times bigger than the Indian watch market, making it an enormously promising prospect.

Tatas' retail mascot makes parts for Boeing 787?

Very few know that along with all these stylish products that Titan makes and markets for India's millions, it also supplies parts for the Boeing 787 aeroplane. Titan's little-known precision-engineering division (PED) is a world-renowned supplier in machine building, automation and complex aeronautical components. Started in the early 1990s to indigenously design machines for the watch division and save nearly 100 per cent import duty imposed on Japanese and German machines, Titan's engineers built over 300 equipment for the watch plant. Over the years, several established companies came to seek its expertise, and its capabilities became well known globally. By 2018, it was exporting parts for over seventy firms across aerospace, automotive, oil and gas, solar, electrical and medical equipment industries in Europe, China and East Asia, including top companies such as 3M, Siemens and Bosch. It was rare to see a B2C company delight its B2B customers with equal promise.

L.R. Natarajan, then chief operating officer (jewellery business) recalled that several of the first set of employees at PED belonged to Titan's erstwhile bracelet-making plant. When Titan started outsourcing the bracelets from China, the plant was closed, and the 100-odd employees that included twenty managers were considered to start the equipment manufacturing for the watch division. It took ten years for the endeavour to take shape as the PED, which eventually spun out of the watch division in 2005. But all through, the company stayed with its 100 employees who would have otherwise lost jobs due to the bracelet outsourcing strategy. 'Any other family-owned company would have said, '*Tala lagao aur ghar bhejo*' (lock the plant and send the workers home). But we won't do that to our employees.'

Power of the Titan brand

'The Titan brand stands for elegance, style, friendliness, innovation and quality. The Titan company is about entrepreneurship, pioneering spirit, innovation, multiple stakeholder view, and having a very nurturing culture.'

Bhaskar Bhat

Summing up Tanishq's success story, Bhat underscored Titan's core competence, 'Our entry into the jewellery business was out of a desire to scale up. But the entire strategy was differentiated when compared to other jewellers. In essence, we excel at approaching an unorganized sector in an organized manner and carving out a niche for ourselves.' Industry after industry, whether watch, jewellery or eyewear, Titan was able to identify the right opportunity in related areas, bring value to customers through design, styling, and with its knowledge and expertise in retailing. It had evolved from being a product-brand company to becoming India's largest speciality retailer. The independent retailers (jewellers and opticians) who had dominated those markets had built systems and processes to induce customer loyalty to their stores. While introducing measures to improve customer experience in these businesses, Titan effectively incorporated this factor in its strategy. The Tata brand brought in the much-needed element of trust in these businesses. Bhat emphasized that Tanishq's 22-karat purity platform was supported by the Tata promise. This thought was echoed by Professor Narayandas, 'When they say that Tanishq comes from the House of Tata, they are providing people with trust in a jewellery market and this is powerful.' Same was the case with eyewear, which was related to the healthcare space, where trust played a major role. The trust reposed by the customers in the Tata-backed Titan brand was visible from the fact that Titan ranked in the top ten among 16,000 brands studied across nine cities of India, and Tanishq was the first Indian brand to enter the list of top-thirty best retail brands in Asia–Pacific in recent years.

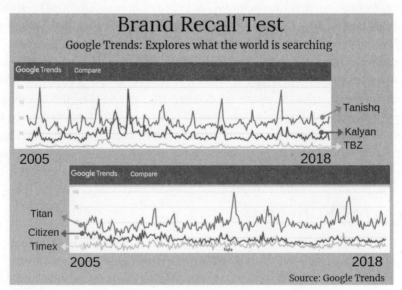

Source: Google Trends

Titan's brand has been built on two distinct touchpoints, both of which play a role in making them the customers' first choice. The first is the outer and more visible aspect of its products—the company's dynamism and capability to consistently launch new products and collections with refreshing designs that service different consumer segments. While it contributed to an innovative idea by launching Raga, an only-women's brand of watches, it continued to build the dynamism around it through annual thematic collections—one year it was pearls, another year aqua, and romantic cities the third. By 2018, Titan designed and developed over 800 new time products every year. There wasn't a dull moment in its designs. Design and style are two intrinsic points that customers looked for in the personal retail space. Titan made these its DNA across businesses and linked them to international styling and design trends and fashion.

Harish Bhat narrated a personal interaction he had had with a Titan customer in Bangalore several years ago.

> That customer acknowledged that he had used a Titan watch for over twenty years, and it continued to function with clockwork precision notwithstanding the passage of time. He further mentioned that once he had dropped that watch into a water tank. When it was found and fished out of the water after a couple of days, it was still working. You should have seen the delight on that customer's face as he narrated to me as to how Titan is a watch that stands the test of time.

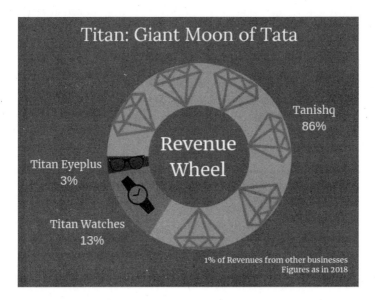

Titan: Giant Moon of Tata

Revenue Wheel

Tanishq 86%

Titan Eyeplus 3%

Titan Watches 13%

1% of Revenues from other businesses
Figures as in 2018

Stories such as these were not uncommon at Titan. Most senior leaders at Titan that I interacted with narrated similar accounts. Chawla shared a story when a customer's watch went inside a washing machine. And when it came out after fifty-five minutes, it was still working! Thus, the second touchpoint of Titan's brand power was the inner invisible aspect of its products—quality. And customers ensured that while they expressed their appreciation, they also expressed their displeasure with equal force. 'You have to keep moving up that quality, it's not a static quality because expectations are changing. If there is any slip up somewhere. the customer first comes and says—"I didn't expect this of Titan",' he admitted.

'There is sufficient evidence to show that the greater the organizational orientation towards the customer, the greater is the company's long-term prosperity and sustainability,' observed Bhat after working in India's top retail company for three decades. And this is indeed true even of Titan. So splendid was its financial performance that by November 2017, it rose to the third spot as the most valuable Tata company after TCS and Tata Motors. By May 2018, its market cap touched ₹85,000 crore with the best ROE in the group after TCS. Between 2002 and 2018, its net profits rose 188 times, from ₹6.2 crore to ₹1163 crore, and dividends to shareholders increased from 10 to 375 per cent. While the TCS wealth-creation story was well known, Titan emerged as the hidden gem in the Tatas' diadem. Ace investor Rakesh Jhunjhunwala, who owned nearly 10 per cent of Titan's shares, often credited Bhat for bringing the company out from the jaws of death on to the road to success. And Bhat believed that strategy was not based on the outcomes of a couple of quarters. He was convinced of Titan's approach to long-term value creation. Within a decade and a half of its worst crisis, it ranked among the most profitable and most valuable retail company in India; it secured a spot in Asia's Fab 50 companies four times and delighted 12-crore customers globally.

Professor Narayandas commended the growth at Titan during his years as an independent director on the company's board.

> That's a direct result of the phenomenal talent of people who are career
> Tata employees in a very competitive lifestyle segment. You might get the
> impression that the Tata Group focuses only on the core sectors. But they can
> be what they have achieved at Titan. This company defined new categories.

Often considered jinxed with consumer-facing and retail businesses,[19] the Tata Group succeeded with Titan by becoming a force to reckon with in super-competitive retail businesses often dominated by foreign brands. Titan truly lived up to its name, in letter and spirit. Every three seconds, someone, somewhere in the world was buying a Titan product.

CHAPTER 17

DELIGHTING CRORES OF CUSTOMERS

A business relationship manager from TCS and his small team of ten members were stationed at the office of Thermo King Corporation in Minneapolis, USA. Towards the end of the project that TCS was doing for them, there emerged a need for undertaking some additional work with an estimated additional cost of ₹1 crore. However, due to budgetary constraints, the customer wasn't willing to go ahead with that part of the project even though it was very important for the company. The relationship manager from TCS knew the importance of that additional portion of the project for the customer's business. So, he called his internal team to his house, along with their families, for dinner. When they were together, he expressed his thoughts on how they could help the customer. By the end of the dinner, the team jointly decided that all of them would spend their personal time to complete that extra part of the project, and give it for free to the customer. They did not even consult their superiors back in India but went ahead as a commitment to the customer's business.

Over the next several weeks they worked over time and completed the task. On 24 December, they called on the customer's team and presented this supplementary part of the project as a Christmas gift. The customer's team was overawed with the service and attitude with which the group of TCS employees had worked. The team members went to the senior leadership of Thermo King and shared what the TCS team had done for the company. 'Can we accept this as a $300,000 Christmas gift from them?' they asked. The company's legal department was in a fix. Never before had they faced such a situation. After some deliberation they suggested that a Christmas gift of $50 or 100 could be accepted. Accepting a $300,000 gift would be unethical. In reality, it wasn't a gift but an entire project that was being given gratis to the company.

Ultimately it was decided that the company would pay a token amount possible within their budgetary constraints for this additional work done by TCS. In addition, to express their delight at the superlative customer service standards displayed by the TCS team, the senior leadership at Thermo King wrote an appreciative letter to S. Ramadorai, then TCS MD. A few months later, when he came to Minneapolis, he told the team, 'You guys have done a tremendous job. Not bothering for hierarchy, you recognized the need of the customer and executed this job, which is amazing.' Such a recognition from the top boss meant much more for the young team than the monetary reward they received for their notable service. After sharing this incident, G. Jagannathan, former global head of business excellence, observed:

> One of the key tenets at TCS is customer satisfaction. If the customer wants something, that stands as the topmost priority irrespective of the time and effort required for achieving it. We ensure that customer requirements are met 100 per cent within the specified time. That is the bible for us.

Let's go to early 1980s. Trucks in India were provided with rugged non-synchronous gearboxes. However, Moolgaokar decided that it was the right time to introduce the much smoother and easy-to-use synchronized gearbox for the convenience of the drivers. In those years, synchronized gearboxes were not available in India. They had to be imported and hence were expensive. The company's management committee was not in favour of importing it. Their concern was that customers may not pay for an additional feature and the company may have to bear the cost. The committee made a recommendation to the chairman that he should not insist on this feature. His reply made them reconsider their approach. The sheer vision communicated through that one sentence made them introspect their approach to product development. Moolgaokar told them, 'Has anyone of you driven a truck continuously for three days? For a single day?' None of them had. He continued, 'Please drive a truck yourself and you'll realize the reason for my insistence.' That was the time when customers had to wait for several years to get a TELCO truck despite making full payment. This was due to the cap on production imposed under the Licence Raj. Even if no additional features were introduced in the TELCO trucks, their demand would have continued to be high. 'Yet, for Moolgaokar, drivers' safety and convenience were of prime importance,' emphasized Chandra Prakash Lohia, former manager.

Moolgaokar believed that even if the customer was not asking for it, and the competition was not providing it, TELCO must work towards product quality that was beyond customer expectations. So extraordinary was his passion and commitment towards customer satisfaction that advocate Charles J.E. Grundy, Moolgaokar's friend for many years, would often share that even on hunting expeditions in Bastar, if Moolgaokar happened to spot a Tata truck, he would buttonhole the truck driver for first-hand feedback on the performance of the vehicle! It was no surprise then that TELCO held 75 per cent market share (Leyland had the remaining) and people were willing to wait for a decade to drive a TELCO truck. In the late 1970s, when Tata trucks were in short supply and sold at a premium of ₹40,000 per vehicle, TELCO refused to raise prices. Moolgaokar underscored his belief, 'Profits should come from productivity, and not by raising prices in a favourable market. Our greatest asset is customer affection.'

Interestingly, the demand for some of the vehicles launched in those years continues to date. One such truck that completed thirty years of non-stop success on Indian roads was TELCO's 407. In the mid-1980s, Prime Minister Rajiv Gandhi relaxed controls on the Indian auto industry. This resulted in four leading Japanese automakers collaborating with local partners—DCM–Toyota, Eicher–Mitsubishi, Swaraj–Mazda and Alwyn–Nissan. In the thick of competition, TELCO decided to independently manufacture its own version of a small truck (LCV—light commercial vehicle) that was in great demand. Developed as Project Jupiter, under the direct guidance of Moolgaokar, several cross-functional teams gave their very best. Proactive collaboration with several suppliers was forged, and a new product was born in 1986. To make the most of the government's policy that fuel-efficient vehicles would pay half the taxes, the 407 met all the ecological norms of the day and emerged among the most fuel-efficient vehicles of its time. It was a classic David versus Goliath situation where localization played a major role.

In a price-sensitive business, affordable spare parts are crucial for long-term viability.[1] Along with a rugged product suited for Indian roads, TELCO's service network gave 407 the upper hand, and it successfully overtook the Japanese quartet. Within a year of its launch, 407 had wiped out all competition from Japanese automobile giants and gained nearly 80 per cent market share. By 2016, when it completed three decades of success on Indian roads, Tata Motors had sold more than 500,000 vehicles of 124 variants and five models of 407 and continued to retain over 75 per cent market share in its category. 'Initially, when we started, we were not sure whether it would survive. But that vehicle pushed the Japanese and their Indian partners out of business. It has been an outstanding success,' admitted Prakash Telang, former managing director of Tata Motors, who was part of Project Jupiter and had seen the three-decade-long successful run of Tata 407.

The letter by J.R.D. Tata to Simone Tata (on page 218) illustrates customer-centric conversations at the level of the group chairman way back in the 1960s.

The three examples of TCS, TELCO and Lakmé, are indicative of the customer focus that existed in Tata companies across all levels of leadership—from a team leader to a company's MD, to the group chairman. And this was at the time when Tata companies operated in a sellers' market. Elucidating the cause of success in those years, Ratan Tata observed, 'We were perceived as being fair and just to our customers, with our products being backed by a concern for quality and credited with being ahead of the times.' After the mid-1990s, India's economic scenario changed with tough competition from global giants, which entered Indian markets across industries and sectors. However, the last quarter-century has been a testimony to their resilience and capacity to excel in changing circumstances.

TO MRS. SIMONE TATA*

Bombay
30 January 1964

Dear Simone

Many thanks for sending me eight samples of Lakmé products for men and asking for my comments.

The Cologne, After Shave Lotion and Talc are excellent. I would, however, give the Cologne a slightly less anaemic colour by making it a little darker in tint.

The Hair Dressing Cream is not right as it is too thick and sticky. Its consistency should be nearer that of Brylcream, although the colour could be a little on the creamy side, if preferred.

As I do not shave with a blade, I have not been able to test the three Shaving Creams....

That leaves only the Pro-Electric Shave Lotion, which unfortunately I do not normally use! Its perfume, however, seems quite pleasant.

On the whole, I feel you have evolved an excellent range of products.

What about a good range of Deodorants? There is nothing we need more in our country! I have tried a number of deodorants made in Europe and America. As you know, they are mostly of three types: spray, roll-on and stick. As the roll-on bottles presumably cannot be made here, we could only produce the stick type, or the simple spray type (not aerosol variety) in a plastic bottle. I hope Lakmé are working on this product. They can count on me as a regular user!

Yours sincerely,
Jeh

*Wife of Naval Tata, Managing Director, Lakmé Ltd., 1964, Chairman, 1982, later Chairman, Trent Ltd.

The Tata Group has not just thrived but has emerged as a market leader across industry categories in which it is present and delighted over crores of customers through its products and services in industrial (B2B) and consumer (B2C) markets.

Understanding customers from gens X, Y and Z

Traditionally, customers have been segmented based on their socio-economic background (a mixture of occupation and income). The five distinct segments are: upper class, upper-middle class, middle class, lower-middle class, working class and subsistence. In several cases, customers are profiled using psychographic segmentation, which involves dividing the market into segments based on different personality traits, values, attitudes, interests and lifestyles of consumers.[2] In current times, there has been an increasing classification of customers based on generational preferences and differences. The largest of the generational group in India are the millennials. Born between 1981 and 1995, the millennials or Gen Y account for nearly 40 per cent of India's population and 50 per cent of its workforce. It is a larger group than the total working population of the USA, western Europe and Japan put together.

These millennials have a strong influence on consumer purchase decisions of people belonging to other generations, especially due to their stage in life, and emerge as a vital segment for every business. Being the largest demographic group in India and globally, millennials are characterized by high levels of disposable income and as digitally connected individuals, driving various consumer segments towards rapid growth and development.[3] 'Collective individualism is at the heart of how millennials behave, and understanding the nuances of this paradox holds the key to determining how companies and brands will connect with this generation in the years to come,' observed Ravi Kant, then CEO (watches) at Titan. With consumer spending in India poised to quadruple to over ₹225 lakh crore by 2020,[4] Tata companies have effectively targeted this group by curating experiences, brands, products, services, distribution channels and communication campaigns that appeal to this demographically significant segment. Fastrack watches (express individuality), Croma electronic and consumer durable stores (online presence and product reviews), Westside lifestyle stores (cool places for shopping), Tata Tea's Jaago Re campaign (a brand good for society), and Tata Cliq (omnichannel convenience) are examples of Tata brands fulfilling distinct millennial needs.

The previous generation, Gen X, born between 1965 and 1980 are referred to as the greying population and constitute nearly 30 per cent of India's population. If one were to extend this to the senior citizens who have just retired from active work life, this number would increase to nearly 40 per cent. According to the 2011 census data, India was home to 10.4 crore elderly people. Referred to as the Baby Boomers in the West, this segment of customers was born in the post-World War II era. In contrast to the millennials' consumption priorities, this segment of consumers believes in savings. The Gen X and those born before World War II years are often referred to as silvers in the Indian marketing context.[5] The average silver (above fifty-five years) is often ignored in market research studies, presuming that due to retirement, she may not be likely to spend money. However, the demographic scenario is totally different. An average silver is far wealthier than the average millennial and has much greater proclivity to spend. Loyalty card data indicates that their ticket size is higher, number of occasions when high ticket items are purchased is higher, and the number of stores from which they buy are far fewer. Adrian Terron, head of customer-centricity at Tata Sons observed:

You can imagine what a company would miss out on if they did not cater to them. Moreover, when you make everything easier for older consumers, it becomes easier for everyone—whether that's more space, easily chewable food or easy-to-open packaging. We want to study this trend and embark on this journey early.

Interestingly, post-demonetization, Gen X consumers have even become digitally smarter. According to a Nielsen report, the percentage of Gen X using digital transaction methods after demonetization had gone up from 68 to 90 per cent.[6]

If we think we have captured the key consumer segments through these three generations, we are sadly mistaken. Even while companies work towards satisfying Gen X and Y, Gen Z has arrived on the scene. A generation of highly educated, technologically savvy innovative thinkers and decision makers, Gen Z are those born after 1996. While millennials embraced technology, Gen Z are digital natives. They don't know a world without computers, mobile phones, gaming devices and social media. To address this emerging segment, brands can't simply 'embrace technology' like millennials have. They must act digitally native too, creating a seamless and strong overarching brand experience across in-store, digital and mobile platforms.[7] With the world's largest Gen Z population at 40 crore, India and Indian companies will have to equip themselves to delight this 'future-ready' generation.

Delighting customers of all genres

Ratan Tata effectively summed up the transformed scenario with respect to customer expectations from companies:

> In today's world, customers are looking for products that suit their purpose best in terms of price, features, quality and appearance. They expect to be treated as kings and to receive sales and service support. They expect to receive timely and competent attention, along with a definite solution to their problems from our service people, dealers or channel partners.

With 65 crore lives touched every single day by Tata companies, 7.5-crore footfalls through over 200,000 retailers and more than 1700 owned retail stores, and a presence in 150 countries across the globe, the Tata Group has been committed to delight customers of all genres and in all sectors. Let's take a quick look at the variety and veracity of their customer-centric approach to business.

Achieving customer affection: Tata Power's mantra

'The electricity customer is unique. They don't miss you till they don't get you. And the moment you don't have electricity, all hell breaks loose, especially in Mumbai, where people are used to 100 per cent availability,' observed S. Padmanabhan with a sagacious smile. The former chairman of Tata Power summed up customer expectations in the power business, 'Electricity should be available at a low price, and should be highly reliable all the time.' Tata Power catered to two categories of consumers. On the one hand are over 600,000 retail consumers, comprising residences, commercial outlets, shops and slums. On the other hand are big industrial consumers, including Indian Railways, Mumbai airport, municipal water pumping stations, sewage treatment plants, fire brigades, hospitals and the refineries of Hindustan Petroleum and Bharat Petroleum. Operating in a heavily regulated industry, where every aspect of running a power company was prescribed by Central and state authorities, the company came up with the approach of 'customer affection' as its mantra. Vivek Talwar, chief culture officer, elaborated on this approach, 'We don't look at power as a commodity. We have realized that there is a superior experience and value that we can provide to our customers that makes us the preferred supplier.' One of the ways in which Tata Power did this was by trying hard to reduce customers' power consumption. Unlike any other company that would make all efforts to increase the sale of its products and services, Tata Power made all efforts to ensure that consumers used less of the product that they were selling! Tata Power consumers could exchange their old energy-guzzling appliances with new five-star rated ones at a discount of 40–50 per cent on the MRP. Over 13,000 consumers availed of this offer in a single year, thereby reducing energy costs by 30–50 per cent without compromising on comfort and convenience. Product-side efforts were complemented with service-side improvement.

'Consumers have become far more vocal. Their expectations of quality and performance are much higher. They want superfast responses. Activism is on the rise. Younger consumers take to the digital media to voice their concerns. Such behaviour is fairly new,' observed Ashok Sethi, chief operating officer. The company used digitization in a big way to delight these GenNext customers with élan. The Tata Power app for customers in Mumbai and Delhi NCR, was one such initiative that gave them access to information, troubleshooting, and even payment facility on the move while engaging directly with the company. By 2018, nearly 20 per cent of its customers were using the app.

Be the farmers' best friend: Rallis India's dictum

By 2050, global population is estimated to cross 900 crore, with India accounting for nearly 170 crore. This would mean an urgent need for better farm productivity—produce more from a lesser area to achieve nearly twice the existing levels of food production. With a conducive natural environment, India has the capacity to sow and reap three crops a year in most parts of the country and emerge as the food bowl of the world. Similar success was achieved in milk and food production to become self-sufficient in the late 1960s and early 1970s through Operation Flood and the green revolution. The future could be to achieve substantial surplus for exports.

To this end, Rallis—the Tatas' agri-solutions company—focused on a threefold strategy: to offer farmers products, knowledge and services. By 2017, Rallis had the largest agrochemicals capacity in India with a direct reach of over 75-lakh farmers. It was a leading player in the industry with a wide range of products in insecticides, herbicides, fungicides, plant-growth nutrients and seeds. However, this success story was achieved after hard efforts. In 2003, Rallis had posted its worst loss of ₹105 crore in its 150-year-long history. A dozen years later, not only had it posted profits for ten successive years, but also had become a success story on the stock markets, by creating a place for itself among the top five best-performing Tata companies. A strong focus on organizational processes and robust international partnerships played a big role in its turnaround.

The senior leadership of the company gave total credit to its customer-centric approach. Venkatadri Ranganathan, chief operating officer, shared a perspective on the true measure of customer-centricity. 'Customer-centricity is when I do things with customers' interests in mind. I develop a level of engagement with them that they can trust me. There is nothing better than a person willing to trust his livelihood on you.' Its success came from a customer relationship management programme—Rallis Kisan Kutumb (RKK), through which all products, solutions and advisories were offered.[8] Initiated in 2006 by R. Gopalakrishnan, then chairman of Rallis, RKK expanded its network from 13,000 to 10 lakh farmers within a decade. Through diverse activities it engaged with nearly 60 lakh farmers and sold products to over 1.2 crore famers.

Project MoPU (More Pulses) was another impressive initiative jointly executed by Rallis and its holding company Tata Chemicals to create shared value for major stakeholders. At the national level, production of pulses would reduce India's dependence on imports and in turn help the exchequer in saving foreign currency.[9] Private sector's involvement brought in technology and transparent practices to enhance farmer incomes and working conditions. For investors, the market for branded pulses estimated at ₹10,000 crore provided a huge opportunity to capture market share, especially for first-movers such as Tata Chemicals. For consumers, unpolished pulses[10] presented a rich source of protein for India's substantive vegetarian population. By 2017, pulses sold under the Tata Sampann brand were available at 128,000 outlets across India, providing sales of over ₹400 crore. On the back end, Rallis engaged with more than 400,000 farmers in ten districts across three states of India. MoPU achieved multiple outcomes for two categories of customers—farmers (of Rallis' agrochemicals)[11] and end-consumers (of Tata Chemicals' Sampann products).[12] Such large-scale value creation for diverse stakeholders set MoPU apart as a fine amalgamation of customer-centric and inclusive business strategies, which was a rarity among Indian business groups.

Tata Sky pioneers innovative infotainment in crores of Indian homes

With over 1.7 crore subscribers, Tata Sky was the largest player in India's direct-to-home (DTH) television services sector, which had nearly 10 crore registered (6.3 crore active) subscribers by 2017. With more than 250 television channels, movies and interactive services for games, learning, recipes, and news, Tata Sky's state-of-the-art digital infrastructure and retail network covered more than 36,000 towns across India. Since its launch in 2004, India's DTH business recorded a fiftyfold growth. At 90 per cent, the country had one of the highest penetration of pay TV in the world. With seven DTH players[13] and thousands of cable operators, the industry remained hyper competitive. Yet, the sector was largely commoditized with content, technology, distribution and pricing being similar across competitors. Content differentiation was not allowed by law in India. So how did a player like Tata Sky differentiate itself from competition? The company identified two areas—value-added services on the network and prompt service on the ground. Ever since its launch in 2006, Tata Sky had been the most innovative operator in the DTH space, and pioneered several value-added services for its customers.[14] It was the first to introduce high-definition (HD) channels, provide personal video recorder services for people not at home when programmes were broadcast, video on demand (VoD), television access on smartphones through TV anywhere, and the first to offer 4K (ultra-HD) set-top box for better picture clarity. With a field failure rate (for set-top boxes in consumer homes) of 0.1 per cent, it had successfully beat the industry average of 5 per cent by fifty times.

'Very often companies discover a technology and look for a need to match that technology. At Tata Sky, we first find the customers' need and then discover the technology to fulfil that need,' observed Vikram Mehra, former chief commercial officer. For customer-centric services on the ground, Harit Nagpal, CEO, encouraged customers to write to him directly for any grievances.

He would review and forward the twenty mails he received every day from consumers to a Bangalore-based team that would resolve matters at the earliest. 'When the aggrieved subscriber gets a call from the company within 15 minutes of sending a mail to the chief executive, and the problem gets solved within an hour, that person becomes a promoter of the company,' observed Nagpal.

It also launched a dedicated Twitter handle for customer service that recorded time of revert and resolution of issues. On 7 October 2014, Visakhapatnam bore the brunt of Cyclone Hudhud, with estimated damages amounting to ₹21,000 crore. Telecommunication channels were severely affected, and thousands of dishes were blown off the rooftops. To ensure speedy recovery to normalcy, Tata Sky sent technicians from other parts of India to the cyclone-affected area and ensured that dishes were replaced even before the trees were cleared from the roads. As a token gesture, the company offered a 50 per cent discount on new dishes to all its customers, which was much appreciated. 'The customer who is quick to react negatively is equally quick to appreciate the swift resolution of the grievance,' observed Nagpal.

Glamourizing steel—Tata Steel's pioneering retail ventures

Imagine buying steel in an air-conditioned showroom with your spouse sipping a glass of cola while the salesmen advises you on options available for your new home—steel doors that have a wooden finish, or better still complete solutions for your new apartment. Sounds appealing, isn't it? That's exactly what Tata Steel envisioned and achieved for its retail customers. They glamourized a commodity like steel and brought it within easy reach. From the dust and grime of *mandis* (wholesale markets) where steel was available in lumpsum quantities and at ever-changing rates, to air-conditioned retail stores with dozens of branded options of exact size and at a fixed price, Tata Steel became the first company in India to de-commoditize steel and converted it to a retail brand accessible to customers across India. This customer-centric transformation of India's largest steel company was game-changing.

In the pre-liberalization era, the typical scene in marketing offices of steel companies was of customers requesting for prior appointments with sales managers, which would be given after a month. When the customer would come to the office after a month and ask '*Sahab se milna hai*' (I want to meet the boss), the secretary's response would be, '*Sahab golf khelne gaye hai*' (Sir has gone to play golf)! The situation was no different in Tata Steel's marketing office at Kolkata. Reminiscing those days, Fusion Engineering's Gautam Mukherjee said, 'In 1989, we ran at 20 per cent capacity and had to almost shut down because there was no steel available. I was called a beggar in the marketing department of TISCO.'[15]

By the mid-1990s, the steel industry got decontrolled, and new players entered the Indian market. Steel was no longer a sellers' market. Prices moved from cost-based pricing to market-based pricing, and devising strategies for ensuring sustained profitability amid competition became the need of the hour. Tata Steel embarked on re-engineering its entire marketing and sales approach to remain competitive and ahead of the pack. The first change it brought was product-related—a transition in its product mix from low-margin, high-volume products such as semi-finished steel to high-value flat products that were used in automobiles and consumer durables. The second change was customer-related. It introduced greater speed in its response to customer requirements for quotations (from a month to twenty-four hours) and flexibility by starting credit sales. Mukherjee was no longer called a beggar at Tata Steel. He had a new title. He was among the 100 'key customers' identified by the company for 'relationship management'. Tata Steel's journey towards customer-centricity had begun.

Intra-company analysis indicated that 20 per cent of the company's business came from over 6000 customers that included wholesalers, traders and small-ticket customers.[16] This segment was highly disorganized and fragmented, and included customers at the base of the pyramid, to which Ratan Tata was consistently drawing the group's attention to. Although their individual per capita consumption was low, there was a huge market that could be tapped. The company identified a remarkable opportunity in this untapped retail market by creating significant differentiation in its products and services, redesigning its distribution network and providing superior value to end-customers. To achieve this end, it began an exercise called retail value management (RVM)[17] in 2000, focusing on low-value, high-volume B2C markets.

Given the sheer scale of targeting 19,000 villages across India, Tata Steel's B2C journey consisted of two key steps—mapping the market and modernizing retail channel partners. To ensure that its products reached end-consumers in the most convenient manner, it studied leading FMCG companies like Procter & Gamble, Hindustan Unilever and Asian Paints, who were highly successful in channel management strategies for B2C products. Tata Steel also became the first company in the world to sell branded steel products.[18] To ensure that consumers got a genuine product, Tata Steel embossed its brand on all products in a way that was impossible to copy. It became the first company in the world to innovate watermark branding on cold rolled steel. In a nationwide study conducted by ORG-MARG in 2005, all brands of Tata Steel—Shaktee, Tiscon and Steelium— emerged as leaders with the highest brand equity in their respective categories. In an industry with a cost-optimization focus, Tata Steel invested about 1 per cent of the total revenue from sales of branded products on branding initiatives. For many

India's Top Steel Companies: Sales

Number of million steel units sold

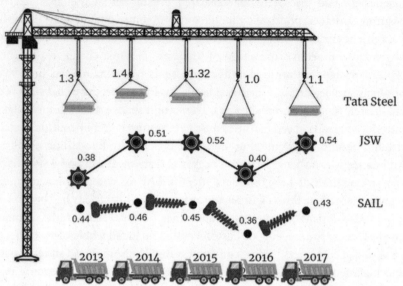

Tata Steel

1.3 1.4 1.32 1.0 1.1

JSW

0.38 0.51 0.52 0.40 0.54

SAIL

0.44 0.46 0.45 0.36 0.43

2013 2014 2015 2016 2017

Indian Steel Companies

Energy Consumption and Co2 Emission CO_2

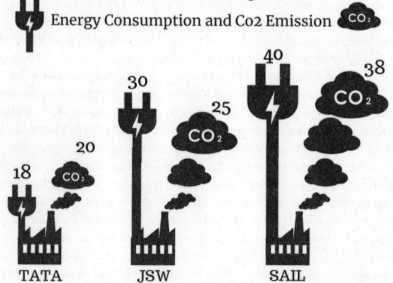

18 20 TATA

30 25 JSW

40 38 SAIL

Source: ESG Reports
Figures are average of 2010-2016

years, the steel industry followed '*Aaj ka bhav*' (today's price). Tata Steel changed and introduced recommended consumer price (RCP) for its products across all Tata dealers. The RCP rates were stable for a quarter and were displayed in stores for greater transparency. The customers benefitted from this price stability.[19]

Prior to Tata Steel's redesigned distribution network, its steel was bought in bulk by traders who sold it to the highest bidder through auctions in mandis at Mumbai and Kolkata. The retailers would travel to these mandis, buy their requirement and return to their geographies to sell the product at inconstant prices. The whole market played on uncertainty and shortage. Sadly, consumers' interests were nowhere in the picture. When Tata Steel introduced its customer-first approach, it met with a lot of resistance as most middlemen made money by hoodwinking consumers on price, quality and quantity. Those traders who were in business for seventy years and were making a crore a month through dubious means, could now earn only a few lakhs. Anand Sen, now president of steel business, reminisced that many of them threatened Tata officers. Some wrote to Ratan Tata seeking redressal. Others filed cases against the company.

Yet, the company stood its ground. It received full support from the top leadership. To ensure rapprochement, Tata Steel counselled its dealers and distributors on the long-term benefits of customer-centric ethical practices. Channel partners eventually realized that branded products, transparent practices and defined prices led to higher footfalls in their stores compared to peers. They were making money not by selling more to one customer at a different price, but by selling to more customers. Between 2006 and 2010, the year-on-year increase in sales to dealers rose from 4 to 40 per cent, inventory requirements reduced by 75 per cent, and return on capital employed (ROCE) increased from 11 to 32 per cent.[20] By 2017, Tata Steel products commanded a premium of ₹10,000 per tonne as compared to the next competitor brand.[21] As if resonating with the company's prudence in proactively targeting retail customers, Tata Steel's sales from branded products increased from 9 to 50 per cent of total sales of over ₹50,000 crore over the fifteen-year period. By 2017, the company had 30 lakh retail customers serviced through a pan-India sales distribution network of 212 distributors and 12,600 dealers and retailers. It had exceeded its own target of 10 lakh retail customers by three times in less than a decade by creating win-win outcomes for consumers, channel partners and itself.

Experience regal luxury—the Taj way

Any story on customer delight is incomplete without a mention of the Taj Group of Hotels, India's first luxury hospitality chain since 1903, and now one of Asia's largest group of hotels. With 150 properties, nearly 18,000 rooms and a presence in sixty-one locations across the globe, the Taj Hotels have been ambassadors

India's Leading Hotel Groups: Room Income

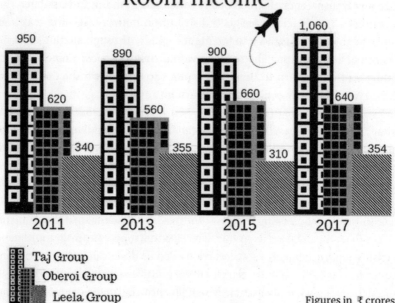

	2011	2013	2015	2017
Taj Group	950	890	900	1,060
Oberoi Group	620	560	660	640
Leela Group	340	355	310	354

Taj Group
Oberoi Group
Leela Group

Figures in ₹ crores

of Indian hospitality. From its very beginning, Taj was a synonym for the 'quintessence of imperial amplitude' and was considered at par with other beacons of global hospitality—Shepherds in Cairo, Raffles in Singapore and the Peninsula in Hong Kong.[22] The Taj Group is the only hospitality chain in the world that has fourteen real palaces—small and big—as its properties. Lake Palace Udaipur, Rambagh Palace Jaipur, Umaid Bhavan Palace Jodhpur and Falaknuma Palace Hyderabad are among the four major palaces. The customer experiences around each palace were uniquely designed to provide an authentic regal experience that guests sought. The most important ritual in erstwhile palaces was the grand welcome for kings. To replicate those moments from another era that guests came to experience, the Taj team did a lot of research and created inimitable arrival experiences for each palace. In Umaid Bhavan Palace, they organized a sword salute under a canopy whenever the guests arrived. In Lake Palace, guests' arrival was heralded by showering petals. In Falaknuma, the team decided that the guests' car would be stopped at a certain point, and they would be ushered in a horse-drawn carriage for the short ride uphill to the main entrance.[23] Taj delivered on the primary pillars of heritage and authenticity so that its guests relived every aspect of the erstwhile royal life. The bathing experience was another specialty.

At these palaces, the Jiva Spa experiences were run on signature themes like the coronation bath ceremony, a special occasion for a young prince on the morning of his coronation. A two-hour coronation bath ceremony at the Jiva Spa within the palace was typically accompanied by live musicians in the background to recreate moments of a bygone era. At the Nadesar Palace, Varanasi, this bathing experience consisted of a royal *abhishekam* (ceremonial bath) with waters of the Ganga. Each of these featured palace experiences were highly appreciated and cherished by guests. This was visible in the increase in company revenues when these exquisite services were created and delivered on-site.

The company innovated at every level to provide bespoke experiences to its guests—in rooms, entertainment, food and beverage, and many more areas. An in-house study at Taj found that on average, across its hotels, a guest encountered an employee forty-one times every day. Taj looked at these as forty-one opportunities to consistently deliver the Taj levels of service to its guests. The company ensured appropriate processes and mechanisms to capture these forty-one 'moments of truth', and rewarded employees who delivered the Taj-ness, the Taj way of hospitality.

Customers trust Tatas

'The Tata name is a household name trusted by millions of customers in India. That is an irreplaceable strength. Trust can never be demanded; it must be earned through consistent behaviour. In our case, that consistent behaviour is outstanding quality of products and services'

Harish Bhat

Providing that quality on a steady basis requires good understanding of customers, the right processes, manufacturing, distribution, marketing, and aftersales service systems; and above all innovative mindsets. All these form vital underpinnings of the customer promise. The icing on the cake is several small actions by a company that convince customers of its genuine intent of building long-lasting relationships based on trust. Here is one such example of prioritizing customer interest over business interest at Tata Motors. This goes back to the late 1990s. A neighbour of Ishaat Hussain had booked an Indica. When the Indica was launched, there was a huge demand for it. People paid money much in advance before they got the car. The company's promise was that customers would get the car by a certain date. However, that did not happen. Eventually, when his car came a few days later, he forgot about the delay in delivery and was excited to receive his brand new Indica. A few days later, he found a cheque in the post with a message: 'We apologize for the delay in delivering your car. Here is the interest for the period of delay in delivery on the advance you paid for the car.' A shrewd Gujarati businessman, he was quite astonished at this gesture. When he met Hussain at the gym later that week he said, 'Who pays interest for a delay in delivering a car? Why do you do such things!' Hussain smiled. He narrated this incident to emphasize that the Tatas' commitment to customers went far beyond the ordinary.

That could be the reason why customers also demand the best from the company. If they don't get it, they unhesitatingly write to the topmost leadership, sometimes even to Ratan Tata, about their lack of satisfaction with a product or service. Hussain highlighted the example of Voltas air conditioners. Being the chairman of Voltas, he had witnessed that when some Voltas air conditioners did not work to customers' satisfaction in the peak of summer months, they would directly write to Ratan Tata stating that they expected much more from a Tata product. Ratan Tata's office would send those letters to Hussain and he in turn would forward the complaints to the CEO of Voltas. The CEO would have to send back a reply on every complaint to the chairman. It's a rarity to see the chairman and the CEO of a company personally attending to routine consumer complaints. Hussain emphasized:

> In the Tatas and perhaps Mahindras, they are a bit like us, there is always a final court of appeal. If there is any injustice, which anybody feels is being done, he can write to Ratan Tata. Even now letters go to him, and he is still held accountable. There is a trust factor. That is what the Tata brand is all about.

Interestingly, the Tata companies were so obsessed with dealing with upset customers that they hardly collated all the positive feedback received from happy customers. One of the reasons was that in the Tata way of things publicly sharing appreciation would appear boastful. Yet another was process-related—a desire to make all customers happy before talking about them. In recent years, the need for sharing these testimonials became vital in its journey of becoming more customer-centric. 'Happy customers become role models. They teach and educate other customers about the functional benefits of using the product that could help them in their lives,' observed Adrian Terron.

Learning from let-downs

> 'Well, somehow, selfishly but because it is close to my heart, something that made me very happy and very sad, was the creation of Nano.'

> Ratan Tata

The story of the Tatas' customer-centricity would be incomplete without reflecting on one of its most promising products envisaged as a game changer in the global auto industry—Nano. 'The Nano, when it was launched, did more for the Tatas in terms of exploding the group in the eyes of the global market, than anything else had done in a hundred years,' acknowledged Ratan Tata during our conversation. The intriguing question one would then ask is that when the same team in Tata Motors led both Ace and Nano projects, how is it that the former became unbelievably successful, and the latter did not. Ratan Tata was as involved with Ace as with Nano. The frugal engineering and market research used in the development of Ace was replicated with Nano too. There are several perspectives that emerge in this discussion. Each of them provides valuable insights on consumer behaviour, especially at the base of the pyramid.

Firstly, the Ace story began when Tata Motors was at its nadir. The company was struggling for survival, was very humble and unbelievably incremental. Advertisements were focused on B2B customers, and manufacturing expansion was gradual. Moreover, Ace hardly received any media limelight. The problems with Nano were the opposite. It started with massive hype and received billions of dollars of free publicity. *Motor Trend*, a UK magazine, even called it the greatest model developed since Ford Model T, launched exactly 100 years earlier. Expectations were sky-high. Marketing scholars believe that commercializing a new product in such a context was very different than commercializing a product when nobody was paying attention.

Secondly, from a management perspective, commercializing an innovation at a high-end is much easier than commercializing an innovation at a low-end. The iPad is a classic example. At the higher end, marketers are appealing to people who can afford to take risk. However, when companies innovate at the lower end of the market, the target customers are among the most risk-averse people in the world. A one-lakh rupee expense for buying a car in India is a big decision in the middle- and lower-middle-class households, who critically analyse the pros and cons of the product. 'Why do you want to buy a Nano? Who else has a Nano? Why don't you buy a second-hand car that has been around for fifteen years than a new unknown car?' Such discussions dampen the desire to be the first mover. It requires amazing marketing capacity to persuade such people to switch their mindset.

Thirdly, the target customer segment for Nano was quite complex. The initial demand for the car came from customers who were not the original target for Nano. The car was designed for people who were riding two-wheelers. Instead, people with Mercedes Benz wanted Nano as a third car. Probably, the marketing team got confused in the initial period about the customer profile. Consequently, the advertising focused on celebrating India rather than selling a car. This adversely affected the launch process, selection of factory site, and capacity decisions.

Fourth was the impact of plant relocation from Singur to Sanand. Tata Motors had already received 200,000 orders with full cash payment within a week of announcing the Nano—the biggest sales uptake in the history of global automobile industry.[24] However, the makeshift facility at Pantnagar had an annual capacity of only 30,000 cars. The company couldn't meet the huge surge of early orders for nearly eighteen months. To make matters worse, some thermal incidents with a few Nano cars created fear in customers' minds that since it was a low-cost car, it was unsafe. By the time Sanand plant began production, mixed opinions in the press, some fuelled by competitors, negatively influenced decisions of prospective customers. Ratan Tata acknowledged that pushing the car through regular dealerships was another blunder as the dealers weren't keen on selling a low-priced car with low margins.[25] Probably, the hardest commercialization challenges got compounded by the hype, which led to complacency and gaps in execution, especially in marketing and sales.[26]

Lastly, the crucial error was allowing the car to be titled as 'the cheapest car'. With eighty-six patents to its credit, Nano and its development process had witnessed unprecedented innovation.[27] However, Nano's price-related identity in the media created a stigma. In India, when someone purchases a car, it's not just for mobility, but also for exhibiting social status. An aspiring middle class did not want to be seen travelling in a 'cheap car' or a '*Lakhtakiya*' (lakh-rupee vehicle). 'The Nano is a brilliant concept, but a monumental marketing blunder,' observed Hormazd Sorabjee, editor of *Autocar India*, after driving his Nano for 16,000 km.[28] In an interview with Harvard Business School, Ratan Tata had reflected on this key learning, 'No one wants to be seen or categorized as getting a handout.' He underscored the point that the approach of trying to show that we're doing it for the person who can't afford something else, is wrong. 'You have to market the product as being just as good as everything else . . . I think the base of the pyramid is keen to have its own place and status in the hierarchy of the consuming public, which one needs to respect more than we have been doing.'

Customer-centricity for the future: Tatas' 3Ds

'A new trend is coming to the fore, paving a fine path between B2B and B2C: the H2H, or human-to-human, engagement. This is a dynamic where buyers are seen as human beings with particular needs. Product content and marketing strategies will necessarily have to be designed to cater to such needs.'[29]

R. Mukundan

In 2015, Tata Sons officially launched the 'Tata promise to every customer' to emphasize customer satisfaction as the core of everything that Tata companies did, and to build a culture where the customer was centre stage. It read as follows:

> Customer centricity is intrinsic to our culture. We promise to: develop a deep understanding of the unique needs of our customers, deliver pioneering products and services of outstanding quality and value and delight our customers with great experiences at every touchpoint. This is how we will always demonstrate responsible leadership with trust.

The 3Ds of the Tatas' customer promise are not indicative of a new journey they begin. Instead they reaffirm the success achieved across Tata companies in each of them. The first D is visible in the efforts of Voltas in developing an all-weather air conditioner that's highly popular for Indian climate. The other example is Tata Ace by Tata Motors to satisfy a unique requirement of last-mile connectivity in the commercial vehicle space. The second D is epitomized by long-standing brands that are admired by crores of consumers across India for several decades. Titan, Taj, Tata Salt and Tata Tea are brands representing products and services that have delivered quality with customer value. The third D is a continuous journey to ensure that customers seeking an experience are delighted at every touchpoint—whether it is the experience of drinking Tata Coffee, flying aboard Vistara, entering a Tanishq showroom, or using a software developed by TCS. There are infinite opportunities for delighting 90 crore customers across over 100 companies in 150 countries. The 3D promise only inspires all Tata companies to focus their 3Ds towards every C (customer).

The Tata Group didn't leave this approach as a directive. It took concrete steps towards encouraging and facilitating implementation within group companies. A ten-point manifesto was designed corresponding to each of the 3Ds. 'It is open enough not to be prescriptive but directional enough to be adaptive in terms of what each company should do,' observed Terron, who anchored this initiative along with Bhat at Tata Sons. Unlike other companies that focus on customer-centricity from an innovation and communication perspective, the Tata Group integrated its customer promise into the group-wide TBEM initiative to ensure assessment and measurement of Tata companies on each of its parameters. The entire customer-centricity exercise for the future aimed not at centralizing data and processes at Tata Sons, but at building company-specific structures and capabilities that would benefit individual Tata companies and hardwire the approach for the long term.

Five game-changing megatrends

To further build on its customer-centric journey, the Tata Group identified five megatrends that would be game-changing in their customer value propositions and become key focus areas on the way ahead. The first megatrend is *premiumization*. Premium did not necessarily mean luxury. 'At any point of time customers are seeking more value for the same price. Brands are exploring ways for providing greater value in whatever they deliver,' observed Terron. Since the turn of the century, the number of upper-middle-class affluent households in India increased from 1.6 crore to 5 crore, accounting for nearly 20 per cent of the population. The aspirational attitude of youth and increased access to premium goods and service contributed to premiumization. Several Tata brands, including Tanishq, Vivanta, Voltas, and Tata Steel, evolved their own successful approaches on making their products and services premium.

The second megatrend is *health and wellness*. An increasing awareness about the negative outcomes of a sedentary life, to which most of today's urban and upper-middle-class working population is prone, has led to changing consumer preferences. Consumers are willing to pay more for a product that is perceived as providing greater health benefits. Numerous Tata companies have launched products, events and campaigns to resonate with these customer priorities. The third and fourth megatrends are *aftersales service and digitization*. Titan and Rallis are examples of companies that have effectively capitalized on these for urban and rural customers respectively.

Given the large proportion of the group's composition that comes from B2B business, the fifth megatrend is *B2B key account management*. Over a dozen years ago, Ratan Tata had foreseen:

> Tata Steel will need to transition from merely being a steel supplier, and become instead a 'solution provider', working together with key customers to 'design and deliver' steel solutions which improve the customer's product more cost effectively.

Tata Steel's success with customer value management (CVM) emerged as a case in point. Intra-company analysis indicated that nearly 200 key customers accounted for 80 per cent of the company's sales. Devised as a strategy for retaining its key industrial customers, CVM aimed at migrating its large and promising customers, especially original equipment manufacturers, from transaction selling to a collaborative mode of consultative selling and eventually to strategic partnerships that would create mutual value by enhancing value chain competitiveness. In August 2004, a group of senior Tata Steel executives even presented insights from its CVM strategy at a Harvard Business School conference. Given the promise of the automobile and construction sectors, it focused on twenty-five promising clients from 1500 business customers it had and targeted high-margin, high-value B2B markets.[30]

The Tata Group identified influencers and resident experts within Tata companies who could use intelligence, information and insights on these megatrends to form subgroups around each of them. The group on premiumization was led by Garth Viegas, global insights director at Tata Global Beverages; digitization by V. Ranganathan, chief operating officer at Rallis; B2B by Peeyush Gupta, chief marketing officer at Tata Steel; and aftersales service by H.G. Raghunath, former CEO at Titan. The subgroup anchors further engaged with companies that held expertise in the identified areas. Each of them studied megatrends in depth, mined data, and fused existing bodies of research into meaningful insights. The knowledge thus gathered was shared through workshops and round-table conferences with representatives across Tata companies so that they could become more customer-centric.

In conclusion, as they say, the proof of the pudding is in the eating. It isn't enough that companies believe they're giving their very best to consumers. Consumers should feel the same. In his sagacity, Ratan Tata effectively captured this unseen measure of customer delight.

I would like the customer to say that the next product he buys will also be a Tata product because of everything that he experienced. That is what customer retention is about. You cannot afford to have a customer say, 'I made a mistake. I'll never buy another product from this company.' You cannot even afford to have him say he is merely happy with your product. It needs to go further than that. He has to say, 'The next product I buy will be a Tata product.'

CHAPTER 18

THE STORY BEHIND NINE DECADES OF INDUSTRIAL HARMONY

The welfare of the labouring classes must be one of the first cares of every employer. Any betterment of their conditions must proceed more from the employers downward than be forced up by demands from below, since labour, well-looked after, is not only an asset and an advantage to the employer but serves to raise the standard of industry and labour in the country. In looking after the labour of today, we are also securing a supply of healthy and intelligent labour for the future.

Sir Dorab Tata

This quote of Dorabji dates back 101 years. The prodigious son who persevered and converted his father's vision of steel making in India into a reality shared Jamsetji Tata's ideals on labour welfare as a vital prerequisite for industrial success. It would be worthwhile acknowledging the contribution of leaders of his ilk due to which Tata Steel celebrated ninety years of industrial harmony in 2018. This means that for the last nine decades, there hasn't been a strike at the Tata Steel plant in Jamshedpur, which till the 1990s, employed nearly 80,000 people. Of these, 93 per cent were members of the Tata Workers Union, the only recognized union by Tata Steel since 1920. This can be considered a remarkable record. Very few companies in the world, if any, can boast of such success. That too in a country that went through three distinct phases of economic development in the last ninety years. Moreover, in a country, where three major trade union movements were controlled by three major political parties, each trying to use the labour force to achieve political ends, it is even more striking that Tata Steel could remain beyond their reach. Their story provides a pathway to companies desirous of optimizing on synergies between the employer and the employee and co-creating value for the firm, labour and economy.

Verrier Elwin, the British anthropologist, who studied India's tribal communities by staying with them in their ecosystem, classified the evolution of labour welfare at Tata Steel into three distinct phases.[1] The first one was from 1907, when TISCO was established in Sakchi, through 1918 when World War I ended. This period was marked by the Tatas' sympathetic approach towards employee welfare that had not been fully converted into tangible processes. The second phase from the 1920s to the 1930s was marked by sporadic conflict between management and labour. The workers fought hard for their rights and the management transitioned into a democratic approach from a purely paternalistic one. The third phase from 1943 ensured the transformation of the Tatas' kindly approach to labour well-being into concrete actions that led to collaborative decision-making, and redefined prevalent labour standards. A fourth phase could be added from the 1990s, which marked a transition to a professional and performance-driven approach to labour welfare. The peaks and troughs of this journey provide abundant insights.

When Gandhi, Bose and Nehru endeavoured for industrial harmony at Tata Steel

Tata Steel's first labour union was established in March 1920 and led by Surendra Nath Haldar, barrister-at-law from Calcutta.[2] It was formed before the All-India Trade Union Congress (AITUC), the oldest trade union federation in India. Even the Communist Party of India was not in existence during that period. The unanticipated demand during the World War I years had forced Tata Steel to expand its operations much faster than it had planned. The employee numbers had also grown faster than the company could provide for housing and other facilities. To manage them, the company continued to hire foreigners as supervisory cadre officers. Below them, the Indian workers operated. The foreign officers had no sympathy and patience for workers who came from rural and tribal areas and were complete strangers to the industrial environment. They believed that the most efficient way to run a plant was to sweat as much labour out of workers for the lowest possible wage;[3] that there was no place for democracy within the industry; and that the right to hire and fire was God-given. Several labour historians called this an act of managerial despotism, which had become a part of the culture in several parts of India.

Around early 1920s, the impact of the Bolshevik Revolution in Russia was seen in the swelling momentum of India's trade unions. Despite labour welfare measures, Tata Steel, then among the leading companies of Indian industry, was impacted by workers' demands for increasing rights. Even sweepers wanted a share in company profits and a say in increments and promotions. The Jallianwala Bagh massacre followed by the Non-Cooperation Movement of 1920 led by Mahatma Gandhi further fuelled the patriotic sentiment among the Indian masses. Of course, there were local factors that added to the workers' anguish, such as what happened between Temple Tutwiler, then general manager at Tata Steel, Jamshedpur, known for his brash language and erratic nature, and Maneck Homi, a foreman. It seems Homi, a Parsi gentleman, had superior sartorial tastes and would come to the plant in tie and collar. One fine day, Tutwiler in a livid mood, caught hold of Homi's tie and said that only he could wear a tie in Jamshedpur and no one else. Homi resigned and formed a labour union, sowing seeds of the first brush between the management and employees at Jamshedpur. Between 1920 and 1924, Tata Steel, the company with the largest industrial force any single Indian company had in those years, witnessed three strikes. At such a tumultuous time, Mahatma Gandhi arrived in Jamshedpur to mediate. Along with eminent freedom fighter Deshbandhu Chittaranjan Das and C.F. Andrews, he tried to rekindle the relationship between the management and the workers. 'I do not regard capital as the enemy of labour. I hold their coordination to be perfectly possible,' Mahatma Gandhi had observed. He told the workers, 'May God grant that in serving the Tatas you will serve India and will always realize that you are here for a much higher mission than merely working for an industrial enterprise.'[4] As an outcome of his efforts, the Jamshedpur Labour Association (JLA) was recognized by Tata Steel, and Andrews, then secretary of AITUC, was nominated its first president.

Intriguingly, Andrews postponed JLA's elections for several years. The need to protect a 'national industry' from avoidable militancy was probably uppermost in his mind. This seriously upset workers who wanted the right to choose their own representatives. Once again, discontent was brewing in the 'proletariat'. On 1 May 1928, things went beyond control and Tata Steel locked out 4000 workers. The workers wanted Homi back as their leader (he was dismissed in 1925), and the management wasn't willing to accept him. The other key demand was higher wages. C.A. Alexander, the new general manager, refused to negotiate with the workers' preferred leader. This prolonged the strike for nearly four months. It cost the company ₹2 crore and the workers over ₹25 lakh. The only solution to break the impasse was to rope in someone else to mediate. That's when Subhas Chandra Bose, the heroic freedom fighter, entered the scene. He sided with the workers and battled for their rights by negotiating a historic settlement. He became JLA's leader and would regularly visit Jamshedpur to engage with the workers. However, Bose's involvement had reduced by 1932. He was also imprisoned by the British government as part of the freedom movement. In the meanwhile, a section of the workers had started a rival union called the Jamshedpur Labour Federation (JLF) under Homi.

At such a time, V.V. Giri, a railway unionist (who later became the president of India during 1969–74), entered the scene and established the Metal Workers' Union in Jamshedpur to ensure there was one union for the entire industry. However, it failed in uniting workers. Around 1937, Professor Abdul Bari, deputy speaker of the Bihar Assembly and a man of passionate convictions, was sent by Congress to organize labour in Jamshedpur. He became the accredited leader of the Tata Workers Union (TWU), the rechristened JLA.[5] Bari had made his debut as a labour leader during the 1929 strike at the Tata-run Tinplate Company in Jamshedpur. Over the next decade, he became the labour leader of over fifty unions across Bihar and Odisha. During his years at Tata Steel, he provoked workers through his fiery speeches, and on several occasions made management negotiations problematic. He led the worker's demand for higher bonuses, a dispute that had gone into adjudication. The labour discontent continued to simmer, at the peak of which the Tatas fired three workers. In retaliation, workers boycotted the centenary celebrations of Jamsetji Tata in March 1939.[6] Perturbed at the developments, the Tatas invited Rajendra Prasad (who later became the first president of India) and Jawaharlal Nehru to arbitrate between the workers and the management. Their prompt arrival indicated the importance of Tata Steel in the larger priorities of national leadership. Bari was a Congressman, and the two senior-most leaders convinced him for greater refinement in communication and negotiations with the management. In the settlement, both sides compromised on certain issues and an imminent strike was averted. There was a token strike in 1942 to support the Quit India Movement. But that was political in nature and supported by the management as well. As a result, the strike of 1928 was the last 'genuine' strike in Tata Steel's labour log.

The first personnel department

After strikes in the 1920s, a 200 per cent increase in wage rate was implemented by Tata Steel. The company also introduced a variety of bonuses for workers, which encouraged productivity and punctuality. In the early 1930s, when the impact of the Great Depression was at its peak, with over 85-lakh people unemployed in Britain and America, the Tatas did not retrench a single person and instead introduced the profit-sharing bonus for the entire staff in 1934. The scheme, on which a number of other schemes elsewhere have since been based, gave 30 per cent of net profits. The workers cooperated by accepting a wage of ₹1 per day, the barest minimum. Those were also the days of increasing camaraderie among the plant workers. An instance recorded by John Keenan, then general manager at Tata Steel, is poignant. During an accident at the plant, Keenan could take only three of the injured men in his car to the hospital. He chose those who seemed to have a better chance of survival. However, one of them, a Hindu, refused to go and indicated that another man, a half-burnt Muslim, should be taken. '*Hamare bhai ko le jao* (Take my brother),' he said. The same spirit continued in the explosive days post-Partition.[7]

The chairmanship of J.R.D. Tata in 1938 marked the beginning of a new era in labour relations at Jamshedpur. His efforts to positively engage with the volatile Bari were fruitful. Once when he asked Bari whether the Tata management truly deserved his harsh language, the latter replied, 'Tata Saheb, I am sorry, but when I get on to a platform I get excited and cannot control myself.' The mutual respect developed into a good relationship that lasted till Bari's tragic death in 1947.

J.R.D.'s concern for a change in approach to labour welfare wasn't just verbal or ideological. The young chairman wanted to make a concrete change to the strife-ridden atmosphere at Tata Steel. This was visible in the letter he wrote to Tata Sons' board in 1943 while convalescing from pneumonia in Ooty.

> . . . We have little cause for self-congratulating or for feeling complacent about the history of our labour relations . . . That we have managed to scrape through without a shut-down during the last ten years or so is mainly because we were riding on a wave of increasing prosperity, which brought increasing employment, security, pay, bonuses, etc.; to the men and which made it possible for us, and worth our while, to give in to their demands from time to time.

He expressed surprise that Tata Steel had never considered a dedicated department to look after labour welfare in the forty years of its existence.

> If our operations required the employment of say, 30,000 machine tools, we would undoubtedly have a special staff or department to look after them. But, when employing 30,000 human beings each with a mind and soul of his own, we seem to have assumed that they would look after themselves and that there was no need for a separate organization to deal with the human problems involved.

Perhaps, Tata Steel became the first company in India to have a personnel department in 1947.

In 1946, Karesasp Naoroji, grandson of Dadabhai Naoroji, attended the International Labour Organization Committees on Iron and Steel at Ohio (USA). He was representing the Employers Federation of India. During one of the sessions on the 'backward' countries of Asia, an American speaker highlighted the conditions of slavery under which Indian labour worked in the steel industry. Having spent nearly two decades with Tata Steel and a stint in Washington as the Government of India's representative director of supplies during World War II, Naoroji knew the ground reality on both sides of the globe. He arose to share his personal experience at Tata Steel and narrated a slew of employee-welfare initiatives implemented by the company even before they were generally accepted in Europe and America. This included the eight-hour working day introduced in 1912, when the legal limit in Britain was twelve hours. A rest house was provided in 1915 for women working at the coke ovens, in which they might rest and sleep, and a crèche for their children, who were cared for by an Indian nurse.[8] Leave with pay and workmen's accident compensation scheme were introduced in 1920, at a time when they were unknown in Britain or America. The Workers' Provident Fund scheme was started in 1920, which was again unfamiliar in England. The former was legally established in India in 1945 and the latter only in 1952. The company empowered its women workers through maternity benefits from 1928, a measure that was made mandatory in Bihar only in 1946. He also elaborated on bounteous bonuses provided to workers along with several free facilities, including housing, healthcare and education for workers' families. The listeners were amazed by the time Naoroji had rested his case. There was no further mention or discussion on 'slavery' in the 'backward' country of India, where a company had far progressive practices than most of the 'advanced' countries of the world.

Industrial relations redefined

'Industry must be not only a source of employment, but a way of life.'

J.R.D. Tata

By early 1950s, the union's leadership had stabilized. Michael John took charge after the death of Bari. He was ably assisted by V.G. Gopal, then a member of the Indian Parliament. The defining moment in Tata Steel's labour chronicle came on 4 August 1956, the anniversary of the outbreak of World War I. On that momentous day, an agreement was signed between

Tata Steel's management and representatives of the union for promotion of closer association through a three-tiered system that had equal representation of management and employees. The system comprised forty-seven joint department councils at the base, the joint works council and the joint consultative council of management at the apex. All issues connected with industrial relations, working conditions, environment, safety and medical facilities would be jointly decided. The media hailed Tata Steel for making 'industrial history', and for 'a major advance towards a socialist pattern of society'. Labour Minister Khandubhai Desai acknowledged it as a unique experiment in Indian industry. Many observers commented that if the spirit displayed by Tata Steel could inspire other employers, industrial disputes would be a thing of the past.

In the same year, while addressing a conference at Oxford University, J.R.D. identified three vital requirements for successful industrial development—all three related to labour welfare. The first one was providing basic material needs of the workers. The second was providing within and outside the factory, the means of satisfying the more intangible but equally strong human desire for self-expression and fulfilment. The third essential was coping with the special problems of workers relocated from a village to a modern industrial community. He believed this was extremely important as village and tribal individuals suffered acutely from the disintegration of their previous background and spiritual values and from the loss of individuality. This was also very pertinent for the region in which Tata Steel was located. An official survey dated 1906 had warned that the district was 'not to be recommended as a field of recruitment for any industry'.

Labour welfare at Tata Steel had been a comprehensive approach of catering to all aspects of the workers' lives—civic, housing, health and education. To begin with, the town of Jamshedpur was created by Tata Steel and is maintained and managed by them. The municipal services are provided free of cost to the employees.[9] In 1917, when much of industrial England was a slum, Dorabji invited social scientist couple—Sydney and Beatrice Webb— and professors from London University to provide recommendations on the establishment of social, medical and cooperative services in Jamshedpur. Their implementation was led by eminent Indian social workers like Thakkar Bapa from the Servants of India Society. Half a century later, when Jayaprakash Narayan, visited Jamshedpur, he remarked, 'More than anything else, the concept of trusteeship fostered by Mahatma Gandhi receives a much-needed fillip in Tata Enterprises.' In 1907, when plant construction began, there was no urban settlement in Sakchi. By 1951, Jamshedpur was a thriving township with a population of 218,000, thanks to the pioneering efforts of the Tatas. Over those four decades, Tata Steel built nearly 20,000 quarters, flats and bungalows for the employees, allotted on the basis of seniority and salary. It even granted loans to workers who wanted to build their own homes. Thirty-nine primary schools and five high schools taught children in eight languages. It wasn't a surprise that when the all-India literacy rate then was about 10 per cent, it was 70 per cent among Tata employees.[10] Even in loss-making years during the 1990s, it continued with annual expenses on maintenance of Jamshedpur's civic amenities to the tune of ₹100 crore.[11]

The Tata Main Hospital, currently a 914-bed secondary care hospital, provided free healthcare services to all employees and their families since 1908. Free medical services were extended even to retired employees and family members of deceased employees. The company's mobile medical vans catered not only to Jamshedpur, but also the neighbouring villages. In 1974, when the Chota Nagpur region had become the epicentre of the smallpox epidemic, the World Health Organization (WHO), requested the collaboration of Tata Steel. The company obliged with resources and manpower. In six months, 20,500 villages and eighty-two towns were inoculated. By 1975, India was declared free of smallpox, for the first time in history. On the education front, the company ran twenty-eight schools for employees' children in Jamshedpur, and even reimbursed fees for those studying elsewhere.

The outcome of Indianization of leadership

In a letter dated 12 November 1928 to the company leadership, Subhas Chandra Bose emphasized the need for Indianization in the company to achieve industrial harmony. One of the earliest challenges facing the company was replacing foreigners with Indians in the management of its steel plant. Some of the earlier labour problems were compounded by the authoritarian approach of the British managers. To achieve this end, Tata Steel embarked on a plan for progressive 'Indianization' at all levels of personnel. The Jamshedpur Technical Institute started in 1921 was aimed at training Indian boys for taking on responsible positions. The Apprenticeship School established in 1927 provided a five-year course of training students to work as skilled operators. The institutions complemented each other in grooming Indian labour from rural and tribal communities to operate and manage the plant at all levels, and free the company from dependence on foreign technical personnel. Jamshed Bhabha, former director of Tata Sons, had admitted that in 1921 it was thought inconceivable that an Indian could lead a full-fledged modern steelworks.

This was achieved in 1938 when Jehangir Ghandy became Tata Steel's first Indian general manager. The tradition continues ever since, and its positive impact was visible in the management and labour relations.[12] In later years, J.R.D. Tata acknowledged with satisfaction that Tata Steel's technical training programmes were the most comprehensive in India. When the government steel plants were commissioned in the 1950s, hundreds of young engineers were trained in Tata Steel's institutions before beginning work at the public-sector units.

In 1957, the Communist Party of India (CPI) emerged as the main opposition in the Lok Sabha. One of the seats they had won was from Jamshedpur. Shripad Amrit Dange, one of the founding members of CPI, initiated efforts to revive its affiliate—the Jamshedpur Mazdoor Union—and break into the Tata Workers' Union. The Tatas requested the Bihar government to intervene, but Dange continued to raise newer demands, a persistent one being that TWU be derecognized. This was an indirect ploy of politically influencing Tata Steel's over 30,000 workers. J.R.D. and John appealed to the workers to reject these efforts and received full support. This was followed by attempts by Dange and his party workers to harass Tata Steel labour and even gatecrash into the plant to damage property. In the violence that ensued, two workers lost their lives. The Tata Steel management shut down the plant on 20 May 1958 as a safety measure. Two weeks later, when the company invited workers willing to resume duty under the unsafe conditions, nearly 9000 workers registered. There was a stampede that day to list their names. The message was loud and clear. The Tata Steel union and workers had far more faith in the company management than a politically motivated outfit. Dange withdrew and called off the unilateral strike.

This incident witnessed the tangible outcome of the company's efforts initiated a decade earlier through the department of labour welfare. Two decades later, an attempt by the Janata Party-led government to nationalize Tata Steel through legislation was unequivocally rejected by the Tata Steel union. From the late 1960s, India witnessed three bandhs almost every year. Yet, work at the plant never suffered. When the transportation system in Jamshedpur got paralysed during the bandhs, the workers would come on foot. Even curfew did not affect attendance. The company initiated a new practice in 1979 where a worker was deemed to be 'at work' from the moment he left home for work, till he returned from work. The company was financially liable for any mishap during such travel. This was another industry first. Tata Steel's workers maintained better conditions of work and pay compared to workers in the Bombay–Thane industrial belt who belonged to trade unions with a confrontationist attitude.[13] There were benefits in harmony than aggression. J.R.D.'s vision of proactively engaging with workers achieved success in the most trying times. When Jayaprakash Narayan failed to gain support from the Tata Steel union for a socialistic trade union, he had remarked, 'In Bihar, except the Tatas, nobody has ever succeeded, not even the gods.'

The majestic man manager

A visit to Jamshedpur wouldn't be complete without a mention of Russi Mody, MD of Tata Steel from 1974 to 1993. Considered a man manager par excellence, his rapport with workers and his concern for their well-being was legendary. An alumnus of Harrow and Oxford universities, he would sit with workers, call them by their first names, sip cups of tea and eat chapattis with them to build a sense of bonhomie. In 1947, J.R.D. had summoned him to his office in Calcutta and enquired whether it was true that the twenty men working directly under him were the only ones who had not joined the recently formed Mercantile Employees' Union. Mody agreed stating that the workers might have been happy with his style of working and did not find the need to join a union. J.R.D. was impressed. To leverage his people skills, he appointed Mody as a labour officer in the newly formed personnel department at Jamshedpur.

In 1955, the Tata Steel coalfields were suffering from very low productivity and incurring an annual loss of ₹50 lakh. Mody, then in charge of the collieries, interacted with workers and their representatives to understand their problems. In a letter to J.R.D., he requested for an expenditure of ₹55 lakh for new roads, electricity in the workers' colony, and drinking water supply for the colliery houses. J.R.D. readily agreed, a statesman-like decision for a loss-making unit. The net result was that after the money was spent and the workers' confidence gained, there was a stark improvement in productivity and production.

In his years as MD, Mody held open houses every day from 7 a.m. to 9 a.m. at his bungalow in Jamshedpur. Anybody could walk in and talk about anything of personal concern. This practice was eventually instituted for all vice presidents of the company. Abanindra Misra, chairman of Tata Sponge Iron, recalled that Mody started the 'dialogue sessions' with the officers of the company. Categorized into junior dialogue and senior dialogue, 3000 people would participate in the dialogue and ask him questions. He would respond with his earthy humour. As for workers, every week, he sat in the Tata Steel plant shops and listened to their grievances. He would even accept written petitions. Workers had faith that Mody would not disappoint them. Whether his reply was 'yes' or 'no', he sent a personally signed letter to every petition.

This amounted to sending out 10,000 letters every year. In 1979, when 10,000 contract workers incensed by communists, entered the plant threatening destruction unless their demand for being made permanent wasn't immediately met, Mody appealed to Tata Steel workers and a major crisis was averted.

He often said, 'What is man management? That one must behave naturally with any human being.'[14] He was a man-manager almost worshipped by the workers and enjoyed the adoration of his managers. He gave opportunities to high-performing middle managers by promoting them to senior positions and giving them greater autonomy. During his tenure, the average age of superintendents reduced from fifty-four years to thirty-five years. N.K. Sharan recalled an incident in the 1980s. For long years, most of the superintendents were coming to work on motorbikes. One became a superintendent after twenty years of experience on the shop floor. In one townhall meeting, Mody shared that a lot of people in Bombay and Delhi were now driving cars. 'I think the time has come when I would like to see all our superintendents coming in car,' he announced. Within a month, one could see hundreds of Maruti 800 vehicles across Jamshedpur. 'He got them for all the superintendents, and I could see the transformation in the quality of life of the senior people in one stroke,' reminisced Sharan.

A humorous anecdote has done its rounds several decades since 1973, when the name of the lane on which Bombay House is located (in Mumbai) was changed from Bruce Street. Hearsay has it that Mody was once pulled up by a policeman as he tried to park his car on the narrow road and reproached with '*Tumhara baap ka rasta hain kya* (Does this street belong to your father)?'[15] Mody gleefully showed the name on the street. It read 'Sir Homi Mody Street'.[16] Sir Homi was his illustrious father, a former governor of Uttar Pradesh, and a director at Tata Sons for two decades, who had mentored J.R.D. in his formative years.

In 1972, the Bihar government took possession of the Jamshedpur township calling it a 'zamindari',[17] though Bokaro, the public-sector steel plant 150 kilometres away, was considered an 'industrial estate'. Despite this, Tata Steel continued to bear expenses of maintaining all civic amenities in Jamshedpur. In the period of uncertainty that followed, there was marked deterioration in the township's functioning as the issue of ownership was unclear. Eleven years later, the government decided to return the township back to the Tatas, thanks to Mody's ceaseless efforts. J.R.D. had given up hope for any reversal in the government's decision. He praised Mody's diplomacy and people skills for this administrative victory.

His popularity with the workers was evident. On his birthday, thousands of workers would pour into his bungalow, garlanding him with marigolds and having him ride an elephant in a procession through Jamshedpur. A bon vivant, he thoroughly enjoyed the warmth he received. In September 1989, when he arrived from Bombay for a celebration of his golden jubilee at Tata Steel, a huge crowd of company officials, town residents and tribal workers had assembled at the tarmac. They had brought with them a unique gift—a 1.7-tonne laddu made in the company canteen![18] Mody's was the longest-ever stint of a senior executive at Tata Steel. He had risen through the ranks to become the chairman of Tata Steel after starting his career on the shop floor with a monthly salary of just ₹100.

Discharging 40,000 workers in a single decade

Tata Steel embarked on a transformative journey around the time Indian economy was liberalized. Rightsizing the labour force was a vital element of this exercise. After taking over as the chairman of Tata Steel in 1993, when Ratan Tata enquired about the size of the workforce, he was met with a stony silence. A few months later, the number 80,000 emerged. Jamshed Irani recalled the reason for the massive labour force at Tata Steel. 'The Tatas never gave any money for political causes and certainly nothing to politicians, who wanted "bribes". I myself dealt with that. But we could give one thing, which they wanted, and that was jobs.'

In the 1960s and the 1970s, labour was cheap and to placate the powers that be, the company willingly gave jobs. Till the wages were low, that wasn't much of a problem. 'I remember J.R.D. exploding one day in the 1980s when we mentioned that Tata Steel's wage bill was ₹100 crore. He said, "100 crore! What are you guys doing?" Three years later the wage bill increased to ₹200 crore,' reminisced Irani. As part of the Tata culture, the company gave more than what was recommended by national wage agreements. From a labour productivity standpoint, Tata Steel was producing 100 tonnes of steel per man-year, compared to 1000 tonnes per man-year by some of the efficient producers in the USA. There were also a lot of redundancies. For example, Tata Steel had some 3000 secretaries and office boys. The accounting department alone employed thirty-two drivers, security personnel and peons.[19] All these were contributing factors to the rising wage bill. Given that the quantum of wages was non-negotiable, the size of the workforce had to be reduced to manage costs. For this a massive initiative was undertaken.

The Tata culture of not retrenching people and its agreements with the union limited any option of laying off workers en masse. Moreover, that wasn't desirable due to the socio-economic consequences for a workforce that did not have many employment opportunities in Jamshedpur outside the Tata plants. Interestingly, there was also a tradition at Tata Steel, once written into the agreement with the union that every retiring worker (having completed twenty-five years of service) could nominate a person (daughter or son) to take his job when he retired. While the one-for-one replacement clause built immense loyalty between the company and several generations of employees, it perpetually prevented the company from achieving any labour force reduction. At Tata Steel, it wasn't just lifetime employment, it was eternal employment. In such a scenario, the company had to persuade its workforce to voluntarily separate. It proposed a very attractive package through its Early Separation Scheme (ESS), and convinced the union led by V.G. Gopal, not to insist on the hereditary employment clause for the sake of the company's survival. The unions also realized that productivity was the key to the company's survival.[20]

Irani personally addressed several meetings to share his concerns about the dire state of affairs and the need to reconsider employment policies for existential reasons. He recalled one such meeting at the plant.

> After I explained my plan, one of the workers stood up and shouted, 'We understand why you are doing it and how the company is gaining. But you are taking away the jobs of my children.' Immediately, on an inspired moment I shot back, 'Look, if you don't do it, your job and my job is at stake. So, forget your children, think about yourself.' That was the turning point.

The narrative was clear. The management was honest. The workers understood the enormity of the situation. To maintain credibility and convey through personal example, throughout his tenure as MD, Irani never bought a car for himself. He used one from the available cars in the company. This gesture conveyed to the workers that his words and actions were in harmony.[21]

Irani maintained absolute transparency with the union and workers. In his presentations with union leaders, he shared details about the cost, sales, profits/losses, expense per employee, and potential expenses with the rising wage bill. He presented facts about competition and international benchmarks vis-à-vis the company's performance. In conclusion, he would ask for suggestions on alternatives possible in the given situation. But there was none. Moreover, Tata Steel wasn't taking advantage of the situation by proposing an apology for a separation scheme. Instead, ESS was so attractive that they had to curtail the exits by deciding who would leave and who would stay. They wanted to ensure that high-performing candidates remained with the company. In effect, it wasn't a voluntary retirement scheme, but a strategic separation scheme.

'Too much money or too little brains?'

What were the key features of the package? The entire workforce was divided into three age groups. For those above fifty-five years of age, they would get their existing salary until the retirement age of sixty-one years. For those below fifty-five and above forty-five years, would get 1.2–1.5 times their salary until retirement. Those below the age of forty-five years would get 1.5 times their salary until retirement. If they died before the notional date of retirement, their families would continue to receive full payment until the retirement date. As for medical services, those who continued to live in Jamshedpur, the company would provide free medical services for them and their dependent family members. For those leaving Jamshedpur, the company would provide free medical insurance. Employees accepting the severance package had to vacate company accommodation. However, they were given three years' time to find alternative housing. After accepting the package, the worker could take another job and even benefit from dual sources of income.

The entire scheme was designed by the personnel department headed by S.N. Pandey, vice president of human resources. The management's role was limited to outlining the retrenchment policy and giving approvals. R.B.B. Singh, then deputy president of TWU, called it the best scheme in the country and a win-win for all. The package was so lavish, that some of Irani's industry peers told him, 'Jamshed, you either have too much money or too little brain that you have offered such a scheme!' However, Ratan Tata firmly stood behind the initiative despite short-term risks.

Given the massive payments entailed by the ESS for long years, one would wonder the quantum of savings it brought for the company. But there were several. One of the key savings was through the constant amount of salary paid to employees until retirement, instead of increasing salaries based on inflation and market parameters. To this, the savings on payroll taxes, and contribution to pension and provide fund were substantial. The savings on housing and other perquisites given to employees also contributed significantly in the cost-cutting drive. Throughout this decade-long exercise, Irani continued to participate in quarterly meetings with all union leaders. He would address groups of 300–400 union representatives in the Michael John Auditorium in Jamshedpur. The union representatives often enquired about the final target. Irani confessed.

If I had said at that time that from 80,000 we want to reach 60,000, there would have been an uproar! So, I would tell them that I would not give them a

final figure, because quite frankly, I did not know the final figure. We worked
on department-wise annual targets.

About 3500 workers and staff accepted the scheme every year. In those years,
during his confidential 360-degree performance appraisal, Irani scored 10 on
10 for decision-making, 9 on 10 for competence and efficiency but just 1 on
10 for social ability. Unfazed, he admitted, 'My wife Daisy could score 10 on
10 on that!'

The greatest business decision of all time?

Misra gave full credit to the union for their cooperation. Despite massive
workforce reduction, not a single day was lost on account of strike. Instead, a
new tradition developed. On the last day at work, unit workers would celebrate
with *bada khana* (grand feast). 'Hats off to the management and the union
for this trust and relationship. On the one hand we were downsizing, and
simultaneously we were setting up new plants with qualified people through
fast ramp-up,' he recalled. Irani believed that a company could buy equipment
and hardware with money. But not software—the trust and mutual respect
between the union and the management.

It was not that the union was a pet union of the management. They didn't
agree to everything we wanted. But in this, they were with us because they
could see that we were careful in selecting the first few workers for the package.
If you are successful with the first 500 or 1000, they spread the word. Word of
mouth is far better than writing essays on the benefits of the scheme.

The scheme was a mega-success. By 2006, Tata Steel's labour force had
reduced to 38,000. In just over a decade, over 40,000 workers had left happily.
Of these, 10,000 were through normal attrition, retirement and death. About
30,000 workers accepted ESS.[22] It was an unheard-of initiative where thousands
of employees left the company without any protests, or disparagement by the
media, politicians and society. A similar initiative called the Performance Ethic
Programme was also implemented for the managerial staff. The eighteen-
month-long exercise led to a reduction of 1000 officers.

ESS received much appreciation. In an era when mass lay-offs, especially
due to industry cycles, were commonplace in developed economies, Tata
Steel's bold decision to engage with the union and devise an amicable
approach to downsize 40,000 workers was adjudged as one of the greatest
business decisions of all time by Forbes. It was considered on par with
landmark decisions taken by top multinationals like Apple, Ford, IBM, and

Johnson & Johnson, by making radical choices that changed the course of business. It not only made the company more competitive, but also created enormous goodwill as an honourable and fair institution.[23] In 2004, when TWU and management celebrated the historic occasion of seventy-five years of industrial harmony, President A.P.J. Abdul Kalam presided over the event that celebrated a relationship built firmly on mutual cooperation, coordination and understanding.[24]

Nearly fifty years earlier, J.R.D. had identified three most important requirements for getting along with people. The first was communication— frank and continuous discussion between people or groups. The second was the need for total honesty and sincerity in dealing with people. The third was trust. In the 110 years of its existence, Tata Steel had evolved to achieve all three in substantial measure.

CHAPTER 19

GROOMING A QUINTESSENTIAL TATA EMPLOYEE

'If I have any merit, it is getting on with individuals according to their ways and characteristics. In fifty years, I have dealt with a hundred top directors and I have got on with all of them. At times, it involves suppressing yourself. It is painful but necessary. To be a leader, you have got to lead human beings with affection.'

J.R.D. Tata

'I remember the year 2003. I had fallen sick, and it was a very serious case. Probably, I would not have survived, if not rushed to the Breach Candy Hospital,' recalled Prakash Telang. It was a Sunday afternoon and Ratan Tata was resting at an Alibaug guest house. Telang was then the plant head, and his colleagues at Tata Motors' Pune plant thought it most appropriate to inform his office. Ratan Tata's team immediately made arrangements at the hospital in Mumbai and also informed him. 'How are they bringing Prakash to Mumbai?' he asked. 'We believe they are sending him in an ambulance,' was his team's reply. 'No. Send a Tata plane immediately to get him to Mumbai,' was Ratan Tata's instant instruction. His team submitted that being a Sunday afternoon, pilots might not be available at such a short notice. 'If you can't get a pilot, I will fly the plane,' was Ratan Tata's assertion. 'Finally, I was shifted to the hospital [. . .] I survived,' shared Telang. The very next day, Ratan Tata was by his bedside at the hospital to wish the convalescing Telang a speedy recovery.

On 1 April every year, Tata Motors organizes an event at the Pune plant where the chairman addresses the senior leadership. In a normal scenario, Telang, as the plant head, would have been by Ratan Tata's side and made the opening speech, followed by Ravi Kant, the MD. At the last moment, Ratan Tata told his colleagues that though Telang was not in Pune, he wanted him to speak. All arrangements were made in the nick of time, and Telang's live message was broadcast. Having lost 15 kg during hospitalization, he was very weak. His voice was very feeble. Yet, the caring gesture of making an ailing employee part of the annual event struck a chord with Tata employees at the plant. Many an eye was wet with emotion. 'This was a huge gesture on Ratan Tata's part. It has left a memory of a lifetime: here is a man I must work for. A role model in terms of a business leader, with immense concern for his people,' said Telang, fourteen years later, while we spoke at Tata Motors' guest house in Pune. If the Tatas' concern for employees was laudable, the employees' commitment to the Tata culture and goodwill was superlative.

Safeguarding the Tata tradition, with blood . . .

Of all the places targeted in Mumbai during the 26/11 terror strikes, the one place where the fight with the terrorists lasted for the longest time was the Taj Mahal Palace Hotel. Like Opera House to Sydney and Eiffel Tower to Paris, for over 115 years, Taj has been a prominent symbol of Mumbai. In attacking Taj and trying to destroy its century-old heritage wing, especially the historic dome, the terror masterminds wanted to leave a visible scar on the success story of India Inc. That night, over 1200 guests and 600 employees were inside the hotel for high-profile functions. All restaurants were full when the first gunshots were heard.[1]

The natural question, then, is: how did the final number of casualties remain as low as thirty-one? With 1800 vulnerable people and four terrorists loaded with advanced ammunition, the fatalities could have been twenty times more. The credit for this astounding achievement goes to Taj employees, who went way beyond the call of duty to save as many guests as possible. All employees knew the exit routes. However, it was beyond comprehension that not a single employee gave in to the natural survival instinct of leaving the premises. Even before the NSG commandos could formulate a strategy to safely evacuate the guests, the employees had used their prudence and ensured that they were safe, until help arrived.

Chef Hemant Oberoi's valiant team formed a human chain to protect sixty–seventy guests while escorting them from Wasabi, the Japanese restaurant, down the spiral steps, into the kitchen and out. Several employees serving the hotel in different capacities for many decades voluntarily faced the line of fire while evacuating guests through the exit routes. They laid down their lives by blocking the gunmen's paths, and were sprayed with bullets. Mallika Jagad, the twenty-four-year-old banquet manager for the Unilever event, and her team used their extraordinary presence of mind and switched off the lights and bolted the doors of the banquet room on the second floor of the hotel where the event was on. For over a dozen hours, they took care of guests who were ducking and squatting below the tables. Early the next morning, they were rescued by firemen through the windows. Amit Peshave, the twenty-seven-year-old manager of Aquarius, Taj's 24x7 poolside cafe, instinctively found his way out of the hotel's transformer room and into a street on Colaba. However, his conscience tugged at him, and he came back to save thirty-one diners at the Shamiana restaurant. He was miraculously saved even though a grenade exploded close to him.[2] The telephone operators risked their lives but continued their service in the control room to ensure that guests in various rooms received real-time instructions.

Who can forget Karambir Kang, the forty-one-year-old general manager of Taj Mumbai? His heroic leadership saved the lives of hundreds of guests, even while his own family—wife, Neeti, and sons, Uday and Samar—were getting asphyxiated on the sixth floor of the hotel. 'At that time, we didn't know the magnitude of the attack, and the number of gunmen. Despite that, we just took the right decisions with whatever knowledge we had. We all felt responsible for each other and for our guests.' Kang recalled with supreme satisfaction writ across his face as we spoke at Taj Boston. Kang believed that what happened that night was a tangible expression of the employees' belief that the Taj was their family. The place had given them livelihood, educated their kids, and enabled them to build their homes. 'The Taj is like a temple. It's revered by the staff,' he told me. Even in adversity, the employees had stood by the company ideals and ethos.

Ratan Tata, Kumar, and senior leaders were standing helplessly on the pavement outside, not knowing what was going on inside, or how many people had been killed. It was a horrendous feeling. At another venue, a crisis and emergency microsite was put together for handling everything from lost baggage to finding people and providing minute-by-minute updates. A lot of requests for help was pouring in from people in hospitals, for whom Taj was paying. Some people didn't have anybody to pay their bills for, and there was no knowing if they were connected to the tragedy in Taj. At that time, Kumar walked in with a message from Ratan Tata that Taj should not discriminate while helping people. A Tata team was constituted to visit every hospital where the injured were being treated. If the hospital hadn't taken care of the bills, Taj would do the needful irrespective of whether the person was injured at the railway station or Trident–Oberoi, Taj's competitor. Even hawkers and street vendors who were injured during the attack were taken care of.[3]

When two-thirds of a hotel is closed, any organization would retrench some part of its employee-base—in Taj's case, as large as 1800 people. However, Taj didn't. Not a single person was retrenched post the attacks. Instead, the period was used to further train the employees and raise service levels. Many were transferred to other Taj properties to continue their good work. 'It was a part of the Tata culture to go beyond the ordinary and contribute. The staff witnessed the company's reaction being in total alignment with their sacrifice for the larger cause of human welfare,' recalled Deepa Misra Harris.

An acknowledgement of the Tatas' endeavours for employee and societal welfare came from a person no less than the President of the USA. In 2010, during his historic ten-day visit to India, Barack Obama chose Taj as his residence in Mumbai to show his solidarity with the victims of 26/11. During his visit, he said, 'To those who have asked whether this is intended to send a message, my answer is simply, absolutely!'[4]

A legacy of employee centricity for fourteen decades

'Any study of Tata Literature will bring out the aspect of "caring for people" as primary to doing business or earning profits.'

Radhakrishnan Nair

The benevolent empress. In the preceding chapters, we analysed far-sighted labour-welfare measures implemented at Tata Steel. The practices that Jamsetji implemented at Empress Mills in Nagpur fourteen decades ago are as incredible. They were ahead of their time even when compared to developed countries. Jamsetji impressed on all around him that in the conduct of relations between employers and employees, the latter's interests and welfare should be borne fully in mind.[5] At a time when employees' personal well-being was hardly considered, Jamsetji implemented a series of practices. This included water filtration through costly Berkfield filters to reduce incidences of diseases, provision of sanitary huts, a dispensary, and a grain depot for millworkers to purchase supplies on credit at cost price or even lower, especially during conditions of scarcity.[6] A reading room, library and recreation ground were also provided.[7]

Jamsetji also believed in the financial security of the workforce post-retirement. At a time when 'capitalism was at its roughest', he introduced a pension and gratuity scheme (1887) and a voluntary provident fund (1901), which was the first of its kind in India's mill history.[8] The accident compensation fund (1895) took care of the disabled and furnished gratuities to families of those who died during service.[9] At a time when textile millworkers in Lancashire were working on cold winter nights without any respite, Jamsetji installed humidifying systems and dust-removing apparatus to protect the health of his employees and machinery. He also made available fire extinguishers and automatic sprinklers throughout the sheds—another first in Indian mills. While this may sound commonplace today, we are referring to the 1880s, a time when there was no electricity!

Building the right chemistry. It won't be a hyperbole if one says that building industrial townships had become a core competence of the Tata Group. The Mithapur township took shape in parallel with the Tata Chemicals factory complex. In 1944, its costs were estimated at ₹2 lakh, of which Tata Trusts, Tata Sons and the Maharaja of Baroda were contributing in the ratio of 2:1:1. Within the next five years, a hospital providing free healthcare to employees was up and running. In the desert, an oasis-like township with roads, electricity, sanitation, gardens, cinema hall, library, post office and even an aerodrome sprang up to cater to the needs of 5000 people associated with the Tatas' chimerical chemicals complex.[10]

By 1951, Tata Chemicals had completed a dozen years of existence, but hadn't earned an annual profit. Unlike entrepreneurs who considered employee-related expenses to be cost-centres, J.R.D. believed in employee welfare as a duty of the enterprise irrespective of its financial situation. He decided to increase employees' compensation even though the labour contract wasn't due for renewal. In the new proposal, workers were given a company-sponsored dearness allowance and those with more than three months of service received an automatic bonus of 5 per cent of their wages. The unions instantly accepted the proposal. As the saying goes, 'Tough times never last, but tough people do,' the Tatas' persistence paid off. Over the next two decades, the company profits increased twenty times. In 1981, Tata Chemicals became one of the first companies in India to provide employee stock options. Employees were even offered loans on lenient terms to buy debentures, along with special assistance of external agencies, who provided them with investor education. It was as if, more than employees, the company was keen that they benefit from the investment opportunity. And they did.

Private sector's first lifelong career programme. In the late 1940s, J.R.D. conceived the superior staff recruitment committee with the objective of attracting the best talent. In 1956, this became what is now known as the Tata

Administrative Service (TAS), a premier cadre-based career path within the Tata Group of companies modelled on the Indian Civil Service.

TAS' goal has been to select and groom young managers, provide them opportunities for growth, and add them to a talent pool that could be tapped into by group companies, thereby creating a leadership pipeline. TAS remains unique in providing recruits opportunities for lifelong mobility across the group.[11] Rajesh Dahiya, former head of TAS, recalled J.R.D.'s hands-on involvement in grooming the careers of TAS managers in the programme's formative years. Any TAS manager could walk into his cabin and say, 'I have worked for two years at Tata Oil Mills. Now for my growth, I should learn steel making.' And J.R.D. would say, 'Why steel making? Why not carmaking?' And they would have a debate on that.[12] Speaking to TAS officers in 1988, J.R.D. said, 'Loyalty is not only to a company but also to an idea, to a life purpose, to the opportunities that one may get.' This message is so much unlike the absolute loyalty that family-owned business leaders expect employees to have towards them.

Every year, from within Tata companies and business school campuses, nearly 1500 candidates apply for TAS, of which only twenty-five or thirty-five get selected. The year-long training programme for these recruits is rotational with classroom and field-study modules (including a rural stint). At the end of training, appointments are made to Tata companies based on candidates' profiles. The companies come with their needs, TAS officers state their aspirations and the TAS office under Tata Sons Group HR plays the role of the matchmaker. 'The key factor that distinguishes TAS is that its officers have an opportunity at a very early age to solve problems or address issues that are worrying the senior-most leadership of the company. As a result, they end up thinking way beyond their years, which instils a sense of maturity and confidence in them and enables them to take up leadership positions early on,' shared Amit Chincholikar, senior vice president, Group HR, Tata Sons.[13] Despite challenges and limitations, over six decades, TAS has created an impressive pipeline of leaders. It has produced stalwarts like Krishna Kumar, Prakash Telang, Harish Bhat, R. Mukundan and K.R.S. Jamwal.

The alma mater of Tata leaders. The first management institutes in India were the Indian Institutes of Management at Ahmedabad (in collaboration with Harvard Business School) and Calcutta (in collaboration with MIT Sloan School of Management), which were established in 1961. Even before them, in 1959, the Tatas envisaged the idea of a staff college. In January 1966, the Tata Management Training Centre (TMTC) was made the permanent base for group-wide leadership development programmes. The venue selected was a heritage bungalow constructed by George Wittet in the tranquil settings of Pune's suburbs. In the initial years, when there weren't many institutions providing management development programmes, TMTC emerged as a hub for training personnel across private and public sector companies. In 1987, it was chosen as one of the centres for advanced training of senior government officials. Prime Minister Rajiv Gandhi had even addressed a course at TMTC. On demand, the centre has continued training programmes for senior IAS officers.

Lt. Col. M. Ravishankar, deputy general manager at TMTC, recalled J.R.D.'s proactive participation in TMTC programmes. They were occasions for the group chairman to interact with senior executives. On one occasion, an army officer running TMTC as its admin head ticked-off the chairman for not wearing a tie to the dining hall, where the dress code was formals. 'But I don't have a tie,' J.R.D. contended. 'I will provide you, sir,' said the officer. J.R.D. obliged. He went back to the room, wore the tie and returned. Later, he took the officer aside and said, 'I would have appreciated if you could have conveyed this to everyone in advance so that you don't leave an opportunity for anyone to be let down before others.' J.R.D.'s characteristic style set high standards for budding leaders. Probably that's why every programme at TMTC has a Tata-specific layer, where faculty and trainers talk about 'Tata-ness' and their aim to inculcate and enhance this quality in the group's leaders.

Over the years, TMTC developed a three-tier leadership programme. At the highest level is the Group Strategic Leadership Seminar conducted in conjunction with Harvard Business School. It caters to senior leaders ready for CXO roles across Tata companies. The next tier is the Tata Group Executive Leadership Seminar in collaboration with Ross School of Business, and focuses on executive leadership development and sharing of global best practices. The third tier is the Tata Group Emerging Leaders Seminar conducted along with faculty from Indian business schools and in-house experts. It focuses on senior managers taking up strategic roles. These are complemented by customized programmes as requested by Tata companies in diverse areas. Its scale of operations can be estimated from the fact that TMTC conducts over 100 programmes each year with an average footfall of 15,000 Tata executives.

A movement called Titan.[14] In a meeting in March 1987 at Titan Industries, Xerxes Desai emphasized that as a Tata enterprise it was their responsibility to empower the people near Hosur, where a Titan watch factory was going to established. To avoid draining the resources of Hosur, Titan even built a model township for its employees. Desai decided that Titan would recruit fresh sixteen-year-old boys from neighbouring villages. Two teams of executives visited village schools near Hosur, and informed students that a watch factory was going to open at Hosur. Those interested could sit for entrance exams. Through this process, 400 rural boys were selected. A new chapter was about to begin in their lives.

Given their backgrounds, the company decided to treat each boy as a child of the family. Foster fathers who would stay with each group of young boys in the transit houses throughout the training period were identified by Desai himself. The boys were to be nurtured in the nuances of city life. At the factory, they were mentored with immense patience by engineers from Bangalore. They were moulded with human values, taught fundamental principles, and trained in the use of advanced precision machinery in watch-making. To create greater social empathy, the trainees were even taken every month to a neighbouring orphanage to serve and eat with young children. The training was truly integrated—personal, professional and social development formed its vital components.

The outcome was impressive. The first stipend of ₹450 that the trainees received was more than what they had ever seen in their lives. A movement of rural skills training and economic empowerment began, which spurred some of the young minds into entrepreneurship. Several others helped their siblings with higher education, while completing their own graduation part-time.[15] Two decades later, 85 per cent of employees at Hosur hold at least one graduate degree. Over 33,000 lives were touched and transformed in the neighbouring districts and over 210,000 across India. This was the Tata way of business—empowering others while achieving commercial success.

These are few among dozens of examples across Tata companies. The prestige of a job with the Tatas was such that for many decades, in parts of India, there was a saying, 'Joota ho to Bata ka, naukri ho to Tata ka' (If you wear shoes, you must wear the Bata brand; if you have a job, it must be with the Tatas).

Meeting changing employee equations

'The Tata employee is not a special guy. I don't want to give the impression that he's a white angel deposited from heaven, and that we are all pure as lily white. We are not, we are just like anybody else . . . But the atmosphere here is such that you'll think twice before doing anything unethical. We create a unique atmosphere of integrity.'

R. Gopalakrishnan

Over the last few decades, the Tatas' people philosophy has transitioned from being paternalistic to one where companies provide opportunities to employees and they decide how they wish to add value to themselves. Conveniences that were considered motivational in pre-liberalization decades, are now hygiene factors. Internationalization with a Tata footprint in 150 countries has brought new challenges. During my discussion with Satish Pradhan, then head of Group HR at Tata Sons, three key focus areas emerged. First, was a need for far greater adjustment to different nuances and norms of diverse cultures. Consequently, Tata companies need to be more focused on being inclusive. Second, millennials, the largest contributing generation to fresh talent, were entering companies with distinct aspirations. Tata companies needed to become more relevant and contemporary in providing alternatives to meet their key expectations. Third, companies needed to create more choices for people to manage their careers. For example, earlier, freshers were encouraged to bring their spouses to Jamshedpur or Mithapur and live in the township. The company would provide accommodation for them, and even provide them community work or a teacher's job in the local school. However, this

A Family of Seven Lakh

Proportion of employees across Tata Companies

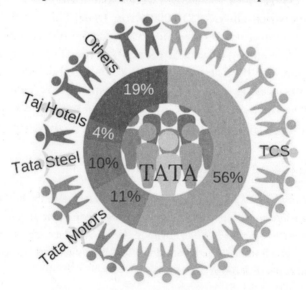

Others 19%
Taj Hotels 4%
Tata Steel 10%
Tata Motors 11%
TATA
TCS 56%

Figures as per financial year 2017

changed over the years. Gen Y employees often said, 'My wife is an investment banker and wants to be in Mumbai. I am not going to go to Jamshedpur. I want to be in Mumbai. If I don't get a manufacturing job here, I will do something else.' People were making different choices, and companies needed to be respectful of that.

In this changing scenario, how did one bring about an alignment between personal and organizational value systems—a high priority at the Tatas? 'There's nothing wrong with the younger generation and its expectations. I was also young someday,' endorsed Gopalakrishnan. During our conversation, three phases of evolutionary expectations emerged. In a thirty-five-year-long career, the first phase is typically about 'I'—my promotion, my salary, my family and so on. To draw a spiritual parallel, the young employee is like a *karma yogi*. He wants to do things, learn things, and get promoted. The second phase is about 'we'—our department, our growth and so on. In this phase, the middle-aged employee is like a *gyan yogi*. He wants to learn and add value to himself. The third part is 'they'—the society, the nation, and so on. In this phase, the senior employee is like a *bhakti yogi*. He is completely dedicated to a cause with little expectation of reward. Companies need to acknowledge this transition. 'If you go to an 'I phase' person and keep talking about the community, he will listen to you but he won't be very interested. As he grows up, the stories will come back to him. It is only in the third phase that he will realize that work is only a means to a higher end,' he explained.

To elucidate how a Tata company with an average employee age of twenty-eight years and 70 per cent of workforce belonging to Gen Y balanced the priorities we just discussed, let's take a sneak peek into India's largest private sector company.

People practices in India's largest private sector company

In a knowledge economy, it is the people who give companies a competitive advantage. The outstanding growth of a company like TCS can be attributed in substantial measure to its investments in human assets for building a knowledge enterprise. The story of how India's largest private-sector employer built an extraordinary force of nearly 400,000 'knowledge workers' is a remarkable one and can be captured through the three Bs—bringing in the right people, building them into skilled people, and bonding multinational knowledge workers into one close-knit TCS family.

Bringing people. In its formative years, TCS needed skilled programmers and software experts for catering to international clients. However, there were handful of colleges in India that offered specializations or dedicated courses in computer science in the 1970s. The job market was full of non-computer science engineers and pure science graduates. To deploy them, TCS had the daunting task of building the right software capabilities in them. It also had to train managers for handling a large base of knowledge workers with unique requirements. For this, it used the twin approach of academia–industry collaboration, and grooming non-IT graduates through focused programmes.

The former began in the days of Faqir Chand Kohli who worked with leading academics like P.K. Kelkar in the establishment of IIT Bombay and IIT Kanpur in 1958–59. He helped in developing India's first MTech programme in computer science at IIT Kanpur. Under Kohli's leadership, TCS contributed immensely to some of these premier institutions. S. Ramadorai extended these efforts by creating a comprehensive Academic Interface Programme (AIP) that brought together top academicians to discuss industry trends, curriculum development and collaboration opportunities. The programme encompassed 535 Indian and 116 foreign academic institutions.[16] Through such investments, TCS contributed substantially to IT education and leveraged these collaborations by recruiting talent directly from academic institutions of eminence rather than from the job market. The seeds of academic alliances sown in the previous century by Kohli, continued to reap benefits for TCS, even fifty years later.

In the noughties, when the demand for software engineers was increasing due to a booming IT sector growing at 40 per cent annually, TCS decided to attract brilliant people who weren't engineering graduates. In 2006, it launched a six-month-long computer science training programme called Ignite, which transformed science and maths graduates into software programmers. The three pillars of Ignite were (1) to have a diverse talent pool (2) make learning enjoyable and (3) make the programme socially inclusive. For the latter, it selected areas in Assam, Meghalaya and Kerala to promote the programme. Between 3 and 13 per cent of those interviewed, were offered jobs in TCS. The first batch of 500 trainees formed a part of the inaugural Ignite programme at the facility in Chennai. Over 60 per cent of these were first-generation graduates, 65 per cent were women and 60 per cent from small towns and rural areas. In those years, initiatives like Ignite helped in meeting the excess requirement of software engineers, and also provided a platform of opportunities for budding engineers in India's hinterland. By 2008, TCS had reached an employee base of 100,000. A decade later, it had nearly 400,000 employees, and was employing twenty-five professionals every hour and over 78,000 new employees every year. The company had witnessed a 14.5 per cent year-on-year increase in employee base between 2002 and 2017.

Building people. TCS wasn't just bringing in the best people but building and empowering them for organizational success. This was the next step in TCS' people story—building competencies and creating coherent teams to accomplish organizational objectives. Given that recruitment numbers were rising, it was a challenging task for TCS to train and coach thousands of young recruits from diverse educational backgrounds and in different TCS offices globally. TCS invested about 4 per cent of its annual revenues in training its workforce. It designed a dedicated training programme for all its employees. By 1997, the company's first corporate learning centre (known as Bodhi Park) was set up in Thiruvananthapuram with a capacity to train 750 personnel (for the initial eight-week training) at any given point of time. The centre's programme portfolio had two target groups. The Initial Learning Programme (ILP) was for fresh engineering graduates. 'We take in rookies and in about one to two years transform them into top flight professionals,'[17] observed Joseph Abraham, former head of HR. The Continuous Learning Programme (CLP) was for existing employees and experienced professionals. It addressed employee learning needs—competency training with hard technical skills and managerial abilities, including generic soft skills. Both ILP and CLP constantly adapted to changing business requirements and inputs from industry leaders and academic experts. Over the next decade, TCS established a dozen domestic training centres in major Indian cities and overseas. By 2014, it began the establishment of its largest corporate learning centre in the world at Thiruvananthapuram with a capacity to train 50,000 IT professionals every year. By then, the company was annually spending 1.5-crore hours on learning and development programmes for its employees. Since 1968, over 500,000 people had benefited from TCS training. Talent building was one of its major contributions to Indian economy.

The other aspect of building efficient human capital was through effective succession planning by making a leadership bench. When Kohli was ready to step down as CEO of TCS at the age of seventy-five, he was clear about the qualities that his successor must possess. He drew up a list of twenty attributes that were necessary for heading TCS, and ranked four or five top executives within the company on those parameters. Ramadorai emerged most suitable and took over as the CEO in 1996. Like his predecessor, Ramadorai too found a great successor in Chandrasekaran to lead the company in 2008. 'In him, I saw excellent execution abilities. He was operationally sound, having wide TCS experience. He was a good team player and, most importantly, had proven himself in the multiple roles he had had in TCS,' he recalled. Interestingly, both Kohli and Ramadorai did not look for top talent outside the company, but considered homegrown leaders for the top job. When Rajesh Gopinathan took over as the fifth CEO of TCS in February 2017, it was in continuation of an unbroken leadership pipeline from within the ranks of TCS for half a century. Compared to TCS, its competitors, Infosys and Wipro, haven't performed as well in terms of internal succession planning.

Bonding people. As TCS grew larger and developed a global footprint, it became increasingly necessary to create a uniform culture of 'one TCS' that would weave together its diverse IT professionals as a single team. For example, project execution style. IT professionals in the Western society prefer working individually unlike the Indian style of working in groups. The Indian IT professionals were also willing to accept a lot of ambiguity, and there was scope for expansion and modification in their assignments. In contrast, employees in the UK and the USA went strictly by job description and preferred to limit their work to the employment contract. In terms of global preferences, majority of Indian employees were keen to go for global projects and even considered migrating permanently to a foreign country. In contrast, European employees did not prefer mobility. With respect to induction and training, the concern for TCS was whether its training framework used for building its India-based human-resource pool would be effective globally, for example in the Chinese context.[18]

Moreover, the Tata brand commanded phenomenal goodwill across India. This was not the case in Western countries, where the brand had gained recent visibility. Hence, any programmes designed around the core Tata brand promise had to be carefully curated. Ramadorai considered the continuous transformation of TCS into a global company without compromising on the Tata values and culture as its biggest challenge. After 2000, when its employee base started increasing phenomenally, it needed to ensure that its ever-expanding family stayed united and connected through sharing of experiences, problems and learnings. Ajoyendra Mukherjee, head of Global HR, underscored three key approaches TCS followed: (1) creating a centralized system of data on human resources, (2) thinking globally yet training locally, and (3) developing initiatives for the younger generation. Three among these initiatives were truly innovative and catered to employees' social, professional and physical domains.

The first was Maitree (meaning friendship), a platform started in February 2002 to engage TCSers and their families in activities that would help them come closer to each other and the organization. It was anchored by Mala Ramadorai, who believed that besides giving employment, a company should also provide cultural moorings and help in assimilation. The first objective of Maitree was to support 'TCS wives' who had relocated outside India with their husbands, through information about their host cities, help in finding appropriate schools for kids, doctors for emergency and Indian spices for cooking. A website was started to share knowledge on such practical requirements. Over a period, Maitree became part of TCS' HR initiatives and was serviced by a corporate team with coordinators in every region. It became a one-stop-shop for all kinds of social activities.

With millennials comprising 70 per cent of its workforce, professional communication and feedback was no longer possible through traditional approaches by 2010. To democratize communication and facilitate bottom-up sharing of views and reviews, TCS launched Knome (pronounced as 'know me') in 2012, as its in-house version of Twitter and Facebook. Despite concerns over Knome becoming a sort of digital water cooler for organizational gossip and a convening platform for raving and ranting against top leadership, Chandrasekaran was convinced that it was through debate and the sharing of ideas that productivity and empowerment could be improved.[19] That's what Knome became. Within three years of its launch, it had 300,000 users, 10,000 interest groups and one-crore social interactions. It had successfully jumped over the hurdles of traditional organizational communication channels by creating a dynamic real-time platform.

A 2013 pan-India study conducted by Assocham indicated that 85 per cent of employees in the private sector were afflicted by lifestyle diseases. An initiative to raise the awareness of TCSers to embrace a healthy lifestyle was most relevant. Using sports as a cohesive force in a large organization was a first-of-its-kind initiative. Chandrasekaran's passion for running became a powerful tool to get TCSers together on a common platform, irrespective of hierarchy. Capitalizing on the common craving for sports, TCS conceived an ambitious programme called Fit4Life with a target of 50-lakh kilometres of collective organizational running in 2013. The MD himself participated in thirteen global marathons. TCS sponsored many of them. By 2017, TCSers had collectively clocked over 30-lakh hours of physical exercise and activity, which amounted to 1.35-crore kilometres. Chandrasekaran believed that Fit4Life[20] wasn't about running, but about team building.[21] He believed that, 'Everyone should try to help one colleague in a way that helps them achieve a little bit more. It need not be work. It can be in any aspect of life.'[22]

The impact of these people practices was evident. In 2010, when India's IT sector was plagued with a high attrition rate of 17 per cent despite providing

India's IT Companies: Employee Growth

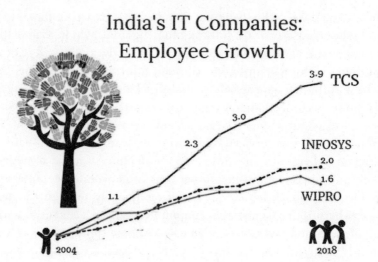

Figures in lakhs

India's IT Companies: Attrition Rate

Figures as in 2018

250,000 jobs annually, TCS had one of the best retention numbers—12–13 per cent (9.9–10.5 per cent in IT services). S. Padmanabhan, former head of global HR, attributed this to TCS' understanding of IT professionals' aspirations at a very differentiated level. 'You must hear the noise (of unfulfilled employee needs) before the noise comes, and plan the individuals' lives in a way that you provide the helical job rotation they're looking for. The sensitivity to understand this was our biggest people-related learning.' In fifty years, TCS had become the largest private sector employer in India, and the fourth largest organization in the country after the Indian Armed Forces, the Indian Railways and the India Post. Its full services capability, broad industry coverage, and large global footprint had offered employees amazing opportunities. Hosting nearly 65 per cent of Tata Group's employees, TCS had created a benchmark through its pioneering people practices.

Factors for critical success as a Tata leader

If we compare the two companies we've explored—Tata Steel and TCS—their people-related priorities were very different given the context of their industries and the time periods they were operating in. While Tata Steel had to focus on Indianization of its labour force during the pre-Independence days, TCS focused on globalization of its workforce in the post-liberalization decades. In the decades when Tata Steel reduced its labour force by half, TCS expanded its workforce nearly ten times. Moreover, one-third of its total workforce, over 134,000 employees, were women, making TCS the largest employer of women in India. Despite the contextual distinctions, the commitment to employee well-being and adherence to Tata values remained the undercurrent in both companies. These are representative examples to communicate the nuance with which the Tatas have dealt with changing employee equations and set industry standards.[23]

During my interactions with Tata leaders across companies, five critical success factors emerged for a quintessential Tata leader. First and foremost was integrity. Not just financial integrity, but intellectual integrity. Second was a commitment to doing business in a manner that was fair to all stakeholders. Third was performance orientation—a burning desire to excel and achieve results. Fourth was marrying personal ambition with the Tatas' pioneering spirit. This could be achieved through two attributes—passion for work and commitment to team members. Finally, developing a complete identity with the group values and becoming an ambassador of the Tata ethos in professional and personal life.

While nurturing these five traits in 700,000 employees, how do Tata leaders ensure that the group's cultural grounding and the focus on founders' values are not diluted in the future? The common conviction across senior leadership is that the Tatas must nurture leadership from within the group from a young age, and ensure that they are in tune with the Tata culture. This would help set the right direction of their value systems.

CHAPTER 20

UNDERSTANDING TATAS FROM EMPLOYEES' EYES

'Remember that everyone who is working in the organization is a human being just like you. It just so happens that God has ordained that you're here and that person is there, that's all. Not necessarily any great difference in intelligence, many a time it is only the background. So be thankful that you are where you are and try and do as much good as you can.'

Prasad Menon

There are hundreds of initiatives across Tata companies that elucidate the Tata way of grooming employees. Instead of attempting to list and elaborate them, I believe the best way to capture the core of the Tata culture would be to understand it from the employees' eyes. Through scores of interactions with employees across companies and hierarchies, I've curated first-hand narratives that provide an engrossing experience of being a Tata employee and the responsibility of being a Tata leader.

Igniting the spark. During conversations with senior Tata executives, I explored the aspect of mentorship they received in their formative years and its impact on their professional journeys. Executives who worked with Tata veteran Krishna Kumar in their initial years mentioned that they learnt several lessons in the Tata way of business as a member of his team. I asked Kumar his approach of mentoring young talent. 'Wherever I have interacted with people who work with me, I've placed tremendous emphasis on character building. We needed to have a sense of idealism in the person, because we were not recruiting just another management trainee, but potential leaders for the group who believe in values,' pointed out Kumar. He gave the example of leaders he worked with through his five decades at the Tatas, and who had succeeded in difficult situations only through integrity. These included J.R.D., Leslie Sawhney, Darbari Seth and Ratan Tata. 'When the new recruits joined my office, nothing was kept from them. Discussions were open to senior managers and others, including my executive assistants. They saw how we implemented integrity, respected values and compassion for the needy in practice. In my view, young people are idealists. That's how I lit them, and I believe those value systems continue to burn even today,' he shared.

Training a young workforce, for life. Sumant Moolgaokar was highly committed to labour welfare. This was at a time when TELCO's Pune plant was getting ready. The workers for the new factory were from villages, not acquainted with life in an industrial set-up. In such a situation, workers tend to involuntarily live in slums. Mumbai is a typical example of this situation. Moolgaokar insisted that in the new TELCO township coming up at Chinchwad near Pune, the apprentices should stay in a proper hostel along with graduate engineers. He ensured a holistic personality development schedule for them in their formative years. He sent them uniforms, organized physical training programmes at 5.30 a.m., ensured discipline in attending theory and practical classes in the evening, followed by sports and games. He believed that once they were used to a disciplined lifestyle, they would not go back to the slums. 'That was the thought process that impressed us very much. I have seen many of them grow very high in stature, not only at Tata Motors but even when they went outside. We still see the benefit of those foundational initiatives. The focus on human beings is something we clearly learned from him,' recalled Telang, who rose up the ranks under Moolgaokar. Remarkably, a 1973 World Bank report on Tata Motors had stated, 'The company's training programmes are among the best in the world considering scope, recruitment and facilities.'

Promotion with permission. G. Jagannathan was serving as the chief value engineer at the MD's office in Tata Steel, Jamshedpur. Jaggu, as he was fondly called, used to play squash in the Beldih Club squash court. It was some time in the 1990s in July. It was raining and suddenly the lights went off in the court. With him were his kids. He was very worried about them because it was pitch dark, and nobody was around. While protecting them and manoeuvring through the darkness, he slipped into a ditch and broke his ankle bone. He somehow dropped his kids home and went to Tata Main Hospital. The diagnosis was a fracture. His foot was plastered, and he was recommended complete bed rest for six weeks. Around 11 a.m., he received a call from Irani's office. It was Krishna Rao, his secretary, who told Jaggu that the MD had called him in his office. Jaggu explained his plight. A minute later, Rao called back to ask if Irani could visit him. 'Why not; he is most welcome,' was his spontaneous reply. Sometime later, he received another call with a message that Irani would be accompanied by his wife, Daisy. 'Are they going to have lunch with me?' he enquired. 'No. Only south Indian coffee.'

Irani came, enquired about his injury and had his favourite coffee made by Lalitha Jagannathan, another lifer in the Tata ecosystem. 'Sir, what was the purpose for which you had called me?' Jaggu asked. Irani said, 'I have been thinking of promoting you as the head of total quality and reengineering. This is a new department and I wanted check with you if you are okay with it?' Jaggu was amazed. During our conversation he told me, 'Here was the MD of Tata Steel appointing me for a particular role. He doesn't have to check with me. He could have just issued the office order and given the letter to me. But he wanted to personally come, discuss and explain what that role was all about, and know my opinion. This is the kind of personal care that the Tatas take.'

'Managing' difficult situations. This is the instance when the Tatas and an international company set up a joint venture. The nature of the business was selling equipment to factories for automation and computers. After the construction of the factory, the CEO couldn't get a single order. Wherever he went to sell, there was some inducement involved. The newly hired CEO was from outside the Tata Group. During a meeting, he mentioned to Ratan Tata, 'We set up the factory, but we can't sell a single item. So, I hope it's all right if I, you know, deal with it.' 'No, it's not all right. How can you even ask such a question?' was Ratan Tata's astonished reply. 'Then the factory will close down,' was the CEO's nonchalant submission. 'For that, if you must close it down, close it down. But we have hired you because we thought you would get an honest order,' the chairman asserted. The CEO was nonplussed. He never expected that the chairman would agree to close a factory, but not indulge in any underhanded dealings. He went back and thought that if Ratan Tata has said, it surely must be possible to get honest orders. He tried again, and that company eventually flourished without having to give in to a backhander. Gopalakrishnan, who became the chairman of that company, shared this instance. 'The company is no longer in the Tata fold. But the *sanskaar* (culture) has been instilled there,' he observed.

Earning respect. Saurav Chakrabarti, former corporate quality head at Trent (Westside), the Tatas' retail arm, recalled his experience. Many of the sales associates who worked at the Westside retail stores were matriculates with a monthly salary of ₹7000. On several occasions, while shopping at the outlets, customers would forget their bags or purses in the changing rooms or the display aisles. Many of these contained high-denomination notes, some even amounting to ₹50,000. Yet, there were no occasions of theft or misplacement. The sales associates would promptly call customers and return their belongings. 'Having worked with us for a year, the Tata values of trust and transparency had percolated into them. I call it the intangible Tata-ness,' Chakravarti said.

Mischievous moments. Amid conversations on ethics and values, there were lighter moments too. Misra recalled one such incident when the jovial Russi Mody pulled a fast one on an unsuspecting general manager of the company. Mody called the general manager to his chamber in Kolkata and said seriously, 'I have got an invitation from the British Embassy. We have to go in an hour in ethnic attire. Since you are from Kerala, you wear your lungi and a T-shirt. I will be wearing pyjama-kurta. We will go together.' The unsuspecting manager arrived at the venue that evening dressed in a lungi. He saw Mody and said, 'Sir, you are wearing a suit!' 'No. I am carrying that pyjama-kurta in a bag,' Mody responded while trying hard to hide his smile. He assured him that he would change his dress at the venue. It was only when they reached the embassy's dining area, where the dress code was 'formals', that the manager realized how effortlessly Mody had fooled him! The gullible man ended up interacting with the dignitaries in his lungi and T-shirt and introducing himself as the general manager of Tata Steel! Mody enjoyed the laughter of a lifetime. 'Was it on purpose?' I asked Misra. 'Ya! Practical fun,' he replied with peals of laughter as we both visualized the situation. 'What was the general manager's reaction?' I asked. 'What could he do, attending the dinner in a lungi as instructed by the MD!'

Follow the conscience. The lungi joke was in a lighter vein. But on matters of principle, the Tatas gave total freedom to their employees to disagree with the topmost leadership, as long as they knew that they did not have a personal agenda, and were arguing from a position of strength. Kumar shared the example of a fellow TAS officer, Shyam Chainani. A brilliant engineer from MIT, he founded the Bombay Environmental Action Group (BEAG) in 1975, while working with at the Tatas. BEAG focused on issues of sustainability and opposed companies doing things that were harmful for the environment. In those years, J.R.D. was the chairman of a committee exploring the construction of a bridge from Panvel that would land near Taj and link Mumbai's mainland with the island. Chainani opposed this project in his publications, speeches, and workshops as BEAG opined that it would harm Mumbai's ecology. The government also listened to the ideas of BEAG. J.R.D. was keen to meet Chainani and understand his perspective. He was called to the chairman's office. Chainani told Kumar, 'I am going to see J.R.D. I know what will happen. I'll have to leave.' He penned his resignation letter before the meeting.

J.R.D. began a genuine conversation. 'Young man, why are you opposing this project? It will be good for Bombay and will solve the problem of commuting,'. Chainani argued against it. Later, he said, 'Sir, if you don't mind, I have got my resignation letter.' J.R.D. took it from him, tore it, came around the table, put his arm around him and said, 'People like you need to be with the Tatas.' 'Who would do this as a group chairman to a young TAS officer?' Kumar asked me. 'The encouragement to articulate your conscience and take the right decisions within the culture of the group has been a very powerful factor,' he emphasized. In 2011, when Chainani passed away, *Guardian* reported, 'Chainani worked briefly for the multinational group Tata, and astonishingly, much of his work thereafter was financed by the company, even when he was apparently acting against its immediate interests.'

The Tata way of business accentuated the importance of doing the right thing without worrying about the consequences or business results. 'That comes much later. First, it should be ethical. It should morally be the right thing to do. Means are sometimes more important than the ends,' Kumar told me.

Saying 'I love you' to wife and 'I am sorry' to son. The most common feedback I received from Tata employees across hierarchies was the comfort they enjoyed with the organization culture because of its strong value systems that resonated with their personal value systems. The recurrent response was, 'We can sleep peacefully at night as we are not asked to do anything that creates conflict with our personal values.' A chairman of a Tata company emphasized, 'I don't follow a particular value because the Tatas say so. I follow it because it is the right thing to do.'

The key issue is aligning personal and organizational value systems whenever there is a dissonance, especially with changing value systems in society and expedient decision-making. In my interaction with Vivek Talwar, I asked him how he brought about this alignment, especially in the blue-collar workers who worked at Tata Power plants hundreds of kilometres away from metro cities. He told me about a four-day programme called LASER (learn, apply, share, enjoy and reflect), which was created to break the routine and bring fresh perspectives on work and life. An interesting exercise was one where workers were asked to go home and tell their wives 'I love you'. The next day, they had to come back to the workshop and share their experience. Some of the workers hadn't said 'I love you' to their wives for thirty years. It was going to be very difficult for them. The next day when the workshop began, one of the workers shared his experience. When he had gone home the previous evening, his wife had opened the door as usual. He smiled and told her, 'I love you'. The wife started crying and said, 'You have definitely done something wrong for which you are feeling guilty. You are probably having an affair somewhere. That's why you told me "I love you".' Another worker shared that once under the influence of alcohol he had severely insulted his son and thrown him out of the house. Inspired by the LASER programme, the previous evening he had gone where his son was staying, begged for forgiveness and brought him home. 'When such powerful transformations happen, people bond well together and believe that if they want to make a difference, they can't just make it in their workplace without making it in their lives, in their homes and in their families; it's all connected,' underscored Talwar.

Practising corporate principles in personal life. 'When the atman (individual soul) merges with the brahman (supreme soul), there is nirvana (liberation). The CEO should look at it as professional nirvana when he echoes the philosophy of the organization and its beliefs, that he and the company become one and the same,' observed T.R. Doongaji, while drawing a parallel between management and spirituality. If you want a credible organization, the CEO must be credible and trusted—both by the external and the internal communities,' he underscored based on his decade-long stint with the Tatas. He recalled an incident that corroborated his thoughts. Forty years ago, when he was a young Tata executive, he had gone to Hyderabad. He was keen to buy a necklace of the locally famous rice pearls for his wife. He negotiated the price with the jeweller, and was getting the gift wrapped when the shop owner looked at him and asked if he was a Tata person. 'I was a little surprised. I asked him, what had made him feel so. He said, "The way you negotiated the price, you got something for yourself and ensured that I too got something."' This is the ultimate stage any organization aspires to reach where employees practice organizational values even in their personal lives. Doongaji's example indicated that the Tatas had been successful in reaching this stage nearly half a century ago.

Love thy labour

'One lesson I have learnt through fifty years of working with people is that
there are no union problems. . . only management problems.'

J.R.D. Tata

While we have seen some enticing examples of employee-employer
bonhomie across Tata companies, it hasn't always been a smooth
ride. Several Tata companies have faced situations of dissonance with
its workforce due to local issues. However, their principled approach
in resolving the dilemmas has been noteworthy. Let us see two such
examples.

Strike of the decade? Rajan Nair had joined the TELCO Pune plant in 1976.[1]
An excellent orator, he received immense support from workers, and within
six years became the general secretary of TELCO Kamgar Sanghatana (TKS),
one of the unions. However, in March 1988, his services were terminated due
to several indisciplinary cases on campus. He left swearing revenge against the
management. Once outside, he continued his activities and started controlling
several external unions. He also managed to get his people elected in the next
round of elections at TKS. Their demand was that Nair should be accepted
as the workers' leader, which the management dismissed. At that time,
Moolgaokar wasn't in good health. Nair and his men thought that they would
be able to bully the management into submission. They started retaliating by
going slow on work inside the plant, and even calling a tool down strike when
Ratan Tata came to the plant in January 1989. 'We requested the new chairman
that we would not want him to compromise, because if he did, there would be
gunda elements controlling the factory. He saw our point and refused to cede
ground,' recalled Telang.

The unfortunate high point came on 15 March 1989, when Nair's men
assaulted and even stabbed twenty-two TELCO personnel in various parts
of the city. Ratan Tata threatened to withdraw operations from Pune if
any Tata personnel were harmed. This was a major headline during the
year-long dispute, which has since been called 'strike of the decade'.
Concerned with economic repercussions of the largest employer in the
Pimpri-Chinchwad industrial belt moving out of the region, which had
2000 industrial units, Chief Minister Sharad Pawar called for a tripartite
meeting—the government, TELCO management and TKS—where Ratan
Tata and Nair would be both present. The latter refused to compromise on

his basic demands and Ratan Tata stood firm on matters of principle. With no resolution in sight, the over 3000 workers supporting Nair announced a hunger strike at the historic Shaniwarwada Fort in Pune. With threats of self-immolation and burning of state transport buses by the protesters, the state government launched Operation Crackdown fearing an uncontrollable outbreak of violence. At 2.30 a.m. on the seventh day of the strike, it rounded up the workers from the venue. The evacuation process continued for fourteen hours. With the strike successfully thwarted, the media hailed Ratan Tata's victory. In retaliation, the workers announced an indefinite strike. TELCO's factory had to be closed.

Telang was then in charge of manufacturing. He reminisced, 'We all huddled together. What can we do while the strike is on? We decided to do what we knew best—manufacture trucks. But how do you do that when most of your workmen are out? We appealed to engineers and white-collared people: "If you have any interest to work on the shop floor we will show you how to do that." They were willing to work.' TELCO hired temporary workers. About 30 per cent of the workforce, who were willing to work but needed protection, also joined the team. The company also signed a three-year retrospective agreement with the other union (TELCO Employees Union) and agreed on lumpsum arrears. Over 2200 workers accepted the offer.[2] Within two months of the strike, TELCO had produced 70 per cent of original capacity. This created headlines in local papers with photographs of vehicles leaving the factory gates, and statistics of daily and weekly production. The Nair group thought that it was a façade and that these vehicles were made in Jamshedpur but displayed as manufactured in Pune. Soon they realized that production was actually happening at the Pune plant. Nair, who had earlier claimed that he would crack the style of functioning of the management, started conceding that Ratan Tata was a straight man who was 'misguided' by the company's Pune management.[3]

It would be topical to mention another strike that happened at NELCO in the 1970s when Ratan Tata was heading the company. During our conversation, he recalled:

> There was a confrontation with Bal Thackeray at that time where he went on strike in NELCO and we declared a lockout in the company the next morning, which he never considered could happen. Then we rented apartments all over Andheri to produce electronic equipment that we had contracted to supply and we delivered virtually about 90 per cent of it. We broke the strike, and everybody came back except the troublemakers. That was my learning curve.

Coming back to the TELCO story, two months after the indefinite strike was called, one fine day, all phones in the Pune factory and homes of senior management started ringing at 5 a.m. The urgent message was that a lot of workers had started arriving at the factory gates. Management thought that they were trying to block the entrance. In reality, those workers wanted to return and commence work. 'If you have to win the battle in the long run, you have to get the workforce on your side. There was a lot of introspection at our end on what went wrong, that our credibility went down, and a goon from outside convinced our workers that he had their interests at heart. A lot of work had to be done to get them back into the mainstream. Since then, we haven't had any problems,' shared Telang.

'What did you do differently since then?' I asked Telang. On detailed analysis, the TELCO management realized that Nair had fuelled cases of workers disgruntled with certain non-transparent decisions taken by their personnel managers. 'We decided that there must be a lot more contact between managers and workmen. We created occasions like 'man of the month' functions, suggestion box schemes, and department picnics to increase interactions. We displayed to them through committed practices that everything was being done in a transparent manner,' he shared.

Analysing the difference in the workforce demographics and cultures of TISCO and TELCO, Sharokh Sabavala, then director of Tata Sons, had observed in the 1980s that unlike TISCO, TELCO did not have workers whose families had been employed in the company for three generations. Moreover, TISCO employed local labour while TELCO people came from across India. Consequently, the TISCO culture was much more paternalistic than TELCO, thereby leading to an enviable industrial relations record.[4]

Love the company, hate the management! In 2003, when Bhaskar Bhat took charge as the CEO of Titan, the company was going through tough times. 'We told our guys that every month we have to generate cash and not just brand image. We must buy less and sell more. Keep less inventory,'[5] he recalled. Bhat reached out to employees to shoulder the responsibility for cost-cutting. Nearly 20 per cent of the workforce was asked to opt for the voluntary retirement scheme (VRS). But VRS was unique. Titan paid the employees what they wanted, and not just a year's salary. 'They wanted an amount of ₹900,000. We agreed. We told them: "You deserve a life beyond this and if this is the amount that you think is right, take it. Because the company has thousands of opportunities to earn,"' observed Bhat.

Consequently, the employees who were left behind wanted the company to give them the money it had saved. Titan was willing to sign a profit-sharing agreement with the union. 'It's the management's job to generate profits, we want our fixed increase,' was their demand. Bhat maintained that Titan would be a different company if the union had agreed to a profit-sharing agreement. However, the deadlock over divergent views led to a sixty-seven-day lockout at the Titan factory. 'The employees love the company, but hate the management!' Bhat jested. This was visible in their actions. Throughout the lockout, there was no violence, not a single day of sloganeering at the gate or raising of red flags. The employees considered the Titan factory their temple and did not touch any machine, leave aside attempting to damage them. 'They knew they would come to an agreement. It was almost like a recalcitrant child saying that I don't want to return,' reminisced Bhat. Eventually everything was settled, and ever since, there has been a bonhomie between the management and the union. A decade later, Titan's profits have soared ten times. The union leaders and the labour regret their decision of refusing a share in profits. If they would have agreed and given up their short-sighted stubbornness, they would have been big beneficiaries of the company's prosperity.

I conclude this employee expedition through the Tatas' plants and factories with an insightful anecdote. This time in the corridors of luxury. While we have analysed J.R.D.'s approach to labour welfare through the example of Tata Steel, here is a simple incident that captures the Tatas' approach to labour welfare. In the late 1980s, Taj Hotels had suspended two employees on charges of theft. Post an enquiry process, the charges were upheld, and their services terminated. They made several appeals, one of which was to J.R.D. directly. On the morning of the day he completed fifty years as chairman of Taj, J.R.D. sent for V.S. Mahesh, then vice president of HR. After an hour spent reading the enquiry proceedings and questioning the main witness, he told Mahesh, 'I am satisfied that you have been fair. Go ahead and terminate them, but please see if we can do something for their families, especially if they have schoolgoing children.'[6] The octogenarian J.R.D. did not want the kids to suffer because of their fathers' follies. This was the quintessential Tata way—'Love Thy Labour'.

CHAPTER 21

WHEN EMPLOYEES BECAME SUPPLIERS; WHEN SUPPLIERS ARE TREATED LIKE EMPLOYEES

In 1983, Tata Tea acquired the Kanan Devan Hills Plantations (KDHP) from the James Finlay Group, its Scottish joint venture partner. KDHP had a lineage that dated back 136 years to the era of the Raj. However, by the late 1990s, Tata Tea transitioned from a predominantly tea plantations company to a branded tea company. This strategy led to its expansion beyond Indian shores, and in the celebrated acquisition of Tetley and several international brands. Divesting from its loss-making tea plantations emerged as a key agenda in the early part of the millennium. The decision to exit plantations was largely because converting green leaf to black tea was a high-cost proposition divorced from cost realization. Despite higher yields, Indian tea had higher costs of production at $1.4 per kg compared to 80 cents in Bangladesh, 90 cents in Kenya and $1.2 in Sri Lanka. China and Vietnam were even lower.[1]

Yet, the Tatas were not willing to exit before a sustainable model of livelihood was chalked out for its plantation workers.[2] For this, Tata Tea had three strategic options. One was an outright sale to another company. This was the option selected by its competitor—HUL. McLeod Russel India, the world's largest tea producer, had picked up HUL's seven tea estates in Assam. Given that KDHP's earnings were in red, the new company would most likely slash wages, shut down social welfare programmes and even relieve thousands of employees. So, Tata Tea decided against it. The second option was to close the plantations. This would again lead to loss of livelihoods for over 13,000 employees working on those plantations, some of whom were third-generation workers. The company ventured for the third option, which involved divesting control to its workforce. It was a first-of-its-kind experiment in the world, at least in the tea plantation business. Tata Tea transferred KDHP ownership, including seventeen tea estates covering a total area of 23,783 hectares located in the high ranges of Idukki district in Kerala, to its workers. Along with the estates, Tata Tea's R & D wing at Munnar, the processing unit and other physical assets were also transferred.

On 1 April 2005, the Kanan Devan Hills Plantations Company (KDHPC) Pvt. Ltd was formed, making it the largest employee-owned tea company in the world. Over 99 per cent of the 13,000 workers owned 68 per cent of the new company. Each worker had to buy a minimum of 300 shares. Tata Tea retained 18 per cent stake in the new entity. The remaining 14 per cent was held by a trust and others. T.V. Alexander, then general manager at KDHP, is supposed to have proposed this audacious plan of employees turning owners. It was accepted by the Tata Tea leadership. Eventually, Alexander became the MD of KDHPC and played a major role in its financial success. The 13,000 employees of Tata Tea at Kanan Devan now became its suppliers. Were they successful?

When the Tatas transferred the ownership to KDHPC, the company was operating at an annual loss of ₹8 crore. The change in ownership marked the beginning of a change in the process of decision-making. What was top-down under Tata Tea, now became bottom-up. Inspired by a successful concept at Tata Steel, the participatory management system was introduced to ensure full participation of employees in company management. Unsurprisingly, within five years, employee productivity increased by 58 per cent, monthly earnings nearly doubled, unauthorized absence from work dropped from 24 to 6 per cent, and the company moved out from the red to a net profit of ₹41 crore by 2010. In the same period, the share price increased seven times. KDHPC also started exporting its tea besides launching its own brand 'Ripple'. Of the 2.5 crore kg of tea produced by KDHPC, Tata Tea was the biggest buyer at 1 crore kg. Over 40 lakh kg were exported and the remaining auctioned. To patronize its erstwhile plantations, Tata Tea launched Kanan Devan as a brand of tea. It was delighted that its decision to transfer ownership to employees had been vindicated. By 2015, KDHPC had become south India's largest producer–exporter of tea.[3] It was the largest producer of green tea in India, and the only branded tea company in the world owned and run by its employees. The company emerged as the poster boy of the employee-run company model in the people-intensive plantations business by providing benefits to all stakeholders. Yet, its Tata connect was palpable. Mathew Abraham, now MD of KDHPC, was a third-generation Tata employee who joined Tata Tea in 1994.

Given that plantation workers at KDHPC were no longer Tata employees, but its suppliers, a prudent decision would have been to absolve itself from investments in existing employee welfare programmes. Over the years, Tata Tea had invested substantial amounts in providing health and education facilities to its plantation employees. Logically, with the formation of a new company, the responsibility of managing these should have been transferred to the new management as the quantum of annual investment was no meagre sum. It involved an annual expenditure of ₹12 crore for a 150-bed secondary care general hospital where workers and immediate family availed free treatment, ₹3.2 crore for the High Range School where half of the seats were reserved for the employees' children, who were exempt from paying fees, and ₹2 crore for the Srishti Trust that ran a school and four vocational institutes for workers' children with disabilities.[4] When Sangeeta Talwar, then executive director at Tata Tea, discussed the matter with Krishna Kumar, then vice chairman of the company, his answer was, 'Continue, whatever it takes.'[5] The Tatas would not withdraw from its commitments to its former employees, now suppliers, even though the new company did not bear the Tata name.[6] They were committed to their well-being, even when employees became suppliers.

From darkness to light

'We look at a *karigar* not as a goldsmith but as a human being who is also contributing to Titan's growth. When you look at him as a human being you care for him.'

L.R. Natarajan

When we admire exquisitely crafted jewellery pieces, we rarely enquire about the hands that created them. The unseen heroes of the jewellery industry are the karigars (artisans) who make the ornaments. Habitually, the gold manufacturing chain in India has been largely unorganized. The karigars typically operate out of dingy and hazardous workspaces in cities, squat on the floor and work in non-ergonomic conditions with little light and ventilation. Over the decades, these artisans hardly made any progress even in the use of tools and machinery. Because of poor working conditions, they developed eye and neck problems that affected hand–eye coordination within twenty years of work. By the time they were forty, they had to quit work and take up other jobs. This scenario discouraged the newer generation of their community from taking up their traditional line of trade. The situation had endangered the existence of skilled craftsmanship and supply of aesthetic products to the industry.

Nobody seemed to bother about the pathetic conditions in which the karigars worked, neither the retailer nor the customer or the government or the middlemen, who gave them business. On introspection, Tanishq (Titan's jewellery division) realized that all its stakeholders had benefited from the company's success, except the karigars. So, it took the responsibility of improving their standards of living and lifestyle, rather than accepting their condition as an occupational hazard. One would wonder why a company should even bother about the work life of its suppliers? They were not its employees, and their well-being was not the company's responsibility. 'The karigars are our vendors, not our employees. But we treat them as our partners, and as part of an extended family,' emphasized Natarajan. During its initial decade in the jewellery business, Titan discovered the karigars' challenges. The leadership believed that when Titan employees retired at sixty, why should the karigars at forty. What can the company do for them? From that analysis emerged an approach that had the potential of being a new model to uplift the lives of karigars and help raise industry standards, at least in the organized jewellery market.

The first requirement was gaining the karigars' confidence. The company undertook several initiatives to convince them of their genuine interest in their well-being. Titan ensured that all karigars had hospitalization insurance and underwent periodic health check-ups. It went the extra mile by arranging loans and sometimes even financing them. The employee suggestion scheme was also extended to them. It took them a couple of years to gain their confidence and trust before they could take this engagement to the next level.

After developing a good rapport, Titan expanded this commitment through a social entrepreneurship project in 2008—establishment of karigar parks and the Mr Perfect programme. In these parks, Titan provided karigars with equipment, material and training (skills and behavioural) along with great working conditions, health and safety practices. The karigars had air-conditioned workspaces, workstations with chairs and work tables, unlike the traditional work-on-the-ground arrangement, adequate lighting and ergonomic seating. They also received identity cards, uniforms, assistance to open bank accounts, and a small canteen. The karigars thus groomed and trained through this ecosystem were Mr Perfect. The Mr Perfect karigars now had to focus only on using their skills in making jewellery of the highest standards and designs.

By 2012, Titan established four karigar centres (an evolved version of the karigar parks). The company constructed four buildings of 11,000 square feet each with world-class amenities at a cost of about ₹20 crore. About 300 karigars worked in this new arrangement. The karigar centres even provided boarding, lodging, recreation, gymnasium facilities, and even guest rooms for visiting family members. Given that 60 per cent of karigars hailed from West Bengal, the centres also had Bengali cooks to make recipes to delight their palate, and even stocked Bengali magazines and DVDs to make them feel at home. '*bhalo laage*' (it feels good), was the usual response of the Bengali artisans to these new arrangements like those seen in a BPO industry.[7] Natarajan recalled:

> When we moved them to the Mr Perfect building, we were asking them about their feelings. One of them said, 'I'll now get a good bride for marriage.' Another said, 'After becoming Mr Perfect, I can work till I am sixty years.' Those were genuine feelings. The karigars were earlier looked down upon. Now they were Mr Perfect.

It was a win-win approach. While Tanishq gained with lower costs and better quality directly impacting productivity and profits, the karigars benefited from holistic improvements. By 2017, Titan had established fourteen karigar parks, four karigar centres and impacted the lives of over 1400 artisans. While this was a small number, the company pitched the karigar centres as an industry model to inspire competition to 'raise the bar'.[8] In 2012, in a competition organized by the California-based Management Innovation eXchange, an independent industry innovation body in collaboration with *Harvard Business Review* and McKinsey & Company, Titan's story of transforming its karigar fraternity ranked among the top ten from 163 global entries on 'innovating innovation'.

From tradition to technology—transforming the supply chain

From the early years of the millennium, along with building a rapport with karigars, Tanishq also worked on process improvements in the supply chain. The transition wasn't an easy one. Having worked in a particular way for decades, it was a big challenge to gain the karigars' confidence and trust. Most of them would say, 'You tell us what you want, and we will give you the end output; don't try and teach us how to go about it. We know our job.' From this mindset to winning their confidence took half a decade. Through a comprehensive change management programme, they were introduced to concepts connected with efficient inventory management.

One would wonder how these management concepts were relevant for goldsmiths and artisans. There were three reasons for this. Firstly, the traditional approach of jewellery making was time-consuming. It took hours of painstaking effort to create a simple design, thereby limiting the number of new designs Tanishq could launch in a year. Secondly, given that karigars worked largely with their hands, the quality of jewellery differed from piece to piece. That put tremendous pressure on the company, as the absence of a karigar who had perfected a specific design would impact sales. Thirdly, in the traditional system, karigars did not have all the facilities under one roof. After getting a design from the company, they would procure various elements like wires and balls that went into jewellery making from different agencies. All this while, the company's gold would be lying idle at the karigars' workplace. This was a dual burden—the cost of carrying a large gold inventory as also the risk of large quantities of gold lying with artisans who were not company employees.

With 70 per cent of its sales coming from the jewellery business, Titan had a huge stake in improving these processes and identified numerous improvement opportunities. Having worked with different karigars on 100,000 designs over several years, the company analysed their requirements. 'It was revealing that with 874 individual elements, any jewellery could be made,' recalled Natarajan who led the jewellery division's innovation journey. Having gained this process insights, Tanishq began to map the consumption of individual elements based on past sales. Thereafter, the trained karigar was given the individual elements along with the design. This saved enormous time for the karigar, who now only soldered various elements as per the design, completed the fabrication and gave the finished product to Tanishq. The outcome was encouraging for both. Following these process innovations, the gold inventory requirement came down from thirty days to three days, which was a huge saving for the company. It also improved the karigars' output. Earlier, the best karigar could make 750 grams of jewellery a month. With the process innovations implemented, they were able to make 4 kg of jewellery every month. Consequently, Titan emerged as a world leader with only 0.15 per cent gold lost in the manufacturing process, compared to 5 per cent loss before the process innovations were introduced. Cumulatively, this amounted to reduction in annual loss of gold to the tune of 50–75 kg.

Along with process changes, Tanishq introduced the use of technology. For example, earlier, sorting of diamonds (of similar sizes) was a time-consuming and painful manual process. The company employed forty people for this job and could pack only 800 bags per day. To overcome this limitation, the company's precision-engineering division produced the world's first automated process for diamond bagging using a robot. Launched in 2006, the robot could pack 2500 bags per day with greater accuracy. Similarly, setting of diamond and stone was a manual process and accounted for 65 per cent of the time and effort behind jewellery making. Tanishq introduced a patented process, which improved speed and quality of the diamond setting process from 150 diamonds in a gold casting per shift to 1800 diamonds per shift, a twelve times improvement in efficiency.

Through rapid prototyping and virtual stone-setting methods, cost of production reduced by 65 per cent, karigar productivity improved by 217 per cent, product introduction cycle reduced from eight months to four weeks, and annual capacity of new design introduction increased from 3000 to 12,000.[9] In one case, the customer placed an urgent order and delivery was completed the same day. This would have been unthinkable in the conventional method of stone setting. Moreover, for the 50 lakh stones set into jewellery using virtual stone setting, there was zero loss of stone, and customer complaints were virtually nil.[10] By 2015, annual process and design development cost savings amounted to ₹10 crore.

In the Tata style, Tanishq shared its prosperity and success with its supply chain. In years when actual company profits exceeded anticipated profits by ₹100 crore, Tanishq gave all the franchisees and vendor partners 50 grams of gold coins. Beside the financial benefits, Tanishq continued to engage with them through several communication platforms, including open houses and quarterly communication of progress. 'We respect them and they respect us. The relationship goes beyond supplier–purchaser relation, it is a family relation,' reaffirmed Natarajan.

CHAPTER 22

THE AVIATION DREAM THAT COULD NOT BE GROUNDED

The year was 1914. World War I had just begun. German Zeppelins were bombing Paris, and French anti-aircraft rifles on the Eiffel Tower were trying to gun them down. Ten-year-old J.R.D. Tata was watching this from the terrace of his family home in Paris. He ran to his mother and complained that if she would have had the good sense to marry his father six years earlier, he too would have been a fighter pilot! Years later J.R.D. recalled his pre-adolescent naïve thoughts, 'I fervently hoped that the war would last long enough for me to become one!'

It wasn't surprising for J.R.D. to have had such a fascination for flying in those early years of life. His friend, with whom he spent time during his summer holidays at Hardelot (northern France) was the son of Louis Bleriot, the first man to fly across the English Channel in 1909. After taking a joy ride in a plane at Hardelot at the age of fifteen, J.R.D. decided to become a pilot and make a career in aviation. A decade later, when the Aero Club of India gave him his flying licence, it had No. 1 written on it, indicating that he was the first Indian to have qualified to become a pilot. The following year, he was among the many participants contesting for the Aga Khan prize to become the first Indian to fly solo between England and India. One of the Indian participants— Manmohan Singh—had left London twice, but lost his way over Europe and returned to London. Those were the days when planes did not have radio, navigation or landing guides of any kind. Much of the flying depended on the pilot's judgement and a simple compass. Punning on the name given by Singh to his plane, the editor of *The Aeroplane* observed, 'Mr Manmohan Singh has called his aeroplane "Miss India" and he is likely too!' The real competition was between J.R.D. and another contestant Aspy Merwan Engineer, whom J.R.D. had met near Alexandria in Egypt. Aspy was stranded and struggling to find spark plugs. In true sportsman's spirit, J.R.D. gave him his spare plugs. Aspy reached Karachi before J.R.D. reached London and won the prize. His achievement gained him admission into the Indian Air Force in 1933. By 1960, he became the fifth chief of air staff in independent India. J.R.D.'s journey was to be very different from his competitor—one that would pioneer India's civil aviation industry.

The first known commercial civil aviation flight in India took place on 18 February 1911 when Henri Piquet flew a Humber biplane from a polo ground in Allahabad carrying mail across the Yamuna to Naini. Two months earlier on 28 December 1910, brothers Jules and Jean Tyck took off two planes from Tollygunge Club's golfing greens at Calcutta and registered their name in India's aviation chronicle. This was exactly seven years after Wilbur and Orville Wright invented the aeroplane and made four brief flights at Kitty Hawk in North Carolina (USA) on 17 December 1903.[1] In the next decade and a half, India took baby steps in the development of aviation-related infrastructure. This included commencement of the first domestic air route between London, Karachi and Delhi in 1912 by Imperial Airways (now British Airways), construction of civil airports in Calcutta, Allahabad and Bombay in 1924, and establishment of the department of civil aviation in 1927.

Tatas pioneer civil aviation in India

In 1929, J.R.D. was approached by Nevill Vintcent, a retired Royal Air Force (RAF) pilot, with a proposal to start air services between Karachi and Bombay. The Imperial Airways had regular service between London and Karachi. Vintcent suggested that the Tata-backed airline could start services to western and southern India. Starting from Karachi, the air service could transport post and people up to Madras on the eastern coast via Ahmedabad, Bombay and Bellary. J.R.D. was convinced of the idea and approached Sir Dorab Tata, then chairman of Tata Sons. Dorabji was hesitant to commit an investment into the embryonic aviation sector. However, Peterson, director-in-charge of Tata Steel and J.R.D.'s mentor, convinced Dorabji for the initial investment of ₹2 lakh. For the next two years, the Tatas tried to persuade the British government to subsidize the fledgling aviation business. They requested an assistance of just ₹75,000 for the first two years. But the government declined. When the Tatas decided to donate a free air service to the government, the proposal was instantly accepted. No airline in the world operated without government support. But the Tatas were willing to accept the financial risk associated with the new venture. Immediately after the government approval, J.R.D. visited England to purchase two Puss Moth aircraft from Sir Geoffrey de Havilland, acknowledged as the father of British aviation. J.R.D. wanted to fly one of them to India, but he fell sick at Naples and the aeroplane came as his personal baggage on-board the Victoria. From Ballard Pier in South Bombay, where the ship had docked, the aircraft was taken to Juhu in a bullock cart![2]

   The Tata Airlines was formed in April 1932. The story of Indian commercial civil aviation began at 6.30 a.m. on 15 October 1932, when J.R.D. took off on his first official Tata Airlines flight from Karachi's Drigh Road aerodrome. He landed ahead of schedule at Bombay's Juhu airstrip by 1.50 p.m. There was a brief stop at Ahmedabad where four-gallon Burmah Shell company cans were brought in a bullock cart for refuelling the aeroplane. The aircraft was a single engine De Havilland Puss Moth and carried 25 kg of airmail letters. Within ten minutes of J.R.D.'s arrival, Vintcent flew the aircraft to Madras with the airmail from Bombay. The government had permitted the Tatas a four-anna postage charge per airmail.

   When one uses words such as 'took off' and 'landed', one presumes the availability of elaborate infrastructure at an airport. In those years, there was none. The Bombay airstrip was the wetlands of Juhu beach. In the monsoon, when the 'runway' was underwater, the Tata Airlines would transfer its base to Poona. An open ground in the neighbourhood of the historic Yerawada Jail acted as the aerodrome. Interestingly, in April 1933, J.R.D. was forced to undertake a night journey to Bellary when the only light available was that provided by the crescent moon. Vintcent was supposed to meet him at the airstrip, but failed to turn up, and J.R.D. ended up spending the entire night in the open under one of the wings of the Puss Moth.

   Despite these difficulties, the performance of Tata Airlines was outstanding. It completed its first year of service with 100 per cent punctuality, even during the difficult monsoon months when the perilous Western Ghats made such journeys dangerous. Of those years J.R.D. had once said, 'I was tense only when there was bad weather. Tenseness because I was so anxious that the mail should not be delayed.' Interestingly, the Directorate of Civil Aviation in India recommended that the Imperial Airways should send their staff on deputation to the Tatas to learn how this was done. In subsequent years, Tata Airlines' services were extended to Delhi and Colombo. Success brought competition from other domestic players. Several Indian airlines like Indian Transcontinental Airways, Madras Air Taxi Services, and Indian National Airways commenced operations in India by 1934.

   May 1936 served a severe blow on the young J.R.D. His youngest sibling, Jimmy Tata, died in an air crash in Austria. J.R.D. considered him one of the finest flyers and was looking forward to involving him proactively in Tata Airlines. But that was not to be. Vintcent became the second-in-command at Tata Airlines. During the World War II years, all air services were commanded by the British government in India. In the restricted environment, J.R.D. and Vintcent considered diversifying into aeroplane manufacturing. In 1942, the Tatas submitted a proposal to the British government to set up an aircraft factory in Poona. The government gave permission and Tata Aircraft Limited was formed. Land was acquired and the factory building constructed. However, a turn of events killed the infant company even before it could commence production. The first was the death of Vintcent, J.R.D.'s business partner in the new venture. The RAF bomber that he was flying in for a business visit to London was shot down in the Bay of Biscay near France. Subsequently, the British-led government cancelled the project citing technical insufficiencies. Years later, J.R.D. confessed, 'Someone in the British government was shrewd enough to realize that once Indians got the know-how, they would be able to compete with British aviation interests.'[3] Had this project been successful, the Tatas would have been pioneers of aircraft production in India.

Air India is born

Tata Airlines continued to perform remarkably well. On completion of five years, its profits had risen from ₹66,000 to ₹6 lakh, and it had maintained punctuality at 99.4 per cent. The Indian princes loved the idea of aeroplanes linking their states with the outside world and the Tatas' business did very well ferrying the maharajas in special chartered planes.[4] In 1938, Bobby Kooka, among the first employees at the company, designed the iconic 'Maharaja' (monarch) as the brand identity of Tata Airlines. It was meant to be symbolic of Eastern hospitality at Tata Airlines' new office at Churchgate in Bombay. The Maharaja continued to remain as the carrier's identity for the next eight decades.

In 1946, Tata Airlines, till then a division of Tata Sons, went public by becoming a joint stock company called Air India Ltd. A year later, in October 1947, Tata Sons proposed the establishment of a new company—Air India International—for international air service to London. In the new arrangement, the Government of India was to have 49 per cent stake, Tata Sons 25 per cent stake and the remaining subscribed by the public. The proposal was accepted within three weeks by the newly formed Government of India, which was busy quelling communal strife in post-Partition Delhi. During the tumultuous and traumatic post-Partition period, Tata Airlines had flown refugees from Pakistan to India and vice versa, a gesture gratefully acknowledged by Prime Minister Nehru.

J.R.D. became the chairman of the new company and the company management was with the Tatas. A few years later, when Defence Minister Baldev Singh offered the chairmanship of Hindustan Aircraft Ltd (HAL) at

Bangalore to J.R.D., he politely declined it on two core counts. First, that the leadership of a defence industry firm should not be with an active businessman. Second, given that Air India and HAL had mutual dealings, it wasn't desirable for both companies to have the same chairman.

Eighth June 1948 was a red-letter day. It marked the beginning of Air India's journey across the oceans. *Malabar Princess*, a forty-seater Lockheed Constellation, Air India International's first overseas flight ascended over the Arabian Sea from the Bombay Airport for London. J.R.D. and his wife Thelma were among the passengers along with Digvijay Sinhji (the Jam Sahib of Nawanagar), Duleep Sinhji (famous cricketer), V.K. Krishna Menon (India's high commissioner to the UK), several industrialists and two Indian cyclists on their way to London Olympics. The airfare to London was a princely sum of ₹1720. J.R.D. landed on time (after stops at Cairo and Geneva) at the London Airport to a battery of floodlights and cameras, which had gathered to welcome the first Asian airline connecting the East to the West.

Over the years, Air India developed a fine reputation for its high-class on-board service that was talked about with admiration and envy by its global competitors. In the 1950s, when British Airways introduced a jet service that cut a few hours off the trip, passengers still preferred to fly by Air India's slower propeller-driven aircraft, simply because of the way they were pampered on-board. Air India's finest service probably was on its transatlantic flights, where it took great pleasure in stealing passengers away from its American and European competitors. Long before Singapore Airlines created an icon of its 'Singapore Girl' in her silk sarong-kebaya, Air India had made an icon of its air-hostesses in their exotic silk saris.[5]

After World War II, availability of cheap planes disposed by the American Tenth Force in India led to the establishment of several domestic airlines. Out of political compulsions, the government allowed most of them. As a result, there were nine airlines at the time of Independence. These included Orient Airways (shifted to Pakistan), Indian National Airways, Air Service of India, Deccan Airways, Ambica Airways, Bharat Airways and Mistry Airways.[6] Most of these were established by leading business families. However, all of them, except Tata Airlines, were running in losses. Demand necessitated the presence of two or three airlines, but the glut led to saturation in the domestic civil aviation sector post-Independence. In 1953, the Nehru-led Congress government passed the Air Corporations Act. As a result, all existing airlines, including Air India and Air India International, were nationalized. Air India and Indian Airlines were formed as independent public-sector enterprises catering to international and domestic services respectively.

Nationalizing India's civil aviation sector

Nationalization was hotly debated since Independence. J.R.D. opposed it on several platforms but wasn't invited by the government to present his views. The decision was a fait accompli. Communications Minister Jagjivan Ram, who supervised modalities of nationalization, did consult J.R.D., but that was about compensation to be given to companies getting nationalized. J.R.D. was disheartened. At a luncheon meeting with Prime Minister Nehru in November 1952, he expressed his anguish that the government had intentionally treated the Tatas shabbily, and that it was a planned conspiracy to suppress private civil aviation, particularly the Tatas' air services. Nehru reassured him of no such intentions. In fact, in a personal letter to J.R.D., he placed on record the high appreciation he had for the Tatas, who had pioneered several projects, and the excellent services rendered by Air India International. In his reply, J.R.D. expressed his disappointment at the government's decision to proceed with such a major step without any consultations with the Tatas, who were pioneers in Indian civil aviation. He emphasized his conviction that nationalization would not result in an efficient and self-supporting air transport system.[7]

All along, J.R.D.'s contention was that the new government of India had no experience in running an airline company, and nationalization would mean bureaucracy and lethargy, decline in employee morale and fall in passenger services. The government maintained that nationalization would bring order to the industry, and that the Congress Party had a policy to nationalize all modes of transport since two decades. In hindsight, the communication between the two stalwarts of Indian polity and Indian business represents perspectives belonging to two ends of the spectrum. It would take six decades to reveal whose viewpoint stood the test of time. For the time being, the discord seriously impacted the warm relationship between India's first prime minister and the leader of India's largest business house.

Air India defined world-class service

To employ his expertise, the government invited J.R.D. to lead Air India and Indian Airlines as chairman. After protracted conversations at Tata Sons, J.R.D. accepted the chairmanship of Air India, and a directorship on the board of Indian Airlines. He was particularly concerned that the high standards of Air India International should not be adversely affected by nationalization. His remarks at the end of Air India's first annual general meeting seemed prophetic, ' . . . Unless the greatest attention continues to be paid to the high standards of training and discipline amongst flying and ground crews, the resulting deterioration might destroy the good name of Indian civil aviation.' Over the next twenty-five years, through personal commitment, he maintained high standards of service at Air India, which enjoyed excellent reputation among passengers.

J.R.D. micromanaged the carrier's operational aspects. He would take great personal care of passengers, even when flying as a passenger himself. Many a times, he wandered about on flights, making notes of tiny details that needed to be fixed, from the level to which wine was poured into a wine glass to the hairstyle of air hostesses. If he saw a dirty airline counter, he would shame everyone by requesting a duster and wiping it himself. On one occasion, he rolled up his sleeves and helped the crew clean a dirty aircraft toilet. From the inside decor to the colour of the air hostess' saris; from wordings on Air India hoardings to the availability of toilet paper in lavatories on-board, J.R.D. set high benchmarks in hands-on leadership. He once remarked that to attribute his interest in airlines to his interest in air hostesses was only a slight exaggeration![8]

In the 1970s, when the Government of Singapore commenced Singapore Airlines to attract global tourists into the little island nation, it chose to collaborate with Air India for learning world-class service standards. Air India had been the inspiration for East Asian carriers such as Cathay Pacific and Thai Airways that began to dominate the skies in 1970s.[9] After all, it was the first Asian airline to induct a jet aircraft in its fleet—a Boeing 707 named *Gauri Shankar*—that was acquired in February 1960.[10] In 1955, when Chinese premier Zhou Enlai was to travel to Indonesia for the first conference of the Non-Aligned Movement, China did not have the required long-distance aircraft. So, an Indian Airlines flight was chartered to fly the Chinese prime minister and his team from Hong Kong to Bandung!

J.R.D. inspired employees to consistently delight customers through safety and service excellence. 'When your excellence comes from the top, it becomes the ethos of the organization,' remarked Bakul Khote, founding member of the customer service department at Air India. In the later years, J.R.D. even admitted that during the vital years of his chairmanship at Tata Sons, he was effactually dedicating nearly 50 per cent of his time to Air India, an entity that provided no financial rewards to him or his fifty-plus companies. Yet, through his personal example, he wanted to communicate that all public-sector undertakings could be profitable by maintaining world-class standards. He epitomized his oft-quoted advice, 'Always aim at perfection for only then will you achieve excellence.'

And the doyen of Indian industry was fired . . .

On 1 January 1978, Air India's first Boeing 747 plunged into the sea off the coast of Bombay, killing all 213 passengers and the crew on-board. One of the greatest air tragedies of its time, the fatal fall was attributed to pilot error. A month later, Prime Minister Morarji Desai-led government dropped J.R.D. from the chairmanship of Air India and the directorship of Indian Airlines. A year earlier, he had already been removed from the board of the Atomic Energy Commission on which he had served since its inception in 1948. J.R.D., who was then at Jamshedpur, came to know of this development on 3 February 1978 from Air Chief Marshal Pratap Chandra Lal (Retd), who was appointed the new chairman of both carriers. Interestingly, Lal was serving as MD of a medium-sized Tata company at Jamshedpur. The radio news on the evening of 3 February conveyed the development to the public, and most dailies carried it the next day. On his return to Bombay House on 9 February, J.R.D. found a letter from the prime minister dated 4 February and dispatched from Delhi on 6 February. The press reports on 11 February finally clarified that he had been removed from the position with retrospective effect from 1 February.

In his letter to J.R.D., Prime Minister Desai placed on record his distinguished services to Air India and clarified that the change was not because of any lack of appreciation of his conspicuous work. In his reply, a terribly upset J.R.D. who had served Air India for a quarter-century without remuneration of a single rupee, stated:

> I hope you will not consider it presumptuous of me to have expected that when the government decided to terminate my services and my forty-five years' association with Indian civil aviation, I would be informed of their decision directly, and if possible, in advance of the public . . .

The decision had a deep impact on the morale of Air India employees. The MD resigned, and the cabin crew and officers' associations protested. The country was outraged at this sudden development as Air India was, at that time, a matter of deep national pride, and J.R.D. was synonymous with Air India's success and service. London's *Daily Telegraph* dated 27 February 1978 carried the headline 'Unpaid Air India Chief Is Sacked by Desai.' Desai's decision had brought him some of the worst publicity since he took office as prime minister.

Irani recalled the day when the news became public. J.R.D. was in Jamshedpur and there was dinner at Russi Mody's bungalow that night. He came in looking a bit glum. One among the twenty people present there picked up the courage to ask, 'Sir, we have heard about your exit on radio. How do you feel about it?' J.R.D.'s exact words were, 'I feel as you would feel if your favourite child was taken away.'

In 1980, when Indira Gandhi came back to power, she reappointed J.R.D. on the board of both airlines, though not as chairman. He continued to serve on the boards till 1986, the year in which Ratan Tata was appointed as chairman of Air India by Prime Minister Rajiv Gandhi. In the concluding decade of J.R.D.'s association with his favourite company—Air India—he re-enacted the solo flight aboard a Puss Moth from Karachi to Bombay to commemorate the golden jubilee of the first flight. The only difference was that in October 1982, India's foremost pilot was seventy-eight years old, and had even suffered from angina pain the previous month. The solo flight was a feat applauded by one and all. When he landed at the Juhu airstrip in Bombay, the governor, chief minister and several dignitaries were present to greet him. J.R.D. had acted as a goodwill messenger between the two countries and carried a mailbag with messages from the president of Pakistan to the president of India, and from the mayor of Karachi to the mayor of Bombay. Of the battery of journalists gathered to report the historic event, BBC correspondent Mark Tully asked him if he expected to be around for the centenary year of Indian civil aviation. 'Of course. I will be there,' was J.R.D.'s spontaneous reply. 'You see, I believe in reincarnation,' said the septuagenarian in a witty repartee.

Turbulent political weather ahead

It was the Parsi New Year day in March 1990. Ratan Tata had completed his term as the chairman of Air India the previous year. B.G. Deshmukh, principal secretary to Prime Minister V.P. Singh, asked J.R.D. and Ratan Tata whether the Tatas would be interested in starting a new domestic airline. The octogenarian J.R.D. and Ratan Tata expressed their interest; an opportunity of this kind had come their way after nearly four decades. The Tatas started putting together a proposal. But before things could take concrete shape, the government fell. Under Prime Minister Narasimha Rao's Open Skies Policy, few private players who were permitted to start operations as air-taxi operators in 1986 could become full-service domestic airlines. Some of these were East West, Damania, Jet Airways, Modiluft, Sahara India and NEPC Airlines. In 1994, Civil Aviation Minister Madhav Rao Scindia announced cancellation of the Air Corporation Act, which led to opening up of the sector to private players. The Tatas too decided to enter the fray. While the father of Indian aviation had passed away the previous year, Ratan Tata, himself an avid aviator, led from the front.

As for Air India, its decline had begun in the 1990s. It faced headwinds from domestic private carriers and global airlines. Passenger complaints, political interventions in day-to-day operations, impracticable policies, and bureaucratic delays severely impacted the national carrier. Yet, it continued to achieve social imperatives with great commitment. Between 13 August and 20 October 1990, the Indian government airlifted over 170,000 Indians from Kuwait with help of 488 flights. Air India entered the Guinness Book of World Records for evacuating the most people to date. However, on the commercial side, passenger numbers declined, and Air India's market share dipped.

During the high-profile meeting of Goh Chok Tong, then prime minister of Singapore, with Prime Minister Rao in January 1994 the idea of Singapore Airlines (SIA) exploring a joint venture in India's domestic aviation sector was first mooted. SIA was keen to collaborate with the Tatas. A team led by S. Ramakrishna, formerly with Tata Industries, and Sujit Gupta, then Tata Industries' resident director in Delhi, along with a senior executive of SIA, was set up to undertake a feasibility study for Tata Airlines, a joint venture (JV) with SIA.[11] The Tatas were willing to grant 60 per cent equity of SIA, with 40 per cent being held by Tata Sons. Since Gulf Air and Kuwait Airways already had a 20 per cent stake each in Jet Airways, it wouldn't be difficult to get approvals, they thought. However, it was just the beginning of a bumpy ride in the thick of inclement political weather.

Between 1994 and 1996, Amar Nath Verma, principal secretary to Prime Minister Rao, and chairman of the Foreign Investment Promotion Board (FIPB) had fifteen meetings with senior executives of the Tata Group, of which four were with Ratan Tata. Based on these discussions, on 7 February 1995, a proposal was submitted by the Tatas to FIPB for necessary approvals, as SIA, an international airline, was going to be a major investor in the JV. Finance Minister Manmohan Singh called the Tata proposal a first-class proposal that would be supported at the cabinet committee meeting. Despite proactive conversations at one end, the bureaucratic game began at the other. During a presentation by Ratan Tata and Joe Pillai of SIA to the civil aviation ministry in Delhi, Yogesh Chandra, then secretary of civil aviation, questioned the Tatas' capacity to invest large amounts of capital and stomach loses in the uncertain airline business. It was ironical that such an observation was made for a business house that had started, developed and succeeded in capital-intensive industries for over nine decades. Ratan Tata assured the ministry that the Tatas were not looking for any government subsidies. During the presentation that ensued, Chandra abruptly got up and left, sending a suspicious signal. At a subsequent meeting, he quoted the statement made by Civil Aviation Minister Ghulam Nabi Azad on the floor of the Lok Sabha that no new airlines would be permitted.[12] The indirect indication was that the Tata Airlines proposal may be rejected.

Over the next several months, bureaucrats, politicians and even promoters of rival domestic airlines opposed the JV on several grounds. While bureaucrats cited inadequate infrastructure and security issues connected with a foreign entity's presence in Indian skies, politicians were opposed to it on ideological grounds. BJP leader Pramod Mahajan objected to foreign equity in the domestic aviation sector as a matter of principle. Even though Gulf Air and Kuwait Airways had invested in Jet Airways, he believed that SIA was an international giant that could influence the sector to its advantage, an opinion echoed by Samajwadi Party MP Amar Singh. Another vociferous opponent was Naresh Goyal, a London-based NRI who held 60 per cent stake in Jet Airways. The airline was registered through Tail Winds Ltd, a private limited company registered in the Isle of Man in the Irish Sea. On the one hand Jet opposed the Tata–SIA JV, and on the other, it gained approval from the government for buying ten new aircraft. This was despite Azad citing limited parking space at airports as a key reason for disallowing imported aircraft.[13] This discourse dominated the remaining term of the Narasimha Rao government, and there was no response from FIPB on the Tata Airlines proposal.

From an industry perspective, none of the key players had a strong foundation in the airline business or a major corporate house supporting their venture. This was unlike the 1940s, and the early 1950s, when two large business houses supported the two largest airlines of those times—Tata Airlines and Bharat Airways (promoted by the Birlas). Most of the newer breed of airlines were founded by small-time entrepreneurs—Jet and East West by travel agency owners, Damania by a poultry farmer, NEPC by a maker of windmills and Sahara by a chit-fund owner. Lack of management expertise in a specialized industry and mandatory flights to non-economical social routes in Kashmir and the Andamans severely affected their financials. Consequently, most of them were grounded or acquired within the first few years of launch, except Air Sahara[14] and Jet Airways. The latter capitalized on industry expertise gained through its nationwide sales experience and eventually developed a reputation for reliability.

In June 1996, the United Front government led by Prime Minister H.D. Deve Gowda came to power. Chand Mahal Ibrahim, the new civil aviation minister, opposed the Tata proposal on two premises. Firstly, that it was providing an opportunity for foreign airlines to enter the Indian aviation sector through the back door. He repeatedly asserted that no Western country allowed a foreign airline to take over a domestic circuit.[15]

Secondly, that there was limited demand (around 4 per cent) in the domestic aviation sector and permitting newer players would lead to losses for Indian Airlines and other players. Both these arguments were factually incorrect. Ratan Tata sent clarifications on both issues to the minister. For the former argument, he stated that Tata Airlines was an Indian proposal with a strong desire to give India the experience of a world-class domestic airline; and that they were willing to reduce SIA's stake to a minority 40 per cent. A list of international airlines that had a large stake holding by foreign airlines was also shared. These included the likes of American Airlines, British Airways, KLM and Swissair. The ₹2400-crore Tata Airlines proposal even included a ₹100 crore commitment to building infrastructure at airports, setting up maintenance and training facilities. As for demand in the aviation sector, leading government agencies, including the Airports Authority of India and the Economic Survey 1996–97, projected annual growth in domestic passenger traffic at 12–13 per cent. The Planning Commission forecast an annual growth of 12 per cent requiring the addition of sixty new aircraft at a cost of ₹6000 crore. This meant that not just one, but three Tata-like proposals were required to meet increasing demand. Facts debunked the argument of insufficient domestic demand. Despite economics favouring growth, politics seemed to be supporting stagnation.

Ratan Tata personally met Prime Minister Deve Gowda in July and August 1996. The principal secretary reassured him that the Tatas' proposal was compliant with the civil aviation policy and would soon be cleared. Tata reiterated that the proposed Tata Airlines was fully committed to flying to the social-sector routes. He also pledged that the Tatas would not recruit pilots and engineers from existing airlines, including Indian Airlines and Air India, a concern often expressed in the media. In December 1996, FIPB approved the Tata proposal. It seemed as if the long thirty-month wait was finally over. However, it was not to be so. The civil aviation minister expressed his angst at this development, and supposedly said that the Tata–SIA project would be cleared over his dead body.[16]

When Prime Minister Deve Gowda attended the World Economic Forum at Davos that year with Finance Minister P. Chidambaram, among other questions, they were asked about the 'stop-go-stop' status of the Tata–SIA venture.[17] Their answer was that it was 'being considered'. It would have been a diplomatic faux pas to say anything else at a venue that was meant to project India as an attractive destination for foreign investments. In the Union cabinet meeting held in April 1997, Finance Minister P. Chidambaram, Industry Minister Murasoli Maran and Foreign Minister Indra Kumar Gujral endorsed the clearance of the Tata–SIA proposal. However, Aviation Minister C.M. Ibrahim had supposedly brought with him papers from four unions belonging to Indian Airlines, which threatened to go on strike if the Tata Airlines proposal was accepted. He contended that workers' interests must be protected. The prime minister conceded to this concern and laid the proposal to rest.[18] Later that month, a formal rejection letter was sent to the Tata Group citing inconsistencies in the proposal with the civil aviation policy. There were strong mutterings in the media that the aviation minister had altered the aviation policy at Goyal's behest to upset the Tatas' aviation dreams.[19] M.K. Kaw, civil aviation secretary under Ibrahim, acknowledged this in his autobiography, 'The minister did not clear the file, despite several attempts on my part. The history of civil aviation in this country would have taken a different trajectory if Tata–SIA had been allowed to float an airline.'[20]

In all this squabbling on what was right for India, no one seemed to be bothered about the 1.3 crore air passengers, and the benefits of lower fares and better services that they would have received. Consumer interests were sacrificed at the altar of political pragmatism. Ironically, consumer interest was at the crux of the Tatas' decision to collaborate with SIA. Ibrahim had repeatedly mentioned that if the Tatas were willing to let go of a collaboration with SIA, they would be instantly granted the licence. In response to that, Ratan Tata mentioned in an interview to *Business India*:

> We don't need Singapore Airlines to help us run an airline. But if we decide that we want to run a world-class airline, then we need them. SIA is one of the world's most admired international airlines; are we serving the country badly by creating an Indian airline that embodies all the expertise that they have to offer?

A bumpy ride

In the 1990s, Air India's market share steadily declined and losses mounted. Between 1995 and 1997, it reported consolidated losses of ₹671 crore. When the Atal Bihari Vajpayee-led BJP government came to power in 1998, it initiated a major disinvestment programme under Union Minister Arun Shourie. In 2001, a decision on divesting 40 per cent stake in Air India was taken. Given its long and rich experience, the Tata Group was specifically encouraged to participate in the process. The national carrier was an attractive investment proposition because of its lucrative slots at key Indian and international airports, flying rights to global destinations, its fleet size and market share. The Tatas were interested in exploring the opportunity and collaborated with SIA to study the feasibility. Its findings revealed that robust middle-level managers at Air India would be an asset in turning around the enterprise. SIA and Tata Sons offered to take 20 per cent stake each in Air India. When their joint proposal emerged as sole bidders, it was almost a done deal. Yet, once again, there was an uproar. Virulent attacks by rival airline lobbyists and opposition from labour unions marred the atmosphere. Discomforted by these developments, SIA withdrew its participation. It offered to assist the Tatas as technical advisers without any equity stake. That too cut no ice with the decision makers. The Tatas' entry into the airline sector was successfully stonewalled one more time.

Mukund Rajan was executive assistant to Ratan Tata in those years. He recalled the composure with which Ratan Tata wrote a letter to the government, stating that the group had waited and waited, and had been effectively blocked at every stage. 'Now there is no basis on which we can be blocked and yet our application is not moving. I am therefore taking the decision to withdraw our application.'

A decade later, in 2010, while addressing the tenth foundation day of Uttarakhand at Dehradun, Ratan Tata shared a conversation he had had with a fellow industrialist during the days when the Tatas had applied for the airline. 'You are stupid people. The minister was asking for ₹15 crore. Why didn't you pay the money?' the industrialist chided Ratan Tata. 'I did not want to go to bed knowing well that I set up an airline by paying ₹15 crore as a bribe,' was Tata's reply. He regretted that despite being a pioneer in Indian aviation, the Tata Group faced enormous problems in gaining approvals for a domestic airline. 'We approached three prime ministers. But an individual thwarted our efforts to form the airlines,' he admitted in public. He did not name the individual.[21] On another occasion he confessed, 'It is not that we were thwarted that bothers me, but that vested interests combined to deny the country the benefit of a world-class competitive airline.'[22]

A new dawn on the horizon

In the last year of the Vajpayee government, India's first low-cost no-frills[23] airline was launched—Air Deccan. With a vision to make flying accessible to the masses, the Captain G.R. Gopinath-led airline commenced operations in August 2003 with a 50 per cent tariff reduction. Low-cost carriers (LCC) were globally popular. The concept was most appropriate for the Indian scenario where regional connectivity was limited and the consumer cost-conscious. India had about 455 airports and airstrips, and thirteen international airports. This vast infrastructure could be optimally utilized. Moreover, the potential demand was substantial. For a 100 crore population, India operated just 500 commercial flights every day. With a third of that population, the USA daily operated 40,000 commercial flights.[24]

The idea became tremendously popular in India across age groups. The next few years saw a dozen new LCCs enter the market, including IndiGo, SpiceJet, GoAir, Paramount and Air Costa. The existing full-service airlines also entered the low-cost fray with differentiated brands such as Jet Lite, Kingfisher Red and Air India Express. Between 2003 and 2010, the market share of LCCs increased from 1 to 70 per cent. During the same period, state-run airlines ceded substantial market share to domestic and global competition. Indian Airlines slipped from the first to the fourth position.

To arrest this decline, the Union cabinet under Prime Minister Manmohan Singh initiated a dramatic step to merge the state-run domestic and international airlines—Air India and Indian Airlines (renamed Indian) into one entity in 2006. A government report highlighted two reasons for the national carriers' sub-optimal performance. One was the ageing fleet of aircraft and the other was the stand-alone operation of the domestic and international services. The civil aviation ministry under Praful Patel initiated the merger to efficiently leverage combined assets and capital.[25] Several other benefits included strengthening brand equity, achieving economies of scale, increasing fleet size, streamlining ground operations and ensuring better utilization of slots and parking rights at major airports.

Despite opposition from both the state-run airlines, a new company called National Aviation Company of India Ltd (NACIL) was formed to manage the combined entity in August 2007. It was later renamed Air India Ltd. The merger process that commenced in 2007 took four years for completion. It unfolded as one of the most complex exercises ever and had disastrous effects on the profitability of the new entity. Between 2007 and 2009, combined losses of the two entities increased from ₹770 crore to ₹7200 crore and borrowings from ₹6550 crore to ₹15,241 crore.[26] Furthermore, the merged company had more than 30,000 employees, i.e. 256 per plane,[27] which was twice the global standard. Air India ended up spending almost one-fifth of its revenue on employee pay and benefits while other private airlines spent about one-tenth. Attempts to streamline employee base and reduce cost led to repeated stirs and hunger strikes from eleven of its twelve unions.

Even before the commencement of the merger, the civil aviation ministry had decided to purchase 111 new narrow and wide-body aircraft for a whopping ₹67,000 crore. In subsequent years, the decision to purchase these planes through debt emerged as a 'recipe for disaster', especially because it was taken at a time when the airlines were already in an appalling financial situation.[28] It even came under the CBI scanner under Supreme Court's directives. The losses that occurred from the merger were estimated to be ₹10,000 crore. Between October 2012 and March 2013, the merged entity suffered an average loss of ₹400 crore every single month. In a bid to save and sustain Air India, the government started a regular cash infusion into the national carrier. Meanwhile, IndiGo, Jet Airways and SpiceJet had captured 70 per cent of the Indian civil aviation market.

Tatas' aviation dream could not be grounded

In the middle of this mayhem, in April 2011, the Department of Industrial Policy and Promotion (DIPP) revised foreign investment norms in India. Foreign carriers could now invest up to 49 per cent in air transport service. This was the 'official' opportunity the Tatas had been waiting for since two decades. There was immense scope for growth. With a 120 crore population, India had about 420 aircraft, compared to 2000 aircraft in China for its 130 crore people.[29] However, the market scenario had changed since the previous decade with combinations of competitors catering to different segments. To effectively compete with the clout of LCCs and address the full-service segment, the Tatas devised a dual service strategy. They mooted 'Vistara', a new full-service airline in collaboration with SIA. The latter had waited fifteen years to collaborate with the Tatas for the Indian aviation market. And it was no ordinary airline. In twenty-four of the previous twenty-five years, SIA had been named the 'best airline in the world' for customer service by *Conde Nast Traveller*.[30] It was a testament to the kind of chemistry SIA enjoyed with the Tatas. Vistara was a JV with 51 per cent stake held by Tata Sons and 49 per cent by SIA. Its inaugural flight took off from Delhi to Mumbai on 9 January 2015. Six months earlier, the Tatas' low-cost airline—AirAsia India was launched on the Bangalore–Goa sector. It was a JV between Malaysia-based AirAsia Berhad and Tata Sons, each having a 49 per cent stake. By 2018, both the Tatas' airlines had gained a combined domestic market share of nearly 7 per cent. Vistara was also acknowledged as the 'best airline' and the 'best regional carrier in Asia'.

In the same year, the Indian aviation sector had grown to become the fourth largest in the world with over 13 crore passengers flying every year with thirteen Indian carriers and 500 aircraft. For the twenty-second time in a row, India was adjudged the world's fastest growing domestic travel market with a year-on-year growth of 26.6 per cent. It replaced Japan to become the largest domestic aviation market globally and was poised to reach the third spot in world aviation by 2026.[31] Steady rise in income levels, stability in global oil prices, development of new greenfield airports, entry of new full-service carriers and LCCs, capacity addition by airline operators, reduction of taxes on aviation turbine fuel (ATF) prices, and new policies from the Government of India such as the UDAN[32] scheme were key drivers of this phenomenal growth.

The story comes a full circle

As for Air India, it had succeeded in accumulating losses of ₹50,000 crore and a debt of ₹55,000 crore by March 2018, a disdainful drain on the honest taxpayers' money that could have been invested in vital social-sector schemes. The carrier had unveiled an ambitious turnaround plan with the help of leading consultants Booz Allen in July 2010 to wipe out ₹14,000 crore of accumulated losses and ₹18,000 crore of debt on its balance sheet by 2015. The targets were never achieved. Instead, debt and losses tripled during that period. Besides the huge debt, some of the key problems plaguing the airline included routing and network issues, lack of decisive leadership, managerial complications, and internal incompatibility between the merged airlines.[33]

In his autobiographical account, M.K. Kaw expressed regret that the history of civil aviation in India had been a story of shameless exploitation and ruthless corruption. He called it 'a fascinating saga of benami ownership of airlines, demands for bribes, destruction of rival airlines one-by-one, unwarranted purchase of aircraft, mismanagement of bureaucrats and politicians, free jaunts on inaugural flights, subsidized travel for many categories of travellers, VVIP flights, Haj flights and so on'.

The Narendra Modi-led BJP government put up Air India for sale by March 2018. Accordingly, private players could pick up a stake of 76 per cent. With a debt burden of ₹33,392 crore, the minimum acquisition price came close to ₹43,000 crores for the airline, which had 12.9 per cent market share.[34] Ironically, the Tatas were actively persuaded to participate in the divestment process, despite having been given a more than unfair treatment by previous governments. At 5 p.m. on 31 May 2018, the last date of submitting proposals, there were no bidders. India's characteristic Maharaja was on sale, yet no one wanted to acquire the once iconic brand that symbolized world-class air travel. One wonders, what if Prime Minister Nehru had yielded to the pleas of J.R.D. Tata sixty-five years ago . . .

CHAPTER 23

THE TATA-GOVERNMENT SAGA: ELECTRIFYING EXPERIENCES

'If I were to attribute any single reason to such success as I have achieved, I would say that success would not have been possible without a sustained belief that what I did or attempted to do would serve the needs and interests of our country and our people and that I was a trustee of such interests.'

J.R.D. Tata

On 4 April 1949, Prime Minister Jawaharlal Nehru was leaving for England. He wrote a letter to J.R.D. requesting his help to procure a parcel of Alfonso mangoes for the Mountbattens, the last British Governor General of India and his wife. J.R.D. joyfully sent many dozens for the prime minister and his hosts in England. A month later, when Nehru returned to India, he wrote another letter to confirm whether J.R.D. had received a thank you note from Lady Edwina Mountbatten, the last vicereine of India. He thanked J.R.D. for the mangoes, which were enough to be given to Princess Elizabeth (now Queen Elizabeth) on her birthday, to Clement Attlee, then prime minister of the UK and Sir Stafford Cripps, Chancellor of the Exchequer. The Princess had in turn shared the mangoes with George VI, King of England. This instance is one among the many that exhibit the access J.R.D. enjoyed with the highest echelons of power, and the warm relationship between J.R.D. and the first prime minister of India.

In 1948, Nehru had even invited J.R.D. as an Indian delegate to the United Nations session in Paris, and six years earlier to the marriage of his only daughter, Indira, at Allahabad. Interestingly, R.D. Tata, J.R.D.'s father, and Motilal Nehru had been friends and had worked together for protecting TISCO against dumping of foreign steel. In a letter to Mahatma Gandhi, Motilal Nehru had called R.D. Tata 'one of the straightest and most charming men I have ever met'. The mutual appreciation existed between the two sons as well. Fifteen years younger to Nehru, young J.R.D. admired him as the heroic knight in armour and an apt leader for independent India.

However, four decades later, while penning the foreword to a compilation of his keynote addresses, J.R.D. wrote, 'I have often thought that if fate had decreed that Vallabhbhai Patel[1] instead of Jawaharlal, would be the younger of the two, India would have followed a very different path and would be in a better economic shape than it is today.'[2] What caused J.R.D.'s opinion to change over the four decades? Well, several factors did. The most central being the approach, or rather the lack of it, towards economic development in the first three decades since Independence.

Nation first

The Tatas were not close to any one political family. They were at equal ease with several prominent leaders within the Raj and after Independence. Fully sympathetic to fellow Parsi nationalist Dadabhai Naoroji, Jamsetji was present at the first session of the Indian National Congress at Tejpal Hall in Bombay in 1885. He shared the outlook of economic thinkers Naoroji and M.G. Ranade, who believed that India had possessed an industrial base that had been destroyed by the malign impact of British trade; and that Indian businessmen could contribute to the national cause by building heavy industries in India staffed and financed indigenously.[3] He remained a lifelong member of the Congress and even supported it financially.[4] At the same time, he had a great rapport with several liberal-minded officers of the Raj. Sir Ratan Tata (Jamsetji's younger son) and Lady Navajbai Tata were close to Queen Mary and King George V. At the same time, Sir Ratan was also the first substantial financial supporter of Mahatma Gandhi's struggle in South Africa around 1910, a gesture he recalled during a visit to Tata Steel in 1924. The same was true of J.R.D. He would spend a weekend with Lord Linlithgow, the Indian viceroy at the palatial Viceregal Lodge (now Rashtrapati Niwas) in Simla, a rare privilege, and with equal conviction write to him pleading for freedom for India, a week before the 1942 Quit India Movement.

The nature of the Tatas' businesses in core sectors such as steel, electricity and locomotives made it imperative for their companies to be heavily dependent on government orders and anti-dumping protection. This required the maintenance of a fine balance between the Raj and the freedom movement. Yet, whether under the Raj or post-Independence, their key focus of dialogue with the government of the day was India's industrial development. Farokh N. Subedar recalled that whenever the Tata Group chairman went to the North Block for a pre-budget presentation before the finance minister, the focus wasn't on a 'wish list' of things that were relevant for the Tatas alone. The interests of the Indian industry at large were always a priority. L.K. Jha, former governor of the Reserve Bank of India, recalled in 1986[5] that when he was a secretary to the government, J.R.D. never approached him on behalf of any Tata company, but for the whole industry. He wanted no favours, only fairness.

Following the Quit India Movement, when Gandhiji was jailed, J.R.D. flew to add his signature to the appeal to the viceroy for his release. But in May 1945, when Gandhiji opposed the visit of leading Indian industrialists to the UK and the USA, the young Tata chairman frankly expressed his displeasure at the language the tallest leader of India's freedom movement had used. J.R.D. believed that 'India could not afford to stand still when other nations were forging ahead.' He was equally cooperative when Sardar Patel wrote a personal letter to him in October 1945 to permit and persuade John Matthai,[6] then director of Tata Sons, for contesting elections as a Congress nominee in the Central Assembly elections held later that year. The Tatas believed that the best of their talent could be made available for nation building, especially during the formative years. During those years, some of the finest knights were directors of Tata Sons—Sir Homi Mody, Sir Ardeshir Dalal, and Sir Jehangir Ghandy. With such eminent men on board of Tata Sons,[7] discussions were usually on national issues. 'You felt that the Tatas belonged to the nation,' observed Sumant Moolgaokar while describing the passion within the group to contribute to the nation. Over the years, the Tata-government saga hasn't probably been a matter of influence, but a battle for nation building through transparent and inclusive industrial and social development.

Building a new India

In 1944, some of the most eminent industrialists of India were hosted by the Tata chairman to propose 'A Plan of Economic Development for India'. This was later known as the 'Bombay Plan' or the 'Tata–Birla Plan'.[8] The team consisted of G.D. Birla, Kasturbhai Lalbhai, Shri Ram and Purshottamdas Thakurdas. The ₹10,000-crore plan put forth several recommendations on improving per capita income, health, education, housing, agriculture and industry.[9] It was probably one of the first plans in the world prepared by capitalists, which laid a strong emphasis on social well-being. It envisaged a largely deregulated economy with government investments in industries of national and strategic importance. When the newly formed Government of India adopted centralized economic planning, there was no precedent of economic planning and liberal democracy going hand in hand. But policymakers found no inherent contradiction among the two.[10]

The First Five-Year Plan (1951–56) of the Government of India was very similar to the Bombay Plan. An important element of this plan was the Industries (Development and Regulation) Act, 1951, which mandated registration of all existing industrial undertakings with the government. Besides, it gave absolute powers to the government to decide the production, pricing, distribution and expansion of all such industries. This eventually came to be known as the 'Licence/Permit Raj' and gave enormous powers to the bureaucracy.

In 1954, Prime Minister Nehru, impressed by his visit to China, incorporated in the draft of the Second Five-Year Plan (1956–61) that India would move towards a 'socialist pattern of society'. The plan focused on massive capital investments through the public sector and increased dependence on deficit financing. The Industrial Policy Resolution, 1956, divided industry into three categories—those that were the exclusive responsibility of the state (railways, defence and civil aviation), those to be progressively state-owned and those left to the private sector. A wave of nationalization[11] followed. The Imperial Bank of India was nationalized as the State Bank of India. The insurance businesses were also nationalized in 1956, which included the New India Assurance Company founded by Sir Dorab Tata in 1919. Air India had already been nationalized a few years earlier. These decisions created the first signs of concern among private sector firms. Moreover, government intervention in private enterprise had reached such ludicrous levels that the finance minister wanted to take the decision of whether Tata Steel's shares should be sold at premium or at par. This happened in 1959. Finance Minister Morarji Desai had delayed Tata Steel's application for a new capital issue for several months. J.R.D. believed that the premium the finance minister wanted on the capital was not justified. But the minister wouldn't relent. In a letter dated 23 July 1959, J.R.D. wrote:

> I hope you will not mind my expressing some surprise that the Government of India should take such detailed interest and intervene in a matter which involved no important question of policy or principle but only commercial and financial judgement on a simple business issue. Would it be wrong of me to regret the passing of the days when businessmen with a good record of efficiency and integrity could be trusted to make such decisions themselves?

Ironically, the outcomes of these economic policies were not encouraging, to say the least. Between 1947 and 1964, the years of Prime Minister Nehru, the CAGR in GDP per capita was a mere 1.68 per cent. During the same period, Japan, another Asian country, that was attempting to emerge from the devastation of World War II, was growing at 7.96 per cent.[12] J.R.D. regretted the disinterestedness of the polity for a dialogue that would benefit India and its young economy.

> I tried to share my views with him [Nehru]. He liked me. I loved and admired him. But [we differed] in the field of economics, of which he knew very little in my opinion, and how socialism[13] could be adopted without the loss of freedom for the majority. Whenever I tried to bring up topics of nationalization and bureaucracy, he wasn't even willing to talk. The moment I would try to tell him something, he would turn around and start looking out of the window or take me to see his giant panda!

Nehru had once told him, 'I hate the mention of the very word profit.' 'Jawaharlal, I am talking about the need of the public sector making a profit!' J.R.D. replied. Nehru reiterated, 'Never talk to me about the word profit, it is a dirty word.'

The Indira years

The post-Nehru years emerged as even more averse to private enterprises and their growth. Between 1964 and 1969, the Government of India appointed four powerful panels to further consolidate its hold on large industrial houses.[14] Reflecting on the developments while addressing the Planning Commission in 1968, J.R.D. delivered a satirical message that clearly reflected the frustrations of India's foremost industrialist with the state of the economy.

> As the head of the largest industrial group in the private sector, I must be possessed of a tremendous concentration of economic power. As I wake up every morning, I carefully consider to what purpose I should apply my great powers that day. Shall I crush competitors, exploit consumers, fire recalcitrant workers, topple a government or two? I wish some protagonist of this theory would enlighten me as to the nature of this great power concentrated in my hands. I have myself totally failed to identify, let alone exercise it . . . In fact, the only fearsome concentration of economic power that exists today, lies in the hands of our ministers, planners and government officials. It is that concentration of economic power which is the real threat to our democracy.

There was resonance from an unexpected quarter, P.C. Mahalanobis, the renowned statistician who had provided the expertise for the economic model used in the Second Five-Year Plan, admittedly wrote in 1969, 'India's promised social and economic revolution failed to materialize.'[15]

Such views did not deter the government that continued its totalitarianism against the private sector. The draconian Monopolies and Restrictive Trade Practices (MRTP) Act legislated in 1969 and implemented by a superlatively dominant bureaucracy, snatched away even the minuscule freedom that private enterprises might have enjoyed. It brought under its purview all undertakings whose assets singly or interconnectedly were about ₹20 crore. In the same year, Prime Minister Indira Gandhi nationalized fourteen major private banks. The high rates of interest, the insistence on the right of conversion of loans into shares, and the government's total monopoly of lendable funds were strong disincentives to growth. Ironically, monopoly under the legislation in the 1960s was interpreted in such a way that even if an enterprise had 1 per cent of the market, it was treated as a monopoly. To restrict dealings and payments in foreign exchange and securities, the Foreign Exchange Regulation Act (FERA) 1973 was introduced. J.R.D. bemoaned the series of regulations as 'the government's inexhaustible ingenuity in devising new taxes and other means of reducing disposable profits.'

Purge the private sector?

J.R.D. lamented at the Tata Steel AGM in August 1972:

> Deprived of the right to decide what and how much to produce, what prices to charge, how much to borrow, what shares to issue and at what price, what wages and bonus to pay, what executives to employ and what salaries to pay them and in some cases, what dividends to distribute, directors and top management from the chairman down have hardly any economic power in our country.

There was a serious concern that government policies would soon lead to a total elimination of the private sector. The regulations at the inputs end combined with one of the most regressive tax systems that left hardly anything in the hands of entrepreneurs after delivering an efficient output, made for an ideal recipe for disaster. In the early 1960s, individual income taxes were increased by 450 per cent. Added to that was a super-profits tax on 50 per cent of income remaining after the initial tax.[16] By 1974, the highest rates of personal income tax had increased to a mind-boggling 97.5 per cent, highest in the world.[17] On top of that, wealth tax had to be paid, thereby raising the taxation level to more than 100 per cent.

The routine approach in such a situation would be to 'manage' the tax system. Yet, the Tatas' approach to taxation was different. One of India's finest tax consultants, Dinesh Vyas, had observed that J.R.D. never debated 'tax avoidance', which was permissible, and 'tax evasion', which was illegal; his sole motto was 'tax compliance'. On one occasion a senior executive of a Tata company tried to save on taxes. Before putting up the case, the chairman of that company took him along to J.R.D. Dinesh Vyas explained to J.R.D.: 'But sir, it is not illegal.' Softly, J.R.D. replied, 'Not illegal, yes. But is it right?'

In the pre-Independence years, J.R.D. had mentioned to his economic adviser, Y.S. Pandit, that if there was nationalization of all industries post-Independence, he was not going to evade it or take money out of his interests before nationalization. He was going to hand over all his businesses to the government intact. J.R.D.'s high level of personal integrity and the Tatas, commitment to nation building was visible from this. Yet, the Tatas opposed such a kind of nationalization that was imposed without any compelling economic or social reasons. In an address to the Ahmedabad Management Association in January 1967, J.R.D. pleaded politicians and bureaucrats to work with and not against business; and to shed their preconceptions that:

> ... profit motive is dishonourable, that profit is synonymous with profiteering, that about 3 per cent net is a fair return on risk capital, that the population problem will solve itself, that mechanization means unemployment, that it is more important to impoverish the rich than to enrich the poor, that a welfare state can be built without first creating the means to pay for it, that nationalisation creates additional wealth.

The inordinate delay in granting consents was the commanding bureaucratic tool. During the British Raj, permissions for a new business were given within roughly forty days. For example, Dorabji floated the Tata Construction Company on 6 July 1920 and it was registered on 16 August. Even during the worst days post-Partition, the Government of India had given permission for starting Air India International within weeks. However, within a decade of Independence, the process had become as slow as molasses in January. In those years, J.R.D. had asked Minister Jagjivan Ram, 'Why is it that if the government could make an important decision on a big scheme like Air India in ten days (in 1947), it now (1960s) takes many years to decide on smaller things.' Ram's answer was, 'In those days, we didn't know any better.'

Despite the differences in opinion, Indira Gandhi and J.R.D. maintained a friendly equation. She once wrote to him after a meeting, 'It was good to see you. Please do not hesitate to write or to come and see me when you want to convey any news—favourable or critical.' She also ensured that whenever a French dignitary or head of state was in Delhi, J.R.D. would be invited as both Indira Gandhi and J.R.D. were francophones. However, procrastination over four specific applications by the Indira Gandhi-led Congress government hugely hurt the Tatas. These critical projects included ACC's plans for a million-tonne cement plant, Tata Power's need to generate 500MW more electricity, Tata Steel's urgent need to modernize its ageing plant, and Tata Motors' plan to cut down lengthy waiting lists by increasing capacity from 36,000 to 56,000 vehicles. But the permissions wouldn't come for years. Some did come, though thirteen years later. Here is an example of Tata Power's frustrating yet committed efforts to expand capacity, and the byzantine maze of political landmines it had to negotiate.

Electrifying experiences

In the mid-1950s, J.R.D. along with Sir Homi Mody, then director-in-charge of the Tata Electric Companies (TEC, now Tata Power) went to meet Morarji Desai, then chief minister of Bombay State (now divided into Maharashtra and Gujarat). J.R.D. submitted to Desai the Tatas' projection on power shortage in the coming years. 'No, there will not be. I have seen to that,' was Desai's curt reply. J.R.D. rose from his seat to leave. 'Where are you going?' asked a surprised Desai. 'We have worked out, sir, the demand for electrical power in the coming years. We say it will lead to a power shortage if additional generating capacity is not created. You say it won't. We do not want to waste your time, leave alone ours,' was J.R.D.'s frank response leaving Desai quite perturbed.

This was only the beginning of a series of developments before the story would come a full circle. In 1965, Tata Power commissioned its fourth thermal unit of 150 MW capacity at Trombay. In those years, any new project required hard bargaining with the governments, often with a quid pro quo in kind. The approvals for TEC's fourth unit came only after it handed over its transmission lines at Ganeshkhind in Pune and the Khopoli Power House to the Maharashtra State Electricity Board (MSEB). Undeterred by these complex situations, and anticipating rise in the power requirements of Bombay, TEC planned to set up its fifth thermal power unit with a capacity of 500 MW at Trombay. It applied for the licence in 1971.

With the MRTP Act implemented, the permission for this expansion had to come from the Central government. A very intriguing development was in the making around the same time. In the general elections of 1971, the fifth since Indian independence, Naval Tata, then chairman of TEC, decided to stand for elections as an independent candidate from the South Bombay constituency.

The Shiv Sena was backing his candidature and Bal Thackeray was supposed to have been the principal campaigner. It was to be a three-cornered election. The Congress candidate was Kailas Narain. The third candidate was George Fernandes representing the Samyukta Socialist Party. Fernandes was a sitting MP and had gained immense visibility as a labour leader. Despite his leanings, he respected J.R.D. A couple of years earlier, in 1969, J.R.D. had personally invited Fernandes at the Safdarjung Road Tata Guest House in New Delhi to request him to lead the Tata Steel workers union, an offer that he had declined.[18] The outcome of the elections was surprising. Fernandes lost his deposit with mere 10.34 per cent votes. Unexpectedly, Naval Tata stood second with 40.38 per cent votes. The Congress candidate won the election with 47.1 per cent votes. It was a reassuring moment for the Tatas and Indian democracy that a values-driven private citizen held a good chance to win elections. Yet, the direct and indirect implications of this experiment would soon emerge before J.R.D. and Naval Tata.

It is believed that Prime Minister Indira Gandhi was displeased with the Tatas' attempt at contesting elections against the Congress candidate. Furious and unforgiving, she is supposed to have told J.R.D. Tata, 'So the Tata Group wants to set up a front against me?'[19] This was history repeating itself. Nearly fifteen years ago, Prime Minister Nehru had reacted in a similar fashion. The context was different. J.R.D. was increasingly disillusioned by the Nehruvian approach to socialism, centralized planning and nationalization of key industries. To add to that, during the 1957 general elections, the Communist Party of India emerged as the second largest party in the Lok Sabha. J.R.D. believed that the country needed a credible opposition, and the leftist parties would further damage the prospect of free enterprise flourishing in India. Around 1959, Chakravarti Rajagopalachari, former Governor General of India, and a Congressman, started a new party in reaction to the Nehru-led Congress' anti-industry and socialistic approach to governance. In a later dated 15 May 1961, he requested J.R.D.'s support to the fledgling Swatantra Party. 'I request you that even if you help the ruling party with funds for its political and electioneering activities, it would also be just and proper for you to help a party that seeks to build an efficient check on its errors.'[20] Naval Tata asked J.R.D. to exercise caution. He was concerned that a public support to Rajaji would earn Nehru's displeasure. J.R.D. took two full months before sending a positive reply. However, the transparent leader that he was, he communicated this decision to Nehru when he met him the next time. On hearing about the Tatas' support to Swatantra Party, Nehru blew up, 'You have no business to do that.'[21] In order to pacify him and clarify his stance, J.R.D. wrote a detailed letter to the prime minister dated 16 August 1961:

... We have been perturbed by the total absence of any responsible and organised democratic opposition which we feel is an equally indispensable element of any permanent democratic organisation of society . . . It is indispensable in the national interest that an effort should be made to displace the Communist Party as the second largest in the Parliament . . . We have therefore come to the conclusion that in addition to continued support to the election funds of the Congress, we should also contribute, although on a lower scale, to the funds of the Swatantra Party . . . [22]

In a letter dated 18 August Nehru responded, '. . . You are of course, completely free to help in any way you like the Swatantra Party. But I don't think that your hope that they will emerge as a strong Opposition is justified . . . '

In 1975, when Naval Tata was following up for permissions, the response was hostile to say the least. Madhav Godbole, Maharashtra's power secretary, threatened to take over TEC's assets. He even explored with the Western and Central Railways if they could make their own arrangements for power. The response was in the negative. Finally, Naval Tata personally went to meet Godbole and presented his case with facts and figures. But Godbole (literally meaning the one who speaks sweetly, in Marathi) wouldn't yield. This agitated Naval Tata so much that he reacted with an emotional outburst, 'Even if I have been adopted into the Tata family from a Parsi orphanage, Mr Godbole, I cannot liquidate the assets created by my ancestors.' This mollified Godbole a bit and he agreed to consider the application. The quid pro quo this time was that TEC's distribution network in Kalyan, Thane and Ulhasnagar was to be taken over by the government.

The threat of nationalization was looming large on most private firms. When energy sector companies like Burmah Shell, Esso and Caltex were nationalized in 1976 as Bharat Petroleum and Hindustan Petroleum respectively, the Tatas were concerned that the government would forcibly take over Tata Power. As a precautionary measure, the Tata Power offices were moved out of Bombay House and relocated to Nirmal Building at Nariman Point, a kilometre away. When the threat ebbed, the company moved back to Bombay House and the Nirmal Building office space was given to TCS.

Despite these efforts, the Central government's approval wasn't coming. The indirect implication of Indira's ire resulted in the permission for the fifth thermal plant of Tata Power getting delayed by full six years, till the Emergency was lifted and the Janata Party had come to power. In an interview with *Hindustan Times* on 1 January 1977, a couple of months before the Emergency was lifted, J.R.D. had appreciated the Emergency era for 'bold steps' it had taken for the economy, the success in reversing inflation and the discipline it inculcated in industry and society at large. He was impressed that throughout the Emergency, the trains ran on time. This earned him the indignation of the new prime minister of India—Morarji Desai—who rode to power in March 1997 with the Janata Party-led coalition on the anti-Emergency plank. In an exciting turn of events, the approval of TEC's fifth thermal plant was now before the new industries minister—George Fernandes, who had secured less votes than Naval Tata in the previous elections. Fernandes' first reaction was to turn down the proposal. It was Viren Shah, chairman of Mukand Iron and Steel Works, who pleaded on behalf of the Tatas. He emphasized that the new power plant would not make J.R.D. or Naval Tata richer by a rupee. Instead it would supply additional power to thousands of small and medium enterprises of Bombay. Fernandes was quite convinced. Yet, he explored whether a government undertaking was willing to take up this project. P. Ramachandran, Union energy minister, declined the proposal that the National Thermal Power Corporation could take up this project. Fernandes is believed to have called Maharashtra Chief Minister Vasantdada Patil to check if MSEB would be interested. The rapid response was that no state electricity board had the ability to take up the project.[23]

Finally, Fernandes himself called Naval Tata to check if Tata Power was still interested to proceed with their six-year-old application. Overwhelmed at the prospect of the project finally seeing the light of day after a seventy-five-month wait, Naval Tata's response was a resounding 'yes'. When Fernandes suggested that a senior executive could come to his office to complete the formalities, Naval Tata, the company chairman, himself landed in Delhi the next day. Business historian Gita Piramal mentions the conversation that followed in Fernandes' Udyog Bhavan office.[24] When Fernandes asked him the reason that had caused the delay in gaining a clearance for the project, Naval remained silent. With a smile on his lips, he raised his hand with the thumb rubbing the index finger. When Fernandes further asked the level at which money was demanded, Naval Tata continued to smile but didn't utter a word. Having understood the situation, Fernandes cleared the proposal. It also sent a strong signal to the government machinery that the Tatas were willing to wait, or even let go off business opportunities, but were not willing to grease palms of decision makers in Delhi.

With the decks cleared, India's first 500 MW thermal plant with multiple-fuel-burning capability was commissioned at Tata Power's Trombay complex in 1984.[25] With its 152-metre chimney, it was twice the height of Qutub Minar. Only Japan had a similar-sized unit in all Asia at that time. India joined the league, thirteen years late.

CHAPTER 24

NATIONALIZING THE NATION'S PRIDE?

The threat of nationalization continued in the Janata Party-led government between 1977 and 1979. This time, the target was the jewel in the Tata crown—Tata Steel. When the Government of India nationalized 937 privately-held coal mines across India in 1972–73, those held by Tata Steel[1] (accounting about 2 per cent of the total mines) were spared. It is believed that when Mohan Kumaramangalam, then minister of iron and steel mines, was asked in the Parliament the reason for which all private coal plants were nationalized except those belonging to the Tatas, he said that the Tata mines served as benchmarks for others in efficiency and productivity. The moment other coal plants matched Tata standards, the Tata Steel-owned mines would be nationalized. That never happened. The minister was killed in an Indian Airlines air crash the very next year.

The nationalization fever had gripped the Indian governments of the 1970s. Kumaramangalam's successor, Biju Patnaik, who was the minister of steel, mines and coal in the Janata Party government, came up with a revolutionary idea—that of nationalizing Tata Steel itself. He convinced his colleague George Fernandes, who was the minister of industries. Sometime in 1978, both invited J.R.D. to Delhi to discuss an important proposal. Once again, the venue was Udyog Bhavan. During the meeting, the two ministers requested him to accept the chairmanship of a public-sector steel conglomerate that would include Tata Steel as one of its divisions. J.R.D. was at a loss of words at the shocking idea of nationalizing Tata Steel, the largest private-sector enterprise in India, and among the most successful. Thoroughly disturbed with the government's intentions, he politely excused himself. The irony was that the proposal was coming from Biju Patnaik, a self-made industrial millionaire, who understood the promise of the private sector. Rahul Bajaj, chairman of the Bajaj Group, was made a similar offer to lead a public-sector conglomerate in the automobile sector, which would include his flagship company Bajaj Auto. He too wasn't pleased with the idea.[2]

Gradually, the nationalization news spread across India through the press. In a swift response, V.G. Gopal, president of Tata Workers Union sent a telegram to Prime Minister Desai on 4 October 1978, which read:

Tata Workers' Union Executive Committee seriously disturbed over press reports that Central government contemplating nationalization of TISCO. TISCO's performance has been the best of all steel plants. Labour relations are also most cordial over the last four decades. In the circumstances, workers most unhappy over Government's contemplated move. Request utmost consideration of our above points before taking firm decision.

This was quite unusual. Nationalization is preferred by labour unions as it brings greater job stability, lifelong employment and post-retirement benefits provided by a government enterprise. That Tata Steel's labour union rejected nationalization could be considered a validation of the Tatas' labour policies.

However, the two ministers were not willing to accept popular opinion. Their contention was that the Tatas held only 4 per cent of Tata Steel, whereas the government-backed financial institutions held over 40 per cent. Hence, management of the company should be passed on to the government. At the Janata Party national executive meeting in December 1978, they proposed to nationalize key industry sectors that were profitable. This included steel (Tata Steel), aluminium (Hindalco) and automobile (Tata Motors). The idea was criticized by several members, including L.K. Advani and Subramaniam Swamy. Prime Minister Desai had already assured the Birla Group which owned Hindalco that nationalization for the sake of nationalization wasn't the government's approach.[3] A lot of politics was at play. At the Tata Steel union's executive meeting in January 1979, the labour leaders passed another resolution emphasizing that nationalization of Tata Steel wasn't in national interest. It was a joint resolution by 65,000 employees. They requested the company to communicate the same to the prime minister and his cabinet colleagues.

Encouraged by the workers' response, the very next day, J.R.D. wrote a personal letter to Biju Patnaik explaining the stance of the company and its employees. He emphasized that there were four government-nominee directors on the board of Tata Steel and that all decisions were taken by professional executives who had risen through the ranks. The low percentage of the company's capital held by the Tata Sons and Trusts was in alignment with Janata Party's own philosophy and wishes. 'What then could be the grounds justifying nationalization? Mismanagement? Industrial sickness? Need for large funds for modernization? Removal of disparities?' he abruptly concluded. The message was loud and clear. There were no technical or administrative grounds that necessitated nationalization. Finally, Prime Minister Desai intervened and overruled the proposal. Tata Steel continued to remain a gem in the Tatas' diadem.

Enlightened capitalism, the need of the hour

Nearly two decades earlier in a letter to veteran socialist leader and Gandhian, Jayaprakash Narayan, on 4 January 1955, J.R.D. had written:

> I sincerely believe that with adequate safeguards, evolved capitalism is the most effective, if not the only form of economic organisation combining decentralisation of economic power with efficiency. State ownership and control of all economic activities cannot exist for long without centralised control of political and social activities. Between the two, enormous powers are placed in the hands of a few, leading ultimately to dictatorship in one form or the other.

His words seemed prophetic when the Emergency was declared in 1975.

While there were instances of malpractice and misbehaviour in a large part of the private sector, the government had been unwilling to differentiate between the black sheep and the white. As a result, India lost a great opportunity for industrial and technological growth compared to other Asian countries. Tata Steel, for example, had got its first post-World War I expansion to 1 million tonnes in 1923. In the 1980s, its manufacturing capacity was 2 million tonnes. In sixty years, it could only double its production capacity, due to lack of government approvals. This cost the country over ₹1000 crore in precious foreign exchange wasted on imported steel.[4] In comparison, Japanese steel plants that manufactured about 10 million tonnes in 1958, had grown to 100 million tonnes by 1980. But for the general suspicion of and hostility to private enterprise as an instrument of growth, the Tatas and several other businesses could have contributed much more to India's industrialization. This was evident from the growth figures. Between 1930 and 1980, the average growth of the Tatas was about 3 per cent. This was analogous to the growth of India during the same period.[5] The cause of the despicable growth rate could be attributed to the impractical interpretation of socialism, which aimed at getting rid of all private enterprise or initiative.[6] The skewed focus on heavy industry inspired by the USSR model had also relegated agriculture to a secondary level. Consequently, despite impressive growth of infrastructure and technological know-how, 80 per cent of the population belonging to the agrarian classes was neglected. J.R.D.'s observation that poverty was not the cause of unemployment, but unemployment was the cause of poverty, was pertinent. With employment, people would have spending power and their needs would promote investment in large and small industries. Prime Minister Charan Singh rightly wanted to focus on creating employment in villages. However, he believed that the one way of achieving that was to ban, by legislation and overnight, the manufacture of consumer products by existing industries. When J.R.D. expressed his concerns that such a decision would lead to a loss of two million jobs in the main and ancillary industries, Singh said, 'What if a million people lose their jobs, if ten million people find jobs in the countryside?' Such impractical ideas were common in political discourse.

It wasn't that the Tatas were against socialism. In their businesses they had practised socialistic principles for decades. Jamshedpur and its people-centric approach was one example. Jamsetji was himself a socialist. Probably, that's why he could think far ahead of his times with respect to labour, human relations and township development, and implement practices that were not considered in the most advanced countries for years. Discarding every initiative by private enterprises as capitalistic and self-serving would amount to throwing the baby with the bath water. 'To the extent that socialism or any part of it demonstrably promotes welfare and brings about economic growth, we should accept it. Similarly, to the extent that capitalistic enterprise serves the people's welfare . . . it should be accepted and encouraged,' was J.R.D.'s firm belief. It was for such a vision and clarity of thought that H.T. Parekh, founding father of India's leading financial institutions such as HDFC and ICICI had called J.R.D. a 'practising socialist'.

Regrettably, in the name of practising socialism, the governments' heuristic policies led to several lost opportunities. Tata Motors and Tata Chemicals are examples of two companies that waited for government permissions for thirty years to deliver automobile and fertilizer projects that could positively contribute to the Indian economy and citizenry.

CHAPTER 25

UNLIMITED WAITS; LOST OPPORTUNITIES

In the 1950s, the collaboration between Tata Motors and Daimler-Benz to manufacture trucks in India had been very successful. The German auto giant was impressed with the quality of output at Tata Motors' Jamshedpur commercial vehicles plant. The Tatas' performance and the relationship between J.R.D. and the chairman of Benz led to an offer to Tata Motors for manufacturing the Mercedes-Benz 180D model in India.[1] However, this wasn't going to be possible without government permission. To convince the powers that be, Sumant Moolgaokar came up with a unique idea. In 1960, he personally gave keys of six Mercedes cars to K.B. Lal, then secretary for commerce and industry. The objective was to enable them to experience first-hand the quality of Mercedes cars and then decide on giving the requisite permission. One of these cars was even used by Defence Minister Krishna Menon. Though much appreciated, the six cars were returned to the Tatas after a year, with no concrete consent. The Germans waited for a while to see if the government permitted the collaboration. However, when no response came for a year, they selected Singapore to establish the plant. India's loss of much-needed foreign exchange was Singapore's gain. History repeated itself in 1985. Tata Motors applied for permission to collaborate with Japanese auto giant Honda to make the Accord model of cars in India. Permission was refused citing FERA laws,[2] despite approvals being given to other carmakers for collaboration with foreign partners such as Suzuki and Fiat. It was only in 1995, when Tata Motors could finally enter into a foreign collaboration. Mercedes Benz E220 luxury cars were wholly assembled at the Pune plant and launched in August 1995. It was an equal joint venture between the two companies. However, J.R.D., who had the vision and passion to bring global technology to India, wasn't alive to see that day. R.M. Lala, the Tatas' biographer reflected on this episode with regret, 'Where would India have been if we had got the technology of Mercedes-Benz in the 1960s!'

It was ironical that a government that disregarded a promising venture by the Tatas, turned to them for guidance when the Maruti project was initiated. On

Prime Minister Indira Gandhi's request to J.R.D., Moolgaokar accepted to become the first chairman of Maruti Udyog Limited. It was Moolgaokar who sent V. Krishnamurthy, R.C. Bhargava and V.S. Krishnan to explore global partnerships. In 1982, a joint venture agreement was signed between Maruti Udyog and Suzuki of Japan. Maruti 800 was launched in 1983. The sequence of events indicates a huge loss of opportunity for the Tatas to be pioneers in passenger cars in India, over two decades ahead of Maruti. Despite its high-quality standards, willingness of international collaborators and availability of resources, Tata Motors was prevented by an unseen yet palpable governmental power. It was also a loss for Indians, who could have accessed premium-quality cars from the 1960s. Whose loss was bigger?

Only twenty-seven years . . .

In 1967, Darbari Seth, then director-in-charge of Tata Chemicals had envisaged a fertilizer-cum-energy complex to complement its core business in inorganic chemicals. One of the key objectives was to start with a fertilizer factory, especially because the government was importing large quantities to meet domestic demand. In J.R.D.'s vision, this was to eventually culminate in an agro-industrial establishment with a large nuclear plant in Okhamandal (where the Tata Chemicals plant was located), which would provide low-cost energy, and even desalinate large quantities of seawater that could be provided to farmers in the neighbouring arid areas for cultivation. The US-based Allied Chemicals Corporation was to be the financial and technical collaborator for the ₹200-crore project.[3] When completed, this complex would be the largest single self-contained fertilizer plant in the world. In September 1967, Prime Minister Indira Gandhi visited the Tata Chemicals plant in Mithapur. The visionary idea was presented before her, and she was mighty impressed assuring her support for beginning the project at the earliest. Encouraged by the prime minister's response, the company submitted its detailed proposal by November 1967 anticipating quick approvals for a game-changing project that would save precious foreign exchange for India and boost Indian agriculture in substantial measure. Regular supply of large quantities of fertilizers would have been most advantageous in those years as the government had just begun a massive project for food self-sufficiency (aka green revolution). In financial terms, it would have saved ₹450 crore of precious foreign exchange for India and facilitated an additional production of 40-lakh tonnes of foodgrains for a country that was suffering from severe food shortage. 'Which government would not support a project with such evident benefits and the proactive initiative of a private enterprise that would contribute to social good?' thought Seth and J.R.D. Little did they realize that their wait had just begun.

For several years, the government did not respond to the proposal. Confused with the state of indecisiveness and lack of clarity on the future of the project, Allied Chemicals backed out. The project had landed under the draconian clauses of the just-implemented MRTP Act. After a wait of five years, the government finally responded to Tata Chemicals, but with several caveats. Instead of the proposed annual production of 20-lakh tonnes, the company could produce only 550,000 tonnes. The government had also decided on behalf of the company that instead of ₹200 crore, just ₹55 crore would suffice for setting up the plant. Unable to relate to the unreasonable preconditions imposed by the government, the Tatas cancelled the project in 1973. Despite an ardent desire to serve the nation through industry, they could just wait in the wings and watch a precious opportunity get frittered away.

While J.R.D. had given up all hope, Seth held on to his vision. His patience was rewarded in 1981, only partially though. The Government of India approached the company to participate in the expansion of fertilizer production in India. This time, Tata Chemicals submitted two proposals—one for a phosphatic fertilizer complex close to its existing plant in Mithapur, and the other for a nitrogenous fertilizer plant in Punjab. The government rejected the former citing MRTP. It couldn't permit concentration of industries from one group in a single region. For the latter, instead of Punjab, the site was mandated at Babrala, in western Uttar Pradesh. It took two years to start the process and another two years before the government sent the 'letter of intent'. By the time 1500 acres of land was acquired, environmental clearances came in, and the government approved the contractor for engineering works, it was already 1987.

In 1982, Tata Sons established a new entity for the ₹765-crore fertilizer project—Tata Fertilisers. By late 1988, the government announced a new pricing policy, which threw the fledgling company's financials out of gear. Industry observers were convinced that Tata Fertilisers would have to be wound up, even before the plant construction began. However, Seth salvaged his long-cherished dream by merging Tata Fertilisers with Tata Chemicals. 'They changed the rules of the game after the game had begun,' regretted Seth.[4] In September 1989, during the last year of his tenure, Prime Minister Rajiv Gandhi, came to Babrala along with J.R.D., Ratan Tata and Seth for laying the foundation stone of the new plant. Over 30,000 people had gathered to witness the grand event in an otherwise desolate town 150 km east of New Delhi.

The challenges were far from over. Kapil Mehan, former COO of the fertilizer business, recounted them. There was widespread theft of construction material before the boundary wall was constructed. The gun culture was prevalent, and several goons came in demanding contracts and employment for their people. There was no telephone connection and electricity in the town till the plant set up its own diesel generators in the early 1990s. The nearest town, Narora, which was home to nuclear power plants set up by the Nuclear Power Corporation of India, was 14 km away. The journey was safe only in the daylight hours as highway robbery was a common phenomenon. During the early years, most Tata Chemicals employees in Babrala could not bring their families with them for these reasons. Yet, Seth had a grandiose vision for this plant. He identified five criteria as prerequisites. These included zero discharge of effluents, state-of-the-art technology, low manpower requirements, maximum energy efficiency, and aesthetics. These were high-end parameters for a plan in the hinterland way back in the 1980s.

The plant construction commenced on 1 November 1991 and the first bag of 'Tata Shudh' urea rolled out of the Babrala plant on 21 December 1994. The Babrala plant was the largest greenfield project undertaken by the Tatas until then. Interestingly, the project costs doubled between 1981, when the Tatas first embarked on the project, and 1994, from the estimated ₹756 crore to the actual ₹1530 crore. The satisfaction was that the plant would provide urea that accounted for half of the country's fertilizer consumption.

It had taken a shocking twenty-seven years for the Tatas to get permissions and implement its vision of a fertilizer complex that would provide the most valuable input to crore of farmers across India. The financial implications of this delay had been immense, more for India than for the Tatas. A rough calculation indicated that between 1970 and 1994, the country spent approximately ₹45,000 crore of valuable foreign exchange in importing fertilizers.[5] If permissions had been given in 1967 itself, the magnitude of savings for the country and the catalysing effect on India's food self-sufficiency would have been considerable. In these twenty-seven years, the country witnessed seven prime ministers. A proposal diluted in the Indira Gandhi regime was permitted in the Rajiv Gandhi regime and inaugurated in the Narasimha Rao regime. At the company-level, J.R.D. Tata was no longer alive to see Tata Shudh roll out from the Babrala plant. Seth had since retired from Tata Chemicals.

Over the next two decades, the Babrala plant increased its annual production capacity to over 1.2 million tonnes of urea, accounting for nearly 12 per cent of the total urea produced by India's private sector. The Babrala township with hundred families had developed around an efficient and aesthetic fertilizer complex, a quarter-century late. In 2005, when the Indian Merchants Chamber awarded the Ramkrishna Bajaj National Quality Award to the Babrala plant, the citation read, 'It had demonstrated that world-class business practices are also applicable in a regulatory environment.'

If this was the personification of patience and postponements, the turn of the millennium was going to throw another Tata company in the political quagmire.

CHAPTER 26

UNDER CROSSFIRE: FROM LEFT, RIGHT AND CENTRE

On 21 February 2006, West Bengal Chief Minister Buddhadeb Bhattacharjee laid the foundation stone of the ₹120-crore Tata Medical Centre at Kolkata in the presence of Ratan Tata. During the conversation, the newly elected chief minister, who had come to power on the plank of industrializing West Bengal, requested Tata to consider developing an industrialized cluster in West Bengal. Though heading a Communist Party of India (Marxist)-led government, Bhattacharjee wanted to positively contribute to the industrialization of the state, an area it had been lagging in for several decades. A former executive in Ratan Tata's office observed, 'A warm and refreshing chief minister, Bhattacharjee wanted to make a difference in his own party, which had been historically opposed to industrialization.'

This was the time when the Nano car was in the planning phase. Pitched as the 'people's car', Tata Nano was going to be the lowest-cost car in the world at ₹1 lakh. The Tatas were considering a fixed investment of ₹1500 crore for its manufacturing plant, that would create over 10,000 new jobs. Naturally, several states were trying to woo the Tatas with incentives and subsidies. The options included Pantnagar in Uttarakhand, Singur and Kharagpur in West Bengal and Sanand in Gujarat. Tata Motors had previously selected Pantnagar for establishing the ₹1000-crore Tata Ace Plant, which was to begin production in early 2007. The Tata Bearings and Tata Metaliks plants were already located at Kharagpur, which also had one of the largest railway workshops in India. The two unexplored options were Sanand and Singur.[1] The former was close to Ahmedabad, Gujarat's commercial capital, which then had an enterprising Narendra Modi as the chief minister. The latter was close to the national highway and to Kolkata, capital of West Bengal, which had been ruled by communist governments led by Jyoti Basu from 1977. Uttarakhand was offering the best package with a ten-year tax holiday. That would have meant savings of ₹16,000 a unit for the manufacturer. However, Tata decided to establish the Nano plant in Singur. He believed that the eastern side of India hadn't seen much development for decades. West Bengal's share in India's net manufacturing output had reduced from 25.8 to 4.1 per cent between 1958 and 2005; and it was reeling under a debt of ₹2 lakh crore.[2] Perhaps, the Nano plant could be the catalyst in its industrial journey.

On 18 May, Ratan Tata publicly announced that Singur was the Tatas' choice for the Nano plant. A comprehensive incentive package had been offered by the West Bengal government. This included reduced electricity charges and a loan of ₹200 crore at a discounted rate. A total of 997 acres of fertile multi-crop agricultural land was allocated for the Nano project. Of this, 645.67 acres were for the main plant, 290 acres for the vendor park and 60 acres for the West Bengal Industrial Development Corporation.[3] The government had invoked the Land Acquisition Act, 1894, while acquiring land from the peasants.[4] It offered ₹8.60 lakh for *sali* (single crop) and ₹12.76 for *suna* (double crop) lands.[5] The rates were so attractive that there were representations from farmers outside the project area to the government to purchase their land as well.[6] The Tatas had presumed that because the intention behind the choice of location and the final product were both in national interests, the local population would be doubly supportive. Instead, it turned out to be a double whammy, which ended up in an uphill battle of prerogatives and perspectives with the Tatas caught in the crossfire.

The Bhattacharjee–Banerjee battle begins

Around 2500 landholders who held about 400 acres of land refused to accept the compensation the government was offering. They felt genuinely aggrieved to lose fertile cropland that gave three crops a year. The discontent brewing among the farmers provided a fertile opportunity for the local political leadership. The fact that Singur was first among 50,000 acres of land the government was planning to acquire for industrialization, added to its importance in the domestic political discourse. Trinamool Congress (TMC), the principal opposition party led by its firebrand chief Mamata Banerjee espoused the farmers' cause and decided to protest the land acquisition drive, while calling for rail and road blockade on 25 September 2006. Her call to protect farmers' livelihoods attracted high-profile activists and intellectuals, including Medha Patkar and Arundhati Roy. Banerjee wanted the government to return 400 acres to those who refused compensation and believed the remaining land would be sufficient for the main Nano plant. From the company's perspective, any increase in distance between the manufacturing plant and the vendor sites would add to logistical costs and would affect the price of Nano, a car for the common man. It would defeat the vision of an integrated complex with vendor parks. The agitators considered the supply chain costs as purely business imperatives, which had nothing to do with their cause of farmers' rights. The Tatas, on the other hand, maintained that land acquisition was managed by the state government, and that they (the Tatas) had been transparent in their dealings.

Unable to diffuse the situation, on 30 November, the West Bengal government imposed curfew on the entire district. Within the next month, the Nano plant land was fenced to protect people, property and plant under construction. In retaliation, Banerjee sat on an indefinite fast to protect the peasant's rights, which went on for twenty-five days. It was called off only after President A.P.J. Abdul Kalam, Prime Minister Manmohan Singh and former prime minister Atal Bihari Vajpayee personally appealed to her. After a personal conversation between President Kalam and Bhattacharya, the latter agreed to discuss the issue with the affected parties, without the option of going back on the project. Tata Motors had been open to discuss the issue with all stakeholders. Since the primary contention was between the government and the farmers, there was little they could do.

The issue was not just of compensation, most of which was given at 143 per cent of market price to landowners. Even sharecroppers[7] were compensated with 25 per cent of landowners' compensation. The real losers were landless labourers who would be deprived of livelihood and lacked skills for a job at the new plant. Prakash Telang shared an insight:

> One of the problems we realized later was that a lot of landowners were not cultivating. The compensation was given as per records, and some landowners sitting in Kolkata were pleasantly surprised to receive it. More than 75 per cent of owners who were not tilling their land, accepted compensation. And the labourers who were actually doing their work were probably left out.

Tata Motors selected several youngsters from Singur and sent them to its plant in Uttarakhand for training. They were going to be brought back to Singur when the plant was functional. They hoped this would eventually lead to attitudinal change. But that was not to be. West Bengal Industry Secretary Sabyasachi Sen had also assured skill building through training workshops in automobile and construction work. But the labourers were not convinced of these assurances as their very existence was at stake. 'A bird in hand is worth two in the bush', goes the popular proverb.

By 2007, the government had paid ₹143 crore to over 10,000 farmers. The protesting farmers led by one Joydeep Mukherjee petitioned the Calcutta

High Court that land had been acquired in contravention of legal procedures. Around this time, there was another major land conflict. On 14 March 2007, fourteen villagers protesting a Special Economic Zone (SEZ), died in clashes with the local police at Nandigram, in east Medinipur district, West Bengal. The killings turned the sentiment against the ruling government's industrialization initiatives. They came in for heavy criticism not only from social activists and intellectuals, but also from the governor and members of the ruling party. In response, Chief Minister Bhattacharjee apologized and scrapped the Nandigram project.[8] This bolstered the Singur protesters' agitation, anticipating a similar decision for the Tata Motors plant.

In a turn of events, the Calcutta High Court ruled in favour of the West Bengal government in January 2008 stating that there was nothing wrong in the acquisition of land by the state government. This brought great relief to the state machinery, but incensed TMC who threatened to go to the Supreme Court and continue their stir. The political battlelines were clearly drawn. The BJP-led NDA supported the farmers' agitation in Singur.[9] The Congress-led Central government maintained a neutral stance, as any confrontation with the ruling left party would affect the Central government, which was running with its support. CPI(M) politburo member Sitaram Yechury charged that the Tatas' corporate rivals were fanning the protests, a claim Ratan Tata accepted in a television interview. The complex political situation raised question marks on the fate of billions of rupees worth of investments that West Bengal had attracted. In an interview in late 2007, Tata observed that the solution to Singur lay in sitting down with the state government and talking about compensation, retraining, re-employment and the rest, with Tata Motors being made a party to this activity. 'Instead, what we have is a chorus of negatives, loose talk of returning the land, women and children blocking roads, and guns, bullets and firings.'

Girish Wagh was leading the Nano project and reported directly to Ravi Kant and Ratan Tata. He shared first-hand memories of the stress under which Tata Motors employees were working on-site at Singur. In those politically charged days, they would travel on-site with a police control van provided by the government. Between February 2007 and July 2008, the number of police personnel on-site increased from 800 to 1200, in addition to 350 locally hired security personnel for night patrolling, to protect 4000 employees working day-and-night to meet the deadline. Despite this, there were instances when protesters breached the compound wall and burned construction machinery, and even set a security post on fire. On one occasion, Amarjit Singh Puri, Tata Motors' liaison officer with the state government, and a Canadian architect were on-site. Suddenly 300 protesters besieged their car and started pounding on the windows, bonnet and the trunk. Thanks to cell phones, which had become commonplace in India by then, Puri called the industry secretary of the government, who sent the police to rescue them. 'It was a chilling experience,' he confessed.[10]

By August 2008, the plant came up and machinery installation commenced. 'It was a full-fledged factory in trial stage,' recalled Wagh. Thirteen vendors had also finished constructing their plants, and seventeen others were at various stages of construction. They had collectively invested about ₹171 crore.[11] Kant and Tata were keeping a close watch on the developments. On 15 August 2008, Tata was in Pune. He discussed the status quo in detail with Wagh. By that time, the situation had deteriorated. Protesters used to beat up Tata employees and even contract labour. On occasions, dead bodies and small bombs were thrown into the plant. Chairman Tata had a simple advice for Wagh, 'Whatever decision you take, employee safety is of paramount importance.' With this message, he returned to Singur, and Tata left for an overseas visit.

When 40,000 protesters surrounded the Tatas' Nano plant

By the third week of August, almost 40,000 protesters[12] had blocked the complete highway leading to the Tata plant and surrounded it, while 5000 riot police were deployed to handle the situation.[13] Tata employees had to take a circuitous route to the plant that would take them three hours one way from Kolkata, a distance that was otherwise covered in an hour. This continued for four days until a reporter from a business channel accompanied Tata employees in the bus to report their troubles. News of media sympathy for Tata employees' travails going public further flared emotions. The protesters blocked all entrance and exit points to the plant.

The lowest ebb came on 25 August. The protestors surrounded the only functional exit of the plant. They were not allowing employees and labour to leave. Wagh tried to negotiate with them for more than two hours, but they were unrelenting. It was evening and employees started getting worried. There were thirty-five foreign consultants on-site from Japan, Korea and Germany. Some of them panicked and said that they would call up their embassies for help. It was a very high-pressure situation. The inspector general of police was there but was extremely cautious after the Nandigram violence. Unexpectedly, it started pouring, and large numbers of protesters dispersed. Capitalizing on this opportunity, the Tata employees' buses quickly left the site. While they were leaving, some protesters banged on the buses. Few of them even boarded the buses and said, 'We request you. Please don't come here from tomorrow'. And true to their 'prayers', the Tata employees never returned to the plant after that day.

The situation had gone beyond control. Wagh decided to stop the plant that day and communicated to Kant that it must be shut down. Nevertheless, protesters continued their siege till 8 September. To salvage the situation, there were hectic discussions between Bhattacharjee and Banerjee under the mediation of Governor Gopal Gandhi. As an outcome, the government offered additional compensation to farmers amounting to 50 per cent of the original price and several other benefits, including jobs. But Banerjee rejected the offer. She insisted that 300 acres must be returned. A section within West Bengal believed that protests at both Singur and Nandigram were aimed at stonewalling the state government's plans for industrial growth. West Bengal's land use patterns indicated that the share of fallow, uncultivable land and pastures constituted only 1 per cent of the total land in the state. In such a scenario, working towards industrialization without acquiring agricultural land was near impossible. Moreover, the leadership behind the Singur movement had shown no inclination to resolve misgivings through discussions, despite repeated requests from the chief minister.[14] Governor Gandhi's efforts to broker an agreement between the government and TMC over a fresh land-for-land deal for unwilling landlosers to the project also failed.

The Tatas were caught in the crossfire between the two political parties. The weapons of bandh (general strike), dharna (demonstration) and gherao (human blockade) had been effectively and chronologically used in the political slugfest. By August 2008, the Tatas had invested over ₹1800 crore on the Singur plant, ready to start production. Yet, six weeks after the plant shut down, the deadlock seemed unresolvable despite best intentions.[15] On 3 October, Tata, Kant and Krishna Kumar met Bhattacharjee and senior bureaucrats at the Writers' Building, headquarters of the government in Kolkata. The ninety-minute meeting had no outcome except an assurance that work at the factory could resume under police protection. Ratan Tata was not convinced. Addressing a press conference thereafter, he said,

> Through these two years we have faced enormous destruction, assault and intimidation to our employees. Taking all things into account, mainly the well-being of our employees, the security of our contractors and, in fact, of our vendors also, we have taken the very regretful decision to move the Nano project out of West Bengal.

He reiterated that the 'great agitation and great aggression' on the part of the opposition parties, led by TMC supremo Mamata Banerjee, was the 'sole reason' for Tata Motors to take the decision. He reiterated what he had said during a television interview in December 2006, 'If somebody puts a gun to my head, you either pull the trigger or take the gun away because I will not move my head. I think Ms Banerjee has pulled the trigger,' Tata said.[16]

From Singur to Sanand

Despite unprecedented developments that delayed their most touted Nano project, Tata Motors was committed to launch the car as announced. An alternative plant had to be commissioned at the earliest. Right after Ratan Tata's announcement, there were calls from Andhra Pradesh, Karnataka and Maharashtra. Kant, Wagh and a small team had to decide the alternative location within a week. The team moved from state to state to explore options. But none could beat the offer at Sanand, 20 km from Ahmedabad. The Narendra Modi-led Gujarat government offered about 1100 acres of a flat stretch of land under a single survey number at ₹3.5 lakh per acre. The government also gave a loan of over ₹550 crore on attractive conditions.[17] Within ninety-six hours, the Gujarat administration completed all procedures and the deal was sealed. On 7 October, the decision to relocate to Sanand was officially announced. While making the announcement, a beaming Tata called it homecoming. It is believed that Chief Minister Modi had sent a one-word text message on Ratan Tata's mobile phone as soon he announced withdrawing from Singur. The one word was 'suswagatam' (Welcome in Sanskrit).[18] With Modi by his side that day, Ratan Tata said in Gujarati, 'Aapde ahiya na chhiye, ane aapde ahiya pachha aavya' (We belong here, and we have come back). Interestingly, the cattle farm at Sanand that was given to the Tatas by the government had a century-old Tata connection. Jamsetji Tata had donated ₹1000 to establish the cattle farm when the state suffered severe drought a 100 years ago.

Wagh and Ramesh Vishwakarma, manufacturing head of the Nano plant, had never imagined that they would have to embark on a logistical assignment, which had no parallel in the world of engineering or business— transplanting an entire auto plant from Singur to Sanand within months. Tata Motors had decided to shift the entire plant to the new location to save on time and retrieve part of the investments made in the project. Till the plant was ready, temporary assembly of Nano cars would begin at the Pantnagar plant, and engine and transmission lines at the Pune plant. Effectively, one project became three projects—planning for productionizing the car from the makeshift facility at Pantnagar and Pune, dismantling the plant in Singur, and starting work at the new Sanand plant.

'If you have to dismantle something for no use later, you can dismantle in any manner. But we had to dismantle the plant, transport it and reinstall it,' recalled Wagh. There were several concerns. Every part and equipment that was going to be removed had to be numbered and stored to be retrieved later. The team prepared detailed documents containing guidelines and processes on safe and damage-free dismantling, transporting and recommissioning of a large auto plant. 'Those documents were as thick as books, and no other company had done such detailed work. We have now patented the entire process,' observed Vishwakarma.[19] In parallel, the team created a 40-acre cement pad at Sanand. Its layout was designed in a manner such that the last equipment container that came in there would be the first to be used during installation.

The next decision was about the transportation route from Singur to Sanand. The two towns were 2100 km apart. There were several routes that could be taken. One of them was through the Naxalite area. Another one was shorter by 300 km but was more prone to accidents. A third route had overbridges that limited the height of the containers. Wagh created a team that travelled on two of the routes that were identified to check which one was better. Finally, the Golden Quadrilateral national highways route via Jaipur was selected. Though a bit longer, it was safer. Safety was paramount because even if one truck carrying an equipment met with an accident, it would put their timeline back by at least a few months. Over the next seven months, all the equipment totalling 3500 tonnes were transported in 3340 trucks and trailers from Singur to Sanand. Structures worth ₹440 crore had to be left behind in Singur. 'In those days, I maintained a daily logistics report that tracked trucks on their way to Sanand,' recalled Wagh. Each truck had security guards, and each driver was given a cell phone to maintain real-time contact. He gave full credit to the Tata Motors team that planned and managed the entire logistics. In parallel, the construction team worked energetically in Sanand. The Singur plant design was mirrored and mistakes made earlier were corrected.

When Chief Minister Modi telephoned the Nano project director

Remembering the commitment of the Gujarat government, Wagh said, 'Initially we had a single-lane kachchha road leading to the site. Before our first truck could come with the equipment from Singur, the government had made a six-lane road. They were superfast. Chief Minister Modi was leading from the front.' The transition from working in an environment surrounded by police patrol vans to one of freedom and cooperation was truly refreshing. Wagh recalled his first meeting with Modi. Kant, Puri, Wagh and M.B. Kulkarni (construction coordinator) were present. During the initial conversation, Wagh shared the experience the Tata team had had at Singur, especially the struggle in managing work and ensuring employee safety. In reassurance, Modi patted him and said, 'Girishji, *aap chinta mat karo. Aap kam pe lag jao. Baki mujh pe chhod do.*' (Girishji, you don't worry. You focus on your work and leave the rest to me.) Modi would often ask the Tata team if they had any requirements; and would ensure they are fulfilled. Years later, in an interview to CNN-News18, Ratan Tata recalled his interaction with Modi:

> I will never forget the way he found solutions for a company that was looking for a home. He had told me that he would get me the land I wanted in three days. He delivered that. On the third morning he said, "Ratanji, here is the land I promised." That just doesn't happen in India.

On Vijaya Dashami, Wagh was with his family in Pune. Unexpectedly, his phone rang. It was the Gujarat chief minister's secretary on the line. He told him that Modi wanted to speak to him. Modi came on the line and enquired, 'Girishji, how is the work progressing? Do you need anything? Can I help you in anyway? There should be good progress.' 'Just imagine. The chief minister was involved at this level of micromanagement. The entire government machinery was behind us. Actually, they were ahead of us,' Wagh confessed. It was no surprise that with such a synergistic collaboration between business and bureaucracy, the new plant, which would have typically taken three years for construction, came up in fourteen months. An absolute record.

A former CXO at Tata Motors contrasted the situation in West Bengal. Though the government was well intentioned, and bureaucrats straightforward, they were inexperienced with on-ground implementation as there had been no industrial development in the state since the 1960s. 'When they said power will be available on certain days, there was no one down the line to implement that. Nobody understood what was involved in making it happen. There were several handicaps, which we learnt about only after we started working there.'

It wasn't as if there were no protests in Gujarat. Within a month, landowners and political leaders from the opposition Congress party petitioned the courts on ownership rights, higher compensation and employment opportunities for the local population. 'But, the government handled it well. That is the contrast between West Bengal and Gujarat,' admitted another senior executive.

This experience was similar to the successful implementation of Tata Power's operations in Delhi, which provided electricity to over 60-lakh consumers.[20] It was a successful turnaround of the erstwhile loss-making public enterprise North Delhi Power Ltd. Vivek Talwar called it a public-private-partnership benchmark in operational excellence and levels of delivery. The senior leadership unanimously credited the role of then chief minister of Delhi, Sheila Dikshit, in reducing red tape, and action-oriented decision-making. Firdose Vandrevala, former managing director of the venture, recalled an instance when Dikshit called him and said, 'I will be away for a number of days from tomorrow. Is there anything you need to be cleared while I am away?' 'Which minister would take this kind of initiative?' acknowledged Vandrevala.[21]

'Let's forget the past . . . '

On 2 June 2010, in the presence of Chief Minister Modi, Ratan Tata inaugurated the ₹2000-crore Sanand plant. 'When I came here first on an industry visit invited by the Gujarat chief minister, I was told that if the Nano plant is not in Gujarat, I will be stupid. I am no longer stupid after investing on the plant in Gujarat,' he said. The Tatas' investment in Sanand brought the Ford plant with an investment of ₹4000 crore in 2011. They were followed by Peugeot, Hitachi, Cadila Healthcare and many others totalling billions of dollars' worth of investments in Gujarat.

In contrast, Singur resembled an industrial wasteland. For nearly a decade after Tata Motors left, the 2200 'reluctant farmers' neither received compensation from the state government nor received the land. They were the biggest victims. On the political front, Singur brought bumper benefits to Banerjee. In the 2009 parliamentary elections, TMC emerged as the largest state party in the Central government. In 2011, Banerjee created history in West Bengal by dethroning the thirty-four-year-long communist-party rule and became the state's first woman chief minister. Singur and Nandigram emerged as her strongholds. Her first announcement was returning the 400 acres of land to the farmers, who were unwilling to allow the takeover. Her government passed the Singur Land and Rehabilitation Act, 2011, to revoke the ninety-nine-year lease given to Tata Motors. Though struck down by the Calcutta High Court, it was upheld by the Supreme Court in 2016, which blamed the Bhattacharjee government for not following proper procedures as laid down in the Land Acquisition Act.[22]

The Tatas were mandated to return the land. After the judgment, concrete structures were demolished and roads on the erstwhile Nano plant were dug up. Cultivation recommenced in over 300 acres of the land at Singur. Banerjee repeated her electoral success in 2016 and became chief minister for a second time. The judgment probably vindicated her stand.

On the industrial front, West Bengal's record remained poor. Half a century earlier, Hindustan Motors, the leading auto producer set up its plant near Calcutta. No new plant had come up ever since. The Singur and Nandigram incidents added to the state's anti-industry image. The state saw a 97 per cent decline in industries between 2010 and 2014. In the Banerjee years as chief minister, the outstanding debt of the state increased from ₹1.86 lakh crore to ₹3.05 lakh crore, a 64 per cent growth, with an annual interest burden of ₹45,340 crore.[23] Its debt to gross state domestic product ratio was the third highest of any state. Perhaps, that was the reason while addressing industrialists in Germany in 2016, she urged Tata Motors and other corporations to forget the past and invest in West Bengal.[24]

As for the key learning for the Tatas from the Singur incident, Telang reflected, 'I think everyone stuck to their own ground, and that's when things didn't happen.' This wasn't surprising in a state that was known for not having bipartisan decision-making. 'We did not understand the politics there. We did not foresee the political situation that would unfold,' admitted Kant. In popular perception, the Tatas' leadership was perceived as willing to negotiate with all stakeholders in a transparent manner. However, when things went beyond control and they were held to ransom, they walked out—chin up, chest out. Regrettably, due to plant relocation delays, Tata Motors was not able to fulfil in time the 300,000 fully paid orders it had received for the Nano.

Managing the political quagmire in a complex government system

'When I joined business, there was no black money. There was no corruption, for whom were you to corrupt? When you did not have a system of government control where you had to get a permit for everything. In the early days, taxes were also very low. Black money will always be there as long as taxes and controls are high,' J.R.D. Tata had affirmed this in the late 1980s, based on his half a century of experience under different systems of government. It was the same during the years when Tata Steel and Tata Power were being established. Dorabji Tata did face political problems with the Raj, but not corrupt officers. The British officers he dealt with were men of their word. The only gift they accepted was a Christmas hamper of tinned ham and wine. Despite differences on political and economic grounds, J.R.D. remained appreciative of the finer qualities of both prime ministers—Nehru and Indira, who led India for thirty-two years. Whenever called upon to advise or assist the government on matters of public interest and policy, the Tata leadership made their services available, much beyond the call of duty.

Between 1947 and 1984, the most difficult days for Indian businesses, the Tatas retained the number one position despite an unsympathetic relationship between business and bureaucracy. Operating in core industries that were governed by strict price controls and severe caps on expansion, their achievement was laudable. Throughout this period, J.R.D. believed in keeping business and politics apart. He felt it was wrong for businessmen to run newspapers, or undertake any activity of a political or quasi-political character.[25] In 1979, when J.R.D. was asked why the Tata Group had not grown as fast as some other groups during the Licence Raj years, he said, 'If we had adopted the means some others have, we would have grown twice as big as we are today, but we didn't.' Then he forcefully added, 'And I would not want it any other way.'

Nearly forty years later, Ratan Tata reaffirmed the Tata approach. In a September 2017 interview he said, 'I would be lying if I said there weren't moments when issues came up and decisions had to be made (on taking shortcuts with the government). Happily, every time, boards and leadership stood together saying—that's not what we (the Tatas) do. Over the years, we have suffered because of that. But, I believe it is very important to come back at night and say—I have not succumbed (to pressure).'

CHAPTER 27

AN ABIDING PASSION FOR NATION BUILDING

'Philanthropy has a more profound meaning than that of mere charity since it means "love for mankind". When that love prevails, wealth assumes a nobler purpose.'

J.R.D. Tata

In 1999, soon after R. Gopalakrishnan joined Tata Sons as a director, there was a war between India and Pakistan in Kargil (Jammu and Kashmir). The atmosphere was tense. Many industry captains were sending cheques to the prime minister's fund to express solidarity. Gopalakrishnan rushed into Ratan Tata's office, which was opposite his own at Bombay House, and suggested, 'We must give a cheque for this cause. You must go to the prime minister for a photo opportunity.' Ratan Tata replied, 'What's the big deal with a photo opportunity and just handing over a cheque? How can we satisfy ourselves with a cheque, instead of money reaching the right people?' This left Gopalakrishnan pondering. It was his first brush with the Tata approach, having spent over three decades with HUL.

Over the next six months, around ten senior leaders of the Tata Group met every month to discuss what could be done to support the cause under consideration. The outcome was the Tata Defence Welfare Corpus, a unique fund set up with three representatives of Tata Trusts and one representative each of the army, the navy and the air force. A total of ₹12 crore was contributed by Tata companies and employees. Every year 80 per cent of income earned by the corpus would be used to assist injured soldiers and their dear ones. Though originally started for the welfare of Kargil martyrs' families, the corpus eventually expanded its scope to benefit those involved since the Bangladesh war (1972). Reflecting on this initiative, Gopalakrishnan said, 'It shows that you just didn't sign a cheque as many people can do. But you did what our great saints have called shram daan (service) and not just dhana daan (charity).' Interestingly, the concept of establishing the Prime Minister's National Relief Fund itself was suggested by J.R.D. to Prime Minister Jawaharlal Nehru in

October 1947 to support the refugee crisis post-Partition. In December 1947, when the fund was finally set up, one seat on the board of trustees was allocated to Tata Trusts!

A passionate legacy of 125 years. . .

Since J.N. Tata Endowment was established by Jamsetji in 1892 to fund Indian students desirous of pursuing higher education overseas, the Tatas have worked towards the provision of sustainable solutions for systemic problems. In the preceding chapters, we explored the story behind the establishment of

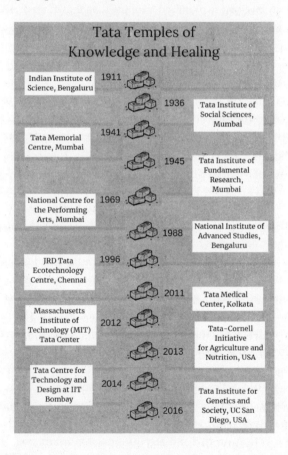

IISc at Bangalore, and the contexts in which Tata Institute of Fundamental Research, Tata Institute of Social Sciences and Tata Memorial Hospital were seeded and supported by Tata Trusts. Each of them has been a pioneer and has risen over the decades as institutions of eminence, not only in India but across Asia. In subsequent years, Tata Trusts funded newer institutions to meet the requirements of a fast-growing nation—the National Institute of Advanced Studies (Bangalore), JRD Tata Ecotechnology Centre (Chennai) and Dorabji Tata Centre for Research in Tropical Diseases at IISc.

Civil society organizations have always considered the Tatas their first resort for funding and mentorship. In post-Independence years, Tata Trusts were one of the primary supporters of NGOs in India. Not many would know that the key funder for establishing the world-famous Jaipur Foot in 1956 was Sir Dorabji Tata Trust (SDTT). Providing rubber-based prosthetics to amputees and polio patients, the institution has benefitted over 15-lakh patients in the last five decades. Pradan (Professional Assistance for Development Action), now a renowned NGO, was initially backed in 1984 by Ford Foundation and Tata Trusts. Started with the objective to systematically groom and enable professionals with empathy towards the poor to work at the grassroots level, Pradan has collaborated with governments and played a major role in developing programmes such as the Integrated Rural Development Programme and the National Rural Livelihood Mission. In the same year, SDTT provided a seed funding to RGVN in Guwahati. Three decades later, its new avatar—North East Small Finance Bank—has become one of the largest small finance banks in northeast India. Similarly, Tata Trusts first backed Vijay Mahajan and Basix in 1997 to seed the then nascent idea of a microfinance company attracting commercial debt and equity investments. Two decades later, it has spawned a ₹1 lakh crore microfinance industry with over three-crore beneficiaries. There are several such anecdotal evidence that indicate the far-sightedness of the trusts in seeding and supporting ideas and initiatives that would have far-reaching outcomes and social impact.

On an interesting note for a sports-loving nation, the Tatas were the first business house in India to support sporting talent in the country in the early 1900s. In continuation with the passion for sports in the Tata family, Tata Trusts and companies have fielded and supported over 400 sportsmen of renown across sports over the last fifty years. These include Test cricketers such as Nari Contractor, Dilip Vengsarkar, Ravi Shastri, Saurav Ganguly and Ajit Agarkar; badminton legend Pullela Gopichand, tennis star Leander Paes, and billiards champions Michael Ferreira and Geet Sethi, among others. Tata Group's support has produced thirty-two Olympians, nine world champions, forty-one Asian game winners, eight Commonwealth winners, eight Padma Shri awardees, and twenty-eight Arjuna award winners.[1] The Tata Sports Club (1937), Tata Football Academy (1987), JRD Tata Sports Complex (1991), Tata Archery Academy (1996), Tata Steel Adventure Foundation (headed by Bachendri Pal, the first woman to climb Mount Everest in 1984), and Naval Tata Hockey Academy (2018) are manifestations of the Tatas' continued commitment to nurture young players with a spark.

Tata Trusts: A structure nonpareil

'I'm very heartened by the fact that a large proportion of our companies'
profits go to Tata Trusts, which use them for philanthropic purposes. That
gives each of our team members and certainly gives me a larger purpose than
just working to make this business successful.'

Harish Bhat

In earlier chapters, Tata Trusts are described as majority shareholders in Tata
Sons. However, the term 'Tata Trusts' has been used to indicate a management
organization. The legal organizations comprise fourteen independent charitable
trusts formed by the contribution of several generations of the Tata family,
who donated all or significant portions of their wealth at different points of
time. Sir Dorab Tata Trust and Sir Ratan Tata Trust are the principal ones
among these fourteen trusts. Each of them has a similar mandate but different
disbursal criteria. The trust deeds, some of which were drafted nearly a century
ago, continue to guide the use of funds for various charitable causes. Over 75
per cent of the trusts' funds come from dividends on shares they own in Tata
Sons. The remaining comes from their own statutory investments. 'We have
certain boundaries in which we can operate or not operate, but we are always
experimenting or testing to see how the boundaries can be pushed. It also
depends on the nature of challenges the country faces at different points of time.
The challenges in 1920s and 1930s were quite dissimilar from the challenges
today,' observed R. Venkataramanan, managing trustee (MT), Tata Trusts.

At an operational level, Tata Trusts are governed by the Maharashtra
Public Trusts Act, 1950, the relevant provisions of the Income Tax Act, 1961,
and the Foreign Contributions Regulation Act, 2010. The board of trustees is
the governing body that sets the strategic direction of activities and provides
the policy and operational framework under which some of the executive
responsibilities are delegated to the MT. The MT conducts the day-to-day
operations of the trusts and is primarily responsible for following the strategic
direction laid down by the board. The project proposals received for funding
requests by Indian and international institutions and individuals are reviewed
by a project management committee. The promising ones are recommended
to the executive committee, chaired by the MT, which in turn seeks board
approval.[2]

The trusts focus on diverse thematic areas such as healthcare, education,
energy, rural upliftment, arts and culture, urban poverty alleviation, water and

sanitation. Initiatives in these areas are supported either through facilitating innovation, assisting institution building or by grants to individuals. By 2018, Tata Trusts had built partnerships in twenty-eight states of India with over 500 partners and implemented over 1000 interventions. Their global partners included World Bank, Gates Foundation, Dell Foundation and Google. According to A.N. Singh, former director at Tata Trusts, between 1931 and 2009, Tata Trusts disbursed ₹1877 crore in grants for various causes.[3] If one compares this figure with the annual funding in 2018, which was nearly ₹1000 crore, it becomes apparent that the financial success of the Tata Group has had a direct impact on the availability of funds for social welfare through the trusts. It validates the virtuosity of the Tata model where profits of individual Tata companies are received as dividends by Tata Sons (proportionate to their holding); Tata Sons' dividends proportionately go to Tata Trusts; and the disbursing mandate of various trusts facilitate the ploughing back of that money into the society. It corroborates an observation J.R.D. made several decades ago, 'We [Tatas] want to make money, because that is the only way to make funds available for the charitable trusts.'

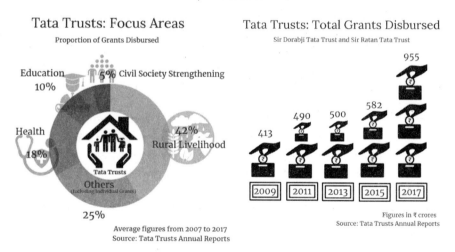

Tata Trusts: Focus Areas
Proportion of Grants Disbursed

Education 10%
Civil Society Strengthening 5%
Health 18%
Rural Livelihood 42%
Others (including Individual Grants) 25%

Average figures from 2007 to 2017
Source: Tata Trusts Annual Reports

Tata Trusts: Total Grants Disbursed
Sir Dorabji Tata Trust and Sir Ratan Tata Trust

2009: 413
2011: 490
2013: 500
2015: 582
2017: 955

Figures in ₹ crores
Source: Tata Trusts Annual Reports

The 'Uberization' of social change

'If we revisit and re-envision ourselves on what our [Tata Trusts] role could be going forward, can we be the Uber or Airbnb equivalent of driving social change?'

R. Venkataramanan

The last five years have seen a major shift in the approach of Tata Trusts—from being a predominantly grant-making institution to one that focuses on participation in the execution process and the outcomes. For nearly a hundred years, their approach was charity-driven. It involved giving support to worthy causes, but suffered from limited direct engagement with the society. The new approach involved shared value creation through sustainable interventions focused on tangible impact at scale, institutional sustainability, catalysing resources and partners, encouraging entrepreneurship and also facilitated direct engagement with community. This could be considered a direct outcome of the hands-on involvement of Ratan Tata in the functioning of the trusts after he stepped aside from executive responsibilities at Tata Sons in 2012. Consequently, even the number of people working in and for the trusts' projects increased from 100 in 2013 to 750 by 2018. Ratan Tata reflected on the need for this transition:

> For the trusts to continue to do what they did at the turn of the century would be like sitting in the twilight thinking that the issues of the country are the same. To me that would have been a disappointment. So, the trusts are going through the transformation that is making them relevant today. If we had not done that, they would have become irrelevant and created edifices that stood up as evidence of what the trusts did but did not contribute to the country.

Any change per se is a challenge. When an institution has been working in a mould for a century, everyone prefers their status-quo—funders and grantees. Moreover, contrary to popular belief, executing collaborative projects in the philanthropy space is probably much tougher than many other industries or environments. Everyone is passionate about what they do and there is a great reluctance to let go of their espoused theory of change. The belief that their idea is the right one and the only idea that would work is dominant. In such a scenario, Tata Trusts have preferred to shift from a programme mode to a platform one. 'Platforms are scalable, but programmes are not. Programmes work only in one set of environments, with a set of constraints, a set of NGOs, and a with the set of persons. If you remove any of these, it may collapse. Hence, platforms are more sustainable. That's what we are intending to migrate to at this point of time,' shared Venkataramanan. NGOs do appreciate if Tata Trusts become the frontend institution in a collaborative project instead of just a funding agency—the initiative could have greater leverage. Simple things like getting an appointment with the chief minister of a state would be far easier as also the ability to mobilize larger capital. It was an interesting paradigm shift, the outcome of which could be measured over a decade. And a couple of interesting partnerships that Tata Trusts have ventured into under the new approach have already yielded impressive results. Let's explore one each with a corporate, a government department and a university.

Google Internet Sathi. This is an initiative by Google India in partnership with Tata Trusts to improve digital literacy among rural women through 'train the trainer' approach. The key feature has been training women on handling digital devices and using the Internet for various purposes, including banking, education, and healthcare. 'To the credit of Google leadership and our trustees and board, we said—"Let's shed what each of us know and put the customers centre stage." It doesn't matter who does what if the objective is achieved in a sustainable way,' shared Venkataramanan while highlighting the synergies that emerged from this partnership. In 2014, only one in ten Internet users in rural India were women. The initiative began in 2015 with an initial target of 4000 villages over twelve months. By March 2018, 40,000 sathis had reached three-crore women across 150,000 villages in fifteen states. 'We converted a programme into a platform so there's very little degree of variability. There will be regional variations in execution, but everybody is looking at the same number. That's why I call it "uberization"[4]—irrespective of the car and driver, you get a standard experience,' observed Venkataramanan.

Zila Swachh Bharat Prerak. In response to Prime Minister Narendra Modi's appeal to the corporate world to sponsor young professionals to facilitate the implementation of the Swachh Bharat Mission, during his Mann ki Baat in September 2016, Tata Trusts collaborated with the Ministry of Drinking Water and Sanitation through Zila Swachh Bharat Preraks (ZSBPs). The ZSBPs form a young cadre of professionals that support district administration across India to ensure effective implementation of the programme. Hired and funded by Tata Trusts, ZSBPs were brought on board to strengthen the capacity of district administrations by providing them technical and managerial support to achieve the open defecation free (ODF) status by improving access to sanitation services in every household. With a monthly stipend of around ₹50,000 paid by Tata Trusts, over 475 preraks were placed across over 400 rural districts in twenty-six states. With an approximate annual outlay of ₹30 crore by Tata Trusts, the impact of the programme can be judged from the outcomes. Since the launch of the programme in 2017, the sanitation coverage increased from 57 to 94 per cent by September 2018. Over 352,800 villages and over 350 districts across seventeen states and union territories were declared ODF. Against a planned target of 15-lakh households, the initiative was able to achieve 13.31-crore households. 'We don't desire to claim credit. It's a true collaborative way on the principles of mutuality that we are able to drive significant levels of change,' admitted Venkataramanan. Interestingly, the project is anchored by Mallika Jagad, who a decade ago worked with Taj Hotels and had anchored a rescue operation during the 26/11 terror strikes on Taj Mumbai. Today, she is one of the leading members of a project on the rescue of Indian women from the shackles of unhygienic defecation practices thrust upon them for centuries. This is also representative of the spectrum of employment options available to those within the Tata ecosystem.

University of California. This cutting-edge collaboration with UC, San Diego, leverages their expertise in advanced genetics, a capability that exists perhaps only in the US. Tata Trusts funded a project to deal with the malaria menace in India. Under this technique, the DNA of a mosquito is reprogrammed so that even during the mating process, it cannot carry the malaria virus. In two generations of a mosquito, which is two or three weeks, a malaria mosquito may bite you, but will not infect you. A similar technique can be extended to handle problems of the Zika virus and many others.

In 2016, the Tata Institute of Genetics and Society was established as a special purpose vehicle by the trusts in collaboration with the National Centre for Biological Sciences, a TIFR-affiliate in Bangalore. 'We believe this institute can be much bigger than the combined strength of TIFR and IISc,' observed Venkataramanan. 'It gives a great degree of computational insights as well as the biology and genetics side of things to drive and look at programmes that have great social relevance.' In response to the concern on Tata Trusts' funds being invested in global research projects, he emphasized that certain technologies and protocols can be contributed and maintained only by global institutions. Such collaboration is necessary for tapping into that degree of capability. 'We have built Indian institutions and are desirous to partner with them. But it is necessary to look at global best practices for the benefit of the Indian population. That's the end objective of all our initiatives.'

Tata companies for society and sustainability

'I suggest that the most significant contribution organized industry can make is by identifying itself with the life and problems of the people of the community to which it belongs and by applying its resources, skills and talents to the extent that it can reasonably spare them to serve and help them.'

J.R.D. Tata

While Tata Trusts are wedded to social welfare by mandate, the same cannot be said of individual Tata companies, which are for-profit commercial entities. Yet, they complement the work of Tata Trusts by contributing to societal well being in substantial measure. This began in a structured way nearly half a century ago. In his first three decades as group chairman, J.R.D. laid enough emphasis on the welfare of Tata employees, workers and families. This was evident through efforts in building strong ecosystems for the townships of Jamshedpur and Mithapur. Having achieved sufficient success, he wanted to extend this focus to the local community beyond the boundaries of Tata plants and ensure better lives for them as well. Accordingly, in 1969, with shareholders' permission, the Memorandum and Articles of Association of leading Tata companies were modified so that company resources could be officially utilized for benefitting the local community and society through CSR activities—probably an unprecedented step in India Inc. Consequently, Jamshedpur and Mithapur plants 'adopted' hundreds of neighbouring villages for integrated rural development. This wasn't a fad, but a commitment that stayed in the best and the worst of the times. This was revealed in 1996, when Prime Minister Narasimha Rao urged industrialists to spend at least one per cent of their net profits for social work beyond employee welfare. Ratan Tata and Jamshed Irani decided to quantify the commitment of Tata Steel to understand where the Tatas stood. When the figures at Jamshedpur were analysed, it emerged that the company had consistently spent between 4 to 21 per cent of net profits for CSR activities unrelated to employees or townships. Noteworthy was the year 1992–93, when Tata Steel had earned its least profits (₹127 crore) but had spent 21 per cent (₹27 crore) of it on CSR.[5] This was more than two decades before the New Companies Act, 2013, mandated profit-making companies to spend two per cent of profits after tax for CSR activities. In 1998, when the clause on corporate citizenship was incorporated in the Tata Code of Conduct, most Indian companies weren't even talking about it. To date, the very first slide in Tata Steel's analyst and investor presentations focuses on its contribution to society.

Over the years, Tata companies' approach to CSR and sustainability became the core of their businesses and not something done in spare time or as an add-on. Throughout this book, a conscious effort has been made to highlight scores of such initiatives that have been undertaken by Tata companies. Whether it is Tata Chemicals' Kisan Sansar Networks, or Tata Global Beverages' community development for tea plantation workers in Kerala, or Titan's livelihood creation programme in Tamil Nadu, or Rallis' Kisan Kutumb programmes, or Taj Hotels' disaster rehabilitation post 26/11 terror attacks through the Taj Public Service

Welfare Trust, or Tata Steel's collaboration with World Bank for eradication of small pox or TCS' Maitree and Purpose4Life community initiatives. With an expanding global footprint, Tata companies have used their global success to contribute to global social welfare—whether through Tata Chemicals' contribution to community development in Kenya through the Magadi Foundation, or TCS' support in providing software for emergency services during Hurricane Katrina in Louisiana State (USA) or greening of the supply chain by Tata Motors' Jaguar plants in the UK.

CSR Spending by Tata Companies

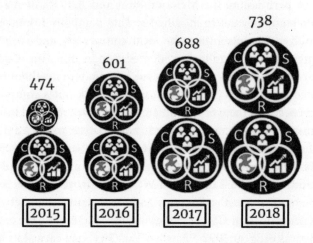

Figures in ₹ crores
Data of Nine Tata Companies

There have been occasions when Tata Trusts and companies worked together—either through contribution of funds or collaboration using common synergies. In 2014, for the first time, a group-wide common CSR platform was established for livelihood training and skill development for employment, entrepreneurship and community enterprise, a crying need for Indian youth. The Tata Community Initiatives Trust was formed to accept CSR funds of Tata companies that did not have independent projects. Now popular as Tata Strive, this initiative aligned with twenty-five focus sectors selected by the Union government as well as skill gaps identified by the National Skill Development Corporation. Its two-pronged approach focused on building Tata Strive skill development centres by leveraging technological competencies and infrastructure of Tata companies and trusts; and helping scale up training capacities of partner centres operated by other NGOs, corporates and governments.

Even the most hardened cynic cannot deny the quantum of social work Tata companies and trusts have done over the last 100 years. Moreover, the Tatas do not advertise their community development and social welfare projects, except the mandatory reporting in company documents and websites. So often, the lay reader is not even be aware of the work that goes on in the hinterland. As Venkataramanan mentioned, 'We wish to be like the intel inside a computer or Qualcomm microprocessor or snapdragon chip inside the smartphone of social change—silently catalysing the outcomes without much visibility.'

Yet, there is a structure that operates at Tata Sons to facilitate this process. Earlier, the Tata Council for Community Initiatives (TCCI) acted as the apex body for evolving a common direction for group-wide CSR initiatives. In 2014, TCCI was replaced by a fifteen-member Tata Sustainability Group (TSG), which focused on thought partnership with group companies for embedding sustainability in business strategies and demonstrating responsibility towards society and environment. The TSG-formulated sustainability assessment framework enabled Tata companies to assess their standing in terms of sustainability and CSR, and fit into TBEM. At the core of TSG are two areas it is directly responsible for: disaster rehabilitation and employee volunteering.

The Tata Relief Committee (TRC), which focused on emergency charity in India and overseas by mobilizing funds in response to natural and manmade catastrophes now operated under TSG. TRC had done a lot of work during the 2004 tsunami in Tamil Nadu or the 2007 Cyclone Aila in West Bengal.[6] In recent times, one of the largest contributions of ₹50 crore was provided for relief purposes during 2013–14 flash floods in Uttarakhand and Kashmir. TRC has been increasingly structured for providing relief and lasting solutions for reintegration of widows and orphans through entrepreneurial opportunities, and long-term rehabilitation and construction efforts led by Tata Housing and Tata Realty. In 2016–18 alone, Tata Group provided relief to 400,000 disaster-affected families in India and Nepal through decentralized state-level disaster management teams across companies.

An important component of the Tatas' commitment to society and sustainability was employee volunteering, christened as Tata Engage. From 2014, the Tata Volunteering Week (TVW) was celebrated group-wide across a four-week period, twice a year. In the first four years, over 150,000 volunteers participated from across Tata companies. In 2017 alone, over 12.4 lakh volunteering hours were clocked by Tata Engage volunteers. The Pro-Engage Project gave options to employees to mentor and coach non-profits to build and sustain their capacity for up to six months mainly during weekends, holidays and after-work hours. Since its launch in 2014, over 500 volunteers worked on 200 projects supporting 130 NGOs in over thirty-five locations.

The Engage+ programme provided qualified employees an opportunity for full-time deputation with a non-profit and spearhead a project of significant social importance for six months. In the experience of Tata leaders, all such initiatives worked as HR enhancement, employee retention and leadership development platforms.

A common question often comes up in academic discussions. Tata Sons does not have majority stake in all Tata companies. Yet, it invests a huge proportion of human and financial resources for social and environmental initiatives, some of which may add financial value, some of which may not. What is the driving force behind this approach? In a 2007 interview, Ratan Tata elaborated:

> Some foreign investors accuse us of being unfair to shareholders by using our resources for community development. Yes, this is money that could have made for dividend pay-outs, but it is also money that's uplifting and improving the quality of life of people in the rural areas where we operate and work. We owe them that . . . It gives the community a sense of belonging and sharing in our growth rather than developing a distaste for us. That's one big reason we've never had problems with the communities around our plants in all the time we've been there.

It's unsurprising then that although 6000 people died in clashes between Naxalites, police and paramilitary groups in Bihar and Jharkhand between the late 1960s and early 2010s not one Tata employee or leader was harmed despite thousands of Tata workers and dozens of Tata companies operating in those geographies. Instead, the Tata Steel Rural Development Society (since 1979) freely engaged with the tribal population and provided health, education and livelihood training programmes. At such a time, the enormous interdependence between a company and surrounding communities becomes evident, that bonding and reciprocity becomes imperative for a company to grow and survive. 'At a time when it is becoming impossible to acquire land and set up green field plants, the Tatas have been successful, thanks to their approach of moving from a negative footprint to a positive handshake,' observed Biren Bhuta, former CSR Head at Tata Steel. Ishaat Hussain shared his decades long experience:

> The whole West Bokaro (Jharkhand) area where we have iron and coal mines, is infested with Maoists. The district collector of that place would not come there without full protection. Our people go around everywhere without any protection! The state has withered away in those places. Tata Steel is virtually

the state. We have our own security, hospitals and schools. The extremist elements have never stopped our mining. They are fully supportive of us and in return we ensure that the local population gets water, electricity, and that their roads are maintained. In all this, there is a bit of altruism, and some self-interest as well.

For the nation, forever . . .

In 1941, when the Tata Memorial Hospital was inaugurated in Mumbai, Sir Roger Lumley, governor of Bombay, said, 'This hospital will spearhead the attack on cancer in this country by providing not only a centre, where specialized treatment can be given, but also one from which the knowledge of new methods of treatment and diagnosis will go out to doctors and hospitals throughout the country.' His vision proved to be prophetic. Not only has the hospital served lakhs of cases in the last seventy-five years (with 70 per cent treated gratis), but also extended its services through the Tata Medical Centre, inaugurated in Kolkata in 2011 with a special focus on northeastern states. The scale would now grow exponentially as Tata Trusts collaborate with the National Cancer Grid, a Department of Atomic Energy project focused on setting up nearly 100 cancer hospitals across India, some in the private and some in the public sector.

As H.S.D. Srinivas, director of health initiatives, Tata Trusts observed, 'We forge partnerships with the governments to implement their programmes more efficiently.' The trusts would provide technical protocols, procure medical equipment, manage operations and quality control these hospitals, which would be manned by trained doctors in oncology. Primary centres for village clusters would be manned by technicians who can wirelessly send images to doctors in hospitals and get a quick response. This would save lives because the disease would be diagnosed early enough rather than mistreated for a year, thereby preventing the restriction of cancer only to palliative care, which is the case today. The 100 hospitals, including district hospitals, government medical colleges and state-of-the-art tertiary care centres, would be an integrated network with 30,000–40,000 beds, making a vast difference. 'We are getting about 80-lakh patients with advanced cases of cancer coming to our hospitals from all over India. What we don't know could be another 80-lakh. Many of these are kids from Assam and Tripura. The real challenge for us is to find a way for cancer treatment, which is becoming treatable, to reach the poorer segments of Indian population,' reflected Ratan Tata. By 2018, over twenty-five cancer hospitals were underway in six states with government contribution of ₹2715 crore and Tata Trusts' contribution at ₹2193 crore. 'Prime Minister Narendra Modi has announced ₹5-lakh health insurance for the families, that's a terrific start,' Ratan Tata complimented.[7]

For long decades, Tata Group has been known for their philanthropic initiatives through the pioneering institutions they have built. However, what is noteworthy is their desire to not rest on their past laurels but to think even bigger for the next century. The abiding passion for building a socially-inclusive nation is palpable. The diversity of initiatives are indicative of the catholicity of their approach. During our conversation, Ratan Tata envisaged that the future focus may be on newer forms of crop development by producing food through bacteria in the lab. The Tatas may contribute the initial funding and research in such areas. He added:

> All of these will not be the sexy part of livelihood, it would be the nation-building part of livelihood. We're looking at producing water out of humidity in air. These may be rural livelihood activities aimed at enhancing the quality of life of the people, but it may be looking at it in a very advanced form, which today one might say that that's not the area the trusts should be looking at. But if we don't, perhaps no one will.

IN CONCLUSION

A WAY OF BUSINESS: AT 150, BEFORE AND BEYOND

'We do not claim to be more unselfish, more generous or more philanthropic than other people. But we think we started on sound and straightforward business principles, considering the interests of the shareholders our own, and the health and welfare of the employees, the sure foundation of our success.'

Jamsetji Tata

After three decades in various capacities as a TAS officer, R.K. Krishna Kumar became the MD of Tata Tea in 1991. It was the time when militancy had started gaining the upper hand in Assam where the company had several tea plantations. The United Liberation Front of Assam (ULFA)[1] had gained control over the southern banks of the Brahmaputra, while the northern banks were under the command of the National Democratic Front of Bodoland (NDFB) militants. The militants demanded what was called 'protection taxes' per kg of tea produced and per hectare of land owned. Kumar observed that most tea companies were paying protection money, which collectively amounted to over ₹100 crore a year. It was common knowledge that big companies had been earlier forced to pay fringe groups to ensure safety in disturbed states such as Punjab, Kashmir and West Bengal. Some like the Goodricke Group even reported the ransom paid in their balance sheet in 1992.[2] The Tatas refused to pay, even though one of their employees was killed by the militants in Nalbari in March 1990. Darbari Seth, then chairman of Tata Tea, had maintained that Tata Tea's policy was not to buy protection but to earn it through the company's goodwill with employees and the local community.[3] This approach did work in the company's favour until April 1993 when Bolin Bordoloi, a Tata Tea manager and the youngest son of Assam's first chief minister, Gopinath Bordoloi, was kidnapped from Guwahati. The Bodo militants demanded a ransom of $15 million (₹54 crore).

347

'We went from pillar to post pleading for support. I went to Mother Teresa, Kanchi Shankaracharya and even met Prime Minister Narasimha Rao to get support. While we got moral support, there was limited help,' recalled Kumar. The company decided not to risk the lives of 175 managers working across the Assam Valley. They were living like prisoners in the estates with the Assam Tea Protection Force shielding them. The company called all the managers to Calcutta and shared with them the company's inability to pay the militants. Conscious of the danger the managers and their families faced, Tata Tea proposed to pay them their full salary and pension, if they opted to retire and withdraw from Assam. The company urged them to return to their native places. 'Interestingly, not one manager responded to that. They all said that they will stand by their duty,' recalled Kumar.

In the meanwhile, the Bodos gradually reduced the ransom for Bordoloi from ₹54 crore to ₹5 lakh, the amount they had spent on keeping him in captivity. The Tatas did not agree even to that. However, they agreed to greater investments for the well-being of the Bodo community. Tata Tea was already managing sixty-three hospitals, 280 adult literacy centres, 173 childcare centres and 110 schools in the region.[4] When Bordoloi was released after eleven months, Tata Tea helped set up a sixty-five-bed referral hospital in the heart of Bodoland at an expense of ₹7 crore. When everyone thought that peace was finally 'achieved', it emerged as too good to last.

In 1995, following the example of Bodo militants, ULFA started demanding money from Tata Tea. ULFA chief Paresh Baruah wrote a letter to Kumar demanding 100 walkie-talkie sets. 'There was no question of buying and supplying military equipment, the value of which was about ₹8–10 lakh. This was an ethical issue. Firstly, it was a supply to militants. Secondly, it meant resorting to illegal means for doing it,' he recollected. The company met and communicated all details to the Assam government. However, most of the information was supposedly leaked from the secretariat of Chief Minister Hiteswar Saikia. One late night, Kumar received a call from someone who claimed to be Baruah himself. He said that he had all the information that the Tatas were giving the government and threatened him. The Tatas now decided to go to the Intelligence Bureau (IB) of the Central government, the agency entrusted with matters pertaining national security. Kumar and his colleagues met IB's additional director several times. Every meeting was followed by letters to them, which were on record. The IB advised two things—don't pay the militants in cash or kind; continue the dialogue with them else they will retaliate.

Tata representatives met with ULFA representatives in different places, including Bangkok, and explained to them that as per the Tata code they would not be able to pay any protection money. Instead, they would willingly undertake work like building hospitals, providing jobs to locals and extending medical support. Consequently, a medical-aid scheme was introduced and funded by the Tatas through which any Assamese could apply for hospitalization within and outside the state. The IB was kept in the loop throughout. A year into this scheme, one of the patients, whose name was registered as Bonti Baruah and was treated in a pregnancy-related blood disorder in Bombay, was found to be Pranati Deka, ULFA's culture secretary. She, along with her baby, and her accomplices were arrested at Mumbai airport. The Prafulla Kumar Mahanta-led Assam government, which had not been kept in the loop due to past experience of information leakage, was furious and alleged collusion between the Tatas and the ULFA, and that the former was funding the latter—a charge of sedition. S.S. Dogra and Brojen Gogoi, Tata Tea managers, were even arrested for 'waging war against the state'.[5] The news hit national headlines—the Tatas were charged for treason! The matter went to the Guwahati High Court and eventually to the Supreme Court, which observed that the Tatas had approached the highest security agencies of the country, the police and the home ministry and provided all supporting documents while engaging with the militants. They could not be funding the ULFA and were not guilty.

Kumar recalled in an interview several years later:

> It is such a paradox that on one hand we had been charged with sedition by the authorities in power at that time, and on the other hand we had been directed and guided by the highest national security agency of the Government of India. We didn't disclose this publicly because we had 175 members of the Tata family across the Assam valley. And to disclose that would have been putting their lives at risk. So we decided not to do that and went through those nine months of gruelling challenges.[6]

The Tatas acted on the belief that the Centre will communicate with the state government, an assumption considered naïve by observers in an era of coalition politics. While the Assam government considered the Tatas' medical scheme a conspiracy to support militants, to many in Assam the real problem was the unflinching Tata principle of not paying.[7]

Yet, this was an example of how a lot of trouble could have been avoided by just paying a small amount of money. When there were large companies that had officially declared ransom payments, declaring the Tatas' actions as seditious just because they continued to engage with the militants on the advice of intelligence agencies smacked of a political witch-hunt. Several industry observers considered the Tatas' decision pragmatic—balancing business obligations with employee safety and fulfilment of social objectives for the local Assamese populace. Had the Tatas decided to exit from Assam, it would have had a serious impact on the local economy and affected the livelihoods of 20,000 labourers who worked in its twenty-one tea gardens. 'This is an example of how moral questions become issues when you run a company. Would you react by taking a soft option or would you take a hard decision based on ethics? The Tatas have taken this stance several times. It is part of our philosophy. It influences every decision we take,' concluded Kumar. It wasn't surprising then that Lalu Prasad Yadav, former chief minister of Bihar, had once observed, 'Going for anything illegal to the Tatas is like going to an Udupi restaurant and asking for a tandoori chicken!'[8]

Redefining the business of business

Three of America's most eminent industrialists were Jamsetji's contemporaries—Andrew Carnegie, J.P. Morgan, and John Rockefeller. Carnegie led the expansion of the US steel industry in the late nineteenth century and is often acknowledged as one of the richest Americans, who in later years donated almost 90 per cent of his fortune (approximately $350 million). Morgan was a financier who founded one of the most powerful banking houses of the world—J.P. Morgan and Company in 1895. Rockefeller is considered the richest person in modern history, who at the peak of his career, controlled 90 per cent of all oil in the USA and amassed a fortune worth nearly 2 per cent of the US national economy. He is also considered one of the greatest philanthropists who donated over $550 million to several causes in his lifetime. While each of these people is considered a titan of the American industry and a benevolent philanthropist, they are often referred to with the unpleasant label of 'robber barons'.[9] The primary reason being that they built their empires and fortunes by adopting tough postures with labour, rigging or breaking rules to favour their own businesses, and eliminating competition through predatory pricing and then overcharging when they had monopoly.

Jamsetji too replicated the wealth-creation characteristics of Carnegie, Morgan and Rockefeller and even their philanthropic priorities, though in much smaller measures. Yet, he can be referred to as a 'benign baron' because the means of earning his wealth were as benign as the purposes for which he bequeathed his fortune. He followed what contemporary organizational theorists refer to as the 'normative approach of stakeholder theory',[10] where managerial relationships with stakeholders are based on normative, moral commitments rather than an instrumental approach of using those stakeholders solely to maximize profits. Such a firm establishes certain fundamental moral principles that guide how it does business—particularly with respect to how it treats stakeholders—and uses those principles to drive decision-making. Through the discussion we've had in the preceding chapters, this resonates with the Tata way of business. It contrasts the instrumental use of ethics.[11] If the purpose of acting ethically is to acquire a good reputation that, in turn, will provide a firm with economic benefits, why not pursue the good reputation directly without the intellectual excursion into moral philosophy?[12]

An alternative view to the purpose of a corporation was proposed in 1970 by renowned American economist Milton Friedman, a Nobel laureate, and a colleague of my late grandfather Professor Chandrahas Shah, at the Chicago School of Economics. Through a widely cited article,[13] Friedman defined the goal of business as the sole pursuit of profit. His views have since been celebrated as 'the business of business is business'. This approach has remained a centre of controversy between economists and organizational theorists at both ends of the spectrum—those believing in a shareholder view of the firm and those convinced of the stakeholder-centric view of a firm. While Friedman's submission may have been relevant to the socio-economic conditions of developed economies like the USA and those in Western Europe, its applicability to underdeveloped and emerging economies of the world is highly debatable. J.R.D. contrasted his views when he said:

> In a poor country like ours in which so many people are economically deprived and oppressed, the social obligations of organized business and industry as I conceive them must go beyond the accepted duties of making a good product, selling it at a fair price, paying fair wages, providing good working conditions to labour and paying taxes in full.[14]

In my interactions with the senior-most executives of the Tata Group, I observed a basic belief that the ultimate objective of the group is to contribute to societal well-being through the Tata Trusts. If this wealth is generated by harming/ negatively impacting any of the stakeholders during the process of wealth creation, and then distributed as charity, it defeats the vision of the founding father who said 120 years ago, 'In a free enterprise, the community is not just another stakeholder in business, but is in fact the very purpose of its existence.' The foresight of a virtuous process of wealth creation was complimented in a lecture to the British Academy by Professor Colin Mayer, former dean of management at Oxford University. He emphasized that controlling ownership of companies should be in the hands of people who can ensure that directors discharge their responsibilities. He identified the Tatas among the world's best firms, owned by foundations pledged to pursue public good.[15]

The Tata approach is distinct from both —the one followed by American industrialists of the nineteenth century and that proposed by Friedman. It resonates with an increasingly popular opinion that beyond altruism or individual philanthropy, the opportunity for the business community is to find ways to leverage their networks, capital, people and technology to help create practical, sustainable, market-based approaches that help benefit society and underserved populations.[16] More than half a century ago, on the occasion of the diamond jubilee of Tata Steel, J.R.D. had defined the Tata way of business as per the fundamental objectives laid down by Jamsetji: To promote India's industrialization, to exploit material and manpower resources in the country's interest, to use the most modern and technological and managerial means, to promote the country's economic self-reliance, to develop human skills and productivity and, last but not the least, to make profits to be ploughed back into growth and modernization as well as to be shared between its shareholders and its employees. He concluded his submission by an assurance, 'It is my privilege to tell you that there is today and there will be in the future no deviation from these fundamental objectives.' Following this path has involved several trade-offs, many of which have been captured in this book. As Krishna Kumar rightly put it, 'There is a natural law where the right things succeed, and you must have belief in it. You may go through a tough time; sometimes face great challenges. But if you firmly hold on to your belief and go forward, you will succeed.'

While a lot of Tata initiatives were driven by the impulse to be charitable and good, some were also borne out of the understanding that they were operating in a country where the role of a corporation had to go beyond just running its core business, unlike advanced economies where developed infrastructure and institutions enabled efficient business operations. Right from inception, either because of its vision or the imperatives, the Tata Group strategically approached its long-term growth by seeing its role, not just as a taker of the ecosystem (society) but also the shaper of the ecosystem. In the process, they also filled several institutional voids. This is what has distinguished them from their peers.

Institutionalizing trusteeship?

'The first thing we look at is what is right for the nation and the larger economy; then we look at what is right for the Group; and then we look at what is right for the company and business. That is how the entire thought-process works in the Tata Group, and that is how this group has been for over a century.'[17]

Veermani Shankar

'A Tata never hoards', wrote an eminent journalist while describing Jamsetji's philosophy, who treated wealth as a trust and believed that what came from the people must, in a quintessential sense, return to them.[18] In a 2017 interview, Ratan Tata reflected:

> The Tata family could have become tremendously wealthy by having distributorships and partnerships in various businesses. But most companies were set up as institutions for the country . . . Personal ownership and personal wealth were never criteria for establishing Tata companies like Tata Steel or Tata Power.[19]

A quarter century earlier, J.R.D. too made a similar observation:

> What makes Indian families start industries? It is the very fact that family members, including children and nephews and the companies in a group can be separated and broken up. This is not the reason why Tata companies have been started.[20]

On another occasion, he had remarked, 'The Tatas are much too big to have a hereditary succession. The Tatas are, thank God, a national institution and must continue to be so.' The appointment of a professional manager as the chairman of Tata Sons is probably a continuation of this legacy.

The ideal of trusteeship owes its origin to the *Isha Upanishad* dating back several millennia.[21] In the twentieth century, Mahatma Gandhi attempted to contextualize it in the light of contemporary capitalism, where trusteeship meant that one owns one's wealth only as a trustee on behalf of others. Some scholars have considered this view of trusteeship as impractical, needing a mature approach that would emerge from smaller experiments whose lessons can provide solutions in implementing the idea.[22] While most corporations and their leaders have called the concept of trusteeship rather utopian, the Tatas' attempts in introducing beneficial labour welfare measures, integration of social welfare as part of its core corporate vision and mandate, standardizing ethical corporate behaviour through a detailed code of conduct, and an ownership structure that perpetuates a positive and synergistic relationship between business and society can be considered fine examples of the successful institutionalization of trusteeship over 100 years. J.R.D. once mentioned in an interview.

> The spirit of trusteeship as envisaged by Mahatma Gandhi is being done in our own House, because of our inheritance and the fact that we are owned by the trust. I think that is the best way to apply the spirit of trusteeship—to act as trustees and to consider the major problems of the country in connection with the operations of the firm as trustees and not as businessmen merely trying to make money for the firm.

A decade ago, international analysts had expressed concern that interesting dilemmas would emerge when the Indian economy slows down. At such times, Tata managers could look at expensive burdens such as Jamshedpur and the rural development projects as tempting targets for cost reduction. Or that Tata companies could lose interest in low-cost and mass market goods without a passionate chairman. Contrary to conjectures, increasing internationalization hasn't diluted the vital tenets of the Tata way of business. Instead, it has inspired international scholars and practitioners to take note of the fact that many of the theories in this field of management research have been vetted on the crucible of practice and measurable outcomes at Tata companies. During our conversation, Gopalakrishnan shared, 'The world is now enchanted with this new concept of "Conscious Capitalism".[23] When they see the Tatas, they are almost saying "Wow, you're already doing it! And doing it for 100 years."' It is no wonder that the Tatas are among the most studied Indian business group in leading business schools globally.[24]

Moreover, the ideal of trusteeship and the Tata way of business have inspired scores of people who have experienced the Tata ecosystem. One such example is Sudha Murthy, who in the early 1970s, was the first female engineer on Tata Motors' shop floor. However, what she recalls most is a single conversation she had with J.R.D. on the steps of Bombay House in 1982, when she had resigned from Tata Motors. 'So what are you doing, Mrs Kulkarni?' J.R.D. asked Sudha. 'Sir, I am leaving TELCO.' 'Where are you going?' he asked. 'My husband is starting a company called Infosys and I'm shifting to Pune.' 'Oh! And what you will do when you are successful?' was J.R.D.'s next question. 'Sir, I don't know whether we will be successful,' she humbly submitted. 'Never start with diffidence,' said J.R.D. 'Always start with confidence. When you are successful you must give back to society. You are only a trustee of that money. Society gives us so much; we must reciprocate.

I wish you all the best,' J.R.D. said while bidding her farewell.[25] That was the last time she met him in her life. However, that inspiration stayed with her. When Infosys superlatively succeeded, she started the Infosys Foundation in 1996. By 2016, it had an endowment of ₹4360 crore. J.R.D.'s words had catalysed the establishment of a foundation that contributed to social welfare at a scale he would never have imagined.[26]

At the other end of this spectrum of influence was a retired employee of Tata Motors, now eighty-two years of age. Satish Bhalchandra, deputy general manager at Tata Motors, shared with me his interaction with this former colleague. Once when he wasn't well, Satish had gone to visit him in Pune. Satish suggested that at that advanced age he should visit a temple or engage himself in some activities. The retired TELCO lifer said that he had only one God and pointed to the sole photo hanging on the wall of his house—that of J.R.D.. He told Satish that every year he visited his village in Konkan and distributed 50 per cent of the pension he received to boys and girls who couldn't pay school fees, and provided career guidance. This was the inspiration of the Tata way. Ravi Shankar Singh, head of HR at Tata Motors, Jamshedpur, shared a similar observation:

> People in Jamshedpur have phenomenal respect for senior leadership. Most of the houses here, besides their own God to whom they would be praying daily, also have the photograph of J.R.D. or Jamsetji. That is the kind of reverence employees have for the Tata family. You can't imagine any other industrialist acquiring a similar status.

He wasn't exaggerating. During my site visits to Tata companies, whether in Jamshedpur, Pune, Bangalore or Mumbai, I witnessed employees and local people touching the statue and photos of Jamsetji and J.R.D. with great reverence.

Perhaps, it was his modesty that had elevated J.R.D. to a seraphic stature. In the early 1940s, when the British government sent feelers to him on how he would respond to being knighted for the considerable support given by the Tatas to Britain's war efforts, J.R.D.'s response was that he wasn't interested. This was like Jamsetji declining the baronetcy in exchange for establishing the IISc. He was not willing for a quid pro quo. Half a century later, in 1992, when Ratan Tata brought him the news that he was being conferred the Bharat Ratna, the highest civilian award by the Government of India, J.R.D.'s first reaction was, 'Oh my God, why me? Can't we do something to stop it?' He remains the sole industrialist recipient of this award to date. On receiving the award, he had submitted, 'I do not want India to be an economic superpower. I want India to be a happy country.'

Phenomenal success in the new world order

> The Tatas are the one company in the world that combine the attributes of old-line industrial giants like US Steel, Dow Chemical and Ford, leading lights in the service sector like Hilton Hotels, major utilities like Commonwealth Edison and highly innovative newcomers like Microsoft and Compaq.[27]
>
> Harry Stonecipher

In the mid-1990s, a group of multinational executives had come to India to explore new opportunities in the country as part of a Harvard Business School executive education programme. Ratan Tata was invited to address them. During his talk, he explained some of the challenges that the group was going through. Up to the 1980s, the Tatas had not been in the highly lucrative businesses that gave enormous profits like fibres and fertilizers. Instead their key focus had been basic industries that were severely affected by bureaucratic controls. The Tatas' strength was in establishing manufacturing facilities and projects of a capital-intensive nature and managing them well. Businesses that required a trading instinct or retail businesses requiring marketing expertise such as textiles and toiletries had met with limited success. Another criticism of the Tatas was that they had lacked as hard a nose for profits as compared to other business groups despite technology leadership.

During that session, most multinational executives started lecturing him on how the Tata strategy would not be sustainable in a more liberalized environment. They suggested that the Tatas should focus on one or two core areas and divest other businesses. Professor C.K. Prahalad had written papers on similar lines. Professor Michael Porter was doing a study on India's competitiveness, and had published a CII report 'Developing India's Competitive Advantages' with Professor Pankaj Ghemawat, now at the Stern School of Business, and Babson College Professor U.S. Rangan.[28] Among other things, the report had suggested that business houses could soon become a thing of the past, and would not survive in new India without radical changes. Asia had witnessed the rise of many soup-to-nuts behemoths that thrived when economic tides were high and eventually fell apart. Some of these included Korea's Daewoo, Indonesia's Salim Group and Thailand's Charoen Pokphand.

Two decades later, most of their recommendations were disproved by the Tata Group by thinking global and implementing best-in-class practices. Under

Ratan Tata, sales had increased from ₹24,000 crore in 1991 to ₹600,000 crore in 2012, with 58 per cent of sales from overseas and worldwide employment reaching 450,000. As Adi Godrej observed, the Tatas' global acquisitions stirred the world into acknowledging the hitherto unknown concept of an 'Indian MNC'.[29] While retaining their top position in basic sectors like steel, heavy vehicles, power and chemicals, the group had substantially overcome their lack of success in certain industries such as retail through Titan or consumer durables through Voltas. Its expertise in the service sector was established through the phenomenal success of TCS. The group not only became globally competitive and globally present, but also gained industry leadership in most businesses. All this, without losing sight of core values and commitment to India. One can only imagine the achievements of J.R.D., had he lived and led the Tatas in the era of a liberalized Indian economy, for which he struggled all his life.

Yet, the period wasn't without mistakes, misjudgements and missed opportunities. We've discussed many in the preceding chapters. Let's look at areas of improvement highlighted by several scholars and industry observers. Incrementalism has been often highlighted as a characteristic of several Tata companies. Management typically tried to take a 360°view for problem-solving and analysed the implications of all actions before decision-making. This is sometimes referred to as 'management by slow manuring'. In the process, the speed of decision tended to slowdown, a handicap in the hypercompetitive era. Consequently, many Tata companies have been slow in restructurings, asset divestitures and efficiency improvements. 'Slimming the group down is one area where I have not succeeded in what I set out to do,' admitted Ratan Tata. The occasional outcome of having a visionary leader at the top can also be that several leaders on the next rung are waiting for instructions, rather than seizing opportunities in their own spaces, as much as they should. Problems may not be addressed as aggressively as it happened in the case of Tata Telecommunications. A former director of Tata Sons observed:

> I think the biggest challenge that we have in the group is that other than Ratan Tata, who has a global mindset and vision, the rank and file of the senior management of the group is extremely risk-averse. Their DNA is set in the accounting environment. They see more risk, more reasons why they shouldn't be audacious.[30]

Perhaps, that's the price one pays for having a big group and a visionary chair? There tends to be a tremendous amount of deference to the group headquarters and the chairman. In such situations, sometimes, CEOs of individual companies tend to behave like COOs, despite having the board's support. These are key challenges for a diversified group.

Oftentimes, there have been comparisons between the Tata Group and other global conglomerates. Given the differences in the macroeconomic situations, this would be a fallacious comparison. A better hypothesis would be: could the Tata Group have grown faster if it didn't have the group structure and was in India versus it had the group structure? The general observation is that most group companies suffer being part of large groups. Yet, well-run group companies benefit rather than suffer. The Tata Group would fall in the second category. Despite some limitations, Tata companies have benefited by being part of the group. They couldn't have done better if they were independent companies. The cohesive group structure facilitated larger investments in innovations, infrastructure and areas benefitting multiple stakeholders, besides giving them the most powerful brand. Putting in place such a cohesive structure can be considered the greatest achievement of Ratan Tata. 'He did a remarkable job,' admired Keshub Mahindra, chairman emeritus of the Mahindra Group.[31]

All along, I had envisaged listing a comprehensive set of operational principles that define the Tata way of business. As I conclude this Tata tome, I realize that these have been elaborately encapsulated in the TCOC, available in the public domain. However, it is the underlying culture that isn't easily measurable, but only anecdotally describable, that captures and communicates the Tata way of business. This unquantifiable undercurrent has been elaborated in this book in substantial measure. It was pithily described by J.R.D. several decades ago when he defined the House of Tata as a group of individually managed companies united by something more metaphysical, an innate loyalty and a sharing of certain beliefs. 'We all feel a certain pride that we are somewhat different from others,' he concluded.

The way forward

'I've spent a lot of time and energy trying to transform the Tatas from a patriarchal concern to an institutional enterprise . . . What I have done is establish growth mechanisms, play down individuals and play up the team that has made the companies what they are . . . If history remembers me at all, I hope it will be for this transformation.'

Ratan Tata

S. Ramadorai, former vice chairman of Tata Sons listed four key strengths of his successor at TCS and now group chairman, N. Chandrasekaran. The first is his ability to think big and consistently raise the benchmark. Second is a passion for excelling in execution. Third is his ability to build teams. 'Chandra will also bring the dimension of disruptions very well. He will not go just the traditional way. And if he does, I will be very disappointed,' he shared. These traits were in full display when at the Tata Group's annual leadership summit held at Taj Swarna in Amritsar in April 2018, he elaborated the 3S philosophy of simplification, synergy and scale to enable the group to scale newer heights. His vision of 'One Tata' aimed at harnessing the potential of firms and ensuring a collaborative approach, apart from simplifying and scaling up operations.[32]

Market observers surmised that Tata companies may be reorganized and brought down to a dozen, a desire Ratan Tata had expressed when he took charge in 1991. Would this be a reality? Only time will tell. Yet, one thing is certain. The Tata Group of the future may look very different from what it is today. Is this a matter of concern? Probably not. Business cycles are inevitable. The current top four Tata companies—TCS, Tata Motors, Titan and Tata Steel—considered a shutdown or merger at some point in their life. We've discussed those situations in the preceding chapters. As I conclude writing, three realignments are underway. In April 2018, there was an announcement of consolidating various businesses across aerospace and defence sectors under a single entity—Tata Aerospace and Defence. In July, there were media rumblings on a proposal to integrate food and beverage businesses under Tata Chemicals, Tata Coffee and Tata Global Beverages into a single company; and to bring the consumer and retail businesses like Infiniti Retail, Landmark and Titan under one umbrella.

In the hypercompetitive era in which modern-day companies operate, such changes may become essential. However, there is a need for constancy in the Tata way of business, even if businesses may change. Ratan Tata's vision clearly communicates this imperative:

> Businesses are cyclic. They will have their ups and downs. The group will look different over the next ten years. There will be companies that were not there earlier, and there will be companies which are there now, but won't be there ten years from now because they aren't relevant or sold to another company. The face of the Tatas may change. But so long as there is still the same drive to make this a conglomeration of enterprises that operate with ethical standards and value systems, I will be very proud.

During our conversation, Professor Narayandas captured this very sentiment about the future role of the Tata Group in one phrase, 'Living by Indian values; being globally competitive.'

A dream come true

In an interview to *Business India* four decades ago, J.R.D. had observed:

> There is no doubt that India has a tremendous future. I am getting old now and there is not much time ahead of me. I hope to get reborn and find myself wrong, but I am convinced that we are not going to grow as fast as we could. If we are less concerned with ideas and ideologies and more with practical down-to-earth programmes, our progress would be much faster.

If Jamsetji and J.R.D. were reborn and around today, they would see that the country they had dedicated their life to has risen from deprivation under colonial rule to become a global power, one of the most attractive investment destinations and the world's third-largest economy after the USA and China. That the institutions they seeded and nurtured have flourished to play a catalytic role in their nation's stupendous growth story—the Indian Institute of Science for which Jamsetji bequeathed half his estate is the topmost university in India; and the Tata Memorial Hospital for which Dorabji endowed a huge sum has emerged as the largest cancer-care hospital in Asia.

They would be proud to see that Tata companies have not only flourished financially but have also achieved gold standards in excellence and ethics as among India's most iconic companies. That Taj has emerged as one of Asia's largest group of hotels, Tata Steel ranks among the top ten steel makers in the world, Tata Power is India's largest integrated power and renewable energy company, Tata Chemicals is world's third-largest producer of soda ash, Tata Motors stands among the world's top ten commercial vehicle manufacturers, Tata Global Beverages prides itself as the world's second-largest tea company, and that TCS has not only been acknowledged as India's most valued company but also the second largest IT services company in the world. If Tata Group companies were listed as a single holding company, the group would be the world's forty-ninth most valuable conglomerate with a ₹10-trillion market capitalization.[33] All this while adhering to the founders' values. The Tata Group has not only been the torchbearers of industrial patriotism and business with a social conscience, but also trailblazers in every sphere of corporate activity—business excellence, globalization, innovation and wealth creation. Indeed, Jamsetji's dream of Tata companies contributing to the building of a new India has come true, 150 years later.

ACKNOWLEDGEMENTS

The world of the Tatas has always fascinated the researcher in me. Not only do they serve every industry—from the seas to the skies (as depicted on the cover page of this book), but also, for fifteen decades, their leadership and management philosophy have balanced the commercial and social imperatives of business. They have distinguished themselves through priorities and processes by evolving and practising an approach that can be referred to as the 'Tata way of business', which effectively combines international best practices with Indian values, and blends the capitalist spirit with socialist primacies. At a time when the world is undergoing serious problems—environmental, social, financial and emotional—corporations, which have been one of the most potent forms of collective effort towards the achievement of focused objectives, can play a major role in contributing to solutions through products, services, processes and practices. In contemporary times, corporations have the opportunity to transition from purely economic and profits-focused entities to those prioritizing value creation for several stakeholders. In the Tata story, I have found a strong resonance to the approach I subscribe to—where profits and social well-being can coexist; where profits are not at the expense of the society, but profits benefit society; where profits are not an end in themselves, but the means to a more noble end. This book has attempted to capture this essence through interactions with scores of Tata leaders, study of Tata literature published by national and international scholars as books, articles, case studies and research papers, and visits to Tata plants, sites, archives, and offices across India. I deem it my responsibility to thank all those who have contributed in substantial measure throughout this process of data collection, triangulation, analysis and publication.

The journey of this book began a decade ago. Ever since, I have personally interacted with nearly a hundred senior executives of the Tata Group. I am obliged to each of them for their participation and time. They were fine ambassadors of the Tata culture and values. In moments of inspired reflection, they shared with me their most valuable lessons, their most exciting experiences and their most difficult dilemmas, that have formed the basis of this book. To acknowledge their contribution, I have listed most of their names and organizational affiliations in the appendix. They are the real protagonists of this book.

I am personally grateful to Ratan Tata, chairman emeritus, Tata Sons, for his time and valuable insights during our personal interaction in August 2018. It was a joyous experience to converse with the tallest leader of India Inc. His humility, vision and commitment to purpose are truly inspiring. The book has truly benefited by his reflective and thought-provoking insights.

I wish to acknowledge the Tata executives who have helped me reach out to the wider Tata ecosystem and connected me with the senior leadership in various Tata companies over the last ten years. These include: R. Venkataramanan, managing trustee, Tata Trusts; G. Jagannathan, former executive vice president and global head of business excellence, TCS; Arun Gandhi, former director, Tata Sons; Satish Pradhan, former executive vice president—Group HR, Tata Sons; Radhakrishnan Nair, former vice president (talent acquisition), Tata Sons; and Siddharth Bhatt, senior consultant, Tata Sons. Rajendra Prasad Narla, archivist, Tata Central Archives, Pune; and Swarup Sengupta, manager, Tata Steel Archives, Jamshedpur, deserve a mention for providing me valuable documents from a rare collection of the Tata story dating back nearly twelve decades. The staff of Tata Motors and Tata Steel coordinated engaging visits to their plants in Jamshedpur and Pune, especially Ram Hudlikar and Satish Bhalchandra (Tata Motors Pune), Kalyan Raman (Tata Motors Jamshedpur); and Merlyn Anklesaria (Tata Steel Jamshedpur).

A special mention is due to Ashok Advani, publisher, Business India Group. He not only introduced me to several Tata stalwarts so that the book may benefit from their rich experiences, but also provided me access to over a thousand issues from the Business India archives published over the last forty years. The book has immensely benefitted from them. I am thankful to him and the Business India team for their time and assistance.

I owe an intellectual debt to my teachers and mentors in India and the USA who introduced me to the fascinating world of management research, inculcated methodological rigour in my approach to research and writing, and opened new vistas in my understanding of the interplay between the commercial and social dimensions of business in the developed and emerging economies. Over the last decade and a half of my association with academia, I have benefited from enriching discussions with my colleagues and stimulating conversations with my students. They are too numerous to be listed here. Yet, I truly appreciate their time and acknowledge their role in catalysing my thoughts.

Several of my former students assisted me in various ways while writing this book. I truly value their enthusiasm and commitment. Amruth Sundarkumar deserves special thanks for collating and analysing financial data across dozens of

Tata companies. Our discussions resulted in interesting insights into the financial successes of the Tata Group. Aditya Arvind has been a great asset and assisted me in designing all the infographics presented in this book. He also contributed markedly to the sections on the TCS story. His novel ideas and creativity are impressive. Aditya Deshpande, an aviation aficionado, contributed to the section on the Tatas' aviation story. Jagannath Srinivas and Kundan Madireddy helped with the transcription of interviews at various stages. Lakshmikant Sharma and Sai Santosh Shetty helped with the audiovisuals. Nikhil Koushik shared many insightful comments on select chapters of the book. It was wonderful working with them in the making of this Tata tome.

The Tata Group portals and publications, including the archival volumes of *Tata Review* provide very valuable information on Tata companies and leaders. I wish to commend the team of writers and editors for their enriching contributions that have immensely benefited this book.

With the information explosion on the Internet, there has also been a meteoric rise in the number of websites providing authentic and referenced information about diverse topics and individuals relating to multifarious fields of study. I have had the benefit of accessing these to cross verify numerous details on individuals, institutions and events. I appreciate the efforts of those who contribute, collate and maintain these high-quality storehouses of genuine information and provide free access to world citizens.

My publishers deserve a special mention. Lohit Jagwani, my commissioning editor, co-created the vision that this book should be a definitive account of the Tata Group in its 150th year. Over the next eighteen months, he shared interesting ideas and highlighted pertinent issues that I could consider. He has made this journey insightful and inspiring. I also thank Indrani Dasgupta, my copy editor, for accommodating many last-minute corrections; and Khyati Behl, my marketing and publicity executive for her ideas on spreading the good word about the book on all platforms. I appreciate the entire team of Penguin Random House for their professionalism and the wonderful format in which the book has been released. They truly deserve being India's leading publisher for delighting their authors throughout a collaborative journey from ideation to distribution.

Finally, I express profound gratitude to my guru, Sri Sathya Sai, for exposing me to the fascinating world of Indian culture and spirituality during the formative years of my life. Our conversations and his discourses have had a profound influence on my life. His message and mission perennially inspire me. For over two decades, I have also been a beneficiary of Sri Sathya Sai educational and service institutions in India and overseas that provide an extraordinary ecosystem for self-discovery and nation building. I am also indebted to my mother, Shefali, for her loving care. Her selfless affection and unconditional support are my greatest strengths.

This book, the third in a series of many more, is an attempt to make business reading more accessible by sharing stories and ideals about institutions and individuals that make every Indian proud. I believe each reader would have found in this book ideas and inspiration based on the success and learnings of India's most-admired conglomerate. I thank my readers for their time and hope they have enjoyed reading this book as much as I did writing it. I'd be delighted to receive your thoughts, comments and feedback. For more stories, interviews, and other audio-visual resources, do visit my website: www. shashankshah.com

APPENDIX

Select Personal Interviews at the Tata Group of Companies (2008–18)

Name of the Interviewee (In alphabetical order)	Current/Last Designation at the Company	Name of the Company
A.B. Lall	Head, Jamshedpur Plant	Tata Motors Ltd
A.N. Singh	Trustee and Adviser	Sir Dorabji Tata Trust
Abanindra Misra	Chairman	Tata Sponge Iron Ltd
Ajoy Chawla	Vice President and Global Business Head	Titan Company Ltd
Alka Talwar	Chief Sustainability Officer	Tata Chemicals Ltd
Alka Upadhyay	Assistant Vice President (Sustainability)	Tata Sons
Amar Sinhji	Head, HR	Tata Capital
Amit Chincholikar	Vice President, Group HR	Tata Sons
Amiya Kumar Singha	Head, Manufacturing Support	Tata Motors Ltd
Anand Sen	President, TQM and Steel Business	Tata Steel Ltd
Anant Nadkarni	Vice President (Group CSR)	Tata Sons
Arun Gandhi	Director	Tata Sons
Arup Basu	President, New Businesses and Innovation Centre	Tata Chemicals Ltd
Avinash Patkar	Chief Sustainability Officer	Tata Power Ltd
Balagopalan	Director (Exports)	Tata Motors Ltd
Bhaskar Bhat	Managing Director	Titan Company Ltd
Biren Bhuta	Chief, CSR	Tata Steel Ltd
C.P. Lohia	Head, Procurement	Tata Motors Ltd

Deepa Misra Harris	Senior Vice President, Sales and Marketing	The Indian Hotels Company Ltd
Dilip Huddar	Head, Purchase and Supplier Quality	Tata Motors Ltd
Durga Dutt Pathak	Head, Corporate HR	Tata Steel Ltd
Faqir Chand Kohli	Director	Tata Sons
Farokh N. Subedar	Chief Operating Officer and Company Secretary	Tata Sons
G. Jagannathan	Executive Vice President and Global Head, Business Excellence and Quality	Tata Technologies
Girish Wagh	Head, Commercial Vehicle Business Unit	Tata Motors Ltd
H.N. Shrinivas	Senior Vice President (HR)	The Indian Hotels Company Ltd
Harish Bhat	Brand Custodian	Tata Sons
Hoshang Sethna	Company Secretary	Tata Motors Ltd
Ishaat Hussain	Chairman	Voltas Ltd
Jamshed J. Irani	Managing Director	Tata Steel Ltd
Jayant Pendharkar	Global Head (Marketing)	Tata Consultancy Services Ltd
K. Ganesan	Vice President (HR)	Tata Consultancy Services Ltd
Karambir Kang	Area Director (USA)	The Indian Hotels Company Ltd
Kishor Chaukar	Managing Director	Tata Industries
K.R.S. Jamwal	Executive Director	Tata Industries
Kulvin Suri	Chief, Corporate Communications	Tata Steel Ltd
L.R. Natarajan	Chief Executive Officer - New Businesses	Titan Company Ltd
Lt. Col. M. Ravishankar	Senior Manager, HR	Tata Management Training Centre
Mukund Rajan	Chief Ethics and Group Sustainability Officer	Tata Sons
Mukundan Ramakrishnan	Managing Director	Tata Chemicals Ltd
N.K. Sharan	Vice President	Tata Business Excellence Group

Prakash Telang	Chairman	Tata Hitachi Construction Machinery Company Ltd
Prasad Menon	Chairman	Vistara
Prasann Kumar Chobe	Senior Vice President and Head Manufacturing Operations	Tata Motors Ltd
Praveen Kadle	CEO	Tata Capital
R. Gopalakrishnan	Director	Tata Sons
R. Venkataramanan	Managing Trustee	Tata Trusts
R.K. Krishna Kumar	Director	Tata Sons
Radhakrishnan Nair	Head (Talent Acquisition), Group Human Resources	Tata Sons
Rajendra Prasad Narla	Archivist	Tata Central Archives
Rajesh Dahiya	Head, Tata Administrative Services and Sourcing – Group HR	Tata Sons
Ranjit Joshipura	Deputy General Manager (Innovation)	Tata Sons
Ratan Tata	Chairman Emeritus	Tata Sons
Ravi Arora	Vice President, Innovation, Group Technology and Innovation Office	Tata Sons
Ravi Kant	Vice Chairman	Tata Motors Ltd
Ravi Shankar Singh	Head, Human Resources	Tata Motors Ltd
Raymond Bickson	Managing Director	The Indian Hotels Company Ltd
S. Padmanabhan	Chairman	Tata Business Excellence Group
S. Ramadorai	Vice Chairman	Tata Consultancy Services Ltd
Sangamnath Digge	Plant Head (CVBU), Pune	Tata Motors Ltd
Sanjay Daflapurkar	Corporate Head (Business Excellence)	Tata Motors Ltd
Sanjaya Sharma	CEO	Tata Interactive Systems
Satish Bhalchandra	Assistant General Manager (Government Affairs)	Tata Motors Ltd

Satish Borwankar	Executive Director, Quality	Tata Motors Ltd
Satish Pradhan	Head (Group HR)	Tata Sons
Saurav Chakrabarti	Assistant Vice President	Tata Business Excellence Group
Shahnawaz Alam	Vice President	Tata Steel Workers' Union, Jamshedpur
Sree Raman	Senior General Manager (Customer Service)	Tata Motors Ltd
Syamal Gupta	Director	Tata Sons
T.R. Doongaji	Managing Director	Tata Services Ltd
Tridibesh Mukherjee	Deputy Managing Director	Tata Steel Ltd
Urmila Ekka	Head, Tribal Culture Centre	Tata Steel Ltd
Vasant Ayyappan	Director, Corporate Sustainability	The Indian Hotels Company Ltd
Venkatadri Ranganathan	Chief Operating Officer	Rallis India Ltd
Vinod Kulkarni	Head, CSR	Tata Motors Ltd
Vishwa Mohan Prasad	Head, CSR (Jamshedpur)	Tata Motors Ltd
Vivek Talwar	Chief Culture Officer and Chief Sustainability Officer	Tata Power Ltd
Wilson J.S.	Head, Car Plant (PVBU)	Tata Motors Ltd

NOTES

[In manuscript form, this book had over 1500 endnotes, including detailed references, meanings of technical terms, elaborations on specific anecdotes and additional fact files. Publishing all of them would have made the book unacceptably bulky. So, at the publisher's instance, it was decided with regret to omit most them, and only retain the most important references. For those interested, most of the omitted notes can be accessed on my website: www.shashankshah.com]

Introducing an Institution That Needs No Introduction

1   Anantha Narayan et al., 'Tata Group: Back to Business', *Credit Suisse Asia Pacific/ India Equity Research Report*, 13 July 2017.
2   The value of a company/group of companies traded on the stock market. It is calculated by multiplying the total number of shares by the present share price.
3   N.S.B. Gras, 'A Great Indian Industrialist: Jamsetji Nusserwanji Tata, 1839–1904', *Bulletin of the Business Historical Society* 23, no. 3 (September 1949).
4   In the late 1910s, lawyer-businessman F.E. Dinshaw had lent over ₹2 crore to the Tata Group when its major companies were in financial trouble. When the Tatas could not repay the loan, the outstanding amount was converted into one-eighth share in Tata Sons' commissions. Dinshaw transferred the rights to the commission to his private company, which was acquired in full by the SP Group by 1965. It is reported that J.R.D.'s siblings also sold part of their shareholding to the SP Group. All these amount to their current holding of 18.4 per cent. In quantitative terms, their investments in Tata Sons appreciated from ₹70 crore in 1965 to ₹58,000 crore in 2016.

Chapter 1: Energy of a Prophet, Courage of a Pioneer

1   Gyaneshwar Chaubey et al., '"Like Sugar in Milk": Reconstructing the Genetic History of the Parsi Population', *Genome Biology* 18, no. 110 (2017).
2   Several biographical facts on Jamsetji sourced from: R.M. Lala, *For the Love of India: The Life and Times of Jamsetji Tata* (New Delhi: Penguin Books, 2004).
3   Dinsha Edulji Wacha, *The Life and Life Work of J. N. Tata* (Miami: Hardpress Publishing, 2013).
4   Angus Maddison, *The World Economy* (Paris: OECD Publishing, 2006).
5   Several facts on the Tatas' history are sourced from the documentary 'Keepers of the Flame' by Zafar Hai.
6   Subrata Roy, 'Tatas' Textile Troubles: Death of the Empress', *Business India*, 2–15 June 1986.
7   N. Benjamin, 'Jamsetji Nusserwanji Tata: A Centenary Tribute', *Economic and Political Weekly*, 28 August 2004.
8   Several facts have been sourced from: *The Golden Jubilee Book of The Empress Mills*, Nagpur (1877–1927).

9   During the course of writing this book, I came to know of a familial bond I have
        with Empress Mills. In the early 1970s, my late great-grandfather Natwarlal Shah
        was invited by Naval Tata, then deputy chairman of Tata Sons, to serve as general
        manager at Empress Mills for two years.

10   R.D. and Jamsetji had a common ancestor in Ervard Tata. Nusserwanji Tata had
        married the sister of R.D.'s father—Dadabhoy Tata.

11   Umakant Varottil, 'Corporate Law in Colonial India: Rise and Demise of the
        Managing Agency System', *NUS Law Working Paper 2015/16*, December 2015.

12   Dwijendra Tripathi and Jyoti Jumani, *The Concise Oxford History of Indian Business*
        (New Delhi: Oxford University Press, 2017).

13   Several biographical facts are sourced from: Frank Harris, *Jamsetji Nusserwanji Tata:
        A Chronicle of His Life* (New Delhi: Penguin Books, 2007).

14   Several biographical facts on Tata Group companies across the book have been
        sourced from: R.M. Lala, *The Creation of Wealth: The Tatas from the 19th to the 21st
        century* (New Delhi: Penguin Books, 2004).

15   Shashank Shah, *Win-Win Corporations: The Indian Way of Shaping Successful
        Strategies* (New Delhi: Penguin Random House India, 2016).

16   *100 Years of Glory*, The Taj Centenary Issue 32, no. 1 (2003).

17   Frederick James, 'The House of Tata—Sixty Years Industrial Development in India',
        Journal of the Royal Society of Arts 96, no. 4776 (27 August 1948).

18   R.H. Mody and S.S. Vaze, 'The Steel Market', *Tata Steel Diamond Jubilee 1907–67*
        (Mumbai: Tata Press Ltd, 1967).

19   R. Balasubramaniam, 'On the Corrosion Resistance of the Delhi Iron Pillar', *Corrosion
        Science* 42 (2000).

Chapter 2: For the Love of India

1   Several historical facts sourced from the Tata Steel Archive in Jamshedpur.

2   It was ten times the amount the world's richest man—the Nizam of Hyderabad—
        eventually gave for IISc.

3   Jamsetji even proposed that an additional five per cent from the profits of Empress
        Mills be diverted to the new scheme. However, his colleagues objected; he was hurt.
        This idea of a proportion of profits being used for a social cause emerged in 2013, when
        the Government of India mandated Corporate Social Responsibility (CSR) spending at
        2 per cent of profits after tax. Once again, Jamsetji's idea was much ahead of his times.

4   Since inception, IISc has been a tripartite venture between the Tatas, the Government
        of India and the Government of Karnataka. Given its national importance, the
        Government of India bears the expenses.

5   Topmost scientists, including M. Visvesvaraya, Homi Bhabha, Vikram Sarabhai,
        Suri Bhagavantam, Satish Dhawan, and C.N.R. Rao, who have played a key role in
        India's scientific and technological progress, have been closely associated with IISc in
        various capacities.

6   Goolam E. Vahanvati, ' . . . And Then the Lights Came on', *100 Years of Glory*, Taj
        Centenary Issue 32, no. 1 (2003).

7   Several facts have been sourced from the biographical account published in the
        centenary year of Tata Power: Anil Dharker, *Invisible Goodness: The Story of Tata
        Power* (New Delhi: Roli Books India, 2016).

8   Tirthankar Roy, *The Economic History of India 1857–1947* (New Delhi: Oxford
        University Press India, 2018).

9   R.M. Lala, *The Heartbeat of A Trust: The Story of Sir Dorabji Tata Trust* (New Delhi: Tata McGraw–Hill, 1998).

Chapter 3: Evolution of India's Numero Uno

1   Several personal anecdotes and quotes of J.R.D. Tata throughout the book sourced from his authorized biography: R.M. Lala, *Beyond the Last Blue Mountain: A life of J.R.D. Tata* (New Delhi: Penguin Books, 1993).

2   Nitin Nohria et al., 'J.R.D. Tata', 9-407-061 (Boston: Harvard Business School Publishing, 2014).

3   Peter Casey, *The Greatest Company in the World? The Story of Tata* (New Delhi: Penguin Books, 2014).

4   Bakhtiar Dadabhoy, *'Jeh' A Life of JRD Tata* (New Delhi: Rupa and Co., 2005).

5   In an interview with Rajiv Mehrotra broadcast on Doordarshan in the late 1980s.

6   Homi Bhabha was the son of Lady Meherbai Tata's brother Jehangir Bhabha. His brother Jamshed Bhabha was the founder of the National Centre for Performing Arts, established in 1980 at Nariman Point in Bombay.

7   Tata chairmen after Jamsetji were not blessed with progeny. Consequently, most of their holdings in Tata Sons were transferred during their lifetime to public welfare trusts.

8   Under Nowroji's chairmanship, the Tatas depended on external experts for key technical advice. J.R.D. believed that such advice should be available in-house.

9   M.J. Akbar, 'A Man Called Jamsetji Tata and His Love Affair with Bombay', *100 Years of Glory*, Taj Centenary Issue 32, no. 1 (2003).

10   Named after an eponymous French Opera, Lakmé also resembled the Sanskrit word 'Lakshmi', the goddess of wealth, also used to refer to women of Indian households.

11   K. Balakrishnan et al., 'A Comparative Study of the Growth and Strategy of Two Large Indian Business Houses, Birlas and Tatas', IIM Ahmedabad, 1980.

12   During this complex exercise, J.R.D. nominated the managing director in each company and another director from the Tata ecosystem. All other directors were from outside the group, thereby giving the companies substantial autonomy. He did not yield to the temptation of appointing family members on the boards of companies, a practice adopted by most other family owned managing houses. He was commended for his statesman-like approach by industry peers.

13   The other eminent Tata leaders of the 1970s and the 1980s included Nani Palkhivala at ACC, Ajit Kerkar at Taj Hotels, P.A. Narielwala at TOMCO, A.H. Tobaccowala at Voltas, Freddie Mehta at Forbes Gokak, and F.C. Kohli at TCS.

14   J.R.D. Tata, 'Ratan is a better manager than I am', *Business India*, 23 December 1991–5 January 1992.

15   Andrew Gowers and Krishna Guha, 'Giant Steps for a Corporate Colossus,' *Financial Times*, 2 August 2005.

16   K.G. Kumar and Madhav Reddy, 'Ratan Tata: The End of Innocence', *Business India*, 23 December 1991–5 January 1992.

Chapter 4: A New Tata for a New Century

1   Ratan Tata has shared this conversation in several interviews. Two of them were an interview on BBC with Karan Thapar (2000) and Rendezvous with Simi Garewal (1997).

2   Naval Burjor Ghiara, 'A Smooth Succession', *Business India*, 1–14 April 1991.

3 Ratan Tata interviewed by Tarun Khanna in Mumbai on 27 April 2015, *for* Creating Emerging Markets Oral History Collection, Baker Library Historical Collections, Harvard Business School.

4 Nazneen Karmali and A.B. Ravi, 'Living in Today's World', *Business India*, 19 June–2 July 1995.

5 Nazneen Karmali, 'A Spoke in the Deal', *Business India*, 21 June–4 July 1993.

6 Azhar Kazmi, *Strategic Management and Business Policy* (New Delhi: Tata McGraw-Hill, 2008).

7 Ratan Tata, 'We Must Keep Questioning the Unquestioned', *Business India*, 19 June–2 July 1995.

8 The Tatas sold their entire stake in Forbes to the Shapoorji Pallonji Group in 2004. Tata Infotech merged with TCS post 2004.

9 Some of these included group strategic sourcing, group legal, group HR, group corporate affairs, the public affairs department, department of economics and statistics, and provision of financial services to group companies.

10 Under subsequent chairmen—Cyrus Mistry and N. Chandrasekaran—this structure has undergone modification.

11 'Brand Name to Survive Personalities: Ratan', *Economic Times*, 14 October 1996.

12 Tarun Khanna and Krishna Palepu, 'House of Tata-2000: The Next Generation (B)', 9-704-408 (Boston: Harvard Business School Publishing, 2006).

13 Morgen Witzel, *Tata: The Evolution of a Corporate Brand* (New Delhi: Penguin Books, 2010).

Chapter 5: Tata Culture, A Way of Life

1 Ratan Tata, 'Industry Has Lived in a Protected Environment', *Business India*, 21 December 1981—3 January 1982.

2 Nirmalya Kumar et al., *India's Global Powerhouses: How They Are Taking on the Word* (Boston: Harvard Business Review Press, 2009).

3 Sunil Kumar Maheshwari and M.P. Ganesh, 'Ethics in Organizations: The Case of Tata Steel', *Vikalpa* 31, no. 2 (April–June 2006).

4 Elankumaran S. et al., 'Transcending Transformation: Enlightening Endeavours at Tata Steel', *Journal of Business Ethics* 59 (2005): 109–19.

5 Arun Maira, 'Complex Conglomerates', *Business India*, 5–18 August 2002.

6 Dev Chatterjee, 'Dilip Pendse (1956–2017): Member of Tata Group's Innermost Circle in 1990s', *Business Standard*, 6 July 2017.

7 Pendse was found guilty in two of the six complaints filed against him and was jailed for eighteen months. Frustrated with legal cases and unable to bear the stress, he committed suicide in July 2017.

8 Harish Bhat, *Tata Log: Eight Modern Stories from a Timeless Institution* (New Delhi: Penguin Books, 2012).

9 Under the original agreement between Tata and NTT DoCoMo, the latter had the right to request a buyer for its stake at a fair market price or 50 per cent of its acquired price, amounting to ₹7250 crore, whichever was higher.

10 Sunil Damania, 'Why Tata Failed in Mobile Services', *Business India*, 23 October–5 November 2017.

11 Deepali Gupta, 'Tata Group Pays Back Rs 17,000 Crore of Teleservices Debt to Banks', *Economic Times*, 11 January 2018.

12 Raveendra Chittoor et al., 'Creating a Corporate Advantage: The Case of the Tata Group', (Hyderabad: Indian School of Business, 2013).

13 Nandita Datta and Srinivas Alam, 'How the Cash Will Flow', *Outlook*, 28 June 2004.

Chapter 6: Decoding India's Number One Brand

1   The value of all brands of the Tata Group can be far more than the value of the Tata corporate brand itself.

2   Naga R. Sandhya and Girija P., 'Tata Tea's Jaago Re! Campaign: The Social-Cause Marketing Initiatives and Long-Term Branding Initiatives', *IUP Journal of Brand Management* VIII, no. 2 (2011).

3   Dina Arzoo, 'The Great Indian Brandwagon is Taking Off', *Business India*, 15–28 September 2014.

4   'From Pupil to Master', *The Economist*, 2 December 2012.

Chapter 7: Wealth Creation, with a Difference

1   As a potential shareholder in the Tata Group in yesteryears, without accounting for any bias, one would prefer to invest their capital equally in all the companies given the uncertainties around the industries amongst other factors. This equal-weighted allocation would also eliminate the bias of studying returns of select few companies that have contributed to higher returns in hindsight and allocating more capital towards them.

2   Annualized returns a.k.a. compounded annual growth rate (CAGR) refers to the growth rate that takes an initial investment to its ending value assuming it compounds over the time period measured. This is a prominent industry metric of investment returns in particular. Our analysis includes reinvesting dividends back into the stocks and thus we compute the 'total returns' a.k.a. compounded annual total shareholder returns (CATSR).

3   It denotes the profitability/profits made per unit of an investment in the company's stock. It takes the net income and divides it by the value of the shareholders' equity and is expressed in terms of a percentage.

4   Among the several conglomerates across India, our criteria saw the Reliance Group and the Aditya Birla Group as the best fit for comparison. The criteria included those with:
    i.   Annual revenues of over $10 billion; and
    ii. At least three entities listed before 2008.

5   Traditional investment literature talks about diversification benefits to reduce risk which brings its own effects through marginally lower expected returns. The case in point with the Tata Group as a whole reduces the risk of the portfolio and provides exceptional returns too—a twofold benefit.

6   Annualized total returns are computed by reinvesting dividends in the respective company stocks in addition to the price appreciation of the stock over the time period in consideration.

7   Three criteria used for shortlisting Siemens, GE and Mitsubishi include:
    i.   All conglomerates have a global presence and are among the biggest, most recognized brands in their continents,
    ii. All are publicly listed with multiple subsidiaries,
    iii. Revenues top $90 billion, and
    iv. All have a history of over 100 years.

Chapter 8: In Search of Excellence: From Existential Crisis to the Zenith of Quality

1   Several facts on Tata Steel have been sourced from: R.M. Lala, *The Romance of Tata Steel* (New Delhi: Penguin Books, 2007).

2   Gita Piramal, *Business Legends* (New Delhi: Penguin Books, 1998).

3   J.D. Choksi, 'Building up the "Mother Industries"', *Tata Steel Diamond Jubilee 1907–67* (Mumbai: Tata Press Ltd, 1967).

4   On two occasions when the government did give permission, geopolitical situations marred the proposals. For example, in 1966 when a 40-lakh tonne strip mill plant was confirmed, the sudden devaluation of the rupee rendered it unfeasible. Again in 1973, when a 50-lakh tonne expansion plan was confirmed with the guidance of Nippon Steel, the Arab–Israel war shot up the fuel prices, thereby making the expansion unfeasible.

5   In 1992, Russi Mody came to know of a 1.5-million-tonne blast furnace ordered by Portugal that was lying unused due to restrictions imposed by the European Union, which did not want any of its member countries to increase steel production capacity. Mody was quick to identify the opportunity and Irani personally visited Portugal to inspect the furnace and negotiate with the sellers. The $700-million blast furnace was acquired for $250 million by Tata Steel. This was a fresh addition to Tata Steel's plant since 1958. This saved precious time and money, which it would have otherwise invested in engineering and building a new blast furnace.

6   Rudrangshu Mukherjee, *A Century of Trust: The Story of Tata Steel* (New Delhi: Penguin Books, 2008).

7   *Business of Excellence: The Tata Journey*, (Mumbai: Tata Group Publications, 2008).

8   Tata Steel's scope of work was broadly classified into five industries within the steel industry: First was core steel making. Second was the engineering industry to feed the steel industry. The third was the mining industry. Fourth were the services such as running townships, hospitals, etc. Lastly, it had small businesses not necessarily connected with steel making, such as anti-friction-bearings industries and selling of ferro-alloys.

9   A holistic and firm-wide approach involving the management and employees that views continuous improvement in all aspects of an organization as a process and not as a short-term goal.

10   R. Jayaraman, 'Impact of Business Excellence on Organisational Excellence', *Drishtikon: A Management Journal* 4, Issue 2 (March–September 2013).

11   Sunil Mithas, *Making the Elephant Dance: The Tata Way to Innovate, Transform and Globalize* (New Delhi: Penguin Books, 2015).

12   *WSD*'s viewpoint was based on a variety of items, including Tata Steel's own raw material supply, low operating costs, a special company culture, good profitability, expansion prospects and location in a country in which demand for steel would grow substantially in the future.

13   Shivanand Kanavi, 'New Steel in Old Bottle', *Business India*, 23 July to 5 August 2001.

14   Robert Kaplan and David Norton, 'The Balanced Scorecard: Measures That Drive Performance', *Harvard Business Review*, 1992.

15   TPM focuses on engaging operators to improve equipment effectiveness with an emphasis on proactive and preventative maintenance.

16   A method that identifies and removes the causes of defects and minimizes variability in manufacturing and business processes.

17   A measure of a company's financial performance based on the residual wealth calculated by deducting its cost of capital from its operating profit, adjusted for taxes on a cash basis.

18   Sudipt Dutta and Ranjan Kocherry, 'Learning to survive', *Business India*, 13–26 July 1998.

Chapter 9: Tatas' First 100-Billion-Dollar Company; India's Most Valued

1   Jatin Desai, *Innovation Engine Driving Execution for Breakthrough Results* (New Jersey: Wiley, 2013).

2   Tata Burroughs became Tata Unisys in 1986. A decade later, Tata Sons bought out Unisys's interest in the company. The new entity was called Tata Infotech Ltd. It was acquired by TCS in 2006.

3   M.G. Arun, 'Tech Giant: What Made JRD Tata Take the "Fateful" Decision to Start TCS', *India Today*, 11 August 2017.

4   Several facts on TCS have been sourced from the autobiographical account: S. Ramadorai, *TCS Story & Beyond*, (New Delhi: Penguin Books India, 2011).

5   Tata Consulting Engineers, Tata Economic Consultancy Services and Tata Financial Services.

6   Anil Dharker, *Invisible Goodness: The Story of Tata Power* (New Delhi: Roli Books, 2016).

7   Vinod Kumar et al., 'The Jewel in the Crown', *Business India*, 10–23 August 1998, pp. 52–61.

8   Shivani Shinde, '40 Years Ago . . . and Now—Faqir Chand Kohli: The Original Indian Techie', *Business Standard*, 4 February 2015.

9   John Roberts and Gary C. Mekikian, 'Tata Consultancy Services: Globalization of IT Services', IB-79 (USA: Stanford Graduate School of Business, 2009).

10   Aroon Sarker, 'The Mode is Upbeat', *Business India*, 16–29 September 1991.

11   Shivanand Kanavi, 'Megasoft', *Business India*, 7–20 June 2004.

12   During our conversation, he deeply regretted the partition of India on religious lines, and ascribed this blunder to the political ambitions of leaders belonging to both religions who wanted to lead their respective countries—Jawaharlal Nehru and Muhammad Ali Jinnah.

13   Shivanand Kanavi, 'TCS@50: Why India Must Be in Eternal Debt to FC Kohli', Rediff.com, 31 March 2018.

14   John Roberts et al., 'Tata Consultancy Services: Globalization of Software Services', S-SM-18, Graduate School of Business, Stanford University, 1995.

15   Subhash Bhatnagar, 'India's Software Industry', in *Technology, Adaptation, and Exports: How Some Developing Countries Got It Right* by Vandana Chandra, ed., World Bank, 2006.

16   Kanta Murali, 'The IIT Story: Issues and Concerns', *Frontline*, 1–14 February 2003.

17   I. Oshri, et al., 'Knowledge Transfer in Globally Distributed Teams: The Role of Transactive Memory', *Information Systems Journal* 18, no. 6 (2008): 593–616.

18   Robert Kennedy, 'Tata Consultancy Services: High Technology in a Low-Income Country', 9-700-092 (Boston: Harvard Business School Publishing, 2001).

19   Vivek Agrawal and Diana Farrell, 'Who Wins in Offshoring', *McKinsey Quarterly*, special edition, 2003.

20   Louis Fernandes and Raju Bist, 'Growing Beyond', *Business India*, 15–28 January 1996.

21   M.E. Porter, 'What Is Strategy?', *Harvard Business Review* 74, no. 6 (November–December 1996): 61–78.

22   N. Chandrasekaran and Geert Ensing, 'ODC: A Global IT Services Delivery Model', *Communications of the ACM* 47, no. 5 (May 2004).

23   An economic phenomenon where a developed nation (like the US) removes its barriers to international trade and integrates its labour market with those of nations with a lower cost of labour (such as India).

24   Michael Chu and Gustavo Herrero, 'Tata Consultancy Services Iberoamerica', 9-705-020 (Boston: Harvard Business School Publishing, 2005).

25   Pankaj Ghemawat and Steven Altman, 'Tata Consultancy Services: Selling Certainty', PG0-004 (Boston: Harvard Business School Publishing, 2011).

26   Vineet Nayar, *Employees First, Customer Second* (Boston: Harvard Business Review Press, 2010).

27   Interview on CNBC TV18, 15 February 2017.

28   Parthasarathi Swami and Soneera Sanghvi, 'Road Warrior', *Business India*, 6–19 January 2014.

29   Shishir Prasad and N.S. Ramnath, 'How Chandra Helped TCS Climb to the Top', *Forbes India*, 11 July 2011.

30   It provided an integrated suite of hardware, network and software solutions; along with business, technical and consulting services.

31   Goutam Das, 'A Fine Run', *Business Today*, 5 January 2014.

32   T.V. Mahalingam, 'Here Is How TCS Bridged the Gulf with an All-Women BPO', *Economic Times*, 2 April 2016.

33   Rohit Deshpande, Tata Consultancy Services, 9-505-058 (Boston: Harvard Business School Publishing, 2009).

34   Saritha Rai, 'After $32 Billion Rally, TCS CEO Sees Path to Even Faster Growth', *Bloomberg Quint*, 31 May 2018.

35   Amit Mudgill, 'Guess What! TCS Alone Is Bigger Than Total M-Cap of All Listed Stocks in Pakistan', *Economic Times*, 23 April 2018.

36   The top ten IT services providers in the world were: Accenture, TCS, Cognizant, Wipro, IBM, HCL, Infosys, CapGemini, DXC Technologies and NTT Data.

37   Clayton Christensen, *The Innovator's Dilemma: When New Technologies Cause Great Firms to Fail* (Boston: Harvard Business School Press, 1997).

Chapter 10: Innovation: Tata Group's Mantra for the Twenty-First Century

1   Presidential address at the first general assembly of the Indian Institute of Science, Bangalore.

2   Kulkarni was responsible for planning and building TELCO township in Jamshedpur during 1953–66. He was nominated by Moolgaokar to lead factory and township planning and construction at TELCO's new Pune plant.

3   Krishna Palepu and Vishnu Srinivasan, 'Tata Motors: The Tata Ace', 9-108-011 (Boston: Harvard Business School Publishing, 2008).

4   N. Madhavan, 'Small Is Dominant', *Business Today*, 25 May 2014.

5   Ashok Pundir, 'Ace Will Help Companies Bring Down Logistics Costs', *Financial Express*, 30 September 2006.

6   C.P. Lohia, former general manager, mentioned that in 1996, Tata Motors was the first company to invest in a crash laboratory of international standards.

7   This contrasted with the 3S dealership model for large commercial vehicles where Tata Motors' dealers offered sales, service and spare parts.

8   Alex Perry, 'India's Tiger', *Time*, 20 November 2006.

9   Jim Collins and Jerry Porras, *Built to Last: Successful Habits of Visionary Companies* (New York: Harper Business, 1994).

10   Jeff Dyer et al., *The Innovator's DNA: Mastering the Five Skills of Disruptive Innovators* (Boston: Harvard Business Review Press, 2011).

11   Some of these include the Pune-based Tata Chemicals Innovation Centre; Tata Motors European Technical Centre at the University of Warwick; the Research, Development and Technology business of Tata Steel Europe that engages 950 researchers in the UK and the Netherlands; and the nineteen TCS innovation labs across India, the US and the UK.

12   Under the Tata Innovation Mission programme, senior Tata executives regularly visit global companies such as Microsoft, Intel, HP and 3M in the US; and Nissan, Fuji, Ito En, Olympus, Toshiba and Hitachi in Japan, to study how they foster innovation.

13   A group-level think tank, it consists of eighteen CXO-level members, one from each Tata company. TGIF organizes many events to facilitate interaction between Tata managers, innovation experts and academicians.

14   'The Ginger Chain—Smart Business at Work', in Prosenjit Dutta's *Innovation: Making Aspirations Count* (New Delhi: Businessworld Publications, 2010)

15   Address delivered at the All India Management Association JRD Tata Award for Corporate Leadership 2016.

16   According to a 2015 Euromonitor International Report, India's bottom-of-the-pyramid population consisted of 38 crore adults living on an annual disposable income of ₹3,25,000. This made India the largest bottom-of-the-pyramid market in the world.

17   Chitra Duvedi et al., 'Swach: Taking Concept to Business Reality', Case Study No. CS/2010-03, Tata Management Training Centre.

18   David Alhstrom, 'Innovation and Growth: How Business Contributes to Society', *Academy of Management Perspectives* 24, no. 3 (August 2010).

19   Run by franchisees, they provide farm extension services and agro-input supplies solutions.

Chapter 11: The Empire Strikes Back?

1   'TELCO Shareholders Reject Ratan Tata's Offer to Quit', *Business Standard*, 15 August 2001.

2   A similar car project by an international major would have cost between ₹3500 crore and ₹5000 crore.

3   Several facts are based on data accessed from archival documents at The Tata Central Archive, Pune.

4   Nazneen Karmali 'Businessman of the Year 1988: Sumant Moolgaokar', *Business India*, 26 December 1988–8 January 1989.

5   Harish Bhat, *Tata Log: Eight Modern Stories from a Timeless Institution* (New Delhi: Penguin Books, 2012).

6   'Tata Indica—Indigenous to the Core', in Prosenjit Dutta, ed., *Innovation: Making Aspirations Count* (Metro Manila: Businessworld Publications, 2010).

7   TELCO imported a second-hand Nissan assembly plant, not being used by its unit in Australia, at a bargain basement price of ₹103 crore. It was upgraded to raise capacity from 1,00,000 to 1,50,000 cars.

8   Roop Karnani et al., 'Racing Ahead', *Business India*, 5–18 May 1997.

9   Prasad Sangameshwaran, 'Getting It Right, the Second Time', *Business Standard*, 14 June 2013.

10 'When "Humiliated" Tata Did "Favour" to Ford with JLR Buyout!', *Businessworld*, 16 March 2015.

11 Gautam Kumra, 'Leading Change: An Interview with the Managing Director of Tata Motors', *McKinsey Quarterly*, 2006.

12 Philip Chacko, Christabelle Noronha and Sujata Agrawal, *Small Wonder: The Making of the Nano* (New Delhi: Westland, 2010).

13 Bala Chakravarthy et al., 'Tata Motors: Becoming a Global Contender', IMD463, IMD Lausanne, 2010.

14 Prashant Salwan, 'Growth and Internationalization: The Case of Tata Motors', *Indian Journal of Industrial Relations* 47, no. 1 (July 2011): 1–19.

15 Vivek Law, 'Three Years After Its Launch, Indica Becomes Top-Selling Car in Its Segment', *India Today*, 24 June 2002.

16 In March 2018, Tata Motors decided to phase out the Indica and the Indigo due to changing market dynamics.

17 Ranjit Pandit, 'What's Next for Tata Group: An Interview with Its Chairman', *McKinsey Quarterly*, 2005.

18 In their widely cited work on 'emerging markets', professors Tarun Khanna and Krishna Palepu from Harvard Business School, have defined economic stage one as markets in less-developed countries in Africa, stage two as countries like China and India, stage three as countries such as Brazil and South Korea, and stage four countries as fully developed markets like the USA and countries in western Europe.

19 The other seven were: HDFC Bank, ICICI Bank, Satyam Computers, Wipro, VSNL, MTNL and Dr Reddy's.

20 It refers to the management, financing and strategy involved with buying, selling and combining companies. Merger is combining two companies to form one, while acquisitions is when one company is taken over by another.

21 Choe Sang-Hun, 'In Daewoo, GM Finds Gold in Overall Gloom', *New York Times*, 23 May 2006.

22 Sanjay Singh et al., 'Tata Motors' Acquisition of Daewoo Commercial Vehicle Company', 908M94 (Ontario: Ivey Publishing, 2017).

23 Ratan Tata interviewed by Tarun Khanna in Mumbai on 27 April 2015, for Creating Emerging Markets Oral History Collection, Baker Library Historical Collections, Harvard Business School.

24 Arijit De and Parvathy Ullatil, 'We Will Like to Better Daewoo HCV Mart Share: Ravi Kant', *Business Standard*, 8 March 2004.

25 In October 2009, Tata Motors acquired the remaining 79 per cent stake in the company.

26 Joe Leahy, 'Tata Near Deal with Ford on Jaguar/Land Rover', *Financial Times*, 27 February 2008.

27 Nick Clark, 'Tata in Pole Position to Buy Jaguar and Land Rover Marques from Ford', *Independent*, 4 January 2008.

28 John Reed and Jonathan Guthrie, 'Land Rover, Jaguar Could Go Separate Ways', *Financial Times*, 13 June 2007.

29 Rina Chandran, 'Tata Motors Completes Acquisition of Jag, Land Rover', Thomson Reuters, 2 June 2008.

30 Joe Leahy, 'Tata Digests Rich Diet of English Takeaways', *Financial Times*, 2 April 2008.

31 'When "humiliated" Ratan Tata did "favour" to Ford with JLR buyout!', *Economic Times*, 15 March 2015.

32   Ray Hutton, *Jewels in the Crown: How Tata of India Transformed Britain's Jaguar and Land Rover* (London: Elliott and Thompson, 2013).

33   Kalyana Ramanathan, 'Tata Ropes in Specialists to Trim Costs at JLR', *Business Standard*, 29 July 2009.

34   Mark Milner, 'Jaguar Land Rover Workers Agree to Four-Day Week and Pay Freeze', *Guardian*, 5 March 2009.

35   'Tata's Takeover of Jaguar and Land Rover: Bumpy Road or Smooth Ride?', Knowledge@Wharton, 3 April 2008.

36   Nevin John, 'Can Cyrus Mistry Reinvent Tata Motors?', *Business Today*, 2 August 2015.

37   Atul Arun Pathak, 'Tata Motors' Successful Cross-Border Acquisition of Jaguar Land Rover: Key Takeaways', *Strategic Direction* 32, no. 9 (2016).

38   For twelve years up to 2005, Ratan Tata held executive responsibility at Tata Motors as both chairman and MD. Tata Motors was close to his heart like Air India was for J.R.D., and TCS for Chandrasekaran.

Chapter 12: When Crores of Teabags Carried the Tata Name into Western Homes

1   China was a close second at 26.1 per cent. Asia accounted for 76.3 per cent of world GDP in 1 AD.

2   Angus Maddison, *The World Economy* (Paris: OECD Publishing, 2006).

3   The latest OECD estimates indicate that 'the economic centre of gravity would further shift towards Asia and by 2060, India and China would account for almost half of the global output'.

4   *Outlook*, November 2001.

5   The idea was to regulate dealings in forex and securities and conservation of forex for the nation.

6   Dan Stone, 'The World's Top Drink', *National Global*, 18 April 2014.

7   Suresh Jayaram, 'What You See When You See: Tea, History in a Cup', *Bangalore Mirror*, 9 April 2018.

8   S.R. Misra, *Tea Industry in India* (New Delhi: Ashish Publishing House, 1986).

9   Aarti Gupta, 'The Person Who Cheers!', *Business India*, 13 August 2006.

10   Aarti Gupta, 'A New Brew', *Business India*, 24 October–6 November 2005.

11   Nazneen Karmali and Madhumita Bose, 'What's Brewing?', *Business India*, 2–15 January 1995.

12   Amitava Chattopadhyay and Wiehr Ulrike, 'Tata Tea Limited (A)', INS582, INSEAD, 2004.

13   Harish Bhat, *Tata Log: Eight Modern Stories from a Timeless Institution* (New Delhi: Penguin Books, 2012).

14   Savio Pinto, 'Tetley Takeover Costs Tata Tea 400 Million Pound', *Business Standard*, 23 August 2000.

15   Shankar Aiyar, '2000-Tata Tea-Tetley Merger: The Cup that Cheered', *India Today*, 25 December 2009.

16   The acquisition of another company using a combination of equity and debt. It involves using a significant amount of borrowed money to fund the acquisition such that the acquired company's future cash flow and its assets are the collateral used to secure and repay the borrowed money.

17   N. Madhavan, 'The Turning Points', *Business Today*, 27 December 2009.

18   Madhumita Bose, 'Tea's Sometime Away', *Business India*, 1–14 April 2002.

19   L.J. Bourgeois et al., 'Tata Tea Ltd. and Tetley Plc. (A).', UV1636 (Charlottesville: University of Virginia Darden School Foundation, 2004).

20   Edna Fernandes, 'Tea Producer Seeks a Stronger Brew', *Financial Times*, 5 December 2002.

21   Amitava Chattopadhyay, 'Tata Tea Limited (C)', INSEAD, 2002.

22   It indicates how much debt a company is using to finance its assets relative to the value of shareholders' equity.

23   S. Elankumaran 'The Bitter Brew', *Asian Case Research Journal* 8, no. 2 (2004).

Chapter 13: Joining the Ranks of World's Most Geographically Diversified Chemical Companies

1   Several historical facts have been sourced from the in-house compilation on Tata Chemicals released on its 75th Anniversary—*Salt of the Earth: The Story of Tata Chemicals* by Philip Chacko and Christabelle Noronha (New Delhi: Westland Publications, 2014).

2   Sarosh Bana, 'Salting a Dream', *Business India*, 11 January 2009.

3   D.R. Pendse, 'Remembering Darbari Seth', *Indian Express*, 15 December 1999.

4   R. Gopalakrishnan, 'Story of 3 Cos: ICI, HLL, ITC', *Economic Times*, 31 March 2008.

5   Milking strategies are used by investors that want to boost stock prices or company revenues in order to create profits quickly.

6   The cost of manufacturing in Magadi was $70 per tonne for soda ash, as compared to $150 per tonne in Mithapur.

7   Prashant Kale et al., 'Don't Integrate Your Acquisitions, Partner with Them', *Harvard Business Review*, December 2009.

8   Siddharth Philip, 'Moving up', *Business India*, 24 February 2008.

9   Vasant Sivaraman and Varun Madan, 'Tata Chemicals Ltd: Global Acquisitions' (Ontario: Ivey Publishing, 2014).

10   Shankar Aiyar, '2000-Tata Tea-Tetley Merger: The Cup that Cheered', *India Today*, 25 December 2009.

11   Nagesh Kumar, 'Internationalization of Indian Enterprises: Patterns, Strategies, Ownership Advantages, and Implications', *Asian Economic Policy Review* 3 (2008): 242–61.

Chapter 14: A Chorus about Corus

1   Sudipt Dutta and Namrata Datt, 'The Big Comeback', *Business India*, 2–16 June 1996.

2   Sumant Banerji, 'Tata's Kalinganagar Steel Plant: A Poor Ambassador of Doing Business in India', *Business Today*, 24 November 2015.

3   Richard Dobbs and Rajat Gupta, 'An Indian Approach to Global M&A: An Interview with the CFO of Tata Steel', *McKinsey Quarterly*, October 2009.

4   S.R. Vishwanath, 'Tata Steel: Financing the Corus Acquisition', *Asian Case Research Journal* 14, issue 2 (2010): 295–312.

5   Rudrangshu Mukherjee, *A Century of Trust: The Story of Tata Steel* (New Delhi: Penguin Books, 2008).

6   Pete Engardio, 'Ratan Tata: The Last Rajah', *Business Week*, 8 August 2007.

7   An amalgamation of fourteen major steel-producing companies in the UK formed in 1967.

8   Kimberly Freeman et al., 'Achieving Global Growth through Acquisition: Tata's Takeover of Corus', *Journal of Case Research in Business and Economics* 1, no. 1 (2009).

9   R. Jagannathan, 'Tatas Trump Brazilian Steel Rival CSN with $12bn Corus Deal',
        DNA India, 31 January 2007.
10   Daksesh Parekh et al., 'Corus' Day Ahead', *Business India*, 25 February 2007.
11   Malcolm Lombers and Andy Radford, 'London's Scheming', *International Financial
        Law Review* 6, issue 7 (July 2007).
12   Ronak Batra and Neera Jain, 'Tata Steel: The Acquisition of Corus', (Ontario: Ivey
        Publishing, May 2017).
13   Muthuraman observed that the acquisition price of 608 pence per share pegged the
        enterprise value at $710 per tonne. A greenfield capacity going downstream as much
        as Corus would have cost Tata Steel $1200–1300 per tonne.
14   Richard Wachman, 'Empire Strikes Back: India Forges New Steel Alliance', *Guardian*,
        22 October 2006.
15   Rashmi Malapur, 'Tata's Acquisition of Corus: A Quantum Leap', *ICFAI Journal of
        Mergers & Acquisitions* iv, no. 4 (2007).
16   Ramnath Subbu, 'Corus Will Facilitate Access to Europe, Says Muthuraman', *The
        Hindu*, 1 February 2007.
17   A.S. Firoz, 'Corus Acquisition: Gambling for Growth?', *Economic and Political
        Weekly* 42, no. 11 (17–23 March 2007).
18   Nevin John, 'Trophy Buy, Distress Sale', *Business Today*, 8 May 2016.
19   Julia Kollewe, 'UK and EU Urged to Act on Chinese Steel Dumping after US Raises
        Duty on Imports', *Guardian*, 18 May 2016.
20   Omkar Khandekar, 'Climate Change Was the Inconvenient Truth that Finally Led to
        Tata Steel's UK Pullout', Scroll.in, 11 April 2016.
21   Stanley Reed, 'Tata Steel Makes a Deal to Stay in Britain, Saving up to 11,000 Jobs',
        New York Times, 7 December 2016.
22   The British Steel Pension Scheme (BSPS) supported 1,30,000 pensioners. At market
        value of £14 billion, the pension assets and liabilities were significantly higher than
        the net assets of Tata Steel Holdings UK.
23   Christoph Steitz and Tom Käckenhoff, 'Thyssenkrupp, Tata Steel Seal Landmark
        Joint Venture Deal', Reuters, 29 June 2018.
24   Megha Mandavia and Baiju Kalesh, 'Tata Steel plans to sell South-East Asia operations
        to focus on Indian market', *The Economic Times*, 12 July 2018.

Chapter 15: Hits, Misses and Lessons

1   Shashank Shah, *Win-Win Corporations: The Indian Way of Shaping Successful
        Strategies* (New Delhi: Penguin Random House India, 2016).
2   International geographies from where Taj gets its major customers.
3   Gabriel Szulanski et al., 'Taj Hotels, Resorts & Palaces: To Pierre or Not to Pierre (A)',
        INS003, INSEAD, 2008.
4   Anil Padmanabhan, 'Tata Buy in NYC', *India Today*, 20 June 2005.
5   Rajiv Singh, 'Brand Wars: Korean AC Companies Feel the Heat', *ET BrandEquity*, 4
        August 2017.
6   Suseela Yesudian, ed., *India: Acquiring Its Way to a Global Footprint* (Basingstoke:
        Palgrave Macmillan, 2012).
7   Prashant Kale, Harbir Singh and Anand P. Raman, 'Don't Integrate Your Acquisitions,
        Partner with Them', *Harvard Business Review*, December 2009.
8   Achal Raghavan, 'Going Global and Taking Charge: The Road Ahead for the Indian
        Manager', *Vikalpa* 33, no. 4 (October–December 2008): 61–68.

9   Ray Hutton, *Jewels in the Crown: How Tata of India Transformed Britain's Jaguar and Land Rover* (London: Elliott and Thompson, 2013).

10   Sunil Mithas, *Making the Elephant Dance: The Tata Way to Innovate, Transform and Globalize* (New Delhi: Penguin Books, 2015).

11   Ming-Jer Chen and Danny Miller, 'West Meets East: Toward an Ambicultural Approach to Management', *Academy of Management Perspectives* 24, no. 4 (November 2010): 17–24.

12   Neelam Singh, 'Emerging Economy Multinationals: The Role of Business Groups', *Economics, Management and Financial Markets* 6, no. 1 (2011): 142–81.

13   Pritish Nandy, 'JRD', *Illustrated Weekly of India*, 31 August–6 September 1986.

Chapter 16: The Making of a Titan

1   Bhaskar Bhat and B. Bowonder, 'Innovation as an Enhancer of Brand Personality: Globalization Experience of Titan Industries', *Creativity and Innovation Management* 10, no. 1 (March 2001): 26–39.

2   Saurav Chakrabarti, then corporate quality head at Trent (Westside), shared a similar focus at Trent's Westside stores across India. Titan's experience and reputation in successfully delighting customers had positively impacted the approach used by other retail companies of the Tata Group.

3   Harish Bhat, 'Timeless Lessons from a Titan', *The Hindu BusinessLine*, 15 July 2016.

4   Samar Srivastava, 'Titan Looking Beyond Tanishq to Fast-Track Growth', *Forbes India*, 23 June 2014.

5   Markides C., 'Strategic Innovation', *Sloan Management Review* 38, no. 3 (1998): 9–23.

6   Mohana Prabhakar, 'Best of Times, Worst of Times', *Business India*, 15–28 December 1997.

7   Anuradha Raghunathan, 'The Man Behind Titan's Success: Bhaskar Bhat', *Forbes India*, 1 October 2012.

8   When I secured a rank among the top ten students at the Class XII Maharashtra State Board exams, I was gifted the just-launched Titan Edge watch by P.N. Shah, former president of the Institute of Chartered Accountants of India. It remains a proud possession two decades later with no servicing requirements, not even a change of strap.

9   K.R. Balasubramanyam, 'Titan Industries' Bhaskar Bhat has made India-manufactured watches respectable', *Business Today*, 12 January 2012.

10   Anshul Dhamija, 'Titan's Attempt to Stay Wristworthy', *Forbes India*, 27 April 2016.

11   Sekhar Seshan, 'Giant Strides', *Business India*, 16–29 March 2015.

12   Mahesh Kulkarni, 'Why Time Ran Out for HMT', *Business Standard*, 14 September 2014.

13   Karat is a measurement for purity or fineness and is used for gold. 1 Karat is 1/24th of pure gold. In the case of 18 karat gold, it is 75 per cent pure. Carat is the term used to measure the weight of diamonds. A carat is 200 milligrams.

14   Mitu Jayashankar, 'Titan: The Golden Cage', *Forbes India*, 20 July 2010.

15   Harish Bhat, *Tata Log: Eight Modern Stories from a Timeless Institution* (New Delhi: Penguin Books, 2012).

16   Samar Srivastava, 'Titan's Wedding Party', *Forbes India*, 24 January 2018.

17   Kumar Ramesh et al., 'Raga and Tanishq-Symbolic Linkages Between Brands (the Indian Context), IMB 427, IIM Bangalore, 2013.

18   The rising prices of gold played a major role in Tanishq's financial success. Between 2000 and 2018, the price of 10 gram gold (22 karat) increased from ₹4400 to ₹34,400.

The senior leadership's persistent efforts in building the business during adverse circumstances paid huge dividends.

19 R. Jagannathan, 'The Tatas Have Broken the Consumer Jinx with Titan', *Forbes India*, 13 June 2014.

Chapter 17: Delighting Crores of Customers

1 Murali Gopalan, 'The Japanese Juggernaut Rolls on beyond Maruti too', *The Hindu BusinessLine*, 28 September 2017.

2 Rama Bijapurkar, *We Are Like That Only: Understanding the Logic of Consumer India* (New Delhi: Penguin Portfolio, 2009).

3 Harveen Ahluwalia, 'Millennials to Redefine India's Consumption Story: Report', *LiveMint*, 20 February 2018.

4 Anjali Kapoor Gaba, 'How to Sell to Millennials', *Fortune India*, 5 February 2016.

5 Kritika Kapoor, 'The Desi Definition of Gen X, Y, Z', *Times of India*, 16 November 2012.

6 Ajita Shashidhar, 'It's Gen X, Not Just Millennials Who Marketers Need to Talk to', *Business Today*, 20 December 2017.

7 Ruth Bernstein, 'Move Over Millennials—Here Comes Gen Z', *AdAge India*, 21 January 2015.

8 Its 4S philosophy focused on sampark, sambandh, santushti and samruddhi (contact, relationship, delight and prosperity), and brought coherence and consistency to its customer-centric endeavours.

9 India's exchequer was burdened with import of pulses estimated at ₹24,000 crore. Interestingly, countries such as Australia and Canada grew pulses only to supply India. They did not consume any!

10 Kruthiventi Anil Kumar, then principal scientist at Tata Chemicals Innovation Centre, shared, 'In our initial trials we found that the wax coating that you see on pulses comes from a chemical that is a proven carcinogen. We needed to educate people and change this perception that polished pulses are of higher quality. Our initial advertisements focused on this specific issue.' Celebrity chef Sanjeev Kapoor was brought in as brand ambassador to endorse the benefits of unpolished pulses, along with several other channels of communication.

11 A FICCI report indicated major advances—productivity improvements ranging from 30 to 60 per cent in total production, and reduction in spending on fertilizers by 30–40 per cent, thereby improving farmer incomes.

12 One worked with farmers to improve productivity and ensure regular supply, the other provided distribution networks and regular demand. This virtuous cycle was a perfect combination for balancing the demand–supply equation in the fragile farm sector.

13 Key competitors include Dish TV, Airtel Digital TV, Sun Direct, DD Free Dish and Videocon D2H.

14 Lancelot Joseph, 'Innovation Impact', *Business India*, 9–22 December 2013.

15 Sudipt Dutta and Namrata Datt, 'The Big Comeback', *Business India*, 3–16 June 1996.

16 Prosenjit Datta, 'Tata Steel—A Peek into the Branding Saga', *A Case Study Special on Innovation*, (New Delhi: Businessworld Publications, November 2010).

17 There were nine levers of RVM—company, distributor, retailer, consumer, opinion leader, value influencer, direct marketing, mass media and word of mouth—that covered the interest of each stakeholder.

18   Several competitors followed suit and introduced their own retail brands such as Jindal Tiger and SAIL Jyoti.

19   Kulvin Suri, recollected the time when the Australian mines were flooded in 2007–08. The ensuing shortage led to skyrocketing of steel prices to ₹7000 a tonne. At that time, Muthuraman decided to roll back prices by ₹2000 a tonne in customers' interest.

20   Prosenjit Datta, 'Tata Steel—Creating Value via Supply Chain', *A Case Study Special on Innovation*, (India: Businessworld Publications, November 2010).

21   Tata Steel's fifteen-year-long retail journey can be classified into three phases. The introductory period between 2002 to 2007 focused on creating brand identity and establishing the channel. The growth period between 2008 and 2012 focused on enhancing capability and consumer experience. The maturity period from 2013 onwards focused on providing customized solutions and redesigning several offerings through innovation.

22   Padgaonkar, Dileep, 'The Splendour That is the Taj', *100 Years of Glory (The Taj Centenary Issue)* 32, no. 1 (2003).

23   Andrew Harper, 'Taj Falaknuma Palace: A New Experience of Palatial Splendor', *Forbes*, 17 October 2012.

24   Robert Bong et al., 'Tata Nano's Execution Failure: How the People's Car Failed to Reshape the Auto Industry and Create New Growth', IN1314, Blue Ocean Strategy Institute, INSEAD France, 2017.

25   Ratan Tata interviewed by Tarun Khanna in Mumbai on 27 April 2015, for Creating Emerging Markets Oral History Collection, Baker Library Historical Collections, Harvard Business School.

26   Ashish Mishra, 'Saving Tata Nano', *Forbes India*, 4 January 2011.

27   Arpita Agnihotri and Saurabh Bhattacharya, 'The Tata Nano: What Went Wrong?' 9B15A03 (Ontario: Ivey Publishing, 2015)

28   'Stuck in Low Gear', *The Economist*, 20 August 2011.

29   R. Mukundan, 'A New Equation Begins to Bloom', *Tata Review*, July 2015.

30   B. Muthuraman et al., 'Understanding the Process of Transitioning to Customer Value Management', *IIMA Vikalpa* 31, no. 2 (April–June 2006).

Chapter 18: The Story behind Nine Decades of Industrial Harmony

1   Verrier Elwin, *The Story of Tata Steel* (Mumbai: Commercial Printing Press, 1958).

2   Several facts in this chapter are sourced from the Tata Steel Union Commemorative Museum, Jamshedpur, gathered during a personal visit.

3   Morgan Witzel, *Tata: The Evolution of a Corporate Brand* (New Delhi: Penguin Books, 2010).

4   Nitin Nohria, Anthony Mayo and Mark Benson, 'J.R.D. Tata', 9-407-061 (Boston: Harvard Business School Publishing, 2014).

5   Dilip Simeon, *The Politics of Labour under Late Colonialism—Workers, Unions and the State in Chota Nagpur 1928–39* (New Delhi: Manohar Books, 1995).

6   Gita Piramal, *Business Legends* (New Delhi: Penguin Books, 1998).

7   Several facts on people practices at Tata Steel have been sourced from: S.N. Pandey, *Human Side of Tata Steel* (New Delhi: Tata McGraw-Hill, 1989).

8   Surtees H.M. Tuckwell, 'The Tata Iron and Steel Works: Their Origin and Development', *Journal of the Royal Society of Arts* 66, no. 3402 (1 February 1918).

9   The erstwhile town services division eventually became India's only comprehensive urban infrastructure service provider—Jamshedpur Utilities and Services Company (JUSCO) in 2004.

10   'The House of Tata', *Fortune*, 1 January 1944.

11   Sudipt Dutta and Ranjan Kocherry, 'Learning to survive', *Business India*, 13–26 July 1998.

12   Jamshed J. Bhabha, 'Harvest of Faith and Courage', *Tata Steel Diamond Jubilee 1907–67* (Mumbai: Tata Press Ltd, 1967).

13   Subrata Roy, 'Russi Mody: Businessman of the Year 1983', *Business India*, 19 December 1983–1 January 1984.

14   Amrita Nair Ghaswalla, 'Russi Mody Was an Institution at Tata Steel: Ratan Tata', *The Hindu BusinessLine*, 17 May 2014.

15   Meher Marfatia, 'Big House in a Little Lane', *Mid-Day*, 17 April 2016.

16   Incidentally, my ancestral family office is also located on Homi Mody Street, just 200 metres from Bombay House.

17   In the Bihar Land Reforms Act, 1956, when the Singhbhum zamindaris were taken over by the government, an amendment was inserted exempting Jamshedpur (located in the East Singhbhum district).

18   Palakunnathu Mathai, 'Chairman Russi Mody Completes 50 Years in TISCO', *India Today*, 14 February 2013.

19   'Taking the Sting out of a Painful Situation' in Verne Harnish's *The Greatest Business Decisions of All Time* (New York: Time Incorporated Books, 2012).

20   Sudipt Dutta and Namrata Datt, 'The Big Comeback', *Business India*, 3–16 June 1996.

21   Several facts in this chapter sourced from the centenary year compilation: R.M. Lala, *The Romance of Tata Steel* (New Delhi: Penguin Books, 2007).

22   There were over a thousand workers who did not accept the scheme. Tata Steel continued to employ them due to its non-retrenchment policy.

23   Verne Harnish, *The Greatest Business Decisions of All Time* (New York: Time Incorporated Books, 2012).

24   Historically, Tata Steel had done well in people management and succession planning from within the company. Over the years, it created a pipeline of leaders and managed the entire leadership development through internal mobility. Compared with other Tata companies that have been in existence for nearly eighty years it has been the only Tata company with leadership at the highest levels that has been developed from within the company. Moreover, leadership for its subsidiaries and associated companies is also provided from within the Tata Steel Group.

Chapter 19: Grooming a Quintessential Tata Employee

1   Several fact files of this episode have been sourced from my previous book: *Win-Win Corporations: The Indian Way of Shaping Successful Strategies* (New Delhi: Penguin Random House India, 2016).

2   Adrian Levy and Cathy Scott-Clark, *The Siege: 68 Hours Inside the Taj Hotel* (New Delhi: Penguin Books India, 2013).

3   The Taj Public Service Welfare Trust, announced on 15 December 2008, has since then supported rehabilitation efforts during 13/7 Mumbai bomb blast, Bihar fire and cyclone, cloud bursts in Ladakh, Uttarakhand and Kashmir, and Sunderbans flood.

4   Meena Menon, 'Mumbai Is a Symbol of Energy and Optimism That Defines India: Obama', *The Hindu*, 6 November 2010.

5   B.S. Saklatvala and K. Khosla, *Jamsetji Tata* (New Delhi: Publications Division, Ministry of Information and Broadcasting, 1970).

6   *The Golden Jubilee Book of the Empress Mills, Nagpur (1877–1927)*, accessed at the Tata Central Archives, Pune.

7   D.E. Wacha, *The Life and Life Work of JN Tata* (Madras: Ganesh and Company, 1914).

8   N. Sivakumar, 'The Business Ethics of Jamsetji Nusserwanji Tata—A Forerunner in Promoting Stakeholder Welfare', *Journal of Business Ethics* 83 (2008).

9   N. Benjamin, 'Jamsetji Nusserwanji Tata: A Centenary Tribute', *Economic and Political Weekly* (28 August 2004).

10   Philip Chacko and Christabelle Noronha, *Salt of the Earth: The Story of Tata Chemicals* (New Delhi: Westland Publications, 2014).

11   Chittoor Raveendra et al., 'Creating a Corporate Advantage: The Case of the Tata Group', ISB005, Centre for Teaching, Learning and Case Development, ISB Hyderabad, 2013.

12   Shashank Shah, 'Employee and Labour Welfare at the Tata Group Companies: A Case Study', *Management and Labour Studies* 35, no. 3 (2010).

13   Pratim Banerjee, a former student of mine now serving as a TAS officer and working at Tata Technologies USA, shared his experience, 'The opportunities that one can come across by being a TAS Officer (TASO) are immense! The scale that the programme provides with its presence in a diverse set of industries through its 100-odd companies is what's very attractive. Besides, the TAS brand is very strong, and can be a great "door-opener" with senior leadership at various organizations.'

14   Several fact files of this anecdote have been sourced from the eponymous documentary.

15   Morgen Witzel, *Tata: The Evolution of a Corporate Brand* (New Delhi: Penguin Books India, 2010).

16   Several facts for this section have been sourced from the autobiographical account: S. Ramadorai, *The TCS Story & Beyond* (New Delhi: Penguin Books India, 2013).

17   Vinod Kumar et al., 'The Jewel in the Crown', *Business India*, 10–23 August 1998.

18   Beng Wee Geok and Ivy Buche, 'Tata Consultancy Services: A Systems Approach to Human Resource Development', ABCC-2008/12-004, The Asian Business Case Centre, Nanyang Technological University, 2008.

19   Parthasarathi Swami and Soneera Sanghvi, 'Road Warriors', *Business India*, 6–19 January 2014.

20   A similar sounding Purpose4Life was created as a TCS volunteering forum for community projects in the areas of education, health and environment.

21   Shyamal Majumdar and Shivani Shinde, 'Lunch with BS: Natarajan Chandrasekaran', *Business Standard*, 21 January 2013.

22   Adam Bryant, 'Natarajan Chandrasekaran of Tata Consultancy Services: Making a Habit of Accountability', *New York Times*, 10 February 2015.

23   Empowering women at the workplace was another area where group companies have initiated several programmes in recent years. The Tata Second Career Inspiring Possibilities launched in 2008 was a unique group-level initiative for women, who have taken a break from their career due to personal commitments, to restart their career. Another key initiative started in 2014 was Tata LEAD. The number of women leaders at Tata companies and number of women directors on Tata boards has been historically minuscule. It is imperative for the group to sustain such efforts to change this demographic skew.

Chapter 20: Understanding Tatas from Employees' Eyes

1   Several facts of this anecdote have been sourced from: Gita Piramal, *Business Maharajas* (New Delhi: Penguin India, 2011).

2   Shekhar Ghosh and Nazneen Karmali, 'Tough Times', *Business India*, 16–29 October 1989.

3   Shiv Taneja, 'TELCO Workers Intensify Agitation', *India Today*, 15 November 1989.
4   Subrata Roy, 'Business of the Year 1983,' *Business India*, 19 December 1983–1 January 1984.
5   Anuradha Raghunathan, 'The Man Behind Titan's Success: Bhaskar Bhat', *Forbes India*, 1 October 2012.
6   V.S. Mahesh, 'The Maruti Strike and an Old Story from the Tata Group', *LiveMint*, 13 November 2011.

Chapter 21: When Employees Became Suppliers; When Suppliers Are Treated Like Employees

1   Aarti Gupta, 'A New Brew', *Business India*, 24 October–6 November 2005.
2   Aarti Gupta, 'The Person Who Cheers!', *Business India*, 13 August 2006.
3   Sajeev Kumar, 'Kannan Devan Appoints New MD', *The Hindu BusinessLine*, 3 August 2015.
4   Indulekha Aravind, 'Kanan Devan: The First Tea Plantation Company to Be Majority-Owned by Workforce, Employee-Stakeholders Launch Their Biggest Agitation', *Economic Times*, 22 November 2015.
5   Morgen Witzel, *Tata: The Evolution of a Corporate Brand* (New Delhi: Penguin Books, 2010).
6   In 2013, Tata Global Beverages increased its stake in KDHPC to 28 per cent to help employee shareholders when they needed money. The management control remained with the employees; but KDHPC became an associate company of Tata Global Beverages.
7   Sekhar Seshan, 'Giant Strides', *Business India*, 16–29 March 2015.
8   Deepa Kurup, 'Titan Pitches Karigar Centres as Industry Model', *The Hindu*, 18 May 2016.
9   'The Craft of Fine Jewellery', Chapter 9, Voyager (Tata Innovista Publication, 2011).
10   Prosenjit Datta, 'Tanishq—Going Virtual in Design', *A Case Study Special on Innovation*, (New Delhi: Businessworld Publications, November 2010).

Chapter 22: The Aviation Dream That Could Not Be Grounded

1   Subhro Niyogi, 'Kolkata Was on Aviation Map Just 7 Years after Wright Bros' Feat', *Times of India*, 3 June 2018.
2   Bakhtiar Dadabhoy, *Jeh: A Life of JRD Tata* (New Delhi: Rupa and Co., 2005).
3   R.M. Lala, *The Joy of Achievement: Conversations with JRD Tata* (New Delhi: Penguin Books, 1995).
4   'The House of Tata', *Fortune*, 1 January 1944.
5   Anvar Alikhan, 'Air India Was Once the Company That Inspired Singapore Airlines and Cathay Pacific', Quartz India, 3 July 2017.
6   Yeshi Seli, 'Round Tripping', *Business India*, 8 April 2007.
7   All excerpts of letters from and to J.R.D. Tata sourced from: Arvind Mambro, ed., *J.R.D. Tata Letters* (New Delhi: Rupa and Co., 2004).
8   Excerpt from *Keepers of the Flame*, a documentary by Zafar Hai.
9   Anthony Sampson, *Empires of the Sky: The Politics, Contests, and Cartels of World Airlines* (New Delhi: Random House, 1985).
10   Sean Mendis, 'Air India: The History of the Aircraft Fleet', Whine and Cheez, 26 July 2004.

11   Surajeet Das Gupta, 'Two Decades in the Departure Lounge', *Business Standard*, 9 January 2015.

12   Sanjeev Verma, 'Who Killed Tata Airlines', *Business India*, 5–18 May 1997.

13   Ranjit Bhushan, 'Ground Realities', *Outlook*, 20 November 1996.

14   In April 2007, Air Sahara was acquired by Jet Airways for ₹1450 crore. It was rebranded as Jet Lite, a low-cost offering from Jet Airways.

15   'Why Should I Allow Singapore Airlines into My Country?', *Sunday Magazine*, 19 February 1997.

16   Sanjeev Verma et al., '. . . over my dead body', *Business India*, 27 January–9 February 1997.

17   Vinod Mehta, 'Gowda Scores for India', *Outlook*, 19 February 1997.

18   Sanjeev Verma, 'Who Killed Tata Airline', *Business India*, 5–18 May 1997.

19   Arijit Barman, 'The Last Jet Engine Sigh', *Outlook*, 29 April 2002.

20   M.K. Kaw, *An Outsider Everywhere: Revelations by an Insider* (New Delhi: Konark Publishers, 2012).

21   'Minister Wanted Rs 15-cr Bribe for Aviation Permit: Tata', *The Indian Express*, 15 November 2010.

22   Sandeep Bamzai, 'Tata Juggernaut Stirring', *Business India*, 30 April–13 May 2001.

23   This meant elimination of all frills associated with traditional air travel, including free meals on-board and frequent flyer programmes. The LCCs provided a single class of service, Internet-based ticketing and point-to-point services. LCC aircraft had limited storage space and no entertainment services.

24   Srinivas Sridharan and R. Chandrasekhar, 'Air Deccan (A): Changing the Face of Indian Aviation', 907A01 (Ontario: Ivey Publishing, 2007).

25   Sumit Mitra and Pradeep Kumar Hota, 'Air India Limited and Indian Airlines Limited Merger: Is It Flying?', W14312 (Ontario: Ivey Publishing, 2014).

26   Manju V., 'What Sent Air India Crashing?', *Economic Times*, 16 July 2009.

27   By 2015–16, Air India's employee-to-aircraft ratio was brought down to 106 per plane, marginally higher than the international standard of 100 per plane.

28   Neeraj Chauhan, 'CBI Files Three FIRs on UPA's Aircraft Buy, Air India Decisions', *Times of India*, 30 May 2017.

29   Yeshi Seli, 'Ready to Fly', *Business India*, 30 September–13 October 2013.

30   Diana Mazutis et al., 'Singapore Airlines (A): The India Decision', IMD724 (Switzerland: IMD Lausanne, 2014).

31   Press Information Bureau, Government of India, Vice-President's Secretariat, 2 November 2017.

32   UDAN—*Ude Desh ka Aam Naagrik* was launched by the Government of India in April 2017 as a regional airport and routes development scheme with capped airfares that would be subsidized where uncompetitive.

33   Vaidyanathan Krishnamurthy and Catherine Xavier, 'Air India: Maharaja in Debt Trap', ISB101 (Hyderabad: Indian School of Business, 2018).

34   Anirban Chowdhury, 'Will Air India Find a Buyer? The Answer Is Worth at Least Rs 33,000 Crore', *Economic Times*, 29 March 2018.

Chapter 23: The Tata-Government Saga: Electrifying Experiences

1   He was enormously impressed by Patel's clarity of mind and the logic with which he addressed and solved seemingly intractable problems.

2   Excerpts of all J.R.D. Tata speeches have been sourced from: S.A. Sabavala and R.M. Lala, eds., *Keynote: J.R.D. Tata* (New Delhi: Rupa and Co., 2004).

3   A.M. Misra, 'Business Culture and Entrepreneurship in British India, 1860–1950', *Modern Asian Studies* 34, no. 2 (May 2000).

4   Sir Dinshaw Wacha, who became the president of INC in 1901, was an employee of the Swadeshi Mills.

5   R.M. Lala, 'The Business Ethics of J.R.D. Tata', *The Hindu*, 29 July 2005.

6   Matthai became the first railways minister in independent India, and later the finance minister. He returned to the Tatas due to a difference of opinion with Prime Minister Nehru. Between 1950 and 1957, he served as the director-in-charge for Tata Steel and Tata Chemicals. As chairman of the Sir Dorabji Tata Trust, he helped establish the International Institute for Population Studies (Bombay) in collaboration with the United Nations.

7   The trend continued in later years as well with Nani Palkhivala and S. Jaishankar.

8   Penguin Books also published it in wartime Britain.

9   Several elements were inspired by the published works of eminent engineer, scholar and statesman—Bharat Ratna Sir Mokshagundam Visvesvaraya (1861–1962).

10   Dwijendra Tripathi and Jyoti Jumani, *The Concise Oxford History of Indian Business* (New Delhi: Oxford University Press, 2017).

11   Transfer of a major branch of industry or commerce from private to state ownership or control.

12   Manas Chakravarty, 'The Nehruvian Rate of Growth', *LiveMint*, 17 November 2014.

13   An economic and political theory advocating collective or governmental ownership and administration of the means of production and distribution of goods.

14   This included the Mahalanobis Committee (1964), the Monopolies Inquiry Commission (1965), the R.K. Hazari Committee (1966) and the Industrial Licensing Committee (1969).

15   Rudrangshu Mukherjee, *A Century of Trust: The Story of Tata Steel* (New Delhi: Penguin Books, 2008).

16   'India: Slow Death by Taxes', *Time*, 12 February 1965.

17   Vineet Agarwal, 'A 50 Year Trend of Indian Personal Tax Rates', *Business Today*, 26 February 2011.

18   George Fernandes, 'Encounters with Tata', *Indian Express*, 8 January 1994.

19   Several facts and anecdotes of the Tata Power story have been sourced from: Anil Dharker, *Invisible Goodness: The Story of Tata Power* (New Delhi: Roli Books, 2016).

20   Guha, Ramchandra, 'When JRD Tata called for a strong Opposition', *Hindustan Times*, 24 September 2017.

21   R.M. Lala, *Beyond the Last Blue Mountain: A Life of J.R.D. Tata* (New Delhi: Penguin Books, 1993), p. 331.

22   In 1996, Tatas Sons established the Tata Electoral Trust to insulate themselves against political pressures. The corpus for this trust was contributed by individual companies. It made grants on an impartial basis to all political parties for administrative costs and overheads.

23   Girish Kuber, *Tatayan* (Jaipur: Rajhans Prakashan, 2015).

24   Gita Piramal, *Business Legends* (New Delhi: Penguin Books, 1998).

25   R.N. Bhaskar, 'A Power-Packed Century', *Business India*, 12–25 October 2015.

Chapter 24: Nationalizing the Nation's Pride?

1   Indian Iron and Steel Company and Damodar Valley Corporation mines were also spared.
2   Gita Piramal, *Business Legends* (New Delhi: Penguin Books, 1998).
3   Dipa Jaywant, 'Failure of Tata Takeover Turns out to Be George Fernandes's Second Major Defeat', *India Today*, 3 January 2015.
4   J.R.D. Tata 'Why . . . Tata Steel?' *Tata Steel Diamond Jubilee 1907–67* (Mumbai: Tata Press Ltd, 1967).
5   This was derogatorily referred to by several economists like Professor Rajkrishna as the 'Hindu rate of growth'. As if the practice of Hinduism by 85 per cent of Indians and its virtues of contentment had negatively impacted the growth rate. The reality was that with the same approach to life and living, India had been the world's largest economy between AD 1 and 1700.
6   This approach did not believe in engaging with industry captains for a holistic and inclusive approach to growth and development. For example, France, which was then a planned economy, considered the views of the Patronat (the employer's organizations) and the syndicates (the unions) during policy formulation.

Chapter 25: Unlimited Waits; Lost Opportunities

1   In a letter to his friend George Woods (who later became the president of the World Bank) written in 1959, J.R.D. observed that the time was ripe for the Tatas to move into the small car field where there was the likelihood of an unlimited market.
2   Edmund Amann and John Cantwell, *Innovative Firms in Emerging Market Countries* (New Delhi: Oxford University Press, 2013).
3   Facts and figures sourced from: Philip Chacko and Christabelle Noronha, *Salt of the Earth: The Story of Tata Chemicals* (New Delhi: Westland Ltd, 2014).
4   P. Shankar and Basudev Dass, 'Seth to the Rescue', *Business India*, 15–25 June 1989.
5   At 2018 rates, this would amount to ₹44 lakh crore.

Chapter 26: Under Crossfire: From Left, Right and Centre

1   Saumitra Jha and Debra Schifrin, 'Managing Local Political Risk: Parking the Tata Nano (A)', P-78(A)m (Stanford: Stanford Graduate School of Business, 2012).
2   Nirmal Kumar Chandra, 'Tata Motors in Singur: A Step towards Industrialization or Pauperization?', *Economic and Political Weekly* 3, no. 50 (13–19 December 2008).
3   Laura Alfaro et al., 'Tata Motors in Singur: Public Purpose and Private Property (B)', 9-709-029 (Boston: Harvard Business School Publishing, 2012).
4   The Government of India had legal means of acquiring land from private citizens. The said Act specified that the government could acquire land for 'public purpose' by payment of 'just compensation'.
5   Rakesh Joshi and Aarti Gupta, 'Face-off at Singur', *Business India*, 31 December 2006.
6   Deb Kumar Bose, 'Land Acquisition in West Bengal', *Economic and Political Weekly* 42, no. 17 (28 April–4 May 2007).
7   A tenant farmer who gives a part of each crop as rent to the owner.
8   Laura Alfaro and Lakshmi Iyer, 'Special Economic Zones in India: Public Purpose and Private Property (A)', 9-709-027 (Boston: Harvard Business School Publishing, 2012).

9   National Democratic Alliance statement on Mamata Banerjee, 27 December 2006.
10   Philip Chacko, Christabelle Noronha and Sujata Agrawal, *Small Wonder: The Making of the Nano* (New Delhi: Westland Ltd, 2010).
11   Ashish Mishra and Archisman Dinda, 'Singur Is Still the Waste Land', *Forbes India*, 19 July 2011.
12   The fact that there were 40,000 protestors when only 2200 landless labourers were aggrieved validated the argument that several outsiders had joined the protest for political reasons. This included Naxalite and ultra-left organizations outside West Bengal.
13   Mehul Srivastava, 'Why Indian farmers Are Fighting Tata's Nano', *Bloomberg Businessweek*, 27 August 2008.
14   Marcus Dam, 'Singur to Nandigram and Beyond', *The Hindu*, 27 September 2016.
15   For those five weeks when the plant was shut down, thousands of Tata employees, including 600 ITI-trained local boys, were sent to Ramakrishna Mission for motivation and training sessions conducted by the company.
16   Suhrid Sankar Chattopadhyay, 'Singur's Loss', *Frontline*, 25 October–7 November 2008.
17   Rutam Vora, 'Sanand Project: Tata Motors Denies Receiving Grant from Gujarat Govt', *The Hindu BusinessLine*, 30 November 2017.
18   Anand Adhikari, 'Supersize Gujarat', *Business Today*, 23 January 2011.
19   A.K. Bhattacharya, 'Singur to Sanand', *Business Standard*, 20 January 2013.
20   Founded in 2002, Tata Power Delhi Distribution Ltd is a joint venture between Tata Power and the Government of Delhi NCR. The former holds 51 per cent stake.
21   Anil Dharker, *Invisible Goodness: The Story of Tata Power* (New Delhi: Roli Books, 2016).
22   The fact that it was prime agricultural land with multi-cropping fertility predominantly cultivated by landless labourers tilted the situation in the farmers' favour.
23   Namrata Acharya, 'West Bengal's Debt Burden Rises 64 Per Cent in Six Years', *Business Standard*, 26 April 2016.
24   Rabi Banerjee, 'Forget the Past: Mamata Invites Tata to Bengal', *The Week*, 7 September 2016.
25   In a 1964 letter to Jayaprakash Narayan, J.R.D. had declined his invitation to be a part of the India–Pakistan Reconciliation Group citing the same reason.

Chapter 27: An Abiding Passion for Nation Building

1   Anil Dharker, *Invisible Goodness: The Story of Tata Power* (New Delhi: Roli Books India, 2016).
2   Several technical details, facts and figures on the Tata Trusts have been compiled based on the information received from the office of the managing trustee.
3   Morgen Witzel, *Tata: The Evolution of a Corporate Brand* (New Delhi: Penguin Books, 2010).
4   Sourav Majumdar and Aveek Datta, 'We Are Re-focusing, Re-purposing Tata Trusts: R Venkataramanan', *Forbes India*, 14 June 2017.
5   R.M. Lala, *The Romance of Tata Steel* (New Delhi: Penguin Books, 2007).
6   Shashank Shah, 'Corporate Social Responsibility: A Way of Life at the Tata Group', *Journal of Human Values* 20, no. 1 (April 2014).
7   Shashank Shah and Ajit Jhangiani, 'The Art of Giving', *Business India*, 26 February–25 March 2018.

In Conclusion: A Way of Business

1 It is a rare coincidence that when I was writing this episode, the Assam issue re-emerged as a heated national discussion. Thirty-three years after the signing of the Assam Accord, the Narendra Modi-led BJP government under the directives of the Supreme Court had conducted an elaborate exercise and detected over 40-lakh 'illegal' individuals in Assam with dubious documents. Surprisingly, the opposition parties led by the Congress, which had committed to the Assam Accord under Prime Minister Rajiv Gandhi, were now opposing the very idea of deporting illegal migrants from Bangladesh detected through proper legal processes.

2 Sudipt Dutta and Madhumita Bose, 'Under the Shadow', *Business India*, 24 May–6 June 1993.

3 Omkar Goswami et al., 'Planter, Police, ULFA, Spy', *Business India*, 20 October–2 November 1997.

4 S. Elankumaran, 'The Bitter Brew', *Asian Case Research Journal* 8, no. 2 (2004).

5 B.P. Patra, 'Conflict of Interest, Corporate Social Responsibility and the Controversial Case of Tata Tea Funding of ULFA Militants: An Ethical Analysis', *Vilakshan, XIMB Journal of Management*, September 2008.

6 Vaihayasi Pande-Daniel, 'While Ratan Tata is Extremely Patriotic, He Loves India, and His Mind Is Global', Rediff.com, 28 December 2013.

7 Swapan Dasgupta et al., 'Assam Govt Mounts Pressure on Tata Tea to Come Clean on Its Alleged Funding of ULFA', *India Today*, 20 October 1997.

8 Shivanand Kanavi, 'New Steel in an Old Bottle,' *Business India*, 23 July–5 August 2001.

9 R. Gopalakrishnan, 'Values Are Forever', Tata Titans, Tata.com, March 2004.

10 Tom Donaldson and Preston Lee, 'The Stakeholder Theory of the Corporation: Concepts, Evidences and Implications', *Academy of Management Review* 20, no. 1 (1995).

11 According to this school of thought, strategically applying ethical principles—that is, acting according to moral principles only when doing so is to your advantage—is not following ethical principles at all.

12 D. Quinn and T. Jones, 'An Agent Morality View of Business Policy', *Academy of Management Review* 20, no. 1 (1995).

13 Milton Friedman, 'The Social Responsibility of Business Is to Increase Its Profits', *New York Times*, 13 September 1970.

14 Gopala Krishna C., *Corporate Social Responsibility in India-A Study of Management Attitudes* (New Delhi: Mittal Publications, 1992).

15 Schumpeter, 'The Business of Business', *The Economist*, 19 March 2015.

16 Nick O'Donohoe, 'What Is the True Business of Business?' (Cologny: World Economic Forum, 25 February 2016).

17 Aman Jhaveri, 'Developing the Concept and Practice of "Inclusive Business" for Poverty Alleviation: A Study of Select Organizations from India', doctoral thesis, Sri Sathya Sai Institute of Higher Learning, Prasanthi Nilayam, 2017.

18 M.J. Akbar, 'A Man Called Jamsetji Tata and His Love Affair with Bombay', *100 Years of Glory*, Taj Centenary Issue 32, no. 1 (2003).

19 CNN-News18 exclusive interview anchored by Suhel Seth, 20 September 2017.

20 Naval Burjor Ghiara, 'A Smooth Succession', *Business India*, 1–14 April 1991.

21 The first verse of Isha Upanishad conveys this ideal succinctly. The approximate translation is 'Everything animate or inanimate that is within the universe is controlled and owned by the Lord. One should therefore accept only those things necessary for himself, which are set aside as his quota, and one must not accept other things, knowing well to whom they belong.' Of this verse Mahatma Gandhi had once observed, 'If all the Upanishads and other scriptures happened all of a sudden to be reduced to ashes, and if only the first verse in the Isha Upanishad were left in the memory of the Hindus, Hinduism would live forever.'

22 Sundar Sarukkai, 'JRD Tata and the Idea of Trusteeship' in *Zoroastrianism: From Antiquity to the Modern Period* (New Delhi: Centre for Studies in Civilisations, 2012).

23 Conscious Capitalism Inc. defines it as, 'A way of thinking about capitalism and business that better reflects where we are in the human journey, the state of our world today, and the innate potential of business to make a positive impact on the world. Conscious businesses are galvanized by higher purposes that serve, align, and integrate the interests of all their major stakeholders.'

24 In my research, I came across nearly a hundred management case studies of leading business schools, including Harvard, Stanford, Darden and INSEAD that focused on insightful analysis of Tata companies, strategies, projects and people.

25 Sudha Murthy, 'Appro JRD', Tata Titans, Tata.com, August 2004.

26 Paran Balakrishnan, 'A Life Less Ordinary', *Telegraph*, 27 April 2014.

27 Nazneen Karmali and A.B. Ravi, 'Living in Today's World', *Business India*, 19 June–2 July 1995.

28 Shefali Rekhi, 'India Has to Identify Its Strong Industries and Leverage Them', *India Today*, 15 November 1994.

29 Adi Godrej, 'Builder Extraordinaire', *Business India*, 6 January 2013.

30 Tarun Khanna et al., 'House of Tata: Acquiring a Global Footprint', 9-708-446 (Boston: Harvard Business School Publishing, 2009).

31 Keshub Mahindra, 'Role Model', *Business India*, 6 January 2013.

32 Shally Seth Mohile and Viveat Susan Pinto, 'Simplification, Synergy, Scale: How Chandra is Planning to Take Tata Ahead', *Business Standard*, 19 April 2018.

33 Krishna Kant and Samie Modak, 'TCS Propels Tata Group into Rs 10-Trillion Club; Shares Hit Lifetime High', *Business Standard*, 21 April 2018.